T3-AKX-755

Great Sites for Kids

Check out these general-interest sites when you want to enjoy the World Wide Web without searching for anything.

4Kids Treehouse
www.4kids.com
Easy to use and lots of good links

Berit's Best Sites for Kids
http://db.cochran.com/li_toc:theoPage.db
Quality links and activities

Cyberkids
www.mtlake.com/cyberkids/
Go shopping and world hopping

Global Show-n-Tell
www.telenaut.com/gst/
Kids' online art gallery

Internet Public Library
www.ipl.org/
A library you can play in

Kid City
www.sftoday.com/enn2/kidcity.htm
Slick city

Kids Korner
www.kids-korner.com
Site for kids of all ages

KidsCom
www.kidscom.com/
Electronic international playground for kids ages 4 to 15

KidsWeb
www.npac.syr.edu/textbook/kidsweb/
A huge collection of sites just for kids

thekids.com
www.thekids.com
Delightful picture stories

Micons Used in This Book

$ Site requires that you pay a fee to use the services offered

Cool site with lots of graphics; may be slow to load

Site requires a little parental guidance or attention

Lots of info for students on this site

Jumping-off point for specialized Web sites

Site requires browser plug-ins or advanced browser capabilities

Great site for 8- to 12-year olds

Appropriate for 2- to 7-year olds

Interesting for 13-year-olds and older

Site requires that you sign in

Family Favorite Sites

Here's a space in which you can make notes about your own favorite sites. As you write them here, don't forget to bookmark them in your browser.

Site Name	
Site Description	
URL	
Site Name	
Site Description	
URL	
Site Name	
Site Description	
URL	
Site Name	
Site Description	
URL	

...For Dummies: #1 Computer Book Series for Beginners

More Family Favorite Sites

Site Name

Site Description

URL

Site Name

Site Description

URL

Site Name

Site Description

URL

Site Name

Site Description

URL

Site Name

Site Description

URL

Site Name

Site Description

URL

Site Name

Site Description

URL

Site Name

Site Description

URL

Site Name

Site Description

URL

Site Name

Site Description

URL

COMPUTER BOOK SERIES FROM IDG

Internet Directory For Kids & Parents ™

Cheat Sheet

The Seven Be's of Safety

Here are the Seven Be's, or my proven safety tips for families to keep in mind when wandering around the Internet:

- ✔ Be selective about offering any personal information online.

- ✔ Be nosy. Check with the kids you love to see what they're doing on the Internet.

- ✔ Be alert to the potential for viruses. Get and use virus-detection software, and always back up valuable data regularly.

- ✔ Be aware of "cookies." Assess your feelings about cookies and find out how to disable cookies by visiting: uts.cc.utexas.edu/~ccfr362/index.htm.

- ✔ Be proactive. If anyone in your family gets abusive online correspondence, print it out and call the police.

- ✔ Be cautious. Just like in real life, you need to be cautious around strangers. Sometimes it's wisest to leave online relationships online, especially when it comes to kids.

- ✔ Be protective. Do whatever it takes to ensure children's safety on the Internet.

Great Sites for Parents

Here's a list of some great general-interest sites for parents. For more sites, see Part VII: The Part of Tens.

Essential Information for Parents
www.mcs.net/~kathyw/parent.html
Provocative look at serious family issues

Family.com
www.family.com
Expansive, family-based resource

National Parent Information Network
ericps.ed.uiuc.edu/npin/npinhome.html
Intelligent guidance for caring parents

Not Just for Kids
www.night.net/kids/
Whimsical site for kids and parents to enjoy together

Parent News
www.parent.net/
Up-to-date parenting info

Parent Soup
www.parentsoup.com
Emphasis on parent-to-parent communication

Parent Zone
www.parentzone.com/index.htm
Links to selected site specialties

...For Dummies: #1 Computer Book Series for Beginners

INTERNET DIRECTORY

FOR

KIDS & PARENTS™

INTERNET DIRECTORY FOR KIDS & PARENTS™

by Barbara Moran

IDG Books Worldwide, Inc.
An International Data Group Company

Foster City, CA ♦ Chicago, IL ♦ Indianapolis, IN ♦ Southlake, TX

Internet Directory For Kids & Parents ™

Published by
IDG Books Worldwide, Inc.
An International Data Group Company
919 E. Hillsdale Blvd.
Suite 400
Foster City, CA 94404
www.idgbooks.com (IDG Books Worldwide Web site)
www.dummies.com (Dummies Press Web site)

Library of Congress Catalog Card No.: 97-80405

ISBN: 0-7645-0218-2

Printed in the United States of America

10 9 8 7 6 5 4 3 2 1

1O/RV/RS/ZX/IN

Distributed in the United States by IDG Books Worldwide, Inc.

Distributed by Macmillan Canada for Canada; by Transworld Publishers Limited in the United Kingdom; by IDG Norge Books for Norway; by IDG Sweden Books for Sweden; by Woodslane Pty. Ltd. for Australia; by Woodslane Enterprises Ltd. for New Zealand; by Longman Singapore Publishers Ltd. for Singapore, Malaysia, Thailand, and Indonesia; by Simron Pty. Ltd. for South Africa; by Toppan Company Ltd. for Japan; by Distribuidora Cuspide for Argentina; by Livraria Cultura for Brazil; by Ediciencia S.A. for Ecuador; by Addison-Wesley Publishing Company for Korea; by Ediciones ZETA S.C.R. Ltda. for Peru; by WS Computer Publishing Corporation, Inc., for the Philippines; by Unalis Corporation for Taiwan; by Contemporanea de Ediciones for Venezuela; by Computer Book & Magazine Store for Puerto Rico; by Express Computer Distributors for the Caribbean and West Indies. Authorized Sales Agent: Anthony Rudkin Associates for the Middle East and North Africa.

For general information on IDG Books Worldwide's books in the U.S., please call our Consumer Customer Service department at 800-762-2974. For reseller information, including discounts and premium sales, please call our Reseller Customer Service department at 800-434-3422.

For information on where to purchase IDG Books Worldwide's books outside the U.S., please contact our International Sales department at 415-655-3200 or fax 415-655-3295.

For information on foreign language translations, please contact our Foreign & Subsidiary Rights department at 415-655-3021 or fax 415-655-3281.

For sales inquiries and special prices for bulk quantities, please contact our Sales department at 415-655-3200 or write to the address above.

For information on using IDG Books Worldwide's books in the classroom or for ordering examination copies, please contact our Educational Sales department at 800-434-2086 or fax 817-251-8174.

For press review copies, author interviews, or other publicity information, please contact our Public Relations department at 415-655-3000 or fax 415-655-3299.

For authorization to photocopy items for corporate, personal, or educational use, please contact Copyright Clearance Center, 222 Rosewood Drive, Danvers, MA 01923, or fax 508-750-4470.

is a trademark under exclusive license to IDG Books Worldwide, Inc., from International Data Group, Inc.

About the Author

Veteran journalist **Barbara Moran** has traveled the real world and the virtual world on assignment. A graduate of Kent State University with a degree in telecommunications, Barbara has been a staff writer with the *Atlanta Constitution* and then the *San Diego Union*. She also has been the editor of a home and garden magazine and a weekly newspaper.

Barbara is a trained horticulturist, naturalist, and member of the Society of Environmental Journalists who publishes science, nature and environmental articles in major magazines and newspapers. She's written educational materials for textbook publishers and science organizations. Most recently, she helped create content and site databases for the science and children's divisions of two search engines.

Known to kids as "Ms. B," Barbara founded the Special Species Project. In this project, after learning about a native plant, animal, or ecosystem with the help of a nature or science expert, kids write and draw what they discovered for publication in books and on the Special Species Web site. Among project awards: the *Newsweek* Environmental Class Act Challenge Award and the KGTV-San Diego Leadership Award.

Barbara and her husband, trauma psychologist Bob "Dr. Bear" Baker, created Operation TeddyCare, which collects new teddy bears and gives them, along with free counseling, to traumatized children throughout the world. Barbara and Bob also coach Little League and volunteer for kid-oriented causes. They have two great kids, Krystee and CJ. The family lives in rural Northern California with (at last count) three dogs, a chicken, a goat, a sheep, a cat, 60+ goldfish, a finch, a cockatiel, and a box turtle.

ABOUT IDG BOOKS WORLDWIDE

Welcome to the world of IDG Books Worldwide.

IDG Books Worldwide, Inc., is a subsidiary of International Data Group, the world's largest publisher of computer-related information and the leading global provider of information services on information technology. IDG was founded more than 25 years ago and now employs more than 8,500 people worldwide. IDG publishes more than 275 computer publications in over 75 countries (see listing below). More than 60 million people read one or more IDG publications each month.

Launched in 1990, IDG Books Worldwide is today the #1 publisher of best-selling computer books in the United States. We are proud to have received eight awards from the Computer Press Association in recognition of editorial excellence and three from *Computer Currents'* First Annual Readers' Choice Awards. Our best-selling *...For Dummies*® series has more than 30 million copies in print with translations in 30 languages. IDG Books Worldwide, through a joint venture with IDG's Hi-Tech Beijing, became the first U.S. publisher to publish a computer book in the People's Republic of China. In record time, IDG Books Worldwide has become the first choice for millions of readers around the world who want to learn how to better manage their businesses.

Our mission is simple: Every one of our books is designed to bring extra value and skill-building instructions to the reader. Our books are written by experts who understand and care about our readers. The knowledge base of our editorial staff comes from years of experience in publishing, education, and journalism — experience we use to produce books for the '90s. In short, we care about books, so we attract the best people. We devote special attention to details such as audience, interior design, use of icons, and illustrations. And because we use an efficient process of authoring, editing, and desktop publishing our books electronically, we can spend more time ensuring superior content and spend less time on the technicalities of making books.

You can count on our commitment to deliver high-quality books at competitive prices on topics you want to read about. At IDG Books Worldwide, we continue in the IDG tradition of delivering quality for more than 25 years. You'll find no better book on a subject than one from IDG Books Worldwide.

IDG BOOKS WORLDWIDE

John J. Kilcullen
John Kilcullen
CEO
IDG Books Worldwide, Inc.

Steven Berkowitz
Steven Berkowitz
President and Publisher
IDG Books Worldwide, Inc.

WINNER
Eighth Annual
Computer Press
Awards ≥1992

WINNER
Ninth Annual
Computer Press
Awards ≥1993

WINNER
Tenth Annual
Computer Press
Awards ≥1994

WINNER
Eleventh Annual
Computer Press
Awards ≥1995

IDG Books Worldwide, Inc., is a subsidiary of International Data Group, the world's largest publisher of computer-related information and the leading global provider of information services on information technology. International Data Group publishes over 275 computer publications in over 75 countries. Sixty million people read one or more International Data Group publications each month. International Data Group's publications include: **ARGENTINA:** Buyer's Guide, Computerworld Argentina, PC World Argentina; **AUSTRALIA:** Australian Macworld, Australian PC World, Australian Reseller News, Computerworld, IT Casebook, Network World, Publish, Webmaster; **AUSTRIA:** Computerwelt Osterreich, Networks Austria, PC Tip Austria; **BANGLADESH:** PC World Bangladesh; **BELARUS:** PC World Belarus; **BELGIUM:** Data News; **BRAZIL:** Annuário de Informática, Computerworld, Connections, Macworld, PC Player, PC World, Publish, Reseller News, Supergamepower; **BULGARIA:** Computerworld Bulgaria, Network World Bulgaria, PC & MacWorld Bulgaria; **CANADA:** CIO Canada, Client/Server World, ComputerWorld Canada, InfoWorld Canada, NetworkWorld Canada, WebWorld; **CHILE:** Computerworld Chile, PC World Chile; **COLOMBIA:** Computerworld Colombia, PC World Colombia; **COSTA RICA:** PC World Centro America; **THE CZECH AND SLOVAK REPUBLICS:** Computerworld Czechoslovakia, Macworld Czech Republic, PC World Czechoslovakia; **DENMARK:** Communications World Danmark, Computerworld Danmark, Macworld Danmark, PC World Danmark, Techworld Denmark; **DOMINICAN REPUBLIC:** PC World Republica Dominicana; **ECUADOR:** PC World Ecuador; **EGYPT:** Computerworld Middle East, PC World Middle East; **EL SALVADOR:** PC World Centro America; **FINLAND:** MikroPC, Tietoverkko, Tietoviikko; **FRANCE:** Distributique, Hebdo, Info PC, Le Monde Informatique, Macworld, Reseaux & Telecoms, WebMaster France; **GERMANY:** Computer Partner, Computerwoche, Computerwoche Extra, Computerwoche FOCUS, Global Online, Macwelt, PC Welt; **GREECE:** Amiga Computing, GamePro Greece, Multimedia World; **GUATEMALA:** PC World Centro America; **HONDURAS:** PC World Centro America; **HONG KONG:** Computerworld Hong Kong, PC World Hong Kong, Publish in Asia; **HUNGARY:** ABCD CD-ROM, Computerworld Szamitastechnika, Internetto online Magazine, PC World Hungary, PC-X Magazin Hungary; **ICELAND:** Tolvuheimur PC World Island; **INDIA:** Information Communications World, Information Systems Computerworld, PC World India, Publish in Asia; **INDONESIA:** InfoKomputer PC World, Komputek Computerworld, Publish in Asia; **IRELAND:** ComputerScope, PC Live!; **ISRAEL:** Macworld Israel, People & Computers/Computerworld; **ITALY:** Computerworld Italia, Macworld Italia, Networking Italia, PC World Italia; **JAPAN:** DTP World, Macworld Japan, Nikkei Personal Computing, OS/2 World Japan, SunWorld Japan, Windows NT World, Windows World Japan; **KENYA:** PC World East African; **KOREA:** Hi-Tech Information, Macworld Korea, PC World Korea; **MACEDONIA:** PC World Macedonia; **MALAYSIA:** Computerworld Malaysia, PC World Malaysia, Publish in Asia; **MALTA:** PC World Malta; **MEXICO:** Computerworld Mexico, PC World Mexico; **MYANMAR:** PC World Myanmar; **NETHERLANDS:** Computer! Totaal, LAN Internetworking Magazine, LAN World Buyers Guide, Macworld Netherlands, Net, WebWereld; **NEW ZEALAND:** Absolute Beginners Guide and Plain & Simple Series, Computer Buyer, Computer Industry Directory, Computerworld New Zealand, MTB, Network World, PC World New Zealand; **NICARAGUA:** PC World Centro America; **NORWAY:** Computerworld Norge, CW Rapport, Datamagasinet, Financial Rapport, Kursguide Norge, Macworld Norge, Multimediaworld Norge, PC World Ekspress Norge, PC World Nettverk, PC World Norge, PC World ProduktGuide Norge; **PAKISTAN:** Computerworld Pakistan; **PANAMA:** PC World Panama; **PEOPLE'S REPUBLIC OF CHINA:** China Computer Users, China Computerworld, China InfoWorld, China Telecom World Weekly, Computer & Communication, Electronic Design China, Electronics Today, Electronics Weekly, Game Software, PC World China, Popular Computer Week, Software Weekly, Software World, Telecom World; **PERU:** Computerworld Peru, PC World Profesional Peru, PC World SoHo Peru; **PHILIPPINES:** Click!, Computerworld Philippines, PC World Philippines, Publish in Asia; **POLAND:** Computerworld Poland, Computerworld Special Report Poland, Cyber, Macworld Poland, Networld Poland, PC World Komputer; **PORTUGAL:** Cerebro/PC World, Computerworld/Correio Informático, Dealer World Portugal, Mac*In/PC*In Portugal, Multimedia World; **PUERTO RICO:** PC World Puerto Rico; **ROMANIA:** Computerworld Romania, PC World Romania, Telecom Romania; **RUSSIA:** Computerworld Russia, Mir PK, Publish, Seti; **SINGAPORE:** Computerworld Singapore, PC World Singapore, Publish in Asia; **SLOVENIA:** Monitor; **SOUTH AFRICA:** Computing SA, Network World SA, Software World SA; **SPAIN:** Communicaciones World España, Computerworld España, Dealer World España, Macworld España, PC World España; **SRI LANKA:** Infolink PC World; **SWEDEN:** CAP&Design, Computer Sweden, Corporate Computing Sweden, Internetworld Sweden, it.branschen, Macworld Sweden, MaxiData Sweden, MikroDatorn, Nätverk & Kommunikation, PC World Sweden, PCaktiv, Windows World Sweden; **SWITZERLAND:** Computerworld Schweiz, Macworld Schweiz, PCtip; **TAIWAN:** Computerworld Taiwan, Macworld Taiwan, NEW ViSiON/Publish, PC World Taiwan, Windows World Taiwan; **THAILAND:** Publish in Asia, Thai Computerworld; **TURKEY:** Computerworld Turkiye, Macworld Turkiye, Network World Turkiye, PC World Turkiye; **UKRAINE:** Computerworld Kiev, Multimedia World Ukraine, PC World Ukraine; **UNITED KINGDOM:** Acorn User UK, Amiga Action UK, Amiga Computing UK, Apple Talk UK, Computing, Macworld, Parents and Computers UK, PC Advisor, PC Home, PSX Pro, The WEB; **UNITED STATES:** Cable in the Classroom, CIO Magazine, Computerworld, DOS World, Federal Computer Week, GamePro Magazine, InfoWorld, I-Way, Macworld, Network World, PC Games, PC World, Publish, Video Event, THE WEB Magazine, and WebMaster; online webzines: JavaWorld, NetscapeWorld, and SunWorld Online; **URUGUAY:** InfoWorld Uruguay; **VENEZUELA:** Computerworld Venezuela, PC World Venezuela; and **VIETNAM:** PC World Vietnam.   3/24/97

Dedication

With love to Krystee and Christopher James ("CJ"), to my husband and soul-mate, Bob ("Dr. Bear"), and to his sisters Denny and Gerry.

Author's Acknowledgments

It takes a village to write a book, and in my case, it took a big village.

First on my list of people to thank is my colleague Barbara Lee Williams, former arts lecturer, museum curator, and international editor for The McKinley Group, which is where we first met. With her extensive background in art history, children's literature, higher education on the Net, and the Internet itself, Barbara made me grateful when she agreed to write sections of this book — particularly arts, language, entertainment, history, government and social studies. In addition to being executive editor of "Millennaire: The Third Millennium Education Project" on the Internet, Barbara contributes art criticism to Microsoft's San Francisco Sidewalk, as well as print publications such as *The ThreePenny Review, The Christian Science Monitor,* and the *San Francisco Chronicle.* I'd also like to thank Barbara's children, Courtney Delano Williams and Milton F. Williams IV, and her spouse, Milton III, for their support and valuable input during the whole process.

Also right up at the tippy top of my list goes a big thanks to my Project Editor Robert Wallace, who manned the helm with grace and good humor. Working with Robert was a pleasure, and I learned a lot from his caring guidance. Others at IDG who did so much to bring the book to life include Darlene Wong, Mike Kelly, Gwenette Gaddis, Diane Giangrossi, Bill Barton, Michael Simsic, Tina Sims, Lee Musick, and Karen York.

The process of writing a book can be both fun and daunting. For their unwavering support, patience, and ability to successfully execute "duck and cover" drills as my deadlines approached, I'd like to extend bundles of love and thanks to Dr. Bob, CJ, and my mom Terry Moran, also affectionately known as Gramzi (and thanks for those bowling and golf leads, too, Grams).

Speaking of Grams, I'd like to thank her and my dad, Arthur George Moran, for instilling in us kids a great appreciation of language, literature, and laughter. My brother Jim Moran and sister Ginny Moran are two of my favorite writers and humorists. And I know Dad is in heaven perfecting new puns for our eventual family reunion there.

And finally, I'd like to thank some special people who shared their time, talents, and encouragement when I really needed it: Jeff Cohen, Darlene Snodgrass, Dr. Lisa Post, Joe Holly, Irene Jackson, David Silva, Bill Adams, and my other dear chums from The McKinley Group.

Publisher's Acknowledgments

We're proud of this book; please register your comments through our IDG Books Worldwide Online Registration Form located at: http://my2cents.dummies.com.

Some of the people who helped bring this book to market include the following:

Acquisitions, Development, and Editorial

Project Editor: Robert H. Wallace

Acquisitions Editors: Gareth Hancock, Michael Kelly

Media Development Manager: Joyce Pepple

Permissions Editor: Heather H. Dismore

Copy Editors: William A. Barton; Gwenette Gaddis; Tina Sims; Michael Simsic; Diane L. Giangrossi; Kim Darosett; Linda S. Stark

Technical Editor: Lee Musick

Editorial Managers: Leah P. Cameron; Colleen Rainsberger

Editorial Assistants: Donna Love; Darren Meiss

Production

Associate Project Coordinator: Karen York

Layout and Graphics: Lou Boudreau, Linda M. Boyer, J. Tyler Connor, Angela F. Hunckler, Anna Rohrer, Brent Savage, Janet Seib, Deirdre Smith

Proofreaders: Kathleen Prata, Michelle Croninger, Nancy Price, Janet M. Withers

Indexer: Sharon Hilgenberg

Special Help

Jason Ely, Media Development Assistant; Joell Smith, Associate Technical Editor; Publications Services

General and Administrative

IDG Books Worldwide, Inc.: John Kilcullen, CEO; Steven Berkowitz, President and Publisher

IDG Books Technology Publishing: Brenda McLaughlin, Senior Vice President and Group Publisher

Dummies Technology Press and Dummies Editorial: Diane Graves Steele, Vice President and Associate Publisher; Mary Bednarek, Acquisitions and Product Development Director; Kristin A. Cocks, Editorial Director

Dummies Trade Press: Kathleen A. Welton, Vice President and Publisher; Kevin Thornton, Acquisitions Manager; Maureen F. Kelly, Editorial Coordinator

IDG Books Production for Dummies Press: Beth Jenkins, Production Director; Cindy L. Phipps, Manager of Project Coordination, Production Proofreading, and Indexing; Kathie S. Schutte, Supervisor of Page Layout; Shelley Lea, Supervisor of Graphics and Design; Debbie J. Gates, Production Systems Specialist; Robert Springer, Supervisor of Proofreading; Debbie Stailey, Special Projects Coordinator; Tony Augsburger, Supervisor of Reprints and Bluelines; Leslie Popplewell, Media Archive Coordinator

Dummies Packaging and Book Design: Patti Crane, Packaging Specialist; Lance Kayser, Packaging Assistant; Kavish + Kavish, Cover Design

◆

The publisher would like to give special thanks to Patrick J. McGovern, without whom this book would not have been possible.

◆

Contents at a Glance

Cartoons at a Glance

By Rich Tennant

"A BRIEF ANNOUNCEMENT CLASS – AN OPEN FACED PEANUT BUTTER SANDWICH IS NOT AN APPROPRIATE REPLACEMENT FOR A MISSING MOUSEPAD."

page 47

"It's a letter from the company that installed our in-ground sprinkler system. They're offering Internet access now."

page 313

"SHE JUST FOUND OUT SHE'D RATHER BE A JET PILOT THAN A FAIRY PRINCESS, BUT SHE DOESN'T WANT TO GIVE UP THE WARDROBE."

page 141

"I COULDN'T SAY ANYTHING – THEY WERE IN HERE WITH THAT PROGRAM WE BOUGHT THEM THAT ENCOURAGES ARTISTIC EXPRESSION."

page 11

"From now on, let's confine our exploration of ancient Egypt to the computer program."

page 257

"He found a dog site over an hour ago and has been in a staring contest ever since."

page 113

"This afternoon I want everyone to go on line and find all you can about Native American culture, history of the old west and discount air fares to Hawaii for the two weeks I'll be on vacation."

page 205

Fax: 508-546-7747 • E-mail: the5wave@tiac.net

Table of Contents

Introduction

●●

*G*reetings, fellow parents and grandparents! Hi kids! Welcome to my book on the Internet. You're about to discover some of the best, most fun, most useful, and most unusual sites on the Internet (also called the *Net*). You'll find places to go, things to see, and people to meet from all around the world.

Is This Book Right for Me?

You have a computer. You know how to find the Internet. You may even know a bit about searching for sites. But pretty much, you're all hooked up computer-wise with nowhere to go. That's where I come in. Think of me as your guide to the World Wide Web.

By using this book, you can find and store the Net's best stuff and you can become very confident about searching for even more things. Plus, with this book you get a CD that contains links to every site listed, neatly categorized for you just like the book is. All you have to do is put the CD in your computer's CD-ROM drive, click the name of the site that looks interesting, and instantly go there! (More on the CD in Appendix B, which is cleverly entitled "About the CD.")

If you think you are almost to this stage, but you aren't quite confident about getting on the Internet or using Netscape Navigator, Microsoft Internet Explorer, search engines, e-mail, or all the audio and visual toys available to you, I highly recommend securing as a companion book, *World Wide Web For Kids & Parents* by Viraf D. Mohta. It, too, is part of the Dummies Guide to Family Computing series and covers in much more detail all the aspects of getting ready to surf the Internet. Mohta's book also details neat activities such as building your own Web site. Then people who read my book can find your site!

What Can I Expect to Gain from This Book?

If your youngster walks up to you and says, "I have to write a report on the scalyhead sculpin," you can instantly transform yourself into Super Researcher! Faster than a speeding connection, more powerful than a 28.8 Kbps modem, you will help your child search the Net and find the ultimate site! (Until then, if your child does need to write about the scalyhead sculpin, visit the British Columbia Creature Page at clever.net/kerry/creature/creature.htm.)

This book contains veritable tons of sites on topics of interest to families, such as homework help, family health, travel, finances, ecology, and so forth. I've profiled many Web sites and pages so that you don't have to spend hours and hours searching for the information you need. Just grab this book, look up the topic that you want to find out about, pick out a site that matches your interest, and type the address in your browser or click on the *URL (Uniform Resource Locator)* for the site, which is available on the CD.

Incidentally, *URL* is only one of dozens (or hundreds) of Web-related terms. ISPs, WWW, HTTP — the Internet is an alphabet soup of acronyms. This book won't bog you down with computer lingo; it will give you clear, simple explanations to terms you need to know. And it will provide you with a well-organized, easily accessible collection of excellent, entertaining, and highly useful family-friendly Internet and World Wide Web sites. If some language used in a site profile doesn't make sense to you, check out Appendix A, "A Surfer's Guide to the Internet," for a little help.

I live within eyeshot of the great Pacific Ocean, so I get to see real surfers instinctively maneuver the waves without necessarily understanding every technical principle of wave dynamics. Likewise, we want to be able to instinctively maneuver the Internet. So grab your mouse. Surf's up!

What Exactly Is an Internet Site?

I will not attempt to dazzle you with a lot of technobabble, mainly because I don't understand a whole lot of the Internet's technical aspects myself. What I do understand quite well — as a consumer, parent, and grandparent, and as someone who makes a living tracking sites on the Net — is how to use the technology to find and store favorite sites.

A *site* is a location on the Internet (otherwise known simply as the *Net*). Sometimes the word *site* is interchanged with the word *home page*. A *page* in Internet lingo is one area within a site or home page. You *click through* the site or home page to get to other pages. For the purposes of this book, I refer to locations produced by organizations, agencies, or businesses as *sites* and to people's personal sites as *home pages*. These general definitions are becoming customary in the search engine industry.

You will see illustrations of actual sites in this book to help you along. I used a Netscape browser for these illustrations; your screen may look different from my illustrations if your browser is different.

Confused? Don't worry. I used to be, too. In fact, I was terrified of the Net. Too big, too confusing, too scary. Trust me, if I got over my Netphobia enough to make a living as a site reviewer for two major search engines, you can, too.

I've Heard the Internet Is Unsafe for Children

Because the Internet represents the largest, freest form of expression in the world, it contains all kinds of information. From my experience, I can say that most of what I've seen is informative, uplifting, entertaining, and creative. But not all sites are suitable for children. And some, as far as I am concerned, aren't suitable for anyone because they are filled with hatred or violence.

I highly recommend that children, including teenagers, always use the Internet under the supervision of an adult. That's why I'm writing this book — so families can learn about the medium together and design its use in a safe, personal way that fits each family's likes and needs.

The sites in this book were chosen for their family-oriented content and, in many cases, because they have excellent links to other sites on the same subject. It is also important to remember that those sites may also link to other sites, which may link to even more sites, and so on. Adult oversight is wise, because using the Net is like traveling down a road that leads to another road that leads to many other roads. The main roads suggested in this book always run smooth and clean, but as you travel down the Information Highway and take links to more links and even more links, make sure you don't hit a dirt trail.

Use this book and its CD as a guide to fun, safe, informative sites suitable for family viewing. The CD provides you with a few proven software filters; Appendix B tells you about these filters and how to use them. (I'm a parent and grandparent, too, so I share your concern for kids' safety.)

Finally, and most importantly, stay involved with your kids' Net adventures. As long as a child you love is on the Internet, take time to ask "What are you looking at?" or "What are you chatting about?" After all, exploring the Net is a terrific journey for the whole family to take together.

Sites Profiled in This Book

Internet Directory For Kids & Parents is designed so that you can skip around, much as you do on the Internet itself. The majority of the book provides you with actual sites to visit, categorized into a convenient hierarchy. Whenever needed, I supply you with descriptive information about the site so that you don't visit it cold. Sites take time to show up on the screen (or *load* to use proper techie jargon), so I don't want you to wait on a site only to be disappointed when you see it. My goal is to help you know in advance what to expect of any site that you visit and offer you the best.

Because of the dynamic nature of the Net, some of the sites may eventually change addresses, typically because they change servers. Most sites make sure you still find them by automatically linking you to the new address or by helping you click your way there. Hopefully, none of the sites profiled in this book will shut down entirely or fail to get you to their new locations, but if that does happen, you will likely get a very computerese-type message telling you the site can't be found (usually a message like "404 error" or "No DNS entry").

This book consists of sites with proven staying power, however, which in the world of the Internet means they have been around for a whole year or more!

How This Book Is Organized

You find six major parts, three appendixes, and a handy-dandy CD-ROM in this book.

Part I — Sports, Toys, Clubs, and Games: Play games and enjoy lots of fun activities online. Connect with the latest in kids' sports, clubs, and organizations. Track down your favorite teams and players in college and pro sports. Window-shop at a never-ending toy store known as the Internet.

Part II — Cool School Tools: A plethora of homework helpers and classroom subject-related sites awaits you (I even looked up the word *plethora* using an online dictionary). From *Roget's Thesaurus* and *Bartlett's Familiar Quotations* to dictionaries and encyclopedias covering many subject areas, you will have all kinds of standard (and not so standard) reference books available to you at the touch of a button. Additionally, visit the best sites for kids related to science, math, language arts, social studies, history, and other curriculum areas. Along the way, you'll find experts for kids to talk to and lots of unique learning activities. Homework can be fun? You bet! Who would have believed it when your parents were kids?

Part III — News, Weather, and Current Events: Not only can you find out what the weather will be tomorrow in your neighborhood, but anywhere on earth — or even on Mars. Various sites teach kids about climate and weather forecasting in fun, creative ways. Then it's on to news and current events, kid-style, at special sites designed just for them. Learn about holidays here and in other lands. And find your own "Net Pals" with whom you can communicate directly about what's happening in their part of the world.

Part IV — Family Life: Find out the latest in preventive health care for the whole family, and all about the particular health and nutrition needs of kids. Pick up some information about financial planning. Get some online career guidance or help in picking a college that's right for you. Visit sites just for kids that explain how the human body works. Explore sites related to the whole family's emotional, physical, spiritual, and mental health. And don't forget that all important family member, Fido! Numerous, high-quality sites are devoted to all kinds of pets, and site topics range from choosing pets to caring for them.

Part V — Entertainment and Travel: Travel the world without ever leaving your chair, or plan actual vacations, hikes, and outings with the kids. Discover all kinds of hobbies and craft ideas. Go cybershopping. Introduce your budding artists and musicians to the finest of the arts, or to classic rock 'n' roll. Help kids master the culinary arts using recipes cooked up just for them. Find quick, nutritious family recipes for everyone, including vegetarians. Seek out the best in TV, movies, videos, and software. Send a fan letter to the hero of your choice. (I'm partial to Kermit the Frog myself.)

Part VI — Mother Earth, Father Sky: Get to know Ma Earth from her early years to the present, and then rocket to outer space. Help people in England save the Sherwood Forest of *Robin Hood* fame. Or ask people all over the world to help you with your own environmental quest. See how kids everywhere are promoting earth stewardship through school and personal projects. Find out about rainforest birds, wildflowers in China, and the trees in your own backyard. Discover how to plant a garden, start composting, pick out a bird feeder, or build a birdhouse. Explore nature museums and public gardens, national forests and parks, and the world's most spectacular natural wonders. Find out which nature-based organizations have educational programs and activities geared especially for kids. Then grab those binoculars and get outside!

Part VII — The Part of Tens: This very brief part of the book contains profiles of very interesting sites that are more global in nature than the other sites profiled in this book. I list ten of the best sites for kids and another ten for parents.

Appendixes: Appendix A is a compendium about the Internet, the World Wide Web, browsers, applications, plug-ins, and the miscellaneous information that some techies take for granted that everyone knows. Appendix B tells how to install the CD which comes with this book. The CD offers software to filter out unsuitable sites and an organized directory of all the sites referenced in this book. It's your passport to adventure on the Net. Finally, Appendix C tells parents about keeping kids from accessing unsuitable material on the Internet.

How to Use This Book

Using this book is easy. Follow these steps:

1. **Open this book and look up the topic that you want to find out about.**

   You can look up the subject in the great index that's in the back of the book, scan through the table of contents, or just flip through the pages until something catches your eye.

2. **Use the micons and the profile information to pick out a site that matches your interest.**

   Say you're looking for info about organizations for kids, and you notice the Boys and Girls Club site, which is profiled in Part I: Sports, Toys, Clubs, and Games. You look at the micons above the profile text and see that the site is good for youngsters and teens (Preteen Cool and Teen Territory), that you can get questions answered at the site (Ask the Experts), and that you need a helper application that plays WAV files (Plug-In Required). Everything looks in order; now you're ready to go to the site.

3. **Type the site address in your browser and press Enter.**

   Your browser goes to the site for which you keyed in the address. You can also use the CD-ROM that's attached to this book as a shortcut to the sites you want to visit. For more information on how to do that, see Appendix B.

If you're having trouble connecting to a site that's listed in the book and you're sure that you've keyed the site address into your browser exactly as shown, you may need to add a slash (/) to the end of the address (for example, www.inkspot.com/), or you may need to add *http://* to the front of the address (as in **http://**www.bgca.org/index1.html).

Icons and Micons Used in This Book

What would a Kids & Parents book be without those cute graphics in the margins? The *Internet Directory For Kids & Parents* uses a handful of icons a few times and a truckload of micons quite often. This section explains all those pictures and what they mean.

The medium-sized *icons* in the margins of certain sections of this book are like road signs for you as you leaf through the pages. The following list explains what each icon means:

Remember: The Remember icon points out information that you probably already know but may not be thinking about while reading the text.

Technical Stuff: Check out the paragraphs marked with the Technical Stuff icon if you want to be bedazzled by nerdy Web terminology or computerese.

Tip: Text marked with Tip icons contain valuable insight into some issue — maybe something that can save you time or money, or both.

Warning: The name says it all. If you don't read anything else on a page, read the paragraph marked with a Warning icon. You can avoid disaster by taking those words to heart.

To make your Web surfing a pleasant experience, I use little graphic symbols that can tell you at a glance something important about a site. These little symbols that appear above site profiles are called *micons,* and here's a descriptive list of them:

Ask the Experts: Sites noted with this micon have ways for you to contact experts for more information about the site's subject matter. For example, if a site focuses on equestrian sports, you may be able to contact a farrier for advice.

$ **Fee Required:** Certain sites require that you pay a fee to use the services offered. You can play at some gaming sites, for example, only if you agree to pay a monthly service charge.

Graphic Intensive: Internet connections vary widely, as do service-provider capacities. Many sites are really cool but have lots of graphics, which can mean very slow loading times. This micon identifies those sites for you.

Heads Up: Parents especially should watch for sites so marked. Something about the site requires a little parental guidance or attention. Perhaps the site requires downloading a *helper application* or *plug-in* (programs that help your browser run certain files), or maybe some of the site's links aren't suitable for certain age groups. The text of the site profile explains why the site warrants a Heads Up.

Homework Helper: Many Web sites have loads of information about a given topic. Students can gain valuable insight, not to mention report-writing material, from a site or page marked with a Homework Helper micon.

Loads of Links: Several Web pages not only contain lots of information about a given topic, but they're also jumping-off points for other, more in-depth or specialized Web sites on the same or related topic. This micon notes sites that have lots of *links,* or clickable items that take you somewhere else.

Plug-In Required: The Web is full of interesting sites, and many of them require browser *plug-ins* (programs that help your browser run certain files) for you to get the full impact of their message. Shockwave and RealAudio are examples of plug-ins. This micon also may mark a site or page that uses advanced browser capabilities, such as frames or Java applets.

Tyke Time: The Web even has places that the littlest of surfers can catch a wave! The Tyke Time micon leads the way to those places.

Preteen Cool: Zero in on sites marked with the Preteen Cool micon if you're anywhere from 8 to 12 years old and you want to have some Web fun. This icon marks sites and pages suitable for that crowd.

Teen Territory: Teenagers can find topics of interest to them in sites marked with the Teen Territory micon. Many game sites — and many educational sites — are highlighted with this icon.

Sign In: Some sites require that you let them know more about yourself before they'll allow you to partake of their splendors. The Sign In micon signals you that a given site has that requirement.

Catch a Wave

Well, here you go. Time to plan those family vacations, see some of the prettiest places on earth, help the kids with their homework, play some games, save the rainforest, do a science experiment in the kitchen, contact kids around the world, find a recipe that the kids can make you for dinner, get the lowdown on mumps (what is a *mump,* anyway?), find out how to choose a pet, check on the weather report before that big family picnic, plant a garden, e-mail a TV star, let a newspaper know what you think, and do a whole bunch more things that you never dreamed were possible.

Have fun! Or as my semi-retired ocean-surfing husband would say, "Here's to consistent four-to-sixers with good morning offshores, glassy afternoons, and all the major pulses you can handle."

Part I
Sports, Toys, Clubs, and Games

The 5th Wave®   By Rich Tennant

"I COULDN'T SAY ANYTHING—THEY WERE IN HERE WITH THAT PROGRAM WE BOUGHT THEM THAT ENCOURAGES ARTISTIC EXPRESSION."

In this part . . .

You're bored? Bummed? Sick? Caught in a blizzard? Dark out? Stuck inside? Your friends busy? Even your dog is busy? Get over it! Play some games. Check out cool clubs, organizations, and toys, and find the latest in sports. Be your own best friend. Enjoy yourself as you browse the sites profiled in this part.

Clubs and Organizations

When kids get together, good things can happen. Reaching out to youth everywhere, many traditional youth organizations are now on the Web. What you once might have thought of as a local event is now a global happening. Here are some proven clubs and organizations to get you started or keep you in touch with your favorite group. And take note: If you're a budding young writer, InkSpot is a Web site dedicated to encouraging and helping you in your craft — and you can even get help in getting published!

Boys and Girls Clubs

www.bgca.org/index1.html

Linking Boys and Girls Clubs on the Net: Find out what the Boys and Girls Clubs are all about. Besides giving the locations of local clubs, check out who used to be a member of the Boys and Girls Clubs. Hear the public service announcement recorded by Denzel Washington, a former member and the spokesperson for the organization. (Note that you need a helper application to listen to some of the WAV files on the site.) Check out the other alumni and alumnae who are now in entertainment, sports, business, and government. After you see that this organization has something to offer any kids, follow the link to the listing of all the clubs around the U.S.

InkSpot

www.inkspot.com/young/

Online support for young writers: From the free biweekly newsletter aimed at young writers to the chat groups where you can discuss writing techniques, to get advice on a current project or just to listen in for some ideas or motivation, this site is a wealth of knowledge and resources for writers. Scan through articles that interview experts in the writing field. Pick up some books from the recommended reading list, or browse through the Classifieds to find places both on and off the Web for you to submit your writing. Some of them even pay money!

InterNETional Scouting Page

scout.strw.leidenuniv.nl/scout/

Links to people, units, and scouting organizations worldwide: Scouting troops with Internet sites are invited to add their URLs to this collection of scouting links. See what scouts are up to throughout the world and connect with a group near you. You can find news about events, camps, mailing lists, newsgroups, chats, and online message boards and can share ideas with others.

National 4-H Council

www.fourhcouncil.edu

Describes the expanded mission of 4-H Clubs: If your image of the 4-H is kids raising animals to sell at the fair, this site may broaden your perspective. Environmental stewardship, sustainable agriculture, and workforce preparation are integral parts of today's program. On this site you will find information on the national programs 4-H has to offer. Check out the links page that can connect you to local and state 4-H programs. After you link to a site, you can browse through the local opportunities that you have with 4-H.

Scouter's Compass

www.scouter.com/sl/

A super scouting site: Topics include campsites, upcoming events, earning and collecting patches, councils, and unit locations for all kinds of scouts. You can add your troop, unit, or pack Web site.

YMCAs On The Web

www2.interaccess.com/ymcaweb/

Worldwide directory of YMCA locations and activities: First begun in London, England, by George Williams in 1844, the YMCA now has 3,000 associations in 137 countries. Over 30 million people exercise and enjoy creative and supportive activities at YMCA locations. The programs that the YMCA has to offer can be unique, fun, and educational. Look up your local YMCA and see what's going on. You can even find out where to take SCUBA lessons! It's fun to play at the YMCA! Find a location near you.

Other Stuff to Check Out

Web sites
www.club-z.com/
www.yak.net/kablooey/scrabble.html
www.frisbee.com/
members.iquest.net/~webweavers/isfa.htm

Newsgroups
alt.games
rec.games

Chat areas
www.peak.org/~platypus/chat.html

Online service areas
America Online: GAMES, KIDS ONLY - Study Break
CompuServe: GO ACTION, GO HOTGAMES

Suggested search-engine keywords
Yahoo!: Yahooligans

Games and Other Fun Activities

Play online or download (copy) games to your computer's hard drive. Some are free; others involve shareware, which means that you can try something and, if you like it, you pay to keep using it. Before you run anything you download, do a virus check.

Some games you can play alone or with people sitting next to you. Other sites team you up with Internet gamesters who may live on the other side of the country, or the other side of the world!

This section also includes sites that sell software games online and sites that give you the chance to download samples and demonstrations of various software products.

Here are a few advisories to keep in mind as you begin exploring game sites. These tips aren't meant to discourage you from visiting these sites, and you may never encounter any of the following situations. But I figure that you want to know all the possibilities, so here goes:

- If you live with a parent or guardian, be sure to ask permission before you commit to spend any money at a site, register with a site, or provide any site with personal information.

- Chat rooms are common to game sites, ostensibly to discuss games, but many are unmoderated. Make sure that the chat room is an appropriate, safe environment to visit.

- Be aware that many game sites (and other sites), with or without your permission, set *cookies* in your hard drive that trace your surfing activities. I resent them, but for now, they are legal, and proponents insist that cookies are helpful to surfers. To learn more about them (and how to defeat them, if you choose), visit internet.junkbuster.com/ cookies.html.

- Sites may or may not work well depending on your computer, modem, and browser systems. Just try another site if one site doesn't work. I've tried to provide you with several alternatives that will work, no matter what.

Mega Game Sites

The following sites describe games or links to games, both online and software.

Electric Playground

www.elecplay.com/

For sophisticated computer gamers: This self-described online game superstore features news, reviews, previews, and interviews, for Sega, Nintendo, Macs, PCs, and more. You can also visit the download area for the latest demos or shareware software for the PC and Mac. Parents should probably look over the shoulder of kids cruising this site.

Entertainment Online

www.e-on.com

Super-sized online entertainment site: Get a 30-day free trial of all the multiplayer games, single-player games, brain games, Java games, which the site rates, and the "best of the Net" games, which the site rates. There are e-zines, digital offerings, chats, broadband services, and an extremely useful help service. Be sure you have a Java-capable browser and get the Multiplayer plug-in to compete online with other gamers.

Gamepower

www.gamepower.com

Lots of game action: Inside the jazzy design is a large collection of game reviews from various sources, updates on games for PC, Mac, Playstation, Nintendo 64, and Saturn, plus an array of demos and promotional items, as well as a chat area and contests. Parents will probably want to screen for age-appropriate language and games.

GamerZone

www.gamerzone.com/

Games for everything: You can find both new and classic PC games and links to game sites, including Nintendo 64, Sony

16 **Games and Other Fun Activities** _____

Playstation, Super Nintendo, Sega Saturn, and Sega Genesis. Get the latest information on hardware, video cards, sound cards, joysticks, and other software accessories. Click to find the hottest driver, to connect with game newsgroups, and to scour online gaming magazines. Because some of the content in some of these games can be high in violence and the language in the newsgroups can be a bit off-color, parental oversight is advised.

Games Domain

www.gamesdomain.co.uk/

The mother of all game sites: Visit this site for flashy, commercial, incredibly action-packed games — both free and fee. The site could be intimidating to the less experienced big-game hunter. But it's still worth exploring, with its 1,300-plus games, thousands of links, access to shareware/freeware/demonstrations, magazines, competitions, FAQs (that's frequently asked questions), walkthroughs (which is usually an animated or interactive file that shows you the game graphics and strategy), charts, and a special kids section. It requires registration, quite a bit of reading, and good comprehension skills. Parents need to help select appropriate games. A Java-capable browser is recommended.

Gamespot

www.gamespot.com/

Extremely well-designed game center: Gamespot offers high-band and low-band versions of games and activities to serve any personal computing system. If you are connected to the Internet with a slower modem or just don't want to wait for the graphics to load, choose the low-band version of this site. Get the latest news, reviews, and previews, as well as demonstrations of puzzles and action, adventure, interactive, sports, simulation, and brand-new games. Take advantage of tips about playing and advice about hardware. Parents are advised to preview games and system requirements. Because many of the games reviewed include demos, movie clips, or sound clips that can be downloaded, not many plug-ins are required. Most Java-capable browsers will handle this site. However, after you download any of the files to your systems, be sure that you have the necessary utilities to play the files.

Happy Puppy

www.happypuppy.com/

Giant online software game store: This site isn't about dogs, but it is brought to you with a theme of puppies throughout. Check out freebies from Cindy Pawford, computer classifieds, online ordering, software reviews from Bark Kent, and information on some 20,000 games. Not all areas are geared to kids, but the site has a special kids section, overseen by Junior, of new downloadable demo software so that you can try it before you buy it. The site features a radio show detailing new games.

Kidsoft

www.kidsoft.com/

Software online superstore with products geared especially to kids: The games range from educational to fun and silly. (How about buying a software cyberpet?) Shop at the simulated Town Square. The Parents Café has an online survey to get parents' feedback and ideas, and a chat room gives parents and educators a chance to discuss issues relevant to kids. The KidSoft Select Sites are tested by kids and approved by parents. About Our Products is a section where software titles are reviewed. It's a family-friendly software environment, though some pages require RealAudio or Shockwave plug-ins.

Webfoot Technologies PC Games

www.webfootgames.com/

Demos of arcade, puzzle, action, and simulation games: If you like the demos you find here, you can buy them and download the full versions of the games. Titles include BLUPPO! (Bluppo must collect all the fish in each level without getting squished or attacked by sturgeon), Yendorian Tales: Chapter 3 (a strategy and RPG, or role-playing game), and Inner Worlds (an action adventure featuring Nikita, the woman warrior who has to defeat a monster). These shareware games are for DOS and Windows. This site has neat graphics and music, plus chat and other activities. Start out at the hints and tips section to get help with utilization and other questions. Parents will want to lead the

visit here in relation to age-appropriateness and suitability of various games and the chat area.

WebFun

www.webfun.com/free.htm

Download free games: Read descriptions of games (for example, 3D Shooters — Games that take a quick trigger finger), what you need to run them, and download free demo versions to try before you buy. Almost all the games require a program like WinZip, which you can download at the WinZip Home Page. There are sports games (for basketball, baseball, and so on), RPGs (role-playing games), arcade style games, adventures (such as Curse of Monkey Island), classics (such as Space Invaders), action and cyber shoot 'em ups, strategy games, and some that are a bit of both (Outlaws, for example, in which you are a former marshal who needs to rescue your kidnapped daughter). One major heads up for parents — at the very end of the list of games is a section classified as "Mature."

Online Activities Just for Fun

Visit these sites for some guaranteed smiles. Most are extremely uncomplicated and offer giggles for even the youngest computer user (or *keyboard pounders,* as I call them).

18 Games and Other Fun Activities _____

Apple Corps

**jubal.westnet.com/apple_corps/
apple_corps.2.html**

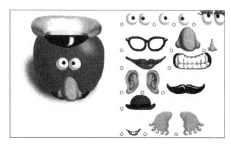

Making faces with fruit: This Java game is based on the same principle as Hasbro's Mr. Potato Head, but you can use any fruit or vegetable. The site features great graphics and is easy to play— sweet and simple, like a good apple. Note that the site contains a few subtle political comments that kids won't get but should amuse parents. Choose your fruit or vegetable (I thought a "Newt" referred only to an amphibian) and then click on a facial feature. Click again where you want the facial feature to appear on your fruit or vegetable of choice. Laugh at the results.

Ask the Eight Ball

www.pe.net/diversions/8-ball/

Have a ball with your future: Type in a question, click "Ask," and the answer is yours for the taking (or leaving). Try to keep your questions to the traditional 8-ball yes-or-no type; this orb won't return winning lottery ticket numbers. The site works okay with 14.4 Kbps modems.

Billy Bear's Playground

**www.worldvillage.com/kidz/bilybear/
wgames.htm**

Free fun and games: Explore traditional paper-reliant games and new online games. The games on this site will keep kids busy for weeks — be sure to go offline sometimes to get some sleep! The site is heavy on the Java applets, so you must have a Java-capable browser before venturing into some of the storybooks, clip art, and creative activities, as well as some of the links to other kid sites. When you load the first Web page of the Playground, it begins playing a great midi file; visitors can get more sound files in the Midi section of the site, and some even come with the lyrics so you can have a sing-along. For kids and adults alike, the Storybook section features information on how to create your own storybook, complete with illustrations, either for the Web or for printing. The Holiday section has coloring pages, games, and clip art for the most popular American holidays.

Blue Dog Can Count

kao.ini.cmu.edu:5550/bdf.html

Blue Dog image © 1992 George Rodgrigue

This doggy does math: Just type in two numbers; the doggy adds or subtracts and then gives you the total by barking.

The site can be a little buggy, especially with Version 3.0 of Netscape Navigator — but then, what dog isn't a little buggy sometimes? Be patient because sometimes Blue Dog needs a minute or so to come up with the answer before she barks out the answer in the form of an AU file. But I adore this site because of the tickled reaction it always solicits from little kids.

Build A Monster

www.rahul.net/renoir/monster/
    monster.html

Create your own animals: What would a duck look like with a frog's head? This simple activity for very young Internet users lets them choose various animal heads, torsos, and limbs and then combine them in funny ways. The site uses CGI scripting and works fine on slow modems.

BU's Interactive Web Games

scv.bu.edu/Games/games.html

Good times with classic games: Old standards gone electronic include Mine Sweep, Battleship, Tic-Tac-Toe, Pegs, and a number of challenging puzzles. Never fear if your browser is Java-challenged; this page comes in both Java and non-Java versions.

Carlos' Coloring Book

www.ravenna.com/coloring/

Stay in the lines every time: This site is another one of my favorites because of its creativity and gentility. It provides a great way for little ones to get comfortable with moving a mouse, clicking, and creating. Choose a drawing, choose colors,

indicate where you want the colors, and the computer does the rest. Remember to set your browser so that it automatically loads the images.

Cartoon Mania

www.worldchat.com/public/jhish/
    cartoon.html

Draw cartoons: Do you like comic books? Why not try drawing your own comic characters? This site shows you step-by-step how to create your own cartoon-style animals by putting a circle here or a squiggly line there. It's not intimidating, so get out your paper, pencil, eraser, and coloring tools of choice and launch your graphic art career!

Castle Infinity

www.castleinfinity.com

Save the dinosaurs: Castle Infinity is the last refuge of the dinosaurs, and it's your job to save the castle and the dinosaurs from some really gooky monsters. The good news is that it's all very exciting but not violent, which makes it great for kids. Sign up for a free CD-ROM starter kit, and then you and your amazing Frisky Broom can sweep justice over the land. You get a four-hour free play period, but after that, if you like the game, you must pay $30 to get the full version. You do need a Pentium PC running Windows 95, 8MB RAM, a 2X CD-ROM drive, and Windows 95-compatible sound card.

CyberJacques

www.cyberjacques.com/

Several kid-friendly games: You can play games including Hangman, Connect the Dots, Simon Says, and Fish! Adults may

20 Games and Other Fun Activities

need to help kids set up to play certain games. Be sure to have the Shockwave plug-in installed before you gather the kids around, or you'll be looking at a mutiny on your hands with CyberJacques leading the group!

Duck Hunt

aurora.york.ac.uk/ducks.html

Find ducks lurking in various photos and art: Okay, I'll admit it. I love Duck Hunt because it's totally dumb. Click where you think a duck drawing is hiding. If you're right, you are congratulated for catching the thing. This game is so silly that it's endearing. In addition to the color version, a black-and-white version is available for slower systems.

Electric Origami

www.ibm.com/Stretch/EOS/

Mindbenders: Twist your mind like a paper origami with this offbeat site that lets you make alien snow, assess the mood of the Internet on a daily basis, or post your art on a cyber-refrigerator door. Brought to you by IBM, this site is very creative, offbeat, and lots of fun. Other activities include a cyber-Kaleidoscope, a tour of spectacular fractals, puzzles, and brain teasers.

Elmo's Playground

members.tripod.com/ ~ElmosPlayground/

Sesame Street's lovable Elmo is here: This fan page is completely devoted to Elmo, the beloved red monster of the Sesame Street TV series. Sing-along to the show's theme song, take the Elmo Lover

evaluation test, visit Elmo's art gallery and download some Elmo graphics for your own homepage, and listen to Elmo talk. You can join in the polls, write a message to Elmo, read poetry written about Elmo, and link to related Sesame Street sites.

Family Games!

www.familygames.com

For family fun: Play these games as a family, including demos of Jumble, Pic-Tac-Toe, a funny word play game, and action adventures featuring Santa (can you rescue Santa's magic items?) and Uncle Julius (with his fabulous Anywhere Machine). Another offering, Twisted Tails, takes a fun-filled look at the classic fairy tales of the Brothers Grimm and Hans Christian Andersen. Try the four-level On-line Science Trivia Quiz! Demo play is free and full versions are reasonably priced. The games emphasize family enjoyment, as well as language and communication skills.

Guess-A-Sketch

showcase.digiplanet.com/ guessasketch.html

Multiplayer drawing and guessing game: You play this game against opponents on the Internet through a chat room. Using Javascript technology, a player can draw a picture while others try to guess what it is. If no one gets it in two minutes, the game starts over. The person who guesses the most drawings in the shortest amount of time is the winner. Because this does involve a chat room used by both adults and kids, parents will want to play along, too. You must sign up to play.

Hangman

www.allmixedup.com/cgi-bin/hangman/ hangman

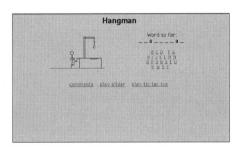

Flawless in its simplicity and enjoyability: Ask for a word. Guess its letters. Every correct letter shows up. Every wrong letter moves your little stick man closer to the gallows. Guess the word, and you win a gold star. Designer Andrew Wilson welcomes your e-mail feedback and word ideas. I give this ingenious little site a gold star. (You can reach three other games from here: tic-tac-toe, connect 4, and slider.)

The Hat: Online Magic Tricks

www.geocities.com/Paris/Metro/8777/

Mega magic site: Now you see it, now you don't. Discover the magic of magic through this extensive Java-enhanced site that features card tricks, illusions, articles about famous magicians, and tips from experts on perfecting your own skills. Submit a trick, chat with others about magic-related topics, and become a member to get even more inside secret information. Poof!

I Spy

www.geocities.com/~spanoudi/spy/

Learn colors and identify objects online: Vibrant, busy pictures contain lots of items for little searchers to find when a grown-up or older sibling says, "I see something. . . ." Choose from two sets of images based on your system capabilities; the smaller set of images loads more quickly, but the larger set has better image quality.

Kendra's Coloring Book

www.geocities.com/EnchantedForest/ 7155/

Interactive coloring book: Select and mix colors, and then choose a picture from a variety of black and white choices. Drop in your colors. If you're happy with the results, you can print your pictures. Though limited in the number of pictures to choose from, this site can keep the kids happy for quite some time. If you want to color the pictures while you're offline, you can print the pictures. You need a Java-capable browser before becoming an online Picasso.

Kids Corner Puzzle

kids.ot.com/

Cute and fun: Put a little puzzle together by picking pieces with a click of the mouse, play hangman, or vent your frustrations or find a penpal by speaking out in the Kids' Speak area, which has separate postings for younger kids and teens. When you are through in the Kids' Corner site, you can visit other kid-related links to Web sites. The site is ever-growing because its content is based on submissions from the kids who use the

22   Games and Other Fun Activities

site. You can send in pictures that will be used for the puzzle page or even featured on the homepage.

MadLibs

www.mit.edu:8001/madlib

Classic party game:. You need to know about verbs, nouns, and adjectives to play. Think of words and fill out a form. The computer takes your words and sticks them into a song or poem. The results can be really hilarious. You can play this game even with a slow modem.

Mr. Edible Starchy Tuber Head

winnie.acsu.buffalo.edu/potatoe/

Based on Hasbro's good ol' Mr. Potato Head: Kids of all have ages can have tons of really goofy fun in honor of the total spud. Choose facial features, stick them on, and customize your tuber man. This game should work reasonably well with any modem speed. If you get bored constructing your masterpiece, you can always read the fan mail, which contains some pretty good humor. Or check out the PotatoCam shots of previous visitor creations. Can't quite master the English language? Try the International Pig Latin version of this site.

Professor Bubbles

bubbles.org/pbfa2.htm

Bubble-based games and activities: Try Tic-Tac-Bubble and then make your own soap solution and bubble blowers for supersized, extraordinary bubbles. The recipe for the solution and some ideas for blowers and bubble machines are posted. Professor Bubbles is an international personality who's capable of blowing

large bubbles that can even surround a person! Be sure to have a frame- and Java-capable browser before blowing over to this site.

Stubbed Toe

www.stardot.com/~lukeseem/ stubbed.html

A variation of Tic-Tac-Toe: Neat graphics and a quick response time make this a fun version of a classic game. You play against the computer. Although the game is fine for any age, other sections of the site invite feedback that may contain blunt language. So parents should check out the management page before the kids do. Tables are used for the Tic-Tac-Toe board, so be sure your browser is capable.

Tarot

205.186.189.2/ms/tarot/tarot.html

Online tarot card reading: Type or think of a question, choose the type of card reading and card deck you want the computer to use, and then await the answer. Parents may want to visit this site first. If you don't object to Ouija boards and palm readings, this site is interesting and graphically attractive. Frames are used for the tarot reading as well as some of the other branches of the home page, www.thenewage.com.

Thunderbeam Kids' Software

www.thunderbeam.com/w/m/ index.html

Java-based games for kids: If you have a Java-enabled browser, you can play online arcade, puzzle, strategy, learning enhancement (don't panic, they're fun), and skill game demos. These games are rated by kids, which is a really nice feature of the site. This site does require you to accept a cookie in your hard drive before you can play. You can shop here, and the site lists itself as having a secure server for worry-free credit-card transactions over the Internet.

Virtual Pizza

www.ecst.csuchico.edu/~pizza/ pizzaweb.html

The ultimate no-cal pizza: Okay, so visiting virtual game sites creates a virtual appetite. Stop by here to order up a customized virtual pizza with the usual, or some highly unusual, toppings. Within seconds, your unique pizza is delivered to your screen. You can almost smell the steaming tennis balls. (I warned you that some toppings were unusual!)

Web a Sketch

www.digitalstuff.com/web-a-sketch/

Based on Etch A Sketch by Ohio Art Company: This online version is a whole lot harder than the handheld toy, which is what makes it both frustrating and addicting. Just view the Sketch of the Week to get properly intimidated before attempting your own drawing. Click your pointer where you want to place a line. Fortunately, the activity comes with an online eraser. It can be maddeningly slow on some systems, but the novelty makes it worth a visit.

Whack-A-Beaver

www.cs.orst.edu/~gottfrhe/java/ whackABeaver.html

Java version of the classic arcade game, Whack-A-Mole: Score points by whacking beavers on the head. Guess where they

will appear next. The site includes a High Score List and source code for anyone interested.

Where's Waldo?

www.findwaldo.com

He's lost again, try to find him: This time, Waldo is hiding at the circus in yet another big crowd. See if you can spot him. Click some of the scenery and you get noises. Try downloadable demos for games on both Mac and Windows platforms, or play the games online. You'll also find a fun geography game.

Online Magazines for Gamers

Sometimes, the best way to keep up to date on new online and video games is by reading magazines for "gamers." Many of these magazines offer online versions, as well as print newsstand versions. Here are some for you to browse. Parents, please remember that games cover a lot of territory and some games or entire sites may be more appropriate than others for your kids.

Computer Gaming World

cgw.gamespot.com/

Reviews, previews, tips, and demos: Get subscription information, as well as the latest news and updates concerning all kinds of games from role-playing, sports, and action/adventure to simulations, puzzles, adaptations of game classics, strategy-based, and online games. This site is easy to understand and navigate with sections for news, features, columns, interactive forums (which parents will

24　Games and Other Fun Activities

want to visit ahead of kids), related hot links, and downloads. Sign up for a free newsletter.

GamePro

www.gamepro.com/

Tips, reviews, and news for video gamers: This site, which is best viewed with Netscape 3.0 or higher, is sponsored by the world's largest interactive entertainment information provider for multi-platform gaming enthusiasts. Founded in 1989, GamePro Media Group produces GamePro magazine, the NetPro supplement and the upcoming NetPro magazine, The GamePro Online Network and GamePro TV. Use this site to find out about magazine subscriptions and current content, see past issues, and get tips, codes, game demos, and lots of game-related questions answered. You can find chat rooms, message boards, and a monthly poll, which parents will want to check out first. Reviews cover all kinds of games including role playing, sports, and (again, heads up parents) fighting. Systems that are reviewed and demoed include Nintendo 64, Playstation, Saturn, 16-bit, PC games, and arcade games.

Inside Mac Games

www.imgmagazine.com/

All-in-one Mac gaming resource: For those with Mac systems, this online magazine offers current and archived news, info on current and past issues of the magazine, original columns and features about topics of interest to Mac gamers, and opportunities to subscribe to the CD-publication and newsletter. Get the latest demos, shareware, new offerings, best offerings, and cool links. This site has chats and other interactive activities that parents will want to scope out first. Inside Mac Games is the only magazine solely geared to Macintosh entertainment. Each issue of the magazine, which comes to you on CD-ROM, includes previews of soon-to-be released games, game reviews of what's hot and what's not, color screen shots, QuickTime movies, hints, tips and tricks, and extensive Mac-related news and extensive feature coverage.

PC Games Online

www.pcgamesmag.com/

All-in-one PC gaming resource: Get game reviews, previews, news, in-depth features, plus the latest shareware and contest information. You can find current information about new releases and upgrades, evaluations of game quality and content, as well as downloads, demos, and all the information you need to subscribe to or buy at the newsstand the print version of this totally gamer-friendly magazine. Parents will want to look over this site first and check out chats and other interactive features. PC Games focuses on online, Windows 95, and DOS titles with its objective coverage of games for the PC. Every major PC game on the market is rated with a letter-grade system to help consumers make good, appropriate choices. Reviews also include game tips and tactics. Through this site, you'll get daily updates, game-review archives, downloadable files, and links to other gaming sites.

PC Multimedia & Entertainment Magazine

www.pcme.com/

Frequently updated online magazine: Stay informed about the newest happenings in the world of computer gaming. Sections include a directory of classic and recently released game demos; columns by Mark Shander, who takes regular looks at behind-the-scenes game development issues; and links to bunches of game-related sites. Easy to use and navigate, this site features various games and includes an illustration from each game, a review of each game, and related internal links to more information, images, demos, and so on. Offerings include sports, action, role-playing, and adventure games, although parents are advised to take a good look with or ahead of the kids to assure the appropriateness of various offerings.

Puzzles, Brainteasers, and Strategy Games

Using your head can be fun, as these sites prove. After all, when you exercise the body, it only gets better, and the mind is no different! Navigating your way to these sites and accepting the challenges they offer keep your brain in tip-top shape. From the classic Chess games to word search and crossword puzzles, these sites can be fun and informative for the entire family.

Caissa's Web

caissa.com/

Full-service chess server: This site has a free 30-day trial. Play games against other chess players anywhere in the world, in real-time, or watch live games as they happen. Additionally, you can sign up for correspondence-style games, get tips from experts, follow chess events, and use the chess library.

GAMEKIDS

www.gamekids.com

Collaborative sharing by kids and teens: The reviews and comments about games, recipes, writing, and other topics are largely written by kids. Add your own ideas and words of wisdom so that kids around the world can read them.

Games Kids Play

www.corpcomm.net/~gnieboer/ gamehome.htm

Rules for classic outdoor and party games: This site requires you to actually go outside and play! Now there's a concept. Rules, folklore, and interesting tidbits about all kinds of classic children's games are here. Passed by word of mouth from parent to child for generations, these are the games thousands of kids have played in the setting light of day or during recess at school. If you remember a game you played and the rules for it, you are invited to submit your memory to this virtual history of play. Among the ones included at this site are the card game 500, Stick Ball, Crack the Whip, Dodge Ball, Duck Duck Goose, Four Square, Ghost in the Graveyard, Hide and Seek, Kick the Can, Marco Polo, Marbles, Mother May I?, Red Light/Green Light, Red Rover, Simon Says, Statues, and Tag.

26   Games and Other Fun Activities

Headbone Interactive

www.headbone.com/zone/games.html

Intelligent, captivating computer games for kids: This site has online scavenger hunts, puzzles, brainteasers, a game chat room, downloadable demonstrations, prizes, links, and free stuff. The Headbone Zone offers bright, positive activities and online and software games for kids — but note that some require a Shockwave browser plug-in.

Imagiware's Game Zone

imagiware.com/games.html

Quick-loading and creative original activities: Fun, educational puzzles, brain scramblers, and visual adventures are presented with style by game/application designers Brian Casey and Tom Tongue. It's a family-friendly site. If you have a Java-capable browser, check out the Java Triangle Puzzle, the electronic version of the game in which you remove all the pegs except one to win.

John's Word Search Puzzles

**www.macconnect.com/~jrpotter/
    puzzles.spml**

Enjoy uncovering and circling words: Look here for copyrighted puzzles for your family to print out and solve with an old-fashioned pencil. Choose from various categories and reading levels. New puzzles are introduced monthly. The best way to view this site is to use Cyberdog or Netscape Navigator.

Netzee

**www.cs.cf.ac.uk/User/G.N.James/
    netzee/**

Get competitive on the Web: Just like the game of Yahtzee that you play around the kitchen table, you can roll the dice with Yahtzee lovers all over the world! This Java applet allows people to play Netzee alone, against the computer, or against an Internet opponent. Click the Start button, get connected, and read the user guide to find out the rules of the game and how to play this version.

Palindrome Home Page

**www.ecst.csuchico.edu/~nanci/
    Pdromes/index.html**

Graphically uncomplicated word game fun: A *palindrome* is a word or sentence that reads the same forwards and backwards. See how many you can think of, enjoy the ones online here, and contribute your own for posting. The postings range from silly to clever. Here are a couple of examples posted on the site: "Some men interpret nine memos" and "Marge, let's send a madness telegram!"

Philly News Crosswords

www.phillynews.com/crossword/

Crosswords in a whole new way: You haven't lived until you've done a crossword online. And, as long as you have a browser capable of displaying tables, you can sling letters around this site with the best of them! Adults can choose from a list of over 20 puzzles from *Philadelphia Daily News* or from smaller ones for a quick puzzle fix. The kids can have a little Word Match action. Pick your own difficulty level, sharpen that mental pencil, and head for 1 across (or 1 down).

Ray's International Web-Chess

www.csd.net/~rayw/joinchess.htm

Free Web chess: This Java applet created by Ray Wilson lets two opponents play chess by using their Java-enabled browsers (Netscape Navigator 3.0 and up, Microsoft Internet Explorer 3.0 and up, or Cyberdog 2.0 and up). Arrange with a partner to set a time for play and then sign on to the site. Play chess with Grandpa even if he lives in another state.

Scrabble

www.cs.mu.oz.au/~dnich/scr_intro.html

Crossword puzzle board game goes online: Play Scrabble (there's even a Scrabble dictionary) and chat with other Scrabblers. To play, you need a frames-compatible browser, the two most popular being Netscape Navigator or Microsoft Internet Explorer (Version 3.0 or higher of either). The site is still experimental and can get a bit unpredictable, but it has improved steadily over time and is certainly worth a try.

Shockwave Yahtzee

www.cln.com/staff/andy/yahtzee.html

Yahtzee with a twist: This online version of the dice game features good graphics and design and the added impact (or frustration) of Shockwave. Go to this site for a great way to spend 10 or 15 minutes a day relaxing and adding up your score.

Smart Games StrataJams

www.smartgames.com/

Puzzles based on games of intellect: Get more than 350 fun puzzles based on Smart Games like Car Jam, Marble Jump, Warehouse, Cash Crop, Traffic, and Sliding Tiles! Play word puzzles, review game products, and play online Java games. Smart Games, Inc., says its mission is to develop mentally stimulating, technology-based entertainment products that emphasize intelligence, achievement, and public recognition. The site has a section of free demos of games such as Smart Games Challenge #1, which features 20 puzzle categories with more than 300 individual puzzles, plus additional word puzzles, strategy puzzles, and perception puzzles.

Susie's Place

www.primenet.com/~hodges/
susplace.html

Variety of traditional word games: Try these fun standards online: Anagrams, Boggle, Doggerel, Stinky Pinky, and Crambo. If you're not sure what they are or how to play, have no fear — Susie helps you with complete online instructions before each game. Some Java applets are featured here, but not enough to prevent you from enjoying the games if your browser is Java-deficient.

Trivia Online

trivia.inetwave.com/

Site for trivia buffs: Share you favorite trivia question and try to guess other people's. New questions and topics are added daily to test your trivia knowledge. The site also features contests and interactive challenges. This is an easy-loading site. You must sign up to participate in any of the activities.

WebChess

www.june29.com//Chess/

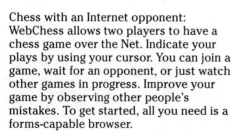

Chess with an Internet opponent: WebChess allows two players to have a chess game over the Net. Indicate your plays by using your cursor. You can join a game, wait for an opponent, or just watch other games in progress. Improve your game by observing other people's mistakes. To get started, all you need is a forms-capable browser.

Yachtzee

www.csun.edu/~mej16489/
yachtzee.htm

Diceless Yahtzee: You click the roll bar icon to play this Java-based game. Select the dice you want to discard and hit the roll bar again. Although the site has attractive graphics and design, it can be a little buggy. Improvements are forthcoming, according to designer Michael Jones.

YahtzREE

uranium.chem.umn.edu/~evan/Yahtzee/

A different version of Yahtzee: Netscape may not display the game correctly on a Mac, but this is probably the best game of Yahtzee on the Web. The graphics are great, the site scores the dice automatically, and a list of top players is updated immediately. This game works best with a Java-enhanced browser or any JDK applet viewer. Try to outperform the top 20 all-time players to this site or get your name in the list of the Top 1000.

Other Stuff to Check Out

Web sites

www.shareware.com
www.shareware95.com
www.gamecenter.com
www.ccweb.com/kuol/
www.meristation.dirac.es/ *(in Spanish)*
www.gdmagazine.com.br/ *(in Spanish)*
www.acertwp.com.tw/sgm.html *(in Chinese)*
www.heiend.com/zoxup/ *(in German)*
www.pczone.co.uk
www.acekids.com/javagame.html
www.maxis.com
www.thunderbeam.com/w/m/index.html

www.acekids.com/javagame.html
www.ibm.com/Stretch/EOS/
www.delorie.com/game-room/chess/
 info.html
www.corpcomm.net/~gnieboer/
 gamehome.htm
www.yak.net/kablooey/scrabble.html

Newsgroups
 alt.games
 rec.games

Chat areas
 www.peak.org/~platypus/chat.html

Online service areas
 America Online: GAMES, KIDS ONLY -
 Study Break
 CompuServe: GO ACTION, GO HOTGAMES

Suggested search-engine keywords
 Yahoo!: Yahooligans, Computer Games,
 Interactive Web Games, Internet Games,
 Word Games

Sports

www.olympic-usa.org

Here are sports sites featuring action, scores, and excitement. You want sports? You can find them here! From the favorites of the armchair quarterbacks to the dreams and ambitions of the young baseball players, you can find a link to most any sport imagined. If you don't know which sport is your favorite, the sites profiled in the General Sports Sites section cover the gamut. The only problem you may have is, do you choose to watch cable TV or surf the Net? Maybe both?

College and Amateur Sports

Want to find out more about your favorite college athlete? Interested in volunteering for the Special Olympics? Or perhaps you want more information about U.S. Olympic Team tryouts in your area? Check out the sites listed in this section. From the NCAA to high school football action, you can find it on the Web.

American Youth Soccer Organization

www.ayso.org/

Youth soccer site: Since 1964, the American Youth Soccer Organization has organized and run youth soccer leagues. Currently some half million boys and girls ages $4^1/_2$ to 18 participate in over 900 local regions nationwide. Find a league near you, visit the online Hall of Fame, and get the lowdown on rules, the league calendar, events, tournaments, camps, and how to participate. You also can link to other soccer sites and soccer chats. A frames-ready browser (such as Netscape Navigator 3.0 or Microsoft Internet Explorer 3.0) is a must for this site.

Archery Links

margo.student.utwente.nl/sagi/arlinks/

Links to archery clubs and organizations: Choose either the frames-based or frameless version of this site that provides links to university and other archery clubs, as well as related sites, including archery history, personal home pages of archers, organizations, events, newsgroups, and traditional and medieval

30 Sports

archery. Sites are marked with icons ranking their usefulness and relevance. You won't find any commercial or bowhunting sites, but this site recommends where to look to find them.

Dick Butkus Football Network — High School Football

www.dickbutkus.com/dbfn/highschool/

High school football action nationwide: You can offer your opinions and discuss your favorite high school football team at the Football Fan Bulletin Board. Enter the Football Fan Challenge contest, check out who is highest ranked by Dick Butkus Football Network editors, and then vote for your own high school football favorites. Stay current on game results, league news, and game forecasts. With adult approval, send a friend a cybergreeting card via e-mail from Dick Butkus or Deacon Jones or shop at the online store for football apparel, collectibles, memorabilia, and equipment. You can also link to other site sections covering Pop Warner, NFL, CFL, arena, and NCAA football. This frames-using site is a must for the avid high school football fan.

College Baseball Pages

www.utexas.edu/students/mohill/
baseball/colpages.html

Links to college baseball sites: Link to sites offering schedules, rosters, standings, scores, news, stats, polls, or pictures (links are coded as to content, so you'll know what to expect if you visit). This site also has a newsgroup. Categories include the Southwest Conference & Big 8 Conference (Baylor, Houston, and Missouri baseball), the Pacific Ten Conference (Arizona State, California, Southern Cal, Stanford, and

UCLA baseball), the Southeastern Conference, East and West divisions (such as Florida, Tennessee, Vanderbilt, Arkansas, and Auburn baseball), the Atlantic Coast Conference (Florida State and North Carolina baseball), the Big Ten Conference (Michigan and Penn State baseball, for example), the Atlantic Ten Conference (such as West Virginia baseball), the Western Athletic Conference (Brigham Young and Hawaii baseball), and the Metro Conference (Tulane and Virginia Tech baseball). Other colleges are also included (such as Harvard and Yale baseball).

College Basketball HQ

www.geocities.com/Colosseum/Field/
6940/

Covering college basketball: Connect with fellow fans through the chat room and message board, and get all the latest news and scores during basketball season, as well as rankings at the end of regular season play. Sections of this site, which opens to one of several musical selections including "Sweet Georgia Brown," cover the NCAA Division I AP poll, NCAA Division I poll, NCAA Division II poll, Men's Division III polls, NAIA Division I poll, NAIA Division II poll, and Junior College Division I Top 20. Stay up-to-speed with the players, coaches, and action as the season progresses. To take advantage of all this site has to offer, especially the chat room, you need a Java-capable browser.

College Basketball Report

www.oaktree.net/morebs/CBR/

Updates on college basketball: Take the College Basketball Report (CBR) Quiz and compare your expertise to others. Participate in the CBR Forum by reading or leaving your own message, or chat with other college game fans through the CBR Chatter. Weekly chat sessions are on Sundays at 2 p.m. Eastern Standard Time. Link to other forums, look back at the the previous season, make and post predictions, and enjoy fan polls. Among the conferences to which you can link are the America East, Atlantic 10, ACC, Big East, Big 10, Big 12, Big Sky, Big South, Big West, Colonial Athletic Association, Conference USA, Ivy League, Metro-Atlantic, Mid-American, Mid Continent, Mid Eastern, Midwesten Collegiate, Missouri Valley, Northeast, Ohio Valley, Pac 10, Patriot League, SEC, Southern, Southland, Southwestern, SunBelt, Trans-American,WAC, and West Coast conferences. Get all the scores and standings, and read articles about on and off the field news related to players. Link to related sites.

College Football Insider

www.collegeinsider.com/football/

News and features about college football: Sections at this site cover schools/schedules, stats, standings, scores, weather at game time, player injuries and stories, viewpoints from columnists, fan polls, message boards, player and coach interviews, promising Heisman potential players, and original features on season highlights. Review the play or player of the week, and enjoy tributes to legendary players. There are Q&A's with coaches and game highlights and lowlights.

College Lacrosse USA

www.centennial.org/lacrosse/mainmenu

Total lacrosse news: Regularly updated, this site offers the latest scores, season schedules, ratings, featured coverage of games, and players for both men's and women's college teams. Get NCAA final statistics for Division I, II, and III Men's leagues, Division III Women's leagues, and National Collegiate Women's leagues. Find out about championships, all-America teams, conference teams, the Lacrosse Foundation, Women's Lacrosse Association, awards, and special events. Link to related sites, and find details on Lacrosse youth camps.

College Soccer

www.collegesoccer.com

Soccer news and features: Get player profiles, coaching interviews, breaking news and background stories, updates on media coverage and exposure, and NCAA tournament information. You can find stats, scores, rankings, and schedules of play, as well as player interviews and related links at this Java-enhanced site.

College Sports Internet Channel

www.xcscx.com/colsport/

College football and basketball: Connect to sites related to college sports, sorted into categories including NCAA Division 1a Football Conference, NCAA Division 1 Basketball Conference, alphabetically by state, or geographically (from a map of the states). Some sites originate from university athletic departments, while others are from newspapers, fans, or student groups.

College/University Volleyball

www.volleyball.org/college/index.html

All about collegiate volleyball: This site serves up the latest news, schedules, and results in women's and men's volleyball.

Link to college and university volleyball sites, as well as media coverage sites. Find out about championships and schools with volleyball programs. Get a history of men's volleyball and link to sites about the Olympics and pro teams.

Little League

www.littleleague.org/

Official Little League site: After opening with a stirring rendition of "Take Me Out to the Ball Game," this Java-enhanced site provides plenty of fun and informative stuff to read and do (such as a site scavenger hunt). Get Little League-related news and season information. Sections for parents tell them how to help their kids get the most from a Little League experience in terms of understanding kids and sports, assessing a child's readiness and growth, and understanding the parents' and coaches' roles in Little League. Visit the Little League Museum and find out about leagues in your area (or how to start one), summer camps, and the Little League World Series. You can link to other Little League-oriented sites.

NCAA Online!

www.ncaa.org/

All NCAA sports: If you like any particular college sport, you can find it here where scores, teams, schedules, tournaments,

games, matches, players, and coaches are all profiled. This site is updated regularly, so you can count on getting the latest college sports-related results and news. Discover NCAA history, programs, services, scholarships, special events, and attractions. Browse the NCAA News online with its weekly articles, commentaries, personnel announcements, and job openings. With a major sports library, the NCAA site offers more than 50 publications and videos covering such things as rules, statistics, sports sciences, research, and records. You can find recruiting information for student athletes, dates and sites of NCAA championships, and related links. Get previews, results, and records for various NCAA sports through the searchable administrative databases. Sports include football, women's volleyball, men's and women's basketball, baseball, softball, men's and women's lacrosse, and men's ice hockey. Link to university, college, and athletic conference sites.

Outside Online

outside.starwave.com/index.html

Subjects of interest to the outdoor enthusiast: Enjoy creative and informative articles on outdoor subjects such as places to hike, camp, backpack, and seek adventure all over the world; how to get there; when to go; and what to take. You can find outdoor news and events, and tips on gear, safety, clubs, and organizations. An internal search box lets you look for your own outdoor interests. Type in

kids to get a whole section of articles pertinent to outside adventures, activities, and travel with children. Choose the Java, non-Java, or text-based version of this site to suit your needs and desires.

Soccer Information Systems

www.soccerinfo.com/

All about amateur-league soccer: Get information about college, high school, and youth league programs, as well as leads on tours to Europe, soccer camps, and recruiting. Find college programs by the name of the college, by division, or by state. This site is very basic but easy to navigate and filled with useful information.

Special Olympics

www.specialolympics.org/

Official Special Olympics site: This international year-round sports training and athletic competition is for children and adults with mental retardation. Its oath is "Let me win. But if I cannot win, let me be brave in the attempt." Check out Special Olympics history, how it operates today, who qualifies to participate, how to get involved, and where chapters and programs are located. This site offers links to related Special Olympic sites. A text-only version of this site is provided for slower computer systems.

Tennis Newspage

www.sportscampus.com/tennis/
tennis_news.html

The latest on college tennis: Get scores, rankings, schedules, and player news for men's and women's tennis. Sections include Final Division II and III, Final Division I Junior, Final Division II Junior, Final NAIA Rankings, and Final California Community College Rankings. This site

has an NCAA Tournament Page featuring player spotlights, ITA National Tournament & Event Calendars and archives, and features on matches and championships. You can click on links to sections on other college sports, and this site also features loads of internal links to its own original coverage.

United States Olympic Committee

www.olympic-usa.org/

Official Olympics site: Get the latest on up-and-coming athletes and famous Olympians. Keep track of competitions, statistics, future Olympics, what's happening at Olympic training facilities, and how to get involved — as an athlete, attendee, or financial supporter. Visit sections devoted to every Olympic sport. Kid Court offers articles fashioned for kids about Olympic athletes and events. Athletes discuss at what age they began their sport, how they train, what they like about it, and what it takes to become an Olympian. Also covered are the Pan American Games, the Paralympics, and the World University Games.

U.S. College Hockey

uscollegehockey.com/

All about college hockey: Get scores, standings, schedules, stats, rosters, and information on recruits and rankings, as well as links to related sites. Youth hockey schools and camps are listed for the up-and-coming Gretsky in your family. Notes and Quotes offers breaking, updated news, and you can link to any press release about hockey on the Internet. Get connected with camps, recruitment information, programs and leagues near you, and read feature articles that take in-depth looks at the sport.

34 Sports

Women's Basketball

www.auburn.edu/~poperic/wbb/
index.html

Links to Women's Basketball: Find lists of U.S. college teams (but not links to sites for them), conference divisions (with links), and link to media coverage (such as GNN Women's Basketball, ESPNet Women's College Basketball, AP Top 25 Poll, Basketball Digest, and Court Awareness Magazine). Get schedules of televised games at this very basic, no-frills, frames-based site.

General Sports Sites

Some people just aren't picky about their sports. Everybody has a friend or relative who will watch sports on television all day if given a chance, even if the only sporting event televised is International Arm Wrestling Regional Semifinals. If you're really into sports, the sites profiled in this section are just what you've always wanted.

Nando Sports Server

www.sportserver.com

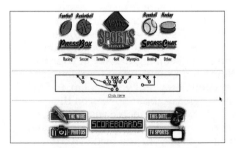

Current sports coverage: View the sports wire and action photos, and check on TV sports coverage and pending sports events of the day. Read sports articles in the Nando Times. Scope the headlines and descriptive graphs and then click topics that interest you to read about the event in more detail. The site is best viewed with a frames-capable browser.

Sports Illustrated for Kids

www.sikids.com

Sports world for kids: Graphically exciting and full of kid-oriented features and activities, this site offers sports-based word games, brainteasers, interviews, articles, trivia, puzzles, and online games. You can ask questions of famous athletes and commentators. Some games may be somewhat confusing to get started, and some games require plug-ins such as Shockwave, so adult assistance may be a good idea.

Total Sports

www.totalsports.net/

Sports news hot off the press: Here's an action-packed, regularly updated sports news site that covers events both on and off the field. It's organized in a fashion that proves comfortable, even familiar, to readers of traditional print sports pages. Scores and stats are posted almost immediately after the event is over. If you can't wait for the evening news to catch up on your favorite team, log on and jump here. Get involved with online sports games like Head-to-Head Baseball and occasional fan polls and chuckle at some sports humor. Be aware, however, that you'll need a Java-capable browser to play baseball!

World Wide Web of Sports
www.tns.lcs.mit.edu/cgi-bin/sports/

Linking digest of various sports: Do you enjoy arm wrestling, cheerleading, or tossing the boomerang? Find organized and individual sporting activities of all kinds. Skiing, walking, table tennis, rowing, softball, fencing, track and field, skating, weightlifting, and shuffleboard are just a few of the hundred or so headings that direct you to relevant links. Submit your own sports site or a favorite if you don't see it here. You can do so simply by clicking the link, filling out the form, selecting the category, and submitting your information. But chances are you will find most of the Web sites that deal with sports are already listed here.

WWW Virtual Reference — General Sports
www.dreamscape.com/frankvad/ reference-sports.html

Listings and reviews for many sports sources: Link up with publications and pro, amateur, and college sports sites that link to even more sites. You also can find information about individual sports, such as running, rollerblading, billiards, and scuba diving. If you want to open a Pandora's Box of Internet links, this is the place. Besides the sports listings, you can find many other categories to choose from.

WWW Women's Sports
fiat.gslis.utexas.edu/~lewisa/ womsprt.html

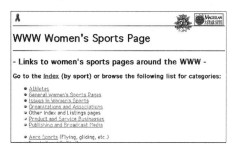

Links to women's sports pages world-wide: Link to sites organized by topic (such as Athletes, Issues in Women's Sports, Organizations and Associations, and sports for the physically challenged) or by sport (for example, flying, gliding, baseball, softball, basketball, cycling, climbing, rugby, field hockey, lacrosse, cricket, ultimate Frisbee, golf, gymnastics, ice hockey, motor sports, boxing, fencing, martial arts, wrestling, racquet sports, skating, soccer, skiing, running, swimming, and other water sports). This site is regularly updated and you are invited to suggest any women's sports' link that you may not find here (but there are plenty).

Online Sports Magazines

Many magazines that serve specific sports now have versions of their print publications online. You can usually read articles from past issues, find out what is in the current newsstand edition, interact with fellow sports enthusiasts, and subscribe to the print magazine through the Internet site. Browse here through the cybernewsstand.

36 Sports

American Track & Field

www.runningnetwork.com/atf/

Professional track-and-field publication: Dedicated to the improvement of the image and performance of American athletes, American Track & Field covers track and field, race walking, cross country, and performance road racing. The site appears to be directed toward coaches and the 3.6 million American athletes involved in sports of cross country and track and field at the junior high, high school, community college, college, and club levels. At this online magazine site, you'll find in-depth listings of events (such as high school, college, and international), results (including high school, college, opens, and international), valuable contacts in track and field, lists of specialty running stores, plus a free e-mail reader service. Additionally, you'll find sport biographies, training tips, features, breaking news on the sports, and special columns. Find out how to subscribe to the print version.

Behind The Boat

www.behindtheboat.com/

Magazine of boat-towed sports: Covering water-skiing and wakeboarding, this online magazine offers original articles, training and performance tips, updates on tournaments, an events calendar, and lots of related links. Graphically intense to the point of being a little confusing, the good news is that the site is packed with information. Get the lowdown on the latest issue, read articles from past issues, check out the calendar of events and competitions, read the athlete profiles and stats, and peruse sections on supplies, boats, and motors. Get advice from experts and reviews of ski videos.

Bicycle Online

www.bicycle.com/

For competitive cyclists: Get news about training techniques and camps, professional level bikes (including quality tests), shoes, helmets and other gear, and read articles, tips and profiles from and about leading pros, trainers, and even cycling-sports photographers. This site has feature stories, updates on events and standings, and related information of special interest to velodrome, street, or trail competitors. You can also get a look at bike maintenance and touring, and you can search bike-related classified ads. Interact with other cyclists through various online forums and discussion groups.

BlackBelt Magazine

www.blackbeltmag.com/

Self-defense for adults and kids: This searchable, online version of several martial arts print publications is graphically dynamic and contains lots of good content. Sections include Martial Arts for Rookies, Merchandise (such as books, videos, and CD-ROMs that you can order online), Subscriptions, and Pro Shop (with martial arts services and links), as well as coverage of events, schools, famous martial artists, martial arts terminology, history, styles, philosophy, and related resources. Click a magazine cover to see the table of contents of the current newsstand edition, which you can subscribe to at this site. Black Belt for Kids is an online version of a regular feature found in *Karate Kung Fu Illustrated Magazine*. The online version contains original training, technique, and history articles, and offers kids a chance to talk to experts and to one another online. An especially nice feature is the Word of Wisdom, a treasure trove of notable sayings about character, discipline, and honor to children.

BoardZ Online MagaZine

www.boardz.com/

The place for people who ride boards: This action-packed site (be sure to read user tips) offers the latest images, mini-movies, and articles about surfing, snowboarding, wakeboarding, and skateboarding. Visit magazine archives for past issues and get related information about equipment, suppliers, events, surf forecasts and projections, and "Surfer Girls" (their word, not mine!). Participate in surveys, find out where the best places to snowboard and surf are (taking into account factors such as El Niño), and link to related sites. This site is best viewed in Netscape 2.0 or greater or Microsoft Internet Explorer 3.0 or better. Subscribe to the e-mail list or offer your feedback to this frequently updated site.

Competitor Magazine

www.competitor.com/

Worldwide source for the triathlete, runner, and mountain biker: Get original features about events and leading athletes, as well as archived stories, club

listings, competitive results, and online radio coverage (requires Real Audio) of running, triathlon, cycling, and mountain biking. Hosted by *Competitor Magazine* publisher Bob Babbitt, "The Competitors" showcases interviews with the world's greatest endurance athletes. Log on anywhere in the world to the site every Sunday night between 9:00 and 10:00 p.m. (Pacific Coast Time) and hear live interviews and training tips from your favorite athletes every single week of the year.

Gold Collectors Series Magazines

www.gcsmag.com/

$

Publishers of special edition magazines: See the special collectible magazines produced by this company that highlight events, teams, and personalities in sporting news. This frames-based site with downloadable photos shows you the covers and details the content of many current offerings (such as its *Pro Hockey Guides, Pro Basketball Guides, Eye On The Tiger: The Tiger Woods Quarterly,* and *Stock Car Guide Quarterly*). Find out about subscribing to the service or ordering individual editions. See past special editions that are still available for sale.

In-Line Skater

www.xcscx.com/skater/

38 Sports

Happenings in the world of in-line skating: Find interviews with some of the sport's best skaters who share secrets about performing new tricks. Get event coverage, profiles of skating personalities, insights about the development of the sport, and information on the latest gear and accessories. You'll also find a comprehensive list of skate shops, links to related skating sites, and even reviews of great music to accompany a skating session. Get a free issue of the print version of *In-Line Skater Magazine.* If you like it, you can get seven more issues for $15.99 (with parental blessing, of course).

International Gymnast Magazine Online

www.intlgymnast.com/

Online version of a magazine for gymnasts: *International Gymnast* was founded in 1956, and by visiting this site's graphic-intensive version or text-only version, you can find out about the print publication and how to get it, as well as find out about the current issue. Check here for an online calendar of events, information about clubs and federations, lots of photographs and personality profiles, as well as a section that enables you to look at back issues. Special features of this searchable site include Gymnast-of-the-Month, Training Tips, Ask Bart & Nadia (yes, *that* Bart and *that* Nadia), Caption Challenge, the International Gymnast Poll, and a Quiz. Also get the latest on upcoming televised events.

National Bodybuilding And Fitness Magazine

nbaf.com/nbaf/home.html

All about amateur and professional bodybuilding: This free, monthly online magazine features original articles and news, the latest on bodybuilding contests, bodybuilding links, and lots of pictures of outstanding bodybuilders, both male and female. It's geared toward readers who want to improve their strength and physique, as well as toward fans of bodybuilders. Interact with the pros through forums, get the lowdown on training techniques and events, and search for other topics of interest. Explore past issues, review the book list, and find out how to subscribe to the print version.

Roller Hockey Magazine

www.rhockey.com/

Online version of *Roller Hockey Magazine:* Find playing tips, coverage of the pros and events, information on the newest gear, and drills to help improve your game. Link to related sites, find out how to subscribe to the newsstand version of the magazine, visit the archives to read past stories and hone in on skills, street games, the latest moves, winning tactics, ways to avoid injuries, stars of the sport, promising newcomers, hot accessories, and game action. Subscribe by calling an 800 number or mailing a check to the address at the site.

Runner's World Online

www.runnersworld.com/

Magazine's online version: Find events calendars and coverage; tips for beginners; advice on preventing and treating injuries; a section just for female runners; the latest road and track results; running links; guides to nutrition, books, and travel geared to runners; and running accessories, clothing, and shoes. The site also has forums where runners can interact with one another and with experts, plus interviews with notables in the sport and the latest on industry developments. Read columns on racing issues and topics of interest, and find out how to subscribe to one of the numerous editions geared to audiences worldwide.

Ski-life

www.ski-life.com/

Online magazine for competitive skiers: No fancy graphics here, but this site contains lots of information about competitive races and other events. Get results for the current season's World Cup events and look at rankings by competitor or by country. Results are updated soon after events so you can keep up to date with the progress of each season's competitions. To use the service, select which type of result you want and click the view button. You'll see sections devoted to upcoming event dates and rules that are relevant to competition skiing across the world. If you want a copy of rules, you can download them in Microsoft Word format and save them on your computer. Some of the sections are quite long and take a while to download, so you may want to just copy and paste instead.

Taper & Shave

www.taper-shave.com/

Covering championship college, high school, club, and international swimming: This detailed site keeps you in the swim of things related to current rankings and competition results worldwide. Among the conferences and championships included here are Men's NCAA I, Women's NCAA I, Ivy League, Big Ten Conference, WAC Conference, Big East, Pac 10, Mid-America, ACC Conference, SEC Conference, US Nationals, Olympic results, and a number of invitationals and other competitions. Read swim-related editorials, original articles, and event coverage. Get the latest on recruiting,

sport developments and personalities, and visit the photo gallery. Find out about related reports and services.

Volleyball Magazine

volleyballmag.com/

Online version of print publication: Get the latest news from the world of competitive volleyball, plus an events calendar, reader poll results, Question and Answer features with veteran volleyball personalities, tips on techniques, training and strategies, and lots of information about the newsstand edition (such as where to get it and how to subscribe). Visit the archive of previous articles, enter contests, participate in online forums, and offer your opinions on a variety of volleyball-related topics (for example, vote for your favorite surface on which to play the game, and then see how your opinion compares to others).

Wind Surfing Magazine

www.worldzine.com/windsurfing/

Online version of magazine for wind surfers: *American Windsurfer* is a leading publication for the sport, and this is the Web site for that magazine. Get a preview of the print magazine, plus tips on high-wind travel spots, training and technique, equipment, competitive events, and specialty shops. This site has good photographs and original articles. You can find out how to subscribe to the print magazine, too.

Yachtingnet

www.yachtingnet.com/

From the publishers of the 90-year-old *Yachting Magazine:* This searchable site features a yacht buyer's guide, a charter

40   Sports

guide, sailing weather reports and features, a competition calendar, news related to racing events and noted racers, forums for powerboaters and sailors, sailing links, a mailing list, and information about subscribing to the newsstand edition. Each day, the editors of *Yachting Magazine* offer a new tip to enhance your time on the water, and news coverage is frequently updated. You will also get first-hand accounts from the magazine's staffers about yacht performance trials and sailing trips. Participate in polls (for example, "Are there enough environmental safeguards in place to keep our waters clean?"). Connect to *Yachting Magazine*'s sister publications online, which cover golf, skiing, and other sports.

Young Equestrian Magazine Online

www.halcyon.com/2001/y.e.index.html

News and information for young riders: This site offers interactive features for young equestrians that allow them to interact with one another and ask questions of riding, training, and horse-care experts. For example, Lyle Petersen, who is a *farrier* or a person who shoes horses, hosts the Ask The Farrier Forum. The site and its print publications are geared to both novice and young riders with articles about training, preparing for competitions, horse selection and care,

and equine safety. If you like the online edition, which is a modified version of the print publication, you can subscribe to the print publication through this site. You'll find fun visuals (such as the flying horse animated GIF, which takes a while to load), related horsy links, and opportunities to help horses in need, even if you don't own a horse yourself.

Professional Sports

The Web is a great place to keep track of your favorite sports and sports figures. From professional tennis to NASCAR, American basketball to world football (also known as soccer), you can find out about the lives of real sports heroes and heroines, read about great teams of the past and present, check on the latest scores, or even shop online. Pick a sport, pick a site, and take your browser out for a game.

ATP Tour

atptour.com/

Men's professional tennis site: This site serves up information on the top competitors and tournaments in 34 countries. The ATP — which governs the men's professional tennis circuit by overseeing rules, prize money, entry requirements, tournaments, the calendar, and rankings — includes that information on its Web site. Check out the tennis newsline, notable quotes, results, rankings, features with top players, and the latest on tournaments, championships, and tennis camps. You can shop online at the Pro Shop. The best way to view these pages is with a browser that has a Shockwave plug-in.

Corel WTA Tour

www.corelwtatour.com/

The latest in women's pro tennis: Find a players guide, tournament information, interactive live chats, and links to other tennis sites. Get news, schedules, match news, player biographies and video interviews, results, and tournament scheduling information. Participate in fun surveys and other online activities. This site is heavy on frames and Java applets; be prepared!

Fastball

www.fastball.com/sitemap.html

All things baseball: Get current scores, link to sports coverage by the Associated Press, interact with fellow fans and players (there's a chat room and discussion area), and read up on injuries, standings, trades, streaks, promising newcomers, All-Stars, and wins and losses for both leagues. You can find coverage of players both on and off the field, as well as archived information and interactive baseball-related activities and games. Check out sections devoted to the Hall of Fame, legendary players, unbroken records, and baseball history.

Football Fans Club

home.netvigator.com/~artyeung/sports/
    football.htm

Who's who in world football: Find links to the world's top leagues, teams, and players in world football, or *soccer* as it's called in the U.S. This well-organized site connects you to soccer home pages worldwide, including fan clubs, official team sites, and personal pages of players.

Instant Sports

www.instantsports.com/

Interactive, real-time baseball reporting: Within minutes of actual game action, Instant Sports shows you statistics, visuals and replays through its play-by-play and an animated Instant Ballpark so you can watch a game in progress as long as you have a Java-enabled browser. Instant Ballpark looks like a video game, but is programmed to repeat the plays of the game that you choose. After you choose the game that you want to view, you can zero in on a particular inning and watch who is batting, pitching, and scoring. Connect to this site when your team's game isn't being telecast or you want to catch up on missed games. (That's right; you can look at games that have already taken place!) Additionally, the site offers personalized fan pages and services. You choose your favorite teams or players and the next time you log in, you can go straight to your saved choices. You can even be electronically notified when your favorite player comes to bat when your team is playing or when your team scores.

Major League Baseball

www.majorleaguebaseball.com/

Official Major League Baseball site: Get scores, statistics, game highlights, schedules, scouting reports, breaking news, a baseball library, an online store, and tributes to great players and to baseball history. The site covers American and international baseball, including both major and minor leagues. Visitors can share strategies and opinions at the Fan Forum. The kids section offers interviews and tips from professional players, video game news, baseball card collecting help, and feedback areas for ideas, questions, and stories. If you plan on downloading any of the videos, be sure to have a player installed on your system that will allow you to play MPEG, QuickTime, or VIVO video. You can create a fantasy baseball team and compare your team with others. A frames-capable browser such as Netscape Navigator 3.0 or Microsoft Internet Explorer 3.0 is recommended for your viewing pleasure.

Major League Soccer

www.mlsnet.com/

Soccer news that spans the globe: Get game highlights, schedules, articles, rules, and scores for worldwide professional soccer. A special section for kids contains advice, tips, and strategies from coaches, along with information on professionally sponsored soccer camps. The site features live audio broadcasts that can be heard through your RealAudio plug-in, QuickTime movies, and a chat group where ichat is needed to participate.

National Hockey League

www.nhl.com/

America's pro hockey organization: Get the latest hockey news and scores, or even listen to a live National Hockey League (NHL) game using your RealAudio plug-in. Downloadable video clips of NHL action, links to your favorite team sites, and Stanley Cup gear can get you tied up in this Web site for quite awhile, and you don't even have to worry about losing

your teeth! Coverage includes not only the men's teams, but the women hockey teams, as well. You can also find an interactive forum and spotlight articles on players.

NBA

www.nba.com/

Official site of the National Basketball Association: Catch all the action of the NBA and find links to the official site of the Women's NBA. Basketball fans find a slam dunk here, with all kinds of features, news, scores, statistics, draft action, interactive activities, and terrific photos. International basketball is covered, too. View AVI or QuickTime video clips and listen to interviews (a RealAudio plug-in is required), participate in polls, and become an expert on the rules and history of the sport.

NFL.Com

www.nfl.com/

Official pro football site: Easily track your favorite teams and players and get the latest news, statistics, game dates, and standings. The Java-enhanced site offers timely features, chats with fans and players, and sections devoted to football's rules and to the Football Hall of Fame. Spend time in the library reading up on the history of football and its all-time great players. You can also go to the Multimedia page and search for AVI and QuickTime movies of you favorite teams.

PBA Tour

www.pba.org/

Pro bowling site: Find chat rooms, archived standings, the latest standings, and news from both the senior and national tours. At Bowlers Journal, you'll get the latest news, comments, and behind-the-scenes articles. Other features include industry news, bowling tips, experts' columns, updates on new bowling equipment, coaching techniques, and fantasy-team bowling challenge information. Turn to this site for news from PBA Regional programs and information on how to participate. Fans can compare their favorite players to local talent in their region. Link to related sites that offer merchandise and other services. Get the latest standings, statistics, and tour schedules at this frames-based site. You can also find information on scholarships for young bowlers.

Professional Golf Association

www.pga.com/

Official PGA site: Enter the Global Clubhouse to find upcoming tournament information as wells as news and background on the PGA, and its senior, pro, team, international, and junior championships. The framed site offers loads of golf-oriented features and services, including the chance to question the country's best professional golfers and receive answers online. You can get help improving your game and send questions about rules to

the PGA Rules Chairman. The Cool Kids with Clubs section explains the Junior Golf program to parents and gives them tips on teaching course etiquette and skills to kids. Find out what's required to become a professional golfer. Visit the Ladies Professional Golf Association page at www.lpga.com/.

REV SpeedWay

www.revspeedway.com/index.htm

Auto racing site: Click your favorite NASCAR driver's photo to link up with the driver's fan club. You can catch up on all the latest news and event tracking and read up-to-the-minute articles. Live scheduled chats with fellow race fans about drivers and race-related topics are a special feature that requires only a frame-compatible browser. You can navigate easily (just as if you were driving a good race car) through this extremely well-designed site. It's packed with special services including an e-mail service that lets you write directly to featured NASCAR drivers.

Other Stuff to Check Out

Web sites

> www.users.nwark.com/~bryan/Colleges/
>   index.html
> www.hockeyguide.com
> www.swimnews.com
> www.USArchery.org
> www.blackbaseball.com
> www.inter.co.jp/Baseball
> www.collegeinsider.com/hoops/
> ourworld.compuserve.com/homepages/
>   JimsQuest/ncaalink.htm
> www.nbc.com/sports/index.html
> www.abcsports.com/
> www.sportsline.com/
> ESPN.SportsZone.com/
> CNNSI.com/

44   Sports

www.usatoday.com/sports/sfront.htm
www.tvguide.com/sports/
www.sport-hq.com/
www.sportschannel.com/
www.1on1sports.com/
www.sportingnews.com/
www.ultsports.com/
www.fastball.com/
www.pro-picks.com/
www.geocities.com/Colosseum/Field/3284/
www.americancheerleader.com/
www.gospelcom.net/gf/sf/
www.cricketworld.com/
www.racqmag.com/
www.gogirlmag.com/
www.theinsidetrack.com/
www.ccsi.com/yeeha/nassa/a1.html
www.lpga.com/

Newsgroups
rec.sport
alt.sports
clari.sports.football.college (NCAA football)
rec.sport.football.college

Mailing lists
emailhost.ait.ac.th/Search/pubmail-
   subj.html#sports

Chat areas
www.sportingnews.com/chat/
www.chatsports.com/
pages.wbs.net/
   webchat3.so?cmd=cmd_doorway:
   College_Football_Chat
www.enternet.com/webchat/chat.html

Online service areas
America Online: SPORTS, TODAY'S NEWS
   — Sports
CompuServe: GO SPORTS, GO NCAA, GO
   FANS, GO SPRTSIMS

Suggested search-engine keywords
Yahoo!: Sports, Kids Sports, NCAA, College
   + name of sport (for example: College
   Swimming and Diving, College Track
   and Field, College Rowing)
search.com (C/Net): Sports

Toys

Beanie Babies, limited-edition Barbies, and Star Wars, Lost World, and Power Rangers action figures. Every week a new toy fad arrives, thanks to TV, movies, video games, and kids talking to kids. Stay current on what's "in" and where to get it with the help of these sites.

FAO Schwarz

www.faoschwarz.com/

Historic toy store goes online: Listen to the store's welcoming ticktock clock and follow the bouncing balls to shopping for all kinds of toys. This framed Web site features online shopping and catalog ordering. Click "Shopping" to view departments organized into collectible and toy dolls, baby toys, preschool and toddler toys, plush animals, books, action figures, arts and crafts, science and discovery toys, musical instruments, games, vehicles, and other novelties. Click a toy to get a better look and to add it to your "bag" if you decide to order it. To view your selections, click the shopping bag icon. Discover store locations and specialized store services, such as personalized shopping, birthday or corporate in-store parties, or retaining a personal shopper.

Toys.com

www.toys.com/

Total online toy-shopping experience:
Browse the online catalog, play online
store games, and order through secure
online connections. This site bills itself as
the largest online toy company on the
Internet, specializing in popular and rare
toys for children and/or collectors.
Product safety and popularity are
contributing factors in the toys selected
for this site. You can special-order many
toys if they're not in the regular toy line.
This site features an internal search box
so you can look for products by name,
category, or manufacturer.

Other Stuff to Check Out

Web sites

www.matchboxtoys.com
www.toymarket.com
www.lego.com
www.bandai.com
www.galoob.com
www.hasbrotoys.com
www.barbie.com
www.hotwheels.com
www.littletikes.com
www.playmobil.de
www.tomy.com
www.vtechinc.com
www.sanrio.co.jp/english
www.ty.com
www.cpsc.gov/kids/kids.html

Newsgroups

www.neosoft.com/internet/paml/groups.K/
kites.html

Online service areas

America Online: MARKETPLACE — ToyNet,
FAO Schwarz, 800-TREKKER

Suggested search-engine keywords

Yahoo!: Toys: Retailers, Toys:
Manufacturers
LookSmart: Toys

46   Toys

Part II
Cool School Tools

The 5th Wave®   By Rich Tennant

@RICHTENNANT

"A BRIEF ANNOUNCEMENT, CLASS — AN OPEN-FACED PEANUT BUTTER SANDWICH IS NOT AN APPROPRIATE REPLACEMENT FOR A MISSING MOUSEPAD."

In this part . . .

*R*esearching your term papers with friends at the public or school library is a great way to enjoy an educational opportunity. But sometimes you just can't find a way to the library — especially when band practice, dance lessons, a football game, or a special after-school date would have to be missed. Your modem and the info in this part can help. Read on to find out just how many homework resources are available on the Web.

Reference Desk

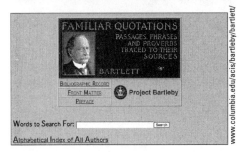

Whether you're working on a homework assignment, hoping to find an inspirational quote to end a speech, or trying to calculate mortgage payments on that dream home, you will find a resource here that can help you. I have included the widest array of reference materials available on the Internet. This cyberlibrary can surely supplement any crowded shelf full of dusty, out-of-date reference books.

Bartlett's Familiar Quotations

"Zounds! I was never so bethump'd with words" as I was perusing this historic resource (by the way, that quote is from William Shakespeare's *King John*. I found it through Columbia University's online Bartlett's, which is shown in the preceding figure). Here are two versions of this famous resource to assist you in finding that perfect popular expression or illustrative quote.

Bartlett's Familiar Quotations

www.columbia.edu/acis/bartleby/ bartlett/

Electronically reprinted version of the 9th edition published in 1901: This is part of Columbia University's Project Bartleby, heralded as one of the largest public collections of original online literature transposed onto the World Wide Web. Use the internal search box to type in requests for an author, phrase, passage or proverb (use any part of the expression you remember). Or scroll down the alphabetical list of all included authors. It might be slow on less powerful computer/ modems. Click the Project Bartleby button for other noted authors and their original works.

Bartlett's Familiar Quotations

www.akweb.com/singles/bartlett.htm

Find a quote: This version may be more user-friendly to computer users on slower systems because it employs a search box rather than an online list of the thousands of passages, phrases, and proverbs. Type in a quotation, noted speaker, or keyword. This site also contains a searchable Webster's Dictionary and *Roget's Thesaurus*.

Dictionaries

You don't have to rely on only one dictionary anymore. Online dictionaries cover a variety of subjects and research needs.

List of Dictionaries

math-www.uni-paderborn.de/HTML/ Dictionaries_noframes.html

Linking list of dictionaries: You can find all kinds of online dictionaries here, from foreign language, Esperanto, and technical, to English language, acronym, and slang. A frames version of this site is also available. The site includes a Thesaurus section and links to dictionaries for medical and other professionals. Parents may want to review the list for suitable offerings; some aren't good for kids, such as The Dictionary of Decadence On Line and Dan's Poker Dictionary.

Maran Graphics Visual Computer Dictionary

www.maran.com/dictionary/index.html

Clear definitions of computer terms and jargon: Illustrated and simple to use, this dictionary defines all the lingo used in the computer world. Just click any letter of the alphabet to get a list of words, and then click the word you want for a definition and illustration.

OneLook Dictionaries

www.onelook.com/

The faster finder: Chances are your word is among the 721,386 defined in the 156 dictionaries categorized here. You can use a search box that has helpful search tips, or you can choose to browse an individual dictionary. You can even link to sites about language use and education.

Pedro's Dictionaries

**www.public.iastate.edu/~pedro/
    dictionaries.html**

Easy-to-use dictionary finder: This is a very straightforward, easy-to-navigate list of online dictionaries. Just scroll and click when you find the dictionary you need. It includes two Webster's Dictionaries and *Roget's Thesaurus*.

Web of Online Dictionaries

www.bucknell.edu/~rbeard/diction.html

Links to over 350 online dictionaries: With so many dictionaries offered in 100 languages, you need only to type in your best guess to get the right spelling and definitions. Or scroll down the page for a massive but well-organized selection of dictionaries you can link to yourself. Preference is given to free online high-quality dictionaries, but there are also downloadable and subscription volumes that are rare or exceptional.

Encyclopedias

Here are two excellent online encyclopedias — one is the traditional type with original researched articles presented online, and the other is an encyclopedia of links to Web pages.

Britannica Online

www.eb.com/

Traditional encyclopedia now online: Get a free seven-day, online trial of this well-known encyclopedia. Britannica Online consists of 32 online volumes, 66,000 researched articles (not links), and 4,000 images. This is an admirable, up-to-date adaptation of the traditional encyclopedia book collection found in many homes and libraries, and you don't have to dust it. You do have to pay for it, however.

Free Internet Encyclopedia

www.cs.uh.edu/~clifton/index.html

Voluminous yet easy to use: Just click the first letter of the subject you're seeking. Or scroll down the entire alphabetized list. When you see your subject of interest, click it to get a list of online links pertaining to your topic. This is a great linking resource to hundreds of informative subjects and sites.

Measurements and Tables

Figure distances, weights, measures, and a whole lot more using these resources.

Martindale's Calculators Online Center

**www-sci.lib.uci.edu/HSG/
RefCalculators.html**

Over 4,500 online calculating tools: Because the site is so extensive, you may need to spend some time fiddling with it in order to get your bearings. Going far beyond adjusting Fahrenheit to Celsius or meters to feet, this site links you to calculating tools of interest to people in agriculture, the arts, the sciences, the gaming industry, automobile building and repair, cooking, manufacturing, finance, and communications. Determine photo depth of field, decipher Morse Code, or consult nine different calendar types (including Aztec and Mayan). What is your shoe size in China? From interest rates and payments to correct speaker sizes for your stereo or how many fish to house in a tank. Factor your net worth, retirement benefits, or how long you'll live. This site is a real measure of how much we measure in life. Be sure to read about the browser plug-ins that the various calculators require; most of them need Java-capable browsers to work properly.

Metric Equivalents of U.S. Weights and Measures

www.amm.com/ref/convert.HTM

Handy reference list: Scroll down or print out this useful listing of many types of measures, including cubic, liquid, linear, nautical, square, and dry measures. Also find equivalents for area and capacity, lengths, volume, and weight. Next time anyone asks you how many grams are in one pennyweight, you'll have the answer handy. Need to do some metric conversions? Try another page on this site: www.amm.com/ref/metric.HTM.

Unit Conversion Form Selector

**dplinux.sund.ac.uk/~manga/refer/
convform.html**

Clear and easy form finder: Choose which type of factoring form that you need — distance, area, volume, mass, speed, temperature, pressure, energy, power, force, activity, and radiation dose or exposure — and click the Get forms button. Then bookmark the form for future use. Or visit the section that has all the forms on it. Click Reference page for links to even more tables and measures, including those serving chemistry and math. You may want to check out the links to dictionaries, atlases, communications codes, computer languages, search engines, and the British Library.

Roget's Thesaurus

Say you're writing a book for kids and parents and are desperately trying to avoid using the word *neat* too much (as in "this is a very neat site"). What can you do? Where can you turn? Try *Roget's Thesaurus* online. Look up the word *neat*. Then you'll discover that you can write that the site is "easy, readable, fluent, flowing, tripping, unaffected, natural, unlabored, rhythmical, felicitous, well put," or "well expressed." Neat, huh?

Roget's Internet Thesaurus

www.thesaurus.com/

Quick-access thesaurus: Both a frames and nonframes version are available at this site, which you search by entering your word into the internal search box. You get a category listing of meanings from which you can then choose. Type in **bug** for example, and you can choose from words with similar context that have to do with uncleanness, fear (as in *bugaboo*), nobility, evil doer, or bad man. However, there is nothing related to insects. And that may bug you if that is the context you need. Still, it's a very useful reference.

Roget's Thesaurus

humanities.uchicago.edu/forms_unrest/ ROGET.html

Easy-to-use thesaurus: Using the internal search box, just type in a word you're seeking and press search. It doesn't get much easier than this to find another way to say the same thing. You can either search for just the word or receive listings of any place the word shows up in the entire Thesaurus.

Other Stuff to Check Out

Web sites
rivendel.com/~ric/resources/dictionary.html
www.uwasa.fi/comm/termino/collect/
www.dictionary.com/

Newsgroups
alt.usage.english newsgroup

Online service areas
America Online: REFERENCE DESK, LEARNING & CULTURE
Compuserve: GO ENCYCLOPEDIA, GO DICTIONARY

Suggested search-engine keywords
Yahoo!: Dictionaries, encyclopedias
Infoseek: Dictionaries, encyclopedias

Specialized Explorations

Arts

Both the visual and the performing arts are using Internet technology to expand and promote their fields in diverse and creative ways. As you explore the arts online, you find museums and other organizations, a vast array of educational materials, professional networks, as well as merchandise and events. One of the most interesting uses of the Net has been the creation of chat rooms where art, dance, and music are passionately discussed. Networking for the arts was never so easy!

Architecture and design

Curious about Frank Lloyd Wright, Julia Morgan, or I.M. Pei? You can check out Web pages dedicated to each of them. Architects and architectural firms, architectural historians and museums, schools, and libraries have made a diverse assortment of images, archives, and exhibitions available for you to peruse.

The Frank Lloyd Wright Page

lcweb.loc.gov/exhibits/flw/flw.html

An American architect: Frank Lloyd Wright designed buildings to relate profoundly to the American landscape. This page documents some of his designs from the decade between 1922 and 1932. The useful information here includes a brief discussion of his life during this relatively quiet period following construction of his design for the Imperial Hotel in Japan. You can view numerous beautiful drawings and architectural models. Projects discussed include the Lake Tahoe Summer Colony and the Doheny Ranch Development for Beverly Hills.

Islamic Architecture at Isfahan

www.anglia.ac.uk/~trochford/
    isfahan.html

A World Heritage City: The city of Isfahan in Iran, proclaimed a World Heritage site by UNESCO, contains a wide range of Islamic architectural styles dating from the ninth century to the eleventh century. This page reproduces several pictures of these architectural styles and explains the fundamental architectural theories and concepts underlying these mosques, shrines, bridges, and palaces.

Lighthouses: A Photographic Journey

www.ipl.org/exhibit/light/

The functional but fascinating architecture of lighthouses: These photographs of lighthouses are inspiring. The tour includes an alphabetical listing of all the lighthouses, a geographical index of the lighthouses listed by bodies of water, and a search engine to look up areas of particular interest in the text. The page also has a lighthouse bibliography for leads on good lighthouse research material as well as a guide to Net lighthouse resources.

Yale Art and Architecture University Library

www.library.yale.edu/Internet/
    architecture.html

Architecture master list: Compiled by Yale University, this list contains entries for architecture schools and museums, archives, libraries, journals, and mailing lists. The Yale collection also links to organizations such as the Society of Architectural Historians and the National Trust for Historic Preservation. This is an excellent place to start serious research.

Other Stuff to Check Out

Web sites
www.gpnet.it/a.nardi/
www.arch.unsw.edu.au/subjects/arch/mm-
    arch/96-s1/students/liu/assign3/imp.htm
www.lib.calpoly.edu/library-info/morgan/
    morgan.html
www.rahul.net/arctour/
www.arch.ethz.ch:80/

Newsgroups
alt.architecture
alt.postmodern
alt.building.architecture
alt.architecture.int-design

54 Specialized Explorations _____

Mailing lists

listserv@jhuvm.hcf.jhu.edu

listerv@suvm.syr.edu

aat-l-request@listserv.uic.ed

Suggested search-engine keywords

Yahoo!: Architecture, architects, plus subtopic (for example: schools or design)

Lycos: Architecture, design, landscape architecture

Art history

Ever go to an art gallery or an art museum and spend your time doing more wondering than wandering? You can save your feet and brain the agony by visiting the galleries and museums of the Internet. You can browse and absorb to your heart's content works that vary from ancient cave-dwelling artists to our contemporary artists. Masterpieces of yesterday and those in the making are illustrated, explained, and put into perspective for your understanding. The sites listed here are only a hair on the brush; keep exploring the various links that some of these sites offer and elevate your artistic and historical knowledge.

Asian ArtIndex

www.ArtIndex.com/

An Asian arts repository: Don't be fooled by the austere home page. This site links to several dozen pages filled with Chinese, Japanese, and Korean art. The museum links are international; some contain outstanding collections of several kinds of Asian art, and others focus on a single artist, such as sculptor Isamu Noguchi. The commercial galleries and auction houses sell ceramics and textiles, paintings and screens, and sculptures. The list of related links includes libraries, bookstores, and organizations such as the Asia Society.

Australia Art Serve

rubens.anu.edu.au/

Art from down under: This site houses more than 26,000 images of art from all times and all nations. Originally free, the page is now viewable by subscription: The more you pay, the greater your resources. Still, for little or no fee at all, you can see a comprehensive sample of art from around the world. The holdings are especially strong in art from the Mediterranean Basin.

The Chauvet Cave

mistral.culture.fr/culture/arcnat/chauvet/ en/gvpda-d.htm

Art from 30,000 years ago: The thrilling discovery of prehistoric cave paintings in the Ardeche in December 1994 may be one of the most significant discoveries in all of art history. We know that the caves, located in south-central France, are possibly the most extensive, well-preserved paintings ever discovered. You can read the text in French or English, but the images speak all languages!

Christus Rex

www.christusrex.org/

Visual arts of the early Christian experience: Created by the Vatican, this unusual Web site is oddly organized: You must scroll by different "messages" and numerous language flags to find the rich art sections. However, it is a wonderful cultural reference for visual arts in the Renaissance. You find Giotto's frescoes, the Vatican collection of master paintings, and pictures of Michelangelo's Sistine Chapel. The site has a gentle reminder that many artistic masterpieces owe their existence to the Catholic faith. The page also links to church documents and the Holy See.

Les Très Riche Heures (Medieval Manuscript)

sunsite.unc.edu/wm/rh/

A book for a lord: This site explains and illustrates a famous medieval manuscript — a book of hours — created around 1414 and owned by Jean, Duc du Berry, the brother of French King Charles V. The manuscript was hand-painted by three brothers — Paul, Hermann, and Jean Limbourg — who came from Flanders. The finely drawn and elegantly painted manuscript illustrations depict the seasons of the year at the duke's turreted castle.

World Art Treasures

sgwww.epfl.ch/BERGER/index.html

Virtual art tours: This thoughtful resource leads you to several programs on art from around the world. The subjects are diverse — Johannes Vermeer, Roman portraits, and Asian art and architecture, for example — but each tour is clearly written and beautifully illustrated. The sections also link to related online Web sites.

Other Stuff to Check Out

Web sites

halai.fac.cornell.edu/scott/BYZART.HTM
www.getty.edu/getty.html
www.tradenet.it/tiepolo/index.html
www.hart.bbk.ac.uk/VirtualLibrary.html
www.welleslian.com/dragontour/china/
architec.html
ic.www.media.mit.edu/Woarch/
womaninarch.html
wsrv.clas.virginia.edu/~umw8f/Cze/
HomePage.html
mondrian.princeton.edu/art430/
lonestar.texas.net/~mharden/74nadar.htm

Newsgroups

rec.arts.fine
alt.art.scene

Mailing lists

fah@netdreams.com
listserv@cunyvm.cuny.edu
caah@pucc.princeton.edu

Suggested search-engine keywords

Yahoo!: Art history, and/or keyword (for example: Matisse, illustrated manuscripts, book arts)

Lycos: Art history, plus keyword (for example: Italy, Cave Paintings, sculpture, or the like)

Artists

Scores of individual artists from around the world — and throughout history — are listed in Yahoo! and in World Art Resources, but the following pages are among the best sites about artists.

Christo and Jeanne-Claude

www.beakman.com/christo/

56 Specialized Explorations _____

Merging art with life: Christo is the famed Bulgarian earthworks artist who, along with Jeanne-Claude, his wife, used fabric to wrap Pont Neuf — one of the oldest and most famous bridges in Paris — and the Reichstag building in Berlin. They also adorned the Japanese countryside with blue umbrellas and decked out southern California with yellow umbrellas. If these artists intrigue you, you may love this information- and image-rich page, which documents several completed projects and presents the artist's plans and sketches for new projects, including "Over the River."

Frida Kahlo Home Page

cascade.cascade.net/kahlo.html

A tale of courage: This famous Mexican painter is best known for her penetrating and dramatic self-portraits and her colorful life. (She was married to the great Diego Rivera and was a friend of many famous folks, including Leon Trotsky.) The page reproduces several of her surreal self-portraits and tells the story of her difficulties and her courage. Don't miss the thought-provoking portraits in which she paints herself as an element in nature, for example, Wounded Deer of 1946.

Georgia O'Keeffe

www.ionet.net/%7Ejellenc/
   okeeffe1.html

Powerful images from a U.S. artist: This page reproduces some of O'Keeffe's powerful images and tells the story of her life before, during, and after her collaboration with photographer Alfred Stieglitz. The paintings include some of her early landscapes and several mature skull images. You also see photographs of O'Keeffe as well, some taken by Stieglitz. The frequent quotes effectively bring the artist to life: "I often painted fragments of things because it seemed to make my statement as well as or better than the whole could. . . . I had to create an equivalent for what I felt about what I was looking at . . . not copy it."

Magritte Home Page

www.virtuo.be/

Charming but illogical art of Belgian artist Rene Magritte: The work of this artist may interest viewers of all ages. This winsome page has useful information and over 250 images, including Magritte's most famous work, a painting of a pipe with the caption "Ce n'est pas une Pipe" (translation: This is not a pipe). The page's authors plan to add more images and expand the art historical information, but even as it is, the whole family will find much to explore.

Michelangelo Buonarroti

www.michelangelo.com/
   buonarroti.html

A man of the Renaissance: The Florentine artist Michelangelo was not only a great sculptor but also a fine painter and passionate poet. This introduction to the artist, his work, and his times is easy to follow and full of interesting tidbits, such as his tempestuous relationship with his demanding patron, Pope Julius II. Michelangelo loved to sculpt, but the Pope's requests that Michelangelo paint the Sistine Chapel (a task that took years) and design the Pope's own tomb kept the

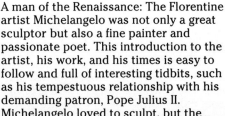

artist from his beloved sculpture. This site illustrates many of the best-known works, including his famous statue David, the tondo (round painting) of the Holy Family, and his sculpture entitled Slaves. The site also offers links to information about Florence.

The Official Picasso Page

**www.club-internet.fr:80/picasso/
homepage.html**

The twentieth century master of painting: This is the official Picasso page; it is sanctioned by the Picasso heirs, who own most of the works on these pages. The virtual exhibition has a number of images of Picasso's two youngest children, Claude and Paloma, and some interesting portraits of women from the 1930s and 1940s. The works are arranged by subject and then by date. One section notes events scheduled around the world that involve the work of this modern master.

The William Blake Page

jefferson.village.Virginia.EDU/blake/

The nineteenth century book: William Blake was utterly unique, a poet, a painter, a mystic, and a bookmaker of the Romantic period. These archives display his illuminated (illustrated) books, which have been painstakingly reconstructed. They have been arranged to allow sophisticated text and image searches. For example, you can search the image database for figures (by types, characters, postures, and attributes), animals, vegetation, objects, and structures, and the texts can be searched for individual words or phrases. The site also contains a select bibliography of articles on Blake.

Other Stuff to Check Out

Web sites
www.book.uci.edu/AdamsHome.html
www.diegorivera.com/
diego_home_eng.html
wwwhni.uni-paderborn.de/cim/privat/
achim/sr/sreng.html
www.noguchi.org/

Music

I know it's a cliché, but it couldn't be truer and more evident than on the Internet. Music is a universal language. Whether you're a budding young songwriter, a musician, or just someone who loves music and has little or no talent for it, you'll find resources here for any level of music appreciation. If you're interested in other music-related sites, check out the music sites profiled in Part V of this book.

American Musicological Society

**musdra.ucdavis.edu/documents/AMS/
musicology_www.html**

The "everything" list of music: The American Musicological Society (AMS) maintains a site that provides a one-stop shop for music links on the Internet. From listing orchestras and universities with music schools, to jokes, music therapy, folk music, instruments, and links for different genres of music, this has to be the grandparent of all music link sites. You can even contact your elected officials from this site. If you decide to join the society, membership dues are prorated according to income. Even starving musicians can afford the dues, but you don't have to be a member to enjoy this great resource.

58   Specialized Explorations

Opera Web

www.opera.it/English/OperaWeb.html

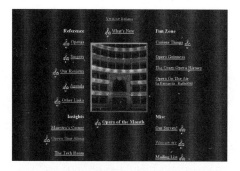

Opera for the serious and curious: If you never understood opera, this is your site. If you love the opera, this is your site. Check out the Opera of the Month to get a synopsis of the story, which great performers have appeared in it, odd facts surrounding the opera, even a musical analysis. For those of you who are shower singers, you can download midi files and lyrics (complete with pronunciations) to liven your next party with an opera karaoke. If the sing-along doesn't work very well, you can always impress your guests with the opera facts listed under the Opera Guinness link. This site comes in two flavors: English or Italian.

Resources for Young Composers

www.geocities.com/Vienna/2095/

Getting past the basics: You've composed a masterpiece. Melody and lyrics are honed to perfection. What's the next step? Apply for a copyright? Enter it into a few contests? Resources for Young Composers is a place that can answer these and other questions. While many young people may have the marvelous talent for music, many don't complete the process of making sure their piece gets

the recognition that it deserves. Download application copyright forms, and run through the list of contests where young music composers can submit their creation for fame and fortune. Some of the contests listed on this site have prizes of several thousands of dollars.

Solomon's Music Theory & Composition Resources

www.azstarnet.com/~solo/#Music Theory

Resources for music development: Composer and teacher Larry Solomon presents a great deal of information and links dealing with music theory, composition, and instruction. His original scores are listed and available for downloading, as is a brief biography on his musical education and teaching. Get advice on choosing a college for music, find out how to train your ear for music, and locate computer software that can help you write your musical score. You can also research composers, find musical scores on the Web, and look for a music festival that's near you.

Other Stuff to Check Out

Web sites

www.middlebury.edu/~lib/
    ethno.html#sectioncontents
www.songhits.com/
math.idbsu.edu/gas/GaS.html
www.geocities.com/Broadway/1336/
www.dfxnet.com/people/johnc/
    playtune.htm
www.billboard.com/

Performing arts

One might think that dance and drama wouldn't translate well to the computer. Not so! As these diverse pages show, information about various dance forms and specific troupes or ensembles is very popular on the Web. Moreover, the use of video enables you to see the troupes in action.

Actors Interactive

www.actors-interactive.com/

Resources for thespians: The life of an actor is a difficult one, and this page was created to aid and inspire these struggling artists. Some of the links — such as movie reviews and trivia — are for fun. But the industry contacts (agencies and casting directors) and frequently asked questions (such as the list of words every actor should know and how to join actors equity) are really helpful. For the history-minded, the site offers archives of Oscar winners and a catalog of over 750 plays with information on their authors.

African Music and Dance

www.cnmat.berkeley.edu/~ladzekpo/
    Ensemble.html

An informative guide to a sacred African war dance: Reviews, pictures, videos, articles, songbooks, and events listings fill this beautiful page dedicated to one type of African dance. The troupe featured is from Berkeley, California, but an online "concert" features ensemble director C.K. Ladzekpo and his 11-year-old daughter, Mawuli Ladzekpo,

performing Adzohu, a sacred war dance-drumming from Benin, West Africa. The site includes a detailed schedule of related 1997–98 performances in the San Francisco Bay Area.

Children's Theater Resources

pubweb.acns.nwu.edu/~vjs291/
    children.html

Encouraging kids to enjoy the theater: This Web page includes a history of children's theater — which is relatively new, having been started in 1918 by speech professor Winifred Ward. You also find links to plays for children. Perhaps most useful is a state-by-state listing of children's theaters and a link to ASSITEJ/USA, the International Association for Theatre and Young People.

Dance Pages

www.ens-lyon.fr/~esouche/danse/
    dance.html

A ballet directory: Estelle Souche, premiere ballet instructor at Ecole Normale Supérieure de Lyon in France, has put together this comprehensive international master list of ballet and modern dance resources. Included are: dance companies, a list of dancers, a list of choreographers, dance history, frequently asked questions about ballet, and a gallery of pictures.

Lord of the Dance

www.lordofthedance.com/index.shtml

The official page of this Irish sensation: Michael Flatley and his Irish dancers amazed us all with *Riverdance*. Here you can learn more about Flatley, considered by many the greatest Irish dancer in the world, about his new show *The Lord of the Dance,* and about Irish dance itself. You also find a photo album, news updates, several reviews, a fan club section, and tour information.

Stomp

**www.usinteractive.com/stomp/
   home.html**

The guide to stomping: "Everything has music to it!" claim the creators of Stomp, the latest hot dance craze. Stomp artists use everyday things — keys, fingers, toes, and furniture — to make music and to inspire dance. You can find out all about Stomp at this page, reserve tickets for Stomp's international tour, read the history of Stomp (which has been around a decade), and check out the pictures of dancers "Stomping."

Other Stuff to Check Out

Web sites
   www.tft.ucla.edu/
   www.artstozoo.org/yoballet/
   www.arts-online.com/bballet.htm
   www2.scsn.net/users/pgowder/dancing.htm
   www.alvinailey.org
   www.iie.org/ai/markson.htm

Newsgroups
   alt.acting
   ba.dance
   alt.music.dance
   rec.arts.theatre.musicals
   rec.arts.dance

Suggested search-engine keywords
   Yahoo!: Performing arts or subtopic (for
      example: dance, drama, acting, theater,
      or Alvin Ailey)
   Lycos: Performing arts or subtopic (for
      example: dance, drama, acting, theater,
      or Merce Cunningham)

Photography

Photography lends itself beautifully to the online world. But you can find more than collections of images here. The sites offer information on photography schools, how-to pages, collectives, and chat rooms. If you're interested in history, some sites celebrating the recent 150th anniversary of the invention of photography have reproduced old images, including daguerreotypes and early documentary images.

Aperture Gallery

www.aperture-photo.com/

reproduced courtesy of Aperture Gallery

Photographic history comes online: *Aperture* has long been one of the most respected photography publications in the world. Their monographs have included the work of Paul Strand, Edward Weston, Frank Horvat, Robert Adams; their modern masters have included John Krill, Anne Leignie, and Tim Booth. This stunning Web site reproduces dozens of photographs, arranged by artist and genre. The authors also provide information on forthcoming photography events and publications.

The International Center for Photography

www.icp.org/

A New York repository of twentieth-century photos: The International Center for Photography, or ICP, was established to collect, preserve, and exhibit notable twentieth-century works, with a special emphasis on documentary photography. It also teaches photography and provides a forum for the exchange of critical ideas and information. Its mission is to present photography's vital role in contemporary culture via its exhibits, its classes, and its Web page. Besides a clear explanation of ICP's history and mission, the page holds wonderful images by artists such as Brett Weston, Marc Riboud, Robert Capa, Weegee (Arthur Fellig), and other documentary photographers.

La Maison Européenne de la Photographie de la Ville de Paris

www.pictime.fr/mep/maps/
    drapeau.map?13,9

Photos from Paris: Don't worry — the text of this wonderful photography museum site is in English, too! Just click the "eye" icon to link to a set of images corresponding to recent shows at this Parisian museum. Photographers in the collection include old masters like Henri Cartier Bresson and new ones like Josef Sudek. The pictures are accompanied by interesting essays by art historians.

Tina Modotti

www.modotti.com/indexeng.html

A revolutionary photographer: This gifted artist is remembered for her touching studies of the Mexican Indians, their land, and their architecture — and for her colorful life. She photographed the murals of Diego Rivera and Jose Orozco; some of these images are here. Modotti was very beautiful, which you can see here from the pictures taken of her in Hollywood, where she had a brief acting career in the 1920s.

William Wegman

sjmusart.org/wegman/

Photos celebrating the dog: The San Jose (California) Museum of Art collected links related to photographer William Wegman, dogs, weimaraners (a breed of dog), and other art/dog things and posted them here for your pleasure. This museum created the site in honor of its exhibition of Wegman's photographs of his weimaraners. Besides discovering facts about Wegman here, you can enjoy his puppy portfolio — including my favorite, "Bad Dog."

Other Stuff to Check Out

Web sites

www.cmp.ucr.edu/
lcweb2.loc.gov/ammem/cwphome.html
www.book.uci.edu/AdamsHome.html
www.gate.net/~eak3/
www.brooks.edu/
www.nyip.com/
www.photo.fr/doisneau

62 Specialized Explorations _____

Newsgroups
> rec.photo.technique.misc
> rec.photo.marketplace
> rec.photo.misc

Suggested search-engine keywords
> Yahoo!: Photography, and specific
> photographers (for example: Edward
> Weston, Cole Weston, or Imogen
> Cunningham)

> Lycos: Photography, and specific keywords
> (for example: photo clubs, markets, or
> tips)

World museums

Over 200 museums from around the world are now online, including the Louvre and the Centre Pompidou in Paris, the Uffuzi in Florence, the Metropolitan in New York, Los Angeles County Museum of Art in southern California, the Nagoya in Tokyo, and the Prado in Madrid. Most offer you tempting highlights from their collections, and the creative ones have put together educational programs, tours, chat rooms, guides, and more. Yes, even the museum shops are online!

Andy Warhol Museum

www.warhol.org/warhol/warhol.html

Celebrating pop art: Andy Warhol was one of the most influential artists of his generation. His pop images, ranging from Campbell's soup and Brillo pads to Marilyn Monroe and Elvis, elevated popular American culture to the status of art. The museum features extensive permanent collections of art and archives as well as changing exhibitions by artists such as Francesco Clemente. Parents may want to screen the film and video section.

Les Musées de Paris

www.paris.org/Musees/

Touring museums in the City of Light: Few cities in the world can match the quality and quantity of Paris's museums. The numerous state museums include the Louvre, Musée d'Orsay, Musée de l'Orangerie, Centre George Pompidou, and Musée national Eugène Delacroix. Small museums include the Musée Rodin, Musée de la Ville de Paris, the Musée Picasso, and Maison de Balzac. The profiles of dozens of museums are arranged alphabetically; several of them have fine Web sites displaying their holdings. If you're planning a trip to Paris, check out the map locating the museums within Paris.

National Gallery Washington

www.nga.gov/

View art from the nation's capital: The NGA Web site features a searchable database of works in the permanent collection. (This includes American, British, Dutch and Flemish, French and Italian, Northern European, and modern art.) The site also has special tours (a select group of related images with explanatory notes) such as "Selections from Audubon's Birds of America," "Pennsylvania German Folk Art," and "Shaker Crafts," as well as other educational material. This is a multilayered, carefully constructed page, so allow yourself plenty of time to peruse it. You also may be interested in the events listing, general museum information, and the museum shop.

Stedelijk Museum

art.cwi.nl/

The collection from the Dutch Stedelijk Museum: Here you find a famed collection of modern paintings and sculptures, drawings, prints, photographs, and so on. You can see highlights from the permanent collection here, including works by Picasso, Mondrian, and de Kooning. What is unique are the special projects, such as "Restoration Matisse," which explains how a conservator goes about restoring a great work of art. Be sure to see the archives with their pictures and notes about a variety of past exhibitions, including photogaphy by August Sandler, sculptures by German artist Imi Knoebel, and photos from the permanent collection. The site text is in Dutch and in English.

WebMuseum

mistral.enst.fr/~pioch/louvre/

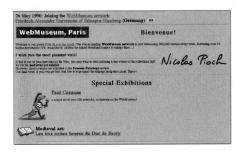

History of art by themes and artist: You find short biographies and images for most Western masters (from Giotto to Matisse) along with some non-Western (specifically Japanese) art and artists. This site is comprehensive, clearly presented, and accurate.

Other Stuff to Check Out

Web sites

www.sfos.ro/culture/roweb/mtr/index.html
www.unt.edu/dfw/dma/www/dma.htm
www.moma.org/
www.mfa.org/
www.lacma.org/
museoprado.mcu.es/
uffizi.firenze.it/welcomeE.html
www.icom.org/vlmp/world.html

Suggested search-engine keywords

Yahoo!: Museums, galleries, plus specific subtopic (for example: Art, Italy, Australia, or Photography)
Lycos: Museums, galleries, plus specific keyword (for example: sculpture, archaeology, or Mona Lisa)

Government and Social Studies

www.demon.co.uk/Itamaraty/

Virtually every country in the world has at least one national page that is both entertaining and educational. Many are official pages, that is, sponsored by the government. You can find many of these pages if you search in Lycos or Yahoo! for *embassies* or *consulates*. Other pages are the work of organizations or institutions, such as universities that specialize in organizing information. Still other Web sites are the creation of individuals who

64 Specialized Explorations

are passionate about one country or culture. The following sections explore Web sites about different countries and about U.S. governmental resources.

Countries and cultures

If you want to discover simple geographic or political facts about any country in the world, you can start at www.odci.gov/cia/publications/nsolo/wfb-all.htm, the CIA World Factbook, which gives you a bare-bones introduction. Alternatively, you can check out www.lonelyplanet.com, Lonely Planet, which also has entries for most countries. Of the numerous countries in Africa, Asia, Australia, Europe, North America, and South America that have established official Web pages to explain their history, government, and cultural traditions, we describe a few to pique your interest. The following sites offer a sample of the amazing diversity of these pages.

The Brazilian Embassy in London

www.demon.co.uk/Itamaraty/

Visit Brazil — land of contrasts: This spectacular-looking site is rich in information and images. For a sense of its diversity, check out the section on football, which is the sport known as soccer to people in the U.S.; the science and technology section; biographies of Brazilian authorities; papers on selected subjects; and cultural events in Brazil, including Brazilian samba and other musical treats. You also find information on the chamber of commerce and surveys and seminars on Brazil.

Canadian Museum of Civilization

www.cmcc.muse.digital.ca/

Canadian history from Norsemen to modern life: This site has information on Canadian peoples, history, and artifacts. The Canada Hall Virtual Tour covers the period from 1000 to 1885, beginning with the Norsemen who sailed to Newfoundland and covers many other topics such as early farm life, the fur and timber trades, maritime shipping, British military presence in the nineteenth century, and life in Victorian-era Ontario. Canadian History Virtual Tour Phase 2 covers 1885 to the present and discusses different industries and religion in Canada. Other sections illustrate old Nova Scotian quilts and hats worn in Canada through the years, the first inhabitants of Canada, and even early watercraft. QuickTime movies are riddled throughout the site, so be prepared for long download times if you want to see them!

Cuba Web

www.cubaweb.com

A look at the diversity, complexity, and cultural richness of Cuba: This site has several informational databases. The Business Library contains U.S. laws and legislation dealing with Cuba, Cuban foreign investment laws, Cuban history, news, financial and trade information, maps, demographics, and other resources relating to business in Cuba. The Culture Library has everything you want to know about Cuban culture, from art and music to food and sports. You can download pictures in the Culture Library (check out the Cuban dancers!), and a list of events may tempt you to visit Cuba.

Cultural Map of Hellas (Greece)

www.culture.gr/2/21/maps/hellas.html

The Hellenic Ministry of Culture's guide to Greece: This page can guide you through your visit — whether it's a virtual visit or an actual one. Information is arranged by region — Peloponnese, Macedonia, and Thrace, for example — and each area has notes on attractions. (You simply click the icons for pictures and text.) Don't miss the famed Palace of Knossos, the Archaeological Museum of Mytilini, or the lovely early Christian basilica of Aghios Andreas. Allow time for downloading the large maps and the numerous links.

The Embassy Web

www.embpage.org

Online embassies and consulates: These pages range from colorful and fascinating re-creations of different cultures to relatively dry statistical databases. However, they can't be beat for getting you the latest accurate statistics about a country. This site brings dozens of countries all together in a searchable database. The site also has bulletin boards and a link to *Washington International* magazine.

France

www.premier-ministre.gouv.fr/

An introduction to France: The governmental links and history section are pretty impressive, and kids can find plenty to discover behind the charming icon of a kangaroo. The texts of recent governmental news bulletins are also reproduced. The download is often slow — probably because this page must transfer from France — but the site is a charming introduction to France and is worth the wait. You can view the page in English, Spanish, German, or French.

In Italy Online

www.initaly.com

Italian e-zine — or electronic journal — with inside information on Italy: You find out about marvelous hidden treasures, such as the rustic villages of Portofino and Viareggio, and how the Italians celebrate Christmas. (Making biscotti is part of the holiday tradition.) In addition, the authors want you to share your own tips about traveling in Italy. You can also practice your Italian in a chat room, check out the many links to sites such as the Ufuzzi Gallery, and view some pages covering Italian opera.

India

www.indiagov.org/

Pages on Indian science and technology, politics, news, culture, and media: In honor of the 50th anniversary of India's independence, this site brings you a wondrous array of pages on Indian science and technology, politics, news,

66 Specialized Explorations

culture, and media. The site includes a country profile section that features facts and figures in a nutshell and a section called "India Towards Prosperity," which discusses India's future in telecommunications, civil aviation, tourism, and other industries. The culture section discusses Indian painting, music, and dance, and the social issues section is dedicated to discussion of social reforms and initiatives to help the poor, women, and children.

Japan Window

www.jwindow.net/

One of the first Japanese Web sites in English: It brings you Japanese Internet and World Wide Web news, as well as special issue coverage. (A special issue may be the XVIII Olympic Winter Games in Nagano in 1998 or a feature on Japanese/English television.) For a glimpse inside the Japan Internet, click the top ten Japanese Web sites of the week — they range from Anime (Japanese animation) to business news sites. Don't miss the "Kids' Window," which has stories, art, and music.

Peru Explorer

www.peru-explorer.com

Land of the Incas: This site is as pretty as it is interesting. Although the pages contain plenty of facts, the authors want

you to have a good time, too. That's probably why they created "Really Cool Stuff," which has features on the path of the Inca, the Colca Canyon, Manu National Park, the Inca Trail, and the Sacred Valley. The government and history sections are hard to find (look under the People and Culture section) but are worth your time.

Si Spain!

www.DocuWeb.ca/SiSpain/

Spain at your fingertips: Created by the Spanish embassy in Canada, this site is the spot to visit to research that Spanish current events paper for your world civilization class. It has information on Spain's history, geography, and society; culture, including links to the Prado (a museum in Madrid) and to pages dedicated to Picasso and Dali; foreign affairs; the Spanish language; food; and tourism. Don't miss the links to bullfighting and Spanish soccer teams (under Other Links). The site is translated into English, Spanish, French, and German.

South Korea

www.kois.go.kr/

 $

The latest news related to Korea: Based on both Korean governmental and international sources, this site has detailed information on the government and history of this country as well as its culture, educational system, and business. At the section titled "Exploring Korea," you can find out about Mask-Dance dramas, traditional musical instruments, Korean martial arts and wrestling, crafts, rites of passage, arts and architecture, literature, calligraphy, and much more.

Tibet

www.tibet.com/

Land of the Dalai Lama: Winner of the Nobel Peace Prize in 1989, the Dalai Lama, the spiritual leader of Tibet, was forced to leave Tibet and now heads his government from exile in India. This is his official Web site, which includes information on the history of Tibet, including the actions of China against the Dalai Lama and other Tibetans. You also find information about Tibetan Buddhism, traditional Tibetan medicine, Tibetan culture (arts and literature), and human rights. The site presents the latest news on the status of Tibet and how you can help this country through letters to various organizations and governments.

Virtual Zimbabwe

www.mediazw.com/index.html

All about Zimbabwe: Zimbabwe in southern Africa is the home of the famous Victoria Falls. The country is also a great place to take a safari adventure. The links

on this site are a source of information for nearly any aspect of the South African country. The link to the National Parks enables you to explore the country's natural beauty and its animal inhabitants. Think South Africa is all jungle and wild animals? Check out the links to commerce and industry. You can take a tour of the shopping mall or discover how to build a Blair toilet — an outdoor latrine that doesn't smell, doesn't attract flies, is easy to maintain, and is a community effort of the country's Ministry of Health. You can even have the *n'ganga* (the tribe healer) throw the Divining Bones or Hakata to help your decision-making (a Java-enabled browser is required for divination).

Other Stuff to Check Out

Web sites

www.utoledo.edu/homepages/achraibi/morocco.html
147.252.133.152/nat-arch/
www.lonelyplanet.com
www.aust.emb.nw.dc.us/
www.denmarkemb.org/
www.indiagov.org/culture/overview.htm
www.nbt.nl/holland/
www.valley.net/~transnat/

Suggested search-engine keywords

Yahoo!: Country or continent and subtopic (for example: culture, history, news, business, or geography)
Lycos: Country and subtopic (for example: government, laws, or statistics)

Government

The U.S. government exists to serve the people, and one way that it does this is by making databases, archives, and exhibitions available for its citizens to use online. The scope of American government resources is pretty impressive — after all U.S. government agencies invented the Internet — but the following resources are good jumping-off places for students (and parents) to begin their research.

68 Specialized Explorations

FedWorld

www.fedworld.gov/

The federal government at your service: Virtually every federal database and online resource is available via this searchable Web site. The resources are comprehensive: Along with specific Web pages, the site has servers listing dozens of related sites, electronic documents, and bulletin boards. Subject areas include international trade, the Internal Revenue Service, the U.S. Treasury, law enforcement, Bureau of Indian Affairs, and so on. A simple keyword search yields titles of numerous related documents.

Historic Documents

**kuhttp.cc.ukans.edu/carrie/docs/
   docs_us.html**

Documents that tell the history of the U.S.: Designed for educators, this page also may interest families. The site contains documents such as a letter written by Columbus to the queen of Spain around 1494, an early discussion of The Iroquois Constitution, the Mayflower Compact of 1620, Chief Seattle's 1854 speech, testimonies of Canadian fugitives from the mid-nineteenth century, Abraham Lincoln's Gettysburg Address, Andrew Carnegie's paper on wealth from the *North American Review* in 1889, the Espionage Act of 1918, the League of Nations treaty, the lyrics to "Brother, Can You Spare a Dime?", and President Franklin D. Roosevelt's statement on the Japanese attack on Pearl Harbor in 1941. Virtually every president — along with other people who helped shape America — is quoted here.

Human Rights Web

www.hrweb.org

A connection to human rights organizations and resources around the world: This page defines human rights and refers visitors to the Universal Declaration of Human Rights in the United Nations Charter. The site also explains why people need to be aware of and concerned about furthering human rights today. The site has several links to other key documents in the history of human rights. Probably the most compelling area of this site contains the real accounts of people who have suffered through human rights violations or who spoke out against the guilty. Parents are strongly urged to review this area in particular before letting a young one browse it; the stories can be very graphic.

Library of Congress

www.loc.gov/

Repository of archived information: Visitors to the site have full text access to current bills under consideration in the U.S. House of Representatives and Senate, and they can view changing exhibitions from the Library of Congress literary holdings, including The Russian Church and Native Alaskan Cultures; Women Come to the Front: Journalists, Photographers, and Broadcasters During WWII; and Frank Lloyd Wright: Designs, 1922–1932. Thomas Jefferson began the Library of Congress back in 1800; he started with his own personal library. Not only can you view these preserved books and documents, but other original historical documents are preserved here, including the Declaration of Independence, the

Constitution, and the Gettysburg Address. Documents are not the only treasures of the library; artifacts of Lincoln's assassination, an early baseball card, and original fabric from the Kitty Hawk airplane can also be found here. The site offers four methods to search the library's huge holdings.

Lycos Government Links

www.lycos.com/government/

Selection of governmental resources and sites from Lycos: Here you can link to federal and state services or visit international political sites, such as India, Current Affairs, or The Inter-America Dialogue. A hefty section on government news includes articles such as "What Did Gore Know?" and "GOP Grabs Money Memo," and "Handgun Bill Passes." You also find coverage of U.S. politics, conspiracy theories, police rights, and sections such as "Nuclear Test Ban Treaty — Has Russia Broken its Word?" On a more practical level, you can locate a nearby consulate or read reports on safety in the workplace.

National Archives Online Exhibit Hall

www.nara.gov/exhall/exhibits.html

Historic documents for grades 6 to 12: Here's where you can find reports such as "A Short History of the Human Rights Movement" and "Biographies of Prisoners of Conscience." The site defines human rights and reproduces documents relating to human rights, including "Universal Declaration of Human Rights" and other UN declarations; the Geneva Convention, which deals with the treatment of prisoners of war; the Convention on the Rights of the Child; and the Charter of the United Nations. This is a great place to start research on human rights. The site doesn't focus entirely on human rights, however. Check out the gifts that 12 of the U.S. presidents have received; some are very touching, others very lavish, but all were tailored to the man in office.

Smithsonian

www.si.edu/

America's Treasure House for Learning: What exactly is the Smithsonian? A collection of museums? A series of databases and archives? A magazine? Of course, it's all of these and more. The Smithsonian collects art, artifacts, documents, and treasures relevant to America and American history. The Air and Space Museum, the National Science Resource Center, the Hirschorn Museum of Art, the Museum of African Art, the Museum of American History, and the Archives of American Art are all part of the Smithsonian. Allow yourself time to explore this site so that you can locate the organization or institute that covers the subject you're looking for.

State and Local Government on the Web

www.lib.umich.edu/libhome/
   Documents.center/state.html

State and local government links: This site is your one-stop shop for almost everything dealing with local government. Links on this site take you to local municipal codes, state laws, professional organizations of elected officials, state tax forms, and even state jobs that are available. The geography student that's in all of us can click a link to a site that lists state capitals, symbols, constitutions, and newspapers. Need to contact your legislator? A couple of links at the primary site will give you phone numbers, fax numbers, e-mail addresses, and even Web addresses . . . oh yeah, and street addresses, too!

UN Links

www.undcp.or.at/unlinks.html

Countries working together: The United Nations is an organization that works to find solutions to international disputes and problems and confronts all kinds of issues that concern humanity. Besides telling you about the UN's history and its 50th anniversary, this information-rich page has links to resources on Activism, Conferences, Human Rights, International Affairs, National Focal Points for Drug Information, Women, and the very cool Model United Nations.

U.S. Census Bureau

www.census.gov/

Your source for U.S. statistics: How many people live in the United States? How do we know? Statistics and facts about U.S. citizens are the domain of the Census Bureau. The bureau can tell you who lives where, what kind of jobs people have, the race or ethnicity and age of the country's population, how people travel, what people do for recreation, and where most crimes happen. How does the Census Bureau find out all of this stuff? This page tells you.

White House

www.whitehouse.gov/

Explore the residence of the U.S. president: This page is really kid-friendly! You can become acquainted with President Clinton and his family (including the family cat, Socks) and explore links to dozens of federally sponsored Web pages on topics such as space and technology, education, and health care. Check out the list of frequently asked questions about the White House and the first family and read news about what's happening at the White House. The site offers a just-for-kids link and a tour of the White House. By clicking the White House History and Tours link, you can find information about the First Family and the First Ladies — and the President, of course. If you want to e-mail President Clinton or Vice President Gore, just click their pictures.

Other Stuff to Check Out

Web sites

www.lib.umich.edu/libhome/
Documents.center/govweb.html

www.odci.gov/cia/publications/nsolo/wfb-
all.htm

www.law.vill.edu/Fed-Agency/
fedwebloc.html

www.congress.org

www.whitehouse.gov/WH/Services/
educate.html#grant

www.halcyon.com/FWDP/cwisinfo.html

sunsite.unc.edu/lia/president/pressites/

www.icrc.org

Newsgroups

gov.us.fed.congress.record.house

gov.us.fed.eop.white-house.announce

alt.politics.usa.congress

alt.politics.usa

Suggested search-engine keywords

Yahoo!: Government, plus subtopic (for
example: civil rights, equal rights, or
women)

Lycos: Government, plus subtopic (for
example: documents or agencies)

History

www.annefrank.com (Anne Frank Home Page)

Historians and history buffs have leaped
onto the World Wide Web with astonish-
ing speed. Kids of all ages have created
Web pages dedicated to a variety of
historical topics, from the history of
aviation to the battles of World War II.
Student projects, oral histories, timelines,
and wonderful collections of images bring
the past to life on the Web.

History Web sites vary from individual
pages dedicated to one person to
comprehensive databases of information
on a historical period. For information on
a specific historical topic, perform a
simple keyword search — like Titanic,
Vikings, or France + History — in one of
the primary search engines (Yahoo,
HotBot, Lycos, and so forth). However,
you may want to start with the general
historical resources listed in this section
to get an overview of available resources.

American history

From the Plymouth pilgrims and the
Native Americans to the cowboys of the
Wild West and today's astronauts,
Americans have left a distinctive and
colorful mark on human history. These
are just a few of the many wonderful Web
pages dedicated to different aspects of
American History. You can find even more
by browsing the section General History
Resources listed later in this part.

African American History

www.cr.nps.gov/delta/afriamer.htm

From roots to civil rights: This clearly
organized and simply written site introduces the African American heritage in
the southern United States. Sections
include Historic Periods, Science, Inventions, and Discoveries, Folklore and
Cultural Traditions, Music of the Delta,
Politics and Civil Rights, and Performing
and Visual Arts. Each section has relevant
links; the link to Related Web Sites takes
you to geographically specific sites (such
as Memphis's African-American Heritage)
and to a page titled "Biographical Profiles
of Some Important 19th Century African
Americans" with information on Nat
Turner, Frederick Douglass, Sojourner
Truth, Mary Ann Shadd, and others.

72 Specialized Explorations

American Civil War: Resources on the Internet

homepages.dsu.edu/jankej/civilwar/
civilwar.htm

A country torn apart: This astounding set of links and documents relating to the Civil War includes pages on Northern and Southern troops and leaders, artillery, sites and events, bugle calls, food, flags, genealogy, medicine, money, stamps, art, and music, and concludes with links to online museums and organizations dedicated to this great and tragic war. Don't miss the extensive group of links on individual battles (Gettysburg, Shiloh, Lee's Retreat); you can also find some touching entries found under "Diaries, Letters and Memoirs."

American Memory (Library of Congress)

lcweb2.loc.gov/ammem/
ammemhome.html

Documents of diversity: Oral histories, maps, papers, videos, photography, and more bring American history alive online at this site sponsored by the Library of Congress. Start by browsing the files and archives of Civil War photographs, Woman Suffrage pamphlets, Walt Whitman's notebooks, panoramic maps, and early motion pictures. To get the full

impact of the site, you need the Real Audio browser plug-in as well as capability to play QuickTime, AVI, and MPEG movies and WAV files. Enjoy!

Colonial Williamsburg

www.history.org

The Revolutionary War period recreated: In Colonial Williamsburg, the people dress and act as people did in Colonial times. Even the children look and behave like children from the 1700s. This Web site shows you soldiers preparing to fight the British, mothers and fathers working, and children in school. It teaches you about food, military life, family, religion, and more! It also contains practical information (maps, directions, hours, and prices) that can help you plan a personal visit to Williamsburg.

The Great War

www.pitt.edu/~novosel/ww1.html

Facts, sentiments, and world social attitude: Growing from a simple site about an author and poet whose focus was on "The Great War," this Web site has expanded to one of the most comprehensive sources of information on World War I (WWI). Uncover not only the American point of view, but also the views of other nations that were involved. Among the must-see listings are the interview with the 103-year-old American war veteran and the section on Victorianism, which explains the time period leading up to WWI. Also available are excellent links to many other sites dealing with this war and with the people who endured it. You need the DirectAudio or Cool Edit plug-ins to get the full impact of the site.

In Memory of World War II

www.islandnet.com/~awong/war/ index.html

Firsthand accounts: Though school textbooks can recount the events and historical figures of World War II, this site can bring one of the most controversial wars into a personal perspective. Dedicated to the individuals affected by the war, In Memory of World War II is a collection of personal stories told by the people who were there. Read about the young German looking for his father; all the young man knew was that his father was an American named David who wanted to take the young man's mother back to America but couldn't. Some accounts are presented in a factual manner; others tug at your heart strings.

Monticello: The Home of Thomas Jefferson

www.monticello.org/

An American architect, farmer, and politician: Join Jefferson for a day on his beautiful farm, Monticello, in the green and rolling hills of Virginia. You can view Jefferson's inventions (like his amazing hall clock), documents relating to his presidency, excerpts from his correspondence with John Adams, a recipe for ice cream, comments on the design of Monticello, and notes on slave life.

Explore the types of plants that Jefferson grew in his gardens. The Garden Shop, run by the Center for Historic Plants, offers bulbs, seeds, and plants descending from Jefferson's own plantings.

Native American History by and about Native Americans

www.lang.osaka-u.ac.jp/~krkvls/ history.html

The first Americans: This list of links related to Native American history is pretty amazing; it ranges from Custer and the Battle of Little Big Horn in 1876, to the American Indian Occupation of Alcatraz 1969–1971. Not all of the pages are historical — for example, Native Web is a cultural page with links relating to politics and law. Examine the links to documents, maps, and timelines, and you won't want to miss the Oral History section or the series of pages on *The West,* a PBS program.

The New Deal Network

newdeal.feri.org

Long struggle out of the Great Depression: A collection of articles, photos, letters to Eleanor Roosevelt from children, and other historic documents provide an understanding of the Great Depression in the United States, the birth of Social Security, and a plan to get the American people back to work and the nation on the road to prosperity. A succinct timeline traces the fall of the economy and the recovery programs that got the country back on its feet. Included in the timeline are the popular songs, movies, and books of the year that echoed public sentiment, as well as local, national, and world historical events.

74 Specialized Explorations

Pioneer Spirit

**www.gps.com/Pioneer_Spirit/
    Pioneer_Spirit.htm**

Stories of pioneer life: Carving out a home in the wilderness, these pioneers showed their grit, courage, and vision. Many of these pioneers were women like Jessamine Slaughter who lived alongside the Missouri River (also called the Smoky Water) from 1863–1877, where people called her "Zezula," which means medicine woman or "one who helps." Several photographs illustrate North Dakota in the 1800s, and most of the stories are told in the words of settlers themselves. Be sure to visit the gallery that compares images of the Dakota territory "then and now."

The Spanish Missions of California

tqd.advanced.org/3615/

The legacy of Father Serra: King Charles III of Spain, Junipero Serra, and the Native Americans who built the missions of California are remembered on this page. You can find out why they built so many missions and where they built them along the California coast. Check out the virtual tour of a typical mission, tips for teachers, and links to other mission sites.

Vietnam Veterans Memorial

www.nps.gov/vive

A country remembers: This site is maintained by the U.S. National Park Service. Like the monument itself, the site honors the 58,196 Americans who died in the Vietnam War or were listed as Missing in Action. You can find a history of the memorial here, as well as links to the Washington Monument, the Lincoln Memorial, the Korean War Veterans Memorial, and other historic sites.

The World of Benjamin Franklin

sln.fi.edu/franklin/rotten.html

An American original: Ben Franklin was a unique American figure — inventor, statesman, philosopher, musician, and economist. You find a QuickTime movie and images of Ben's inventions, as well as quotes from his humorous *Poor Richard's Almanack*. The Franklin Institute's educational mission shines throughout this site, which not only introduces kids to Franklin's personality and work but also illustrates his impact on our culture. It's a funny and fascinating site. To view some of the movies on this site, you need a program capable of playing QuickTime files. Sounds can be heard if your computer can play files with the .AU extension.

Other Stuff to Check Out

Web sites

www.osv.org/
www.isu.edu/~trinmich/Oregontrail.html
www.vboston.com/boswalks/blackhtrail/
www.capecod.net/~rcubelli/ann/
    trypage.htm
www.AmericanWest.com/index2.htm

Newsgroups
alt.history.future
alt.history.what-if
soc.history
soc.history.war.vietnam

Mailing lists
H-CIVWAR@uicvm.cc.uic.edu
H-ETHNIC@uicvm.uic.edu
H-SOUTH@uicvm.uic.edu
H-WEST@uicvm.cc.uic.edu
LISTSERV@UBVM.CC.BUFFALO.EDU

Suggested search-engine keywords
Yahoo!: History, plus subtopic (for example: maps, timelines, Statue of Liberty, or George Washington))
Lycos: history, plus subtopic (for example: Pilgrims, Mayflower, or Cowboys)

General history resources

Each of these general history resources leads you to dozens of Web pages where you can read some amazing facts, whether you are interested in what happened in 1942, in 1492, or ten thousand years ago!

Discoverers Web

www.win.tue.nl/cs/fm/engels/discovery/

Explorers on land and sea: What do Queen Hatshepsut, the Vikings, Christopher Columbus, Francesco de Coronado, Marco Polo, Zhang Quin, Roald Amundsen, Daniel Boone, and David Livingstone have in common? Curiosity, courage, and a great love of adventure! Discoverers Web teaches you about these and many other explorers, military leaders, and diplomats who had a profound impact upon human history. Check out the pictures, drawings, and photos of many of the explorers — and a list of those who died on their adventures so that you don't forget just how courageous they were.

The History Channel

www.historychannel.com/

History comes alive: The History Channel Web site — counterpart to the History TV Channel — is run by people who love to have fun with history. You find descriptions of upcoming TV programs on topics like Ellis Island, women's suffrage, slavery in America, and the Sioux Indians, as well as a terrific list of history hotlinks. (The section on 19th century American history has tons of Civil War links.) Be sure to check out the educational section, the "This Day in History" feature, upcoming events, and other great stuff that this site contains. Also available are trivia games for the older members of the family in addition to the exploratory games designed for the younger Internet explorers. Browse the historical speech archives or listen to the speech of the day. (Note that this site features Shockwave and RealAudio files, and that you need the appropriate plug-ins to enjoy them.)

The History Net — Where History lives on the Net

www.thehistorynet.com/

Voices of history: History Net, sponsored by the National Historical Society, covers American history particularly well, but it also contains concise, illustrated articles and references to little-known events in world history — events that are considered historical turning points. You can browse your way through biographies of historic personalities, eyewitness accounts of important historical events, and descriptions of great battles, arms, and more. The article index includes over 300 articles on topics ranging from America's Civil War and aviation history to WWII and women's history.

HNSource — The Central Server for Historians

history.cc.ukans.edu/history

An overview of history: The University of Kansas site is comprehensive (with over 1,900 links) and alphabetically organized on one Web page. The site is a joint effort by this university and the Lehrstuhl für Ältere deutsche Literaturwissenschaft der Universität Regensburg, so you can find many international links here. Though not rated for the quality of any of the links, no other site can give you as immediate a sense of the variety and depth of history online. Favorites include: Ancient Egypt (with over 60 links), the diverse Asian studies list, the Archives section (here you find the Exhibit Hall of the U.S. National Archives with historic photographs and documents), and the Maps list (over 80 Web sites with maps from throughout history). With a page this big (over 125 screens tall at a monitor resolution of 800 x 600 pixels), allow a lot of time to download.

Other Stuff to Check Out

Web sites

library.byu.edu/~rdh/eurodocs/
www.msstate.edu/Archives/History/
www.wco.com/~ejia/EDU/history.htm
www.teleport.com/~arden/antiquity.htm
portico.bl.uk/

Newsgroups

soc.history
alt.history.living
soc.history.what-if
alt.bible

Suggested search-engine keywords

Yahoo!: History, plus subtopic (for example: Australia, Germany, Ireland, or Vietnam)
Lycos: History, or subtopic (for example: Celts, Muslims, Women, or Native Americans)

History of the ancient world

Great ancient civilizations — like Mesopotamia, Ancient China, and Rome — were populated with fascinating and courageous people who made great discoveries that affect us even today. These sites explore these ancient and modern worlds and reflect the passion and imagination of the historians, archivists, educators, and students who created the sites.

(For other, related sites, check under archaeology in Part VI.)

Byzantium: The Shining Fortress

www.serve.com/byzance/

The beauty finally fades: After the fall of the Roman Empire, the Byzantine Empire stood against Muslim expansion for a thousand years. This page explores the history of Byzantium, its architecture, its early Christian art, and its ultimate fate. You can follow the lineage of Byzantine rulers and their battles from Constantine I to its final ruler, Constantine XI Palaeologus.

China: History in General

darkwing.uoregon.edu/~felsing/cstuff/
history.html

From dynasties to modern times: A country rich in history, mystique, and controversy, China's ancient traditions and their erosion are resourced beautifully in this site. The site is well organized and has plenty of material about China, ranging from concise timelines tracing the political leadership, to their advancements in science and medicine. Try out the links about women in Chinese history and environmental issues in China that are traced back 15 centuries, as well as the country's geography, industries, and economy.

Dead Sea Scrolls Exhibition

sunsite.unc.edu/expo/
    deadsea.scrolls.exhibit/intro.html

Ancient texts explained: This simple Web page explains the history and meaning of the scrolls and provides background on the times in which they were written. One of the most interesting sections, The Qumran Community, has images of artifacts including pottery, basketry, and textiles, largely drawn from the collection of the Library of Congress.

Diogenes' Links To The Ancient World

www.menagerie.net/lyceum/

Leap into the past: Author Raymond Williams guides you to Web sites of note on Mesopotamia, The Holy Lands, Ancient Egypt, Ancient Greece, and Ancient Rome. Some links are a bit scholarly, but others such as Diotima, a study of women in the ancient world, and the Trojan Treasure, about the ancient gold from Troy (also called Priam's Treasure) that was scattered about Germany and found by the Russians, will spark your imagination. The site has links to Greek mythology, treasures in the Vatican, and even a gallery of photos on the Gulf War. How'd that get in there, you ask? When it's your site, you can do what you want! The site is easy to navigate and is well illustrated, too.

Egypt and the Ancient Near East

www-oi.uchicago.edu/OI/DEPT/RA/
    ABZU/YOUTH_RESOURCES.HTML

From pharoahs to pyramids: This University of Chicago page for young people is sure to inspire future Egyptologists and archaeologists. The site contains sections on life in ancient Egypt, myths, writing (hieroglyphics and texts), pyramids, and mummies, as well as stories, puzzles, and links to museums with other kids-friendly pages.

The New Jerusalem Mosaic

jeru.huji.ac.il/open_screen2.htm

Understanding a holy city: This fascinating tour of Jerusalem summarizes its lengthy history, explains its diverse and remarkable landmarks, and introduces some of its most prominent characters. You can also learn how the diet of the city's residents has changed over the centuries and about the importance of water in this city. Sections include Roman Byzantine, Crusader Period, Ottoman, Early Muslim, and the State of Israel.

Odyssey On-Line

www.emory.edu/CARLOS/ODYSSEY/

Ancient odyssey: This online journey (with RealAudio & QuickTime) explores ancient Near Eastern and Egyptian cultures; the Greek and Roman sites are still under construction. Designed generally for the younger crowd in your house, this site contains games and puzzles, as well as pictures and text to introduce these ancient civilizations to youngsters. Most of the games and puzzles are thought-provoking and educational, based upon the Web site's content. The artifacts are from the Michael C. Carlos Museum at Emory University in Atlanta, Georgia, and the Memorial Art Gallery of the University of Rochester in Rochester, New York.

Seven Wonders of the Ancient World

pharos.bu.edu/Egypt/Wonders/

See the seven wonders: If you have always wondered what the seven ancient wonders were — and which one still exists — this is the Web page for you. Ever since Antipater first referred to these seven monuments as wonders in the second century BC, the monuments may have crumbled, but their fame has grown! Click here to read a short history of each wonder and to see images of what they probably looked like when first created. After you're finished with the Seven Wonders of the Ancient World, be sure to check out the Seven Natural Wonders of the World and the Seven Modern Wonders of the World. The easiest way to get to these links is through the FAQs (frequently asked questions).

Medieval and Renaissance history

The medieval era, often (and erroneously) referred to as the Dark Ages, was an age of great political and theological change in many cultures all over the world. The Renaissance was a time of incredible discovery and creativity in every area of study — geography, sculpture, mathematics, astronomy, philosophy, and any other scientific, religious, and artistic pursuit imaginable. Sites profiled in this section explore these historical periods from the perspective of many different cultures. Be forewarned: Browsing these sites can be addictive and time-consuming!

Empires Beyond the Great Wall — The Heritage of Genghis Khan

vvv.com/khan/

A Mongol emperor: Born in 1167 A.D., the Mongol Temujin had earned the name "Genghis Khan," or "universal or oceanic ruler" before he was 40. For another 20 years he ruled an empire that reached from Hungary across Asia to Korea, and from Siberia to Tibet. This lucid, well-illustrated site makes Khan come alive while teaching about the rich culture and history of Mongolia.

Sworn to Serve

**www.itdc.sbcss.k12.ca.us/curriculum/
  sworntoserve.html**

Experience the life of a serf: This amusing two-week course lets students "experience" life as a tenth century vassal to an

English lord. Though aimed at seventh graders, the rich and colorful links (Timeline of Anglo-Saxon England, Medieval/Renaissance Food Homepage, Footwear of the Middle Ages, List of Feudal Obligations) fascinate students of all ages. The page is designed as a school group project, and it contains helpful notes for teachers, but families also enjoy this lively approach to history.

Tower of London Virtual Tour

www.voicenet.com/~dravyk/toltour/

Tools of torture and famous jewels: Both parents and kids love the Tower of London Virtual Tour, in which this infamous landmark comes to life. Stories of England's darker history alternate with images of the crown jewels and pictures of the tower as it stands today. The award-winning Kids tour, an alternative version of the original tour, is guided by a cartoon character and aimed at children in grades 3 through 5.

The World of the Vikings

www.pastforward.co.uk/vikings/ index.html

Heartless raiders or adventuresome inventors: Were Vikings bloodthirsty and cruel? These pages link you to resources on the mythology and history of these early Scandanavian explorers and, hopefully, answer that question. You can learn about the Vikings' beautiful longships, how they farmed, their villages and homes, their runes, and other artifacts as well. The ample links lead to museums and Viking reenactments, both live ones and the online kind. If you can't travel to one of the reenactment locations, then at least one Web site is designed to give the viewer an "interactive experience" on the lives and times of the Vikings.

Modern history

The history of the world since the Renaissance has been divided into many categories: the Enlightenment, the Romantic Period, the Victorian Era, the Modern Era, and so forth. For the past 200 years or so, humans have experienced a time of great advances in many scientific, technological, and humanistic fields; people have also experienced destructive wars, horrifying plagues, and great political upheavals. These sites detail many world-changing events of recent history.

Anne Frank Online

www.annefrank.com

Remembering a young girl's courage: This handsome site brings together the best online references to Anne Frank, a German-Jewish teenager who hid from the Nazis for over two years in an Amsterdam attic only to perish near the end of the war. The tragic story is retold at several Web sites; one link suggests ways children can learn from and take action against bigotry.

The Berlin Wall

www.uncg.edu/~lixlpurc/GIP/ berlin_wall.html

The Berlin Wall 1961-1989

Mauer, Wende und Vereinigung: Texte, Bilder, Kommentare

1. The Berlin Wall Falls. Multimedia Exhibit. Patch High School Stuttgart
2. Cold War: Postwar Estrangement

© Dr. Andreas Lixl, German Internet Project

A country reunited: Sponsored by the University of North Carolina at Greensboro and the German Internet Project, this site links to various pages that recount the history and ponder the significance of the Berlin Wall. The Tour of the Berlin Wall is a long MPEG file download but is an excellent place to start, as is the fine multimedia exhibit "The Berlin Wall Falls." You may want to examine some interesting articles on the Cold War, including one on the Cuban Missile Crisis, which incorporates information from Soviet premier Nikita Khrushchev's memoirs. A few of the links are in German.

A History Place: World War II in Europe

www.historyplace.com/worldwar2/

The great war: The History Place section on WWII has three parts: The Rise of Adolf Hitler, a complete history in 24 chapters; World War II in Europe, a comprehensive hyperlinked list with photos and text; and the Holocaust Timeline with over 150 photos and text. The photographs are vivid, and the explanatory texts, though fairly short, are clearly written and packed with facts.

Remembering Nagasaki

www.exploratorium.edu/nagasaki/

Lessons of war in the atomic age: In honor of the 50th anniversary of the bombing of Hiroshima and Nagasaki, this somber page reproduces photographs of Nagasaki taken the day after the bombing. Get firsthand reactions and accounts of those who survived or knew of someone who experienced the bombing. Check out the forum about issues pertaining to the atomic age. Links are provided for more information on the event or other commemorative sites.

Treasures of the Czar

www.sptimes.com/Treasures/

Last days of a dynasty: The Romanov's rule began in 1613 and ended with the Bolshevik Revolution of 1917. This virtual tour shows you pictures and artifacts from the life and times of Nicholas and Alexandra, the Last Czar and Czarina of Russia.

Other Stuff to Check Out

Web sites
> remember.org/
> marauder.millersv.edu/~columbus/
> www.niagara.com/%7Emerrwill/
> www.serve.com/Threshar/napolean.htm
> www.teleport.com/%7Emegaines/
>   women.html
> world.std.com/~sheal/sutton/
>   armsbycem.html
> www.geocities.com/TheTropics/7557/
>   page1.html
> grid.let.rug.nl/~welling/maps/maps.html
> userwww.sfsu.edu/~lindamar/joan.html

Newsgroups
> bit.listserv.history
> soc.history.medieval
> soc.history.war.misc
> soc.history.war.world-war-ii

Mailing lists
> H-LATAM@uicvm.uic.edu
> LISTSERV@MSU.EDU
> listserv@uicvm.uic.edu

Suggested search-engine keywords
> Yahoo!: History, plus specific subtopic (for example: Holocaust, Russian Revolution, Mahatma Ghandi)
> Lycos: History, plus specific subtopic (for example: Titanic, Industrial Revolution, Explorers)

Language Arts

If you want to know more about literature, languages, or writing skills — subjects collectively known as *language arts* — then turn to the World Wide Web. In this section, you can find some sites that you may actually enjoy visiting when you need help with your homework. Whether you want information about Shakespeare or the author of *Winnie the Pooh,* Web sites may have the answer to your questions. In addition, language arts sites can coach you in a foreign language, give you advice on how to improve your writing, and help you get your work published online.

Great literature for kids and parents

Literature sites on the Web can provide hours of entertainment. You can find both familiar works that have endured the test of time and new stories that may eventually become classics. Check out the following sites for a variety of tales and stories.

Berkeley Digital Library

sunsite.berkeley.edu/Collections/

Books and literary papers online: Although this site is designed for high school students, much here may interest middle schoolers and parents. A large section of this site contains the Emma Goldman papers. Goldman was a well-known activist during the early 1900s. This digital collection includes her documents, along with the California and American Heritage materials that archive historical photographs, manuscripts, and pictures; the Jack London collection, which includes letters, photographs and manuscripts; and the Online Medieval and Classical Library, with works of Chaucer, Gower, and more. That's right — entire books can be read in this online library. The site is organized in a straightforward way and is easy to use.

Children's Literature Web Guide

www.ucalgary.ca/~dkbrown/

Internet resources related to books for kids and young adults: If you love children's books, allow plenty of time to

82 **Specialized Explorations** _____

explore this site. The awards link takes you to information about the H.C. Andersen Medal, the Caldecott and Newbery Medals, and the Canadian Library Association Book of the Year. Check out the links to authors, stories, journals, sections for teachers and parents, and plenty of good reading. Don't miss the recommended reading section, where you find a list that includes *Anne of Green Gables, The Wizard of Oz* books, and *The Wind in the Willows.*

Folk and Fairy Tales from Around the World

psa-usr12.ucdavis.edu/richard/tales/

Tales of wonder from around the globe: Stories from Africa, the Middle East, Siberia, central Europe, England, China, and several other regions of the world are gathered here to entertain and enchant children of all ages. Most of the stories are not illustrated, but the large typeface should help young readers. The stories are neatly organized by geographic region, starting with Africa.

Folklore and Mythology Electronic Texts

www.pitt.edu/~dash/folktexts.html

Folklore with a twist: This story site is pretty bare-looking, but it contains amazing and unusual myths and folktales. The tales are presented in a list. The section called "Bald Stories" is indeed about hairless men. The section titled "Night-Mares" contains stories about the spirits that cause scary dreams. You also can read stories about frog kings and fairy gifts, werewolves and witchcraft, and about little people and changelings. And be forewarned, one section is called "Breaking Wind." All in all, more than 100 legends and myths are collected here.

Literary Resources on the Net

www.english.upenn.edu/~jlynch/Lit/

A collection of English and American literary references: This site is organized by topic — classical and biblical, medieval, American, women's literature, ethnicities' and nationalities, theories, and so on. To make your search easier, you can search by keyword. Each section contains an impressive number of links, and a section called General Resources links to calls for papers, literary mailing lists, syllabi, and other resources. If you're looking for a T.S. Eliot page or the Virginia Woolf Web site, start your research here. This site also links to pages on Alfred Hitchcock, Ian Fleming, Robert Frost, and many more literary figures.

Pulitzer Prizes

www.pulitzer.org

A record of literary, journalistic, and musical achievements: The Pulitzer Prize is known and respected the world over; to win one is a tremendous honor for American writers. Funded by American newspaper publisher Joseph Pulitzer who died in 1917, the awards are given to recognize outstanding achievements in American journalism, letters (fiction, nonfiction, poetry, biography, and autobiography), drama, and music. (Though the site features some of the greatest writing in this century, many topics awarded the Pulitzer are controversial; younger members of the family may want to surf this site with a parent.) This site has summaries, photos, and lists the judges of the winning entries from 1995 through 1997. Also on this site is a timeline of years that the Pulitzer Prize has been given and the winners in those years. It's interesting to go to a year that has special meaning to you and see who the winners were.

Storytellers Sources on the Internet

users.aol.com/storypage/sources.htm

A list of traditional and new stories: Storytelling is a dramatic art, but first you must have stories. This site includes tales such as *Aesop's Fables;* Afghan folklore; Celtic, Greek, and Irish mythology; and Haitian proverbs. Classic fairy tales, Homer's *Iliad,* riddles, jokes, folktales, and *Politically Correct Bedtime Stories* are other resources at this site. Some of the links include audio clips from the stories, and thus may require certain plug-ins or applications.

Other Stuff to Check Out

Web sites

www.odci.gov/cia/publications/nsolo/wfb-all.htm
mgfx.com/kidlit/
www.netten.net/~dpickett/narnia.html
www.cc.swarthmore.edu/~sjohnson/stories
www.sdcoe.k12.ca.us/score/stories.html

Newsgroup

alt.folklore.ghost-stories

Mailing lists

CHILDLIT@RUTVM1.RUTGERS.EDU
JACK-LONDON-REQUEST@SONOMA.EDU
storytell-request@twu.edu.

Suggested search-engine keywords

Yahoo!: Literature or books and/or subtopic (for example: Hans Christian Andersen or E.B. White)
Lycos: Literature or books and/or subtopic (for example: stories, folktales, France, England, or Brothers Grimm)

Individual author and character pages

Most of us have a favorite children's book or author. For example, you may like *Charlotte's Web* by E.B. White, *A Wrinkle in Time* by Madeline L'Engle, or *Treasure Island* by Robert Louis Stevenson. Sometimes our favorite authors create a series of books using the same characters, such as the Boxcar Children, Nancy Drew, the Baby-Sitters Club, or the Littles. Other series may share not characters but a kind of adventure or a subject. These series include the sports books by Matt Christopher and the popular *Goosebumps* books. Many popular authors have Web sites that are either official (approved by the author) or the work of an inspired fan.

AVI

www.avi-writer.com/

The official page of Avi: This award-winning author of mysteries, historical fiction, and comedies for young readers wrote *The Confessions of Charlotte Doyle, Emily Upham's Revenge, No More Magic,* and *Beyond the Western Sea.* The site includes an interview with the author, a list of Avi's works, and information on ordering books.

84 Specialized Explorations

Cyber-Seuss Page

www.afn.org/~afn15301/drseuss.html

The Great Glorious and Gandorious Dr. Seuss site: What's your favorite Dr. Seuss book? *The Cat in the Hat?* But what about *The 500 Hats of Bartholomew Cubbins?* Or *Green Eggs and Ham?* Well, you don't have to decide. You can come to this site and read about all of these delightful stories and about their creator. Watch your browser's cursor as you pass it throughout this site. Move it everywhere; the poems and pictures have lots of links in addition to the obvious ones. The site has other fun stuff to do, too, such as taking the Grinch quiz or playing some Seuss games. What's the best thing here? The stories, of course.

Goosebumps — The Official Site

place.scholastic.com/goosebumps/
index.htm

The book series that's so scary, it's cool: Maximum horror ahead: That's the warning on this site's home page. *Goosebumps* is the number-one selling children's book series in the world, and this site shows you why. The site contains news and information on the books, a bit about *Goosebumps* author R.L. Stine and the *Goosebumps* fan club, and other delicious stuff. The most fun section is called "Field of Screams." Here you find games, puzzles, and gruesome grub — recipes your mother may *not* want to try! Though intended for children, some really small tykes may get a little scared with some of the content in this site. Parents may want to review it first.

Laura Ingalls Wilder

www.vvv.com/~jenslegg/

The story behind *Little House on the Prairie:* This page, which is dedicated to the author of the *Little House* stories, tells the author's real life story and has charming pictures of Wilder's characters. However, the most original aspect of the page is its links to the sites of the stories; each section links to more relevant notes on the real Laura, Almanzo, and other family members who inspired these wonderful pioneer stories.

The Lewis Carroll Page

www.lewiscarroll.org/carroll.html

Adventures with Lewis Carroll and Alice in Wonderland: Look to this site for everything you might want to know about this author and his famous Alice. Artwork includes classic illustrations and photographs of the writer. The site features serious discussions of Carroll's work as literature and also offers logic, mathematics games, riddles, and a charming and funny section dedicated to photos of Carroll, his images, words, and characters incorporated into the popular culture. Links take you to Carroll's best-loved books and his photography, but parents should be aware that links also connect to a discussion of Carroll being a pedophile.

The Page at Pooh Corner

www.public.iastate.edu/~jmilne/ pooh.html

Everything there is to know about Winnie the Pooh: This Pooh page even reveals much about Winnie the Pooh, including the source of his name. (You have to visit to find out.) The unexpected variety of goodies here includes lyrics to Kenny Loggins's song, "The House at Pooh Corner," and a study of the life of author A.A. Milne. Plenty of familiar Pooh images make you feel at home — friends of Piglet, Tigger, Eeyore, and Christopher Robin will feel welcome, too.

Shakespearean Homework Helper

members.aol.com/liadona2/ shakespeare.html

Guide to Shakespearean sites: Shakespeare is a favorite topic on the Net, and this page can direct you to dozens of sites featuring the man, the plays, the poetry, the times, and even Shakespearean insults. Check out the movie and theater links, too. One of the most useful features is a dictionary of Shakespearean English — what a relief! If you have a question about your Shakespearean assignment, you can e-mail the author of this page.

The World of Peter Rabbit

www.peterrabbit.co.uk/

The animated world of Peter Rabbit: The contents of this site include Beatrix Potter's biography, theatrical performances, art shows, Peter Rabbit products, and a playground with games and puzzles. Because the illustrations here are exactly like those in Potter's books, this site should bring back fond memories — or create new ones.

Other Stuff to Check Out

Web sites

www.ala.org/alayou/best/newcald.html
place.scholastic.com/magicschoolbus/
    index.htm
www.scholastic.com
seamonkey.ed.asu.edu/oz/
www.coppersky.com/louisa/
www.tridel.com.ph/user/bula/dahl/
    index.htm
www.ipl.org/youth/AskAuthor/
    AskAuthor.html
www.janbrett.com/

Suggested search-engine keywords

Yahoo!: Books, plus subtopic (for example: authors, Jan Brett, or Hans Christian Andersen)

Lycos: Books, plus subtopic (for example: series, Little Women, Treasure Island, or Winnie the Pooh)

Study languages online

From French to Mandarin Chinese, from Spanish to Swahili, you can study amazing languages over the World Wide Web. Web sites offer programs, courses, and tutors; some even have audio to help improve your pronunciation. Foreign dictionaries also are available. You can search for the foreign language sites or the dictionaries by keywords (for example, "Spanish language" or "French dictionary") and by linking from the sites below.

Dakota

www.geocities.com/Paris/9463/

Hau Koda, or Welcome, to the Dakota language site: This site can help you learn the Dakota (American Indian) language by using a simple method of repetition. This method is traditional and stresses respect rather than the use of a dictionary. The method also uses color charts to help you recognize and repeat the correct sounds, first singly and then in combinations. The site offers two sound lessons and one reading lesson, and the authors suggest that students try to learn without writing down anything at first. Above all, they encourage students to "be patient!"

French Lessons Home Page

www.kd.qd.se/iii/languages/french/ course/flavours.html

Lessons in speaking and understanding French: "You too can learn French!" So promises Jacques Leon, who takes you under his wing and teaches you this charming if elusive language. Leon also has links to an excellent French Web site with loads of information on French Web resources. For those who are ready to dive right in, you can start with a test in French grammar. The site also offers an introductory article on language lessons on the Web. In all, you find nine lessons plus information about additional vocabulary and idioms.

Human Languages Page

www.june29.com/HLP/

A resource guide to language information on the Web: One of the oldest language arts sites on the Web (it was established in 1994), the Human Languages Page is also one of the best. Frequently updated, it contains many of the finest Web resources, including organizations, linguistic resources, multilingual sites, schools, projects, and commercial resources. Be sure to check out some of the site's intriguing links.

Japanese

www.missouri.edu/~c563382/

Free Japanese language lessons: Sponsored by Japan's largest newspaper, *The Yomiuri Shinbun,* this site can teach you Japanese at no cost. One teaching tool is a set of pictures. Audio files give you a chance to hear everyday words and simple phrases the way they should be spoken. After you've learned a bit, you can relax and absorb the cultural information at this site, including instructions on cooking and manners.

Russian Dictionary — With Sounds and Images!

www.wavefront.com/~swithee/dictionary/welcome.html

Instruction in Russian: This site teaches the Russian language through the use of simple pictures and audio files. Children may be impressed with the Cyrillic alphabet and proud that they can learn a few words in such a seemingly difficult language. The site includes a dictionary for your use. If you are using very recent versions of either Netscape Navigator or Miscrosoft Internet Explorer, the sound files should present no problems. If you have any doubt, a link on the site will get you the necessary information and files to make the sound work with your browser.

Spanish Lessons

www.hardlink.com/~chambers/Spanish/

  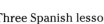

Three Spanish lessons for beginners: Each of these lessons is based on a central theme. The course combines

text — simple vocabulary and sentence structure, as well as verb conjugation — with audio files. The page links to two online Spanish language dictionaries and to the outstanding Human Language Page, which is described elsewhere in this section. If you have an early version of Netscape Navigator or Microsoft Internet Explorer, or if you have another browser that doesn't have a helper application for sound files, note that this site uses sound files with the .AU extension; the spoken work is being taught here as well as the printed word.

Swahili

conn.me.queensu.ca/kassim/documents/ kiswa/swahili.htm

The place to study an African language: Swahili (also Kiswahili) is an African language spoken mainly by the people of eastern and central Africa (the countries of Kenya, Uganda, Rwanda, Tanzania, and so on). The Queen's University Black History Collective presents these Swahili/ Kiswahili lessons taught at this page. The site offers nine lessons and Swahili exercises for reading and listening. You also find a Swahili dictionary and links to other practical Swahili pages, such as a Swahili grammar notebook, Swahili pronunciation, and useful Swahili words. The sample pronunciations are in WAV file format, so prep your browser before you listen to the Swahili vocabulary.

Travel Languages
www.travlang.com/languages/

A traveler's guide to basic foreign
phrases: Click your way to a new language. This site offers instructions in
basic phrases and vocabulary in over 50
languages. First, you indicate your native
language and then you select the language you want to learn. This selection
includes rarely heard languages such as
Magyar, Welsh, and Zulu, along with the
popular romance, eastern European, and
Asian languages. The technique is simple
and absolutely addicting — try it. Foreign
words and phrases are doled out to your
speakers using RealAudio files. If you
haven't already, install the RealAudio
plug-in before you check out the language
pronunciations. A link to the appropriate
site is provided for your convenience.

Other Stuff to Check Out

Web sites
www.jajz-ed.org.il/hebrew.html
www.ild.com/index.html
www.nyise.org/blind.htm
pasture.ecn.purdue.edu/~agenhtml/
   agenmc/china/ctutor.html
www.nd.edu/~archives/latgramm.htm
www.soton.ac.uk/~scp93ch/refer/
   morseform.html
info.utas.edu.au/docs/flonta/DP,1,1,95/
   dictionary.html
sunsite.unc.edu/gaelic/

Newsgroups
sci.lang
soc.culture.french
sk.talk.slovak-world

Suggested search-engine keywords
Yahoo!: Language, plus subtopic (for
   example: French, Mayan, Tagalog,
   sanskrit, Pidgin, or Nordic)
Lycos: Language, plus subtopic
   (for example: classes, schools, or
   organizations)

Writing aids and kids publications

Kids, have you always wanted to write?
The Internet can help you polish your
prose — and actually publish online. Of
course, publishing may require some
work, but, at some of these sites, you can
read stories by people just like you.

Internet Public Library Youth Division
www.ipl.org/youth/

An opportunity to publish online: The
University of Michigan's Youth Division is
designed for kids ages 4 through 14 and is
user-friendly. Here you can submit poetry
and short stories for publication on the
Web. The site also presents a story hour
and information about your favorite
authors, and you can send questions to JJ
the librarian and to some authors, if you
like. Select questions and answers are
posted online. Teens can visit the link
http://ipl.org/teen for help in researching
papers and for recommended Web pages
for teens.

Inkspot — For Young Writers
192.41.39.106/young/

Advice on how to become a writer: Inkspot has gathered together articles and resources to encourage young writers, who can discuss their work with other aspiring writers at a forum at this site. You can submit your writing to the various online and print publications and search for writing jobs that pay! Don't forget to check out Inkspot Writers' Bookstore Recommended Reading for young writers. It has more tips on how to get published.

KidPub WWW Publishing

www.kidpub.org/kidpub/

Publishing site for works by children: KidPub is so proud of its writers — all under the age of 21 — that it archives all pieces accepted for publication. Since it came online, KidPub has published over 14,000 stories by kids of all ages. The site is searchable, and you can click frequently asked questions to learn about publishing. KidPub proudly notes that its site has been visited over a half million times, so your work has a good audience. If you like collaborating with other writers, you may want to contribute to "Return to Gateway Mansion," a continuing saga at KidPub.

Other Stuff to Check Out

Web sites
 www.kidstory.com/write.html
 www.stonesoup.com/

Newsgroups
 alt.publish.books
 alt.writing
 rec.arts.books.childrens
 misc.writing

Suggested search-engine keywords
 Yahoo!: Writing, plus subtopic (for example: poetry, publishing, or kids)
 Lycos: Writing, plus subtopic (for example: stories or tips)

Math and Science

Math, science, and technology skills are becoming increasingly crucial for many of the world's better, more challenging, well-paying jobs. The Internet enhances visualization and comprehension of many theories and processes. The Internet also allows fields such as engineering and mathematics to reach new levels of complexity in terms of calculations and projections. In addition to all that highfalutin' stuff, the Internet makes math and science more fun and easier to understand. Here are some sites to prove it.

Earth sciences

Ma Earth has been around a long time — about 4.5 billion years, scientists estimate. Our home planet is both tough and fragile, complex, and ever-changing. Studying the history, evolution, dynamics, and physical properties of the earth constitutes earth science. Here are some sites to put you on solid ground with that next homework assignment.

Earth System Science Community

gaia.circles.org/Round3/Resources/ samples1.html

Research results from teams of students and scientists: Funded by NASA's Earth System Science Community (ESSC), this multimedia curriculum and support network teams students with global scientists. They conduct research and publish their findings at this site. See what they discovered by clicking the names of any of the participating schools.

90 Specialized Explorations

Helping Your Child Learn Geography

www.ed.gov/pubs/parents/Geography/

Online geography booklet for parents: Sponsored by the U.S. Office of Educational Research and Improvement, this easy-to-read, idea-filled booklet gives parents creative guidance for teaching kids where they live and where other nations of the world are located. You can follow the guide from top to bottom or choose topics — such as map reading, Faraway Places, or Physical and Cultural Regions — that seem most age appropriate.

How Far Is It?

www.indo.com/distance/

Fun way to track the distance between two locations: Type the name of two cities or locations into the To and From boxes, respectively, and get calculations "as the crow flies" of the distance between them. For example, type **Indianapolis, Indiana** in the From box and type **Foster City, California** in the To box. Then click Look it Up! Within seconds, you discover that the distance between them is 1,946 miles (3,131 km or 1,691 nautical miles). See both cities on a map courtesy of Xerox PARC and get driving directions courtesy of MapQuest. You also can get basic data on geographic locations, including county seats, state capitals, populations, and elevations.

Learning Web at the U.S. Geological Survey

www.usgs.gov/education/index.html

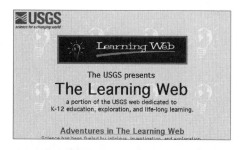

Official public education site of the U.S. Geological Survey: This federal agency is principally charged with keeping track of many natural forces on earth that impact our lives. At this site, you can see what these scientists do and get rock-solid information about volcanoes, earthquakes, faults, plate tectonics, hydrology, geography, and geology. Special features include Ask-A-Geologist and the Children's Butterfly Site. Visit the section titled This Dynamic Earth and view satellite images of our changing earth. Find out how to use maps and compasses, color infrared photos, and false color composites. Lots of well-researched and kid-friendly articles address subjects including acid rain, paleontology, geophysics, and understanding our planet through chemistry. This site is easy to navigate and to comprehend. It's a real public service.

National Geographic.com Kids

www.nationalgeographic.com/kids/

Science-based action for kids: Part of the larger *National Geographic* online site, this section is strictly for kids, who can enjoy mystery games, puzzles, discussions, and fancy graphics. Kids get their own versions of tales about pirates, planets, famous people, mummies, animals, and the earth. Frequently updated, the site enables kids to click through Java-scripted adventures by typing in ideas and answers or clicking on items that move the action along. Solve science- and nature-based puzzles and discuss science and nature topics online with other kids. Grown-ups can link to the main site for science-related news and articles from the *National Geographic* magazine and television show.

Rob's Granite Page

uts.cc.utexas.edu/~rmr/index.html

A roadcut on the information superhighway: That's how Rob, a real live geologist, describes his site, and he should know. In addition to sections of technical information for science professionals, Rob (otherwise known as Robert M. Reed, Ph.D. candidate, Department of Geological Sciences, University of Texas at Austin) has set aside areas and activities for kids and amateur geologists. Enjoy his Enchanted Rock virtual field trip and great images of the many kinds of granite. Do you know how granite is like ice cream? You will after you visit here. Link to related sites of interest to rockhounds and geologists. Rob ranks the related sites as good or not-so-good.

Rockhounds

www.rahul.net/infodyn/rockhounds/

Information page for rock collectors: Things get a little rocky here, but no one's complaining, because this site is for people who like rocks (not to mention gems, semiprecious stones, and minerals). Very nicely presented and easy to understand, this site features frequently asked questions (FAQs), mailing lists, information about trade shows, and links to quality sites about rock shops, galleries, clubs, groups, societies, software,

rock images and photos, books, articles, and publications. You can find details about rock-collecting trips and sites (outdoor sites, that is), plus general earth science and paleontology-related sites. You can also link to the personal home pages of collectors.

Other Stuff to Check Out

Web sites

info.er.usgs.gov/network/science/earth/
earth.html
www.ciesin.org/
www.tiac.net/users/rand50/fimage.htm
agi.umd.edu/agi/agi.html
www.realtime.net/~revenant/geo.html
www.icomos.org/
WWW_VL_Geography.html

Mailing lists

www.rahul.net/infodyn/rockhounds/archive/
rh_index.html
www.neosoft.com/internet/paml/groups.E/
earth_and_sky.html

Newsgroups

sci.geo

Online service areas

America Online: LEARNING & CULTURE

Suggested search-engine keywords

Yahoo!: Earth science, geology, geography
HotBot: Earth science, geology, geography

General math resources

Doesn't *googol* sound like a funny word? Actually, it's a math term that a boy named Milton Sirotta thought up because his uncle, famed mathematician Edward Kasner, was trying to come up with a brand-new term for the number 1 followed by 100 zeroes. It's never too early to make your own mark in math! Here are some math-oriented homework helper sites that you can count on to get you started!

92 Specialized Explorations

Chaffey High School Fractal Links

www.chaffey.org/fractals/

Explore fractal geometry: This site was created by teenagers for youth everywhere. It explains, in very clear language and with wonderful organization and illustrations, the new and exciting world of fractal geometry. In traditional geometry, classic shapes such as squares and triangles were all that you could measure. Now with computers, you also can quantify and illustrate irregular shapes such as leaves and mud pies and the goo in your lava lamp using mathematical equations. And some of those equations make great-looking art! Check out this exciting new math that combines geometry, computers, nature, and the arts in ways never possible before. If you have Netscape 3.0 or Internet Explorer 3.0, you should hear fractal music upon opening this site. Crescendo is the recommended player plug-in to use.

Furman University's Mathematical Quotations Server

math.furman.edu/~mwoodard/
    mquot.html

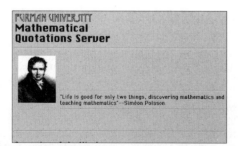

Famous math sayings and quotes: Acting as a sort of *Bartlett's Familiar Quotations* for the math set, this easy-to-navigate,

attractive site is a nifty source of memorable quotes by mathematicians and/or about mathematics. Check the Quotation of the Week or the entire collection, which you can search by clicking the alphabet for the first letter of the last name of your desired speaker or author. Hit the Random Quote link just for fun. (The quote changes regularly.) If you don't have a particular speaker or author in mind, just review the selection under any letter of the alphabet.

History of Mathematics

aleph0.clarku.edu/~djoyce/mathhist/
    mathhist.html

A thorough, well-organized compendium of math history links: Go back in mathematical history by online volume (for example, 1995), timeline, chronology, region (for example, Babylonia, Egypt, China, Greece, or India), or subject. Track down books, historic publications, other math history sites, and a variety of related mathematics pages on the Internet. Also find mailing lists, newsletters, and newsgroups related to math history.

Math Forum

forum.swarthmore.edu/

Huge collection of resources sponsored by National Science Foundation: Explore this academic-community-driven virtual hub for the study of mathematics. First-time visitors are advised to click the annotated home page to get familiar with the site. The Student Center features an interactive forum and math projects (handy for homework assignments). Student-oriented math activities and links include online competitions of weekly math problems, challenges to encourage problem-solving between teams of students, and math tips, tricks, puzzles, and hints. The site features a showcase of student work. Parents may appreciate the discussion groups on math education issues and how to help children excel. You can find links to math sites organized by subjects such as K-12, Arithmetic, Algebra, Geometry, Pre-Calculus, and Calculus. Also you can find college-level and advanced Internet lists, which are only the best Internet resources for each topic. To obtain more extensive lists or to conduct searches for specific materials, go to Steve's Dump (really!).

Math-On-Line Resources for Parents & Families

www.kqed.org/fromKQED/Cell/math/ resources/parent.html

For parents and guardians to help their kids with math: Valuing the importance of parental involvement in math education of kids, this site presented by The KQED Center for Education & Lifelong Learning presents a selected list of links that parents and kids can use together. Among the exceptional, carefully selected links are Family Math, a program developed by EQUALS — at Lawrence Hall of Science, University of California, Berkeley, California — to encourage girls and minority students to enter math-based careers; Ask Dr. Math, a project of the Geometry Forum that is organized into math-related linking categories for all school ages and helps kids with homework questions; and EPGY: Education Program for Gifted Youth, Stanford University's computer-based courses in mathematics for bright, young students. Link back to the main site for even more resources, although many are geared mainly to teachers and to other subjects.

Mighty m&m Math Project

www.hypersurf.com/~gconklin/school/ mm.htm

Math equations using M&M's: Which M&M color is most prominent in the world? Who has the same number of each color of M&M's in their bags as you do? Compare your bag's contents with others worldwide and check in with what the Mars candy company says each color percentage should be. Then eat the data! This site offers a truly unique way to get problem solving, measurement, and statistics and probability skills under your belt. You can find something for kids of all ages here, although to use the fanciest version, you need Netscape 3.0 or above. There's a text-only version, too, that won't make you feel as hungry!

Monster Math

www.lifelong.com/lifelong_universe/ AcademicWorld/MonsterMath/ default.html

Math challenges in English and Spanish: Don't worry: It's not called Monster Math because it's too hard, but because it's an online adventure involving story problems about a Monster party. If you don't get the right answers, you get to try again after receiving helpful feedback. The game is designed to introduce and review basic math concepts, including counting, addition, and multiplication. The activities let the player be a problem solver and move the adventure along. If you want the monsters to talk (an optional feature for the Macintosh only) in English or Spanish, you'll have to get the Talker and Text-to-Speech plug-ins. Don't worry; the home page has links to these utilities.

Online Mathematics Dictionary

www.mathpro.com/math/glossary/
glossary.html

Math dictionary: This voluminous if plain-looking resource is a very useful way to demystify or clarify math-related terms. Click the letter that begins the word you need and chances are, it's here. An internal search box would be helpful, but the site doesn't have one, so just scroll down the list of alphabetized terms until you find the one you're seeking. You may find it interesting just to read the terms after clicking any letter in the alphabet. (Know what a *joule* is? You will if you click the letter *J*.)

Past Notable Women of Computing & Mathematics

www.cs.yale.edu/HTML/YALE/CS/
HyPlans/tap/past-women.html

Get to know women in mathematics: Biographies and links honor the contributions women have made to the advancement of computing and mathematics. Who says girls don't like math? The site includes a photo gallery and related historical links. Read about a wealth of female brilliance, from women such as mathematician and scientist Hypatia of Alexandria (A.D. 370–415) and Sonya Kovalevskaya, a great nineteenth century mathematician, writer, and advocate of women's rights. And did you know that it was Grace Hopper who coined the phrase "computer bug?"

Other Stuff to Check Out

Web sites
www2.hawaii.edu/suremath/home.html
www.ncrel.org/ncrel/sdrs/areas/issues/
content/cntareas/math/ma100.htm

www.fi.edu/qa97/me4/
www.fi.edu/qa97/spotlight4/
freeabel.geom.umn.edu/
csr.uvic.ca/~mmania/
pegasus.cc.ucf.edu/~mathed/problem.html
www.c3.lanl.gov/mega-math/index.html

Newsgroups
k12s.phast.umass.edu/gui/newsgroups/
scied.html

Online service area
America Online: LEARNING & CULTURE

Suggested search-engine keywords
Yahoo!: YAHOOLIGANS — Science and
Oddities, Mathematics
Infoseek: Mathematics

General science resources

"The most exciting phrase to hear in science, the one that heralds new discoveries, is not 'Eureka!' (I found it) but 'That's funny. . . .' " Isaac Asimov, "The Eureka Phenomenon"; *The Magazine of Fantasy and Science Fiction,* June 1971.

That quote by scientist Isaac Asimov has always been one of my favorites because it describes the adventure of discovery that awaits budding — and veteran — scientists. I like scientists because they are truth seekers. So are kids. Kids and scientists seek truth by experimenting and by asking questions. Kids try to count stars and stop to look at bugs and wonder what Saturn's rings are made of — and so do scientists. That makes kids and scientists two of my favorite groups of people. And here are some of my favorite general science sites.

African Americans in the Sciences

www.lib.lsu.edu./lib/chem/display/
faces.html

Collection of articles, bibliographies, and links pertaining to the past, present, and future status of African Americans in the sciences: A version with tables is provided for those browsers that can display them. If not, a text version is here, too. Presented by Louisiana State University Libraries, this site offers information about men and women who have advanced the sciences in biochemistry, biology, chemistry, physics, engineering, entomology, genetics, oceanography, computers, space, medicine, zoology, and technology. Read an assessment of the present challenges facing minorities in the sciences and suggestions for improving minority opportunities in the field of chemistry. Find out about electronic conferences and papers geared to help African American students in pursuing a career in chemistry. The Webliography supplies links to many business, government, arts, social science, and science sites, as well as reference materials.

4000 Years of Women in Science

www.astr.ua.edu/4000WS/4000WS.html

Tracing women's long history as scientists: Get to know 125 women who, prior to the twentieth century, broke with tradition and bias to study science. Based on public talks given by Dr. Sethanne Howard, currently with NASA, the articles describe female inventors, scholars, writers, mathematicians, and astronomers. For part of the site, you have the option of using a frames-based display if you prefer. To access the information, click the Biographies, References, or Photographs links. Just for fun, try the interactive quiz. Get all the answers right and win the "Hypatia Award," which enables you to enter your name in the Hall of Fame and presents you with a certificate that you can print. (Hypatia was a woman natural philosopher and mathematician in Egypt around 400 A.D.) You can also work a crossword puzzle with clues relating to the site (although your browser must be Java-enabled — JavaScript won't help — to run this). Learning Links takes you to related sites. And the Did You Know section offers little-known tidbits of history. For example, did you know that the original idea and patent leading to cellular phone technology came from classic movie star Hedy Lamarr?

Beakman and Jax

www.beakman.com

Science that's strictly for kids: Associated with the kids' science television show *Beakman's World,* this site makes good use of science links and images and keeps kids posted on the show. Visitors can click links to see images of planets, to find out how the human body works, or to explore other kid-geared science topics. Netscape is the best way to view this site. Check out the 50-terrific-questions section for answers to stuff that kids want to know, such as "Why is a diamond so hard?" or "How does soap work?" or "Why does my voice sound different on a tape recorder?" If you have Shockwave, you can enjoy interactive demonstrations of science topics, such as relativity, magnetism, and the workings of the human body.

Bill Nye The Science Guy

nyelabs.kcts.org/

Science made fun for kids: Based on the television show, Bill Nye's site is full of the same high-quality, entertaining science exploration activities as his show. You can find science news, show updates, interactive science demonstrations, a virtual lab, selected Web links, and brainteasers. View this site with Netscape 3.0 or Microsoft Internet Explorer and various plug-ins (QuickTime, RealAudio, VivoActive Player, VDO Live, and Shockwave, for example). Visit the tech section for downloads and assistance.

Discovery Channel Online

www.discovery.com/

Official site of the Discovery Channel: The stories about science and nature that you can find here include lots of graphics and are clearly organized. Sections are devoted to the Discovery Channel, Animal Planet, their various other television shows, and the Kids Channel. It's an ever-varied, huge collection of articles and program notes relevant to fans of these television channels. You can find out what upcoming television shows may help with a homework assignment or term paper.

Fisher Science Education On-Line

www.fisheredu.com

Laboratory science supplies and science links: Here's a vast links library of over 5,000 staff-selected biology, chemistry, physics, earth, and space resources. Use the Sci-Ed Site Explorer by entering keywords of your own or by clicking any combination of suggested keywords, including anatomy, museums, astronomy, physics, biology, chemistry, space science, earth science, mathematics, kids, or primary, secondary, or college education. Other sections include online supply, gifts, and gadgets catalogs for science educators or interested parents. Fisher Scientific is Fisher Education's parent company. Research laboratories and industries worldwide use Fisher products and catalogs.

Great Thinkers and Visionaries on the Net

www.lucifer.com/~sasha/thinkers.html

Discover more about the great thinkers in history: What qualities inspire us? Who are the greatest minds in science, philosophy, and the arts? What constitutes important scientific thought, theory, research, or philosophy? This massive resource (which takes a while to load) contains a list of some of the world's greatest thinkers and visionaries. Locate their books and publications, visit Web sites by or about them, and click enlargeable photos of many of them. Find science-based Usenet discussion links. If you have a favorite, or if you've always wanted to know more about people such as Albert Einstein, Isaac Newton, Stephen Hawking, Isaac Asimov, Carl Sagan, Leonardo da Vinci, Linus Pauling, or Buckminster Fuller, you'll appreciate this site. Note to parents: This resource draws on many perspectives, including views of some controversial people (Timothy Leary, for example), so oversight is advised.

Hands-on Science Centers Worldwide

www.cs.cmu.edu/~mwm/sci.html

International listing of public museums with strong interactive science components: Want to visit a museum in Singapore with fun science exhibits? Try the Singapore Science Centre. Museums around the world are listed here. Although most museums have links to other sites, some do not. From Asia and Australia to Europe, South America, and North America, you can electronically visit science exhibits and read reviews about many of the museums' sites. The list takes a while to scroll down, but at the very bottom, you find links to science sites.

ION Science

www.injersey.com/Media/IonSci/

Science news and selected links creatively presented: This fun online magazine monitors science and nature news and developments. Its staff of writers and artists presents complex and entertaining topics for average readers who like science and nature and want to understand both better. One key objective is to put things in perspective and explain the impact of news and breakthroughs on people's lives. In Focus takes an in-depth look at special subjects (earthquakes, for example), and Hot Links relates to subjects covered at this site. Read about Jersey during the Jurassic period, the Roswell incident, or the Chemistry of Bad Hair Days. The site is updated monthly and is best viewed with Netscape Navigator.

Mad Scientist Network

128.252.223.239/~ysp/MSN/

Real scientists answer your questions: Graphically delightful, good-natured, and packed with solid science, this site may shatter any illusions that you may have about scientists being stuffy, distant types. Experts from many disciplines assist and inspire kids. Sponsored by Washington University Medical School in St. Louis, Missouri, this site has articles (for example, "Chromoplasts and Leucoplasts — What Are They?") and three sections: Ask-A-Scientist, MAD Labs, and MadSci Library. Ask-A-Scientist lets you see what other kids have asked and had answered and gives you a chance to then post your own new inquiry topic. Kids are encouraged to review current (within the last three weeks) and past questions by scrolling or using an internal search mechanism. They can read all subjects in all age categories or just pick subjects and answers for their own age group. Questions from kindergartners through third graders may be "How do skunks make smell?" Tenth to twelfth graders may ask something like "What causes energy to form a visual image?" MAD Labs has fun experiments and activities. MadSci Library has science and science career links. You can best use this site with a frames-compatible browser.

New Scientist

www.newscientist.com

Online magazine of science happenings: You can find plenty of sections to scour here. The Insight link offers science articles, live events, and selected Web links where topics range from the serious

98   Specialized Explorations

(origins of the universe, the basis of emotions, and cloning) to the not-quite-so-serious (*Star Trek* physics). The searchable database of 350 questions and answers includes the ever-popular query, "Why is the sky blue?" Get expert looks at social, economic, practical, and technological impacts of the Internet. You can read reviews of science books and purchase selected book titles online. You also can buy *New Scientist CD-ROM*, a searchable collection of the magazine's complete text and graphics since 1989. Try Shockwave tours of Britain and Australia. Enjoy math- and science-based cartoons, photographs, illustrations, puzzles, and artistic endeavors. The site also includes science job listings, courses, events, editorials, letters, and discussion forums. If you like the online version, you can subscribe here for the print magazine. This site was designed for Netscape 3.0 and Microsoft Internet Explorer 3.0, or better.

PopSci (Popular Science Magazine Online)

www.popsci.com/

Popular Science magazine goes online: Long a favorite with science buffs, even before "techie" was trendy, *Popular Science* describes the latest in automotive technology, appliances and other electronics, and aspects of science to which everyday folks can relate. Now that same everyman approach is online, so staying up-to-speed with science and computers is easier than ever. You can search related links, forums, and Essential Guides to testing your drinking water, using your camera, or assessing the best auto engines. Use the internal search box to find topics covered in the past. You can subscribe online to the print magazine for old-time's sake.

Russian Friends and Partners in Science

solar.rtd.utk.edu/friends/science/
   science.html

You too can be a Russian comrade: With the fall of the Iron Curtain and the dissolution of the Soviet Union, Russia's scientists are freer to develop working relationships with scientists of Western nations. This site (which also has sections devoted to the arts and business) focuses on current and potential projects involving space, telecommunications, agriculture, environmental sciences, health sciences, nuclear sciences, physics, and astronomy. Get the lowdown on the space station MIR and how it was a historic multinational collaboration! Planning a trip to Russia? Here are some thoughts and ideas for your travels. You can also link to related associations, publications, and organizations. English and Russian versions of this site are available, and you can choose either a text-only version or a text-with-graphics version.

Science and the Environment

www.voyagepub.com/publish

Electronic news summary: Read summaries of articles from over 500 magazines, specialty journals, and newspapers. Presented concisely with color images, maps, and graphics, each bimonthly issue contains 80 articles organized into chapters. Chapters include Biodiversity and Wildlife, Alternative Energy and Fuels, Marine Ecology, Health, Population, Agriculture, Climate Change and Atmospheric Studies, and Waste Management and Recycling. It's designed for the classroom, but goes great with home study and enjoyment. All 320 previously published articles are available for sale on CD-ROM.

Science Bytes

loki.ur.utk.edu/ut2kids/

University of Tennessee scientists share their work with kids: Through articles geared to kids, the research being done by scientists at UT is clearly and entertainingly explained. Link internally to articles with titles such as "UT researchers are barking up the dogwood tree!" (plant pathologists studying a dogwood disease) and "He's Nothing But a Rock Hound, A Diggin' All The Time" (profile of a geology researcher). From stream restoration to mapmaking, wildlife conservation, and aerospace technology, you can find high-quality articles guaranteed to show kids how scientists "do" science. Kids and parents are welcome and encouraged to submit feedback on the site and its usefulness.

Science Daily Magazine

www.sciencedaily.com/

Hot-off-the-presses online science news: Get online news, receive e-mail news, or tune into Web broadcasts for breaking news about discoveries and research in disciplines from astrophysics to zoology. Dependent on news releases from leading universities and research organizations, this site posts releases along with contact information. Find links to major science media and science sites. Created in 1995 by Canadian-American science writer/editor Dan Hogan and his schoolteacher wife, Michele Hogan, this site is produced in the couple's home in Connecticut. Hogan is also managing editor of *Current Science,* a biweekly science news magazine for junior high school students published by the Weekly Reader Corporation.

Science Hobbyist

www.eskimo.com/~billb/

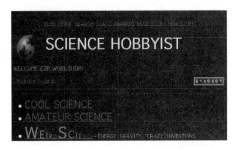

Eclectic collection of fun and practical science resources: This site offers a list of Insanely Great Science Web Sites, links of interest to amateur scientists (including kids), and weird science sites (for example, crazy inventions). A special emphasis is placed on energy-related sites, but you can also find science museums, home schooling links, science fair resources, articles and editorials on science education, and some unique science projects (for example, how to make your own hologram plate). This site is filled with humor, curiosity, and good science.

Science Web Links

www4.ncsu.edu/unity/users/a/
ambodzin/public/sciencesites.htm

Links to some fine science sites: A long list, in no particular apparent order, of some really terrific science-based Web sites. Most come complete with a brief but descriptive summary of what you can find. If you are coming up empty after doing the usual search of topics from one of the Internet search engines, this site may be the place to find the answers to your science homework or term paper. Just about every major science discipline

100 **Specialized Explorations**

is represented, and the sites selected are admirable for their content as well as, in most cases, their creative use of the Internet as an instructional tool. This list was compiled by veteran science and technology educator Al Bodzin and is part of his site for science educators.

Why Files

whyfiles.news.wisc.edu/

Science news for kids and parents: Priding itself on illuminating the science, math, and technology lurking within everyday news, this site does a terrific job. Funded by the National Science Foundation, it's bright, informative, and hip. Discover science projects, revealing articles (for example, a story about the Environmental Protection Agency research into chemicals that may have hormonal effects and the impact of those chemicals on people), and special features, including Cool Science Images, a library of past stories, and forums for feedback, questions, and ideas. Twice a month, new features are published.

Other Stuff to Check Out

Web sites
unr.edu/homepage/jcannon/
    bodzin.html#chatareas
fas.sfu.ca/css/gcs/main.html
malthus.stisd.k12.tx.us/innovations/
www.middleweb.com
www.areacom.it/html/arte_cultura/loris/
    armchair.html
www.helios.org/
www.spe.sony.com/Pictures/tv/beakman/
    beakman.html
ericir.syr.edu/Projects/Newton/
www.nextstep.com/
www.earthsky.com/
www.npr.org/sfkids/

Newsgroups
search.dejanews.com/bg.xp?level=sci

America Online: KIDS ONLY, LEARNING &
    CULTURE, NEWSSTAND
CompuServe: GO SCITRIVIA

Suggested search-engine keywords
Yahoo!: Science
Infoseek: Science

General resources for both math and science

Cornell Theory Center Math and Science Gateway

**www.tc.cornell.edu/Edu/
    MathSciGateway**

Useful list of math and science links for grades 9–12: Easy to use, with good site descriptions, this linking resource is well organized into the categories of Astronomy; Biology; Chemistry; Computers; The Earth, the Ocean and the Environment; Engineering; Health and Medicine; Mathematics; Meteorology; and Physics. You can also find a section devoted to Scientists and the History of Scientists, Ask an Expert, and Encouraging Kids (in science and math, of course). The site also offers links to other K–12 Internet resources, including virtual Field Trips, Museums, Schools on the Web, College and Financial Aid Information, and math- and science-related publications for kids, parents, and teachers.

ENC for Mathematics and Science Education — Digital Dozen

www.enc.org/classroom/index.htm

Monthly list of 12 notable science and math sites: Although most of this site is geared to teachers, one notable area that kids can enjoy is The Digital Dozen. The Eisenhowser National Clearinghouse's (ENC) selection team, consisting of scientists and educators, searches the Net for new and fascinating resources, which they present monthly. If you missed the previous months' choices, don't worry; they are archived so you can go back and visit what you missed. You can nominate sites that you think are high quality, well organized, easy to use, graphically appealing to kids, cutting edge, and scholastically superior. (Check the selection criteria section for more specifics.) Parents may enjoy linking to other parts of this site to read about current issues and directives in science and math education.

MIMS Hub Category Search

scssi.scetv.org/mims/ssrch2.htm

Consortium dedicated to improving math and science education: This site is primarily for teachers and backed by the Midlands Improving Math and Science Hub (MIMS), a group of educators, schools, and businesspeople. However, it still has much to offer students and parents. Of principal interest are the Internet links organized into categories such as Botany, Zoology, Chemistry, Physics, Earth, Space, and Math. The database is searchable. The complexity of the sites varies: In math, for example, you

can find categories for number/numeration systems, numerical/algebraic concepts, probability, and statistics; or you can go to MIMS Gems to find kid-oriented sites such as Math Magic Activities and Math in the Home. Also of interest to students are the puzzles, which are links to math and science brainteasers, trivia, and riddles designed to strengthen reasoning and problem-solving skills. Here's an example of one of the puzzles: If a fish weighs eight pounds plus half of its weight, how much does the fish weigh? MIMS knows.

Other Stuff to Check Out

Web sites
mmm.cs.orst.edu/SMILE/home sci and math
www.learner.org/

Newsgroup
search.dejanews.com/bg.xp?level=sci

Online service area
America Online: LEARNING & CULTURE

Suggested search-engine keywords
Yahoo!: Science
Infoseek: Science

Life sciences

Life sciences focus on what grows, respires, reproduces, and requires nutrients, in other words, whatever is alive. An aardvark is alive. A backpack is not. A daisy is alive. A bicycle is not. You get the idea! Biology is a big part of the life sciences, so many students explore it in school. Plant biologists are called botanists. Animal biologists are called zoologists. Zoologists can specialize — mammalogists study mammals, ichthyologists study fish, and ornithologists study birds. Oh, and don't forget primatologists, herpetologists, and conchologists. Whew! That's a lot of "ologists"! Hunt for your favorite "'ology" among these "lively" sites!

BugWatch

bugwatch.com/bugindex.html

All about bugs, spiders, and insects: Click any of the lovely illustrations of ants, butterflies, wasps, bees, dragonflies, flies, bugs, mantids, hoppers, beetles, cicadas, or spiders, and up pops a wonderfully written, descriptive article and a selection of images of the species of your choice. Click the images to enlarge them. This site is elegant in its simplicity and charm, so whether or not you think you like bugs, you'll enjoy seeing and reading about them here. Link to a selected list of sites of interest to gardeners, entomology professionals, and hobbyists, including sites with areas for kids.

Butterfly Website

mgfx.com/butterfly/

Expert information about butterflies: The resources here tell you about gardening for butterflies, raising butterflies, and helping butterflies survive. This attractive site includes images, inspirational stories, books, a newsletter, an online store, discussion and chat areas, research articles, and butterfly conservation news. Be sure to visit the Picture Galleries.

Fish: A Quick Course on Ichthyology

www.odyssey.ycg.org/fish.htm

All about fish in one easy troll: Scroll down this site to get your hooks into some really great information about fish. For example, you can find out what exactly a fish is, for starters, and how they breathe underwater. The site takes a while to load, but the resulting images and well-organized on-site resources, interspersed with clear writing and diagrams, make it worth your time. If you need a good concise primer on fish or the science of ichthyology, start scrolling here.

Froggy Page

frog.simplenet.com/froggy/

Leap into lots of froggy fun and biology: Probably one of the most comprehensive frog sites on the Internet, this site includes images and frog calls.(Note that all the sound clips are in Sun AU format and may require a plug-in or helper application for your browser.) You also find links covering frogs in classic literature; songs about frogs; frog research, conservation and distribution; real dissections (heads up, parents; the images can be graphic); virtual dissections (so you don't have to cut up the real thing); famous frogs (yeah, Kermit!); frog events; frogs as pets; herpetology; and loads of cute graphics. If you need to do a report on frogs, look here for online resources. Hit the word *ribbit* to hear a frog say it! From here, you can also link to All About Toads.

Human Anatomy Online

www.innerbody.com/

Explore the body's inner workings: This first-ever human anatomy Java site lets you roam inside the human body without downloading software or paying a user fee. This boldly illustrated, relatively easy-to-use Internet application lets you pick a certain body system (for example, the skeleton or the muscular cardiovascular system) and then guides you along to related illustrations or anatomy descriptions. See the heart pumping or lungs working or a baby developing in the womb. Parents will probably want to oversee the journey and help with navigation for younger explorers.

In Search of Giant Squid

seawifs.gsfc.nasa.gov/squid.html

Help scientists find one of the ocean's biggest inhabitants: Dive into this site to explore the myths and realities of the squid, one of the ocean's most mysterious creatures. This highly graphic and interactive site relies on backgrounds, font colors, tables, and Java applets. It's a beautiful online adventure that takes you below the ocean without getting you wet!

Internet Resources for Conchologists

fly.hiwaay.net/~dwills/shellnet.html

Mollusk and shell links: Come out of your shell and discover great links organized into categories. For example, the Mollusk/Mollusc sites include online books, journals, conference proceedings, newsletters, newsgroups, mailing lists, discussions, specimen catalogs, collections, databases, pictures, information on endangered species and conservation, virtual libraries, and biology sites. At the Shellers site, you can locate clubs, dealers, collectors, books, and publications. You also find organizations, associations, societies, research, museums, libraries, university programs, and related government resources.

Living Things

www.fi.edu/tfi/units/life/

Principles of the life sciences: Part of the Franklin Institute's site, this section is devoted to helping people understand the dynamics involved in life science research and observation. Best of all, the site is designed in a student- and parent-friendly way. Have fun exploring the site's options for discovery. One such option, the keyword index, allows you to click any of an impressive list of life science words and terms — for example, anatomy, biome, metamorphosis, migration, carnivore, cells, earthworms, fruit fly, genus, and backbone. Click whatever term interests you and get a comprehensive yet easily understandable definition and a list of links to sites that further illustrate the meaning of the term. This resource provides carefully selected links.

Microbe Zoo

commtechlab.msu.edu/CTLprojects/dlc-me/whatis.html

Zoo that you can fit on your fingertip: This "zoo" features microscopic creatures that live around, inside, and on us. Microbiologists study these nearly invisible beings that you can see at this site. You can examine images of microbes and get data about their size, scientific classification, and feeding habitats. You also find out how they live in their environments and among other microorganisms. Visit the zoo "pavilions" arranged according to natural habitats. There's Water World, DirtLand, and the Animal Pavilion. From the compost heap and toxic waste dump to us, microorganisms live in some strange locales. Check out the House of Horrors if you dare.

New Jersey Online: Yuckiest Site on the Internet

www.nj.com/yucky/
index.html?06192215

A guide to worms, cockroaches, and other yucky stuff: This site has good scientific information, but it's definitely fashioned for kids, so grown-ups may need time to adjust to features such as Your Gross and Yucky Body. That section explains on a kid's level subjects such as what spit is, why we burp, and what *regularity* means. Other sections of the site are called Yucky Bug World, where you get to know cockroaches, among other insects, and Worm World, which includes "interviews" with leeches and tapeworms. Kids can ask the roving worm reporter, Wendell, weird or gross biology questions that they can't really ask anyone else without hearing, "Why do you want to know THAT?" Wendell understands. After all, he's a worm. This site has a proven track record with kids, so it must be doing something right! Grown-ups, keep those senses of humor handy and remember, it *is* biology! Some of the interactive activities require WPlany (Windows Play Any) or Sound Machine, and QuickTime.

The Official Pacific Northwest Slug Page

www.WebElegance.com/slug/slug.html

  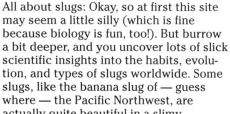

All about slugs: Okay, so at first this site may seem a little silly (which is fine because biology is fun, too!). But burrow a bit deeper, and you uncover lots of slick scientific insights into the habits, evolution, and types of slugs worldwide. Some slugs, like the banana slug of — guess where — the Pacific Northwest, are actually quite beautiful in a slimy, squished banana sort of way. View images, sing slug songs, laugh at slug jokes, and find out interesting things such as where slugs go in the winter. If you get really inspired, you can shop here for sluggish gifts.

Safari Touch Tank

oberon.educ.sfu.ca/splash/tank.htm

Virtual tide-pool adventure: Click any of the images in this graphically stunning little tide-pool and instantly get your choice identified and detailed. Find out about starfish, eelgrass, and — oops, I don't want to give too much away. Animate the tide-pool (a 533K QuickTime file) if you'd like, but it's still beautiful and enjoyable whether it's moving or not. You can even enjoy the animations of the individual plants and animals that are in the tide-pool!

The Searching Wolf

www.iup.edu/~wolf/wolves.htmlx

Articles, news, and links about wolves: If wolf information is on the Internet, chances are it's cataloged among the over

200 sites you find here. Additionally, get lists of wolf resources, books, articles, research and conservation organizations, and wolf illustrations and images. Get the latest wolf-related headlines, opinions, and analyses and discover the best places to actually see wolves. Kids will enjoy finding out how to howl like wolves and understanding what the calls mean. Take the Wolf Test to see how much you know about them.

Seeds of Life

versicolores.ca/SeedsOfLife/

Visually inspiring look at seeds: Presented both in French and English, this photo-rich site presents in artistic fashion an intuitive and sensitive look at the birth and growth of plants. See images of little seeds that resemble fuzzy baby birds and that could almost be described as cute! Discover how seeds sprout, travel, mature, and grow into the plant life upon which we humans depend for survival. This site is a reminder of the miracle of life and the gifts that plants give us, including oxygen and food, for starters.

WhaleClub

www.whaleclub.com/

Get to know whales, dolphins, and manatees: These animals are mammals, just like humans are. But their home is the ocean, and humans are not always their friends. Through articles, links, images, audios, online movies, online discussions and chats, and creative activities (for example, the coloring book), you can find out how these animals live, the challenges they face, and what kids and parents can do to care about them. Sections of the site require various plug-ins, although you can discover plenty to do without plug-ins.

Wildflowers

www.sccs.swarthmore.edu/~tkorn/
wildflowers/

A garden of American and European wildflowers: This site will really grow on you, with its stunning photos of wildflowers and links to wildflower-related sites. Among the flower families represented in this lovely photo array are the lily, orchid, and gentian families.

The Wonderful Skunk and Opossum Page

elvis.neep.wisc.edu/~firmiss/mephitis-
didelphis.html

Uncommon insights about skunks and opossums: Be forewarned: After you visit this site, your perceptions of skunks and opossums probably will change. Both creatures play an important role in the food chain, and they are much more intelligent than often believed. Get links to sites where experts answer your questions, find out how to identify skunk and opossum tracks, clear up some common misconceptions, and collect little-known facts. Know the difference between a possum and an opossum? Technically, there is a big difference, which this site explains. What exactly is skunk scent, and how can you get rid of it? Enjoy revealing and appealing pictures, stories, and folktales about these mostly misunderstood creatures.

Other Stuff to Check Out

Web sites

herb.biol.uregina.ca/liu/bio/idb.shtml
www.usgs.gov/network/science/biology/
    (or)
info.er.usgs.gov/network/science/biology/
    index.html
biotech.chem.indiana.edu/

www.abc.hu/biosites.html
www.data-transport.com/
curry.edschool.Virginia.EDU/go/Whales/
    Contents.HTML
curry.edschool.virginia.edu/go/frog
www.euronet.nl/users/mbleeker/
    fotom_e.html
iip.ucsd.edu/personal/vanderschaegen/
    home/links.html
cvs.anu.edu.au/andy/beye/beyehome.html

Newsgroups
alt.animals
alt.animals.dolphins
alt.animals.bears
sci.agriculture.beekeeping
sci.bio
sci.bio.entomology.misc

Mailing lists
www.neosoft.com/internet/paml/groups.F/
    fungus.html
www.neosoft.com/internet/paml/groups.A/
    arachnid.html

Chat areas
mgfx.com/butterfly/entercon.htm
members.aol.com/dinarda/ant/index.htm

Online service area
America Online: LEARNING & CULTURE

Suggested search-engine keywords
Yahoo!: Science: Life sciences,
    YAHOOLIGANS — Science and Oddities
Infoseek: Biology, animals, plants

Physical sciences and technology

Welcome to the online worlds of physics, chemistry, engineering, and technology. Even if you're not a physicist, chemist, or engineer, you may enjoy exploring these sites. The physics sites, for example, focus on the study of the relationship of matter and energy in the fields of acoustics, mechanics and motion, electromagnetism, thermodynamics, and other areas involving force, radiation, light, and atomic energy. The chemistry sites may help you understand what happens when you mix stuff together and it reacts. At

the engineering and technology sites, you can read about engineers, who study movement and materials and then figure out how to build new things such as better running shoes, robots, computer equipment, solar-powered houses, and lifelike puppets.

Character Shop

www.character-shop.com/

Engineering special effects: This company specializes in animatronics (that's when mechanical and/or electrical components are assembled to move in a realistic manner), makeup effects, puppets, and robotics. See examples of its better-known, believable engineering, design, and construction feats, which you may have seen in movies such as *Operation Dumbo Drop* and *The Santa Clause*. Although this site has many things of interest to kids, it wasn't written specifically for kids; it references beer commercials and contains some indelicate language on the page featuring links. For that reason, parents may want to visit here with younger children. The site includes links to related sites. Many images on the site are clickable if you'd like to see larger versions. It's best viewed in Netscape.

Chem-4-Kids

www.chem4kids.com/

Chemistry made easy: Get kid-oriented explanations and activities on elements and how they combine to make compounds, as well as basic terminology and novel ways to comprehend chemistry concepts, such as bonding and electron orbitals. Read how the periodic table got its name and why it's organized the way it is.

Chemicool

the-tech.mit.edu/Chemicool/

The ultimate Periodic Table of the Elements: Two graphic editions (fancy and less fancy — choose the version that works best on your computer) check the elements for you. In either case, just enter an element name or symbol or click one of the provided images. Within seconds, you get the name, atomic number, density, group, melting point and other states, energy properties, oxidations and electrons, appearance description and characteristics (for example, hafnium is silvery and hard), any reactions or other forms, and facts concerning radius, conductivity, and abundance. Can you guess which five elements are looked up most frequently? Get the answer here!

Cog Shop

www.ai.mit.edu/projects/cog/

Meet Cog the Robot: The Cog Shop is part of the Artificial Intelligence Laboratory at the Massachusetts Institute of Technology in Cambridge. Engineers there are developing and experimenting with Cog, a humanoid-type robot sort of reminiscent of C-3PO in the *Star Wars* movies (except Cog isn't played by an actor). Enjoy a friendly, informative, image- and text-based tour of The Cog Shop, the (real) people of The Cog Shop, and, of course, Cog himself (or itself). You can also review Cog-related papers and publications, Cog's photo album, Cog's coverage in the news, and Cog's latest improvements. Along the way, you also discover why scientists want to build a human-like robot at all.

Energy Quest

www.energy.ca.gov/education/ index2.html

Energy in all its forms: This site, which is geared to students, parents, and educators, offers games, puzzles, and other interactive activities that demonstrate how physics deals with the properties and interactions of matter and radiation. Do you know how much energy is in a peanut? Want to build a solar hot dog cooker or make plastic out of milk? Pop into this site and enjoy the science experiments (under adult supervision, that is). Cars only run on petroleum-based fuels, right? Nope! Check out the alternative fuel vehicles on this site. Of course you can find out how physics provides the groundwork for other sciences, and see how physics is applied to fields such as engineering and health. But that doesn't sound very exciting, does it? Drop in this site and find out that science can be a blast!

EREN Kids' Stuff

www.eren.doe.gov/kids.html

Renewable-energy topics of special interest to kids: Brought to you by the Energy Efficiency and Renewable Energy Network (EREN), this section of the larger site uses articles and links to give kids solar energy science projects and to introduce them to "Earth Dog" and to concepts such as understanding and using renewable energy and transportation systems. Some activities rely on various plug-ins (Adobe Acrobat Reader, for example).

108 Specialized Explorations

From Windmills To Whirligigs

www.sci.mus.mn.us/sln/vollis

Kinetic energy and art: Blow into this in-depth exploration of physical science and art that uses whirligigs, windmills, and kinetic sculpture. Meet Vollis Simpson and tour his yard full of all kinds of wind gadgets! Geared to kids from kindergarten through grade 12, the site was created by the Science Museum of Minnesota and a partnering magnet school for use by teachers, but parents and kids can use its teaching principles, too.

Global Energy Marketplace

www.crest.org/

Focus on alternative-energy engineering and use: This site explores the development of technologies to supplement or one day supplant the world's current dependence on fossil fuels. You can find out about renewable energy alternatives and research, how to increase energy efficiency, and how families can adopt more energy-efficient lifestyles in their homes through recycling, new residential building methods, and consumer practices. Find documents, databases, discussion groups, related sites, software, and organizations devoted to energy research, development, and conservation. See what energy-saving technologies the White House is adopting.

The Internet Pilot to Physics

www.tp.umu.se/TIPTOP/

Mega-resource site for physics: Online and other resources of interest to scientists and students are cataloged here. Track down important events; books and publications; grant and other deadlines; mailing lists and forums; documents and studies; bulletin boards; organizations and societies; job announcements; institutes; forums; research and education programs; conferences; news; and dates of historic significance in physics. The Virtual Laboratory offers visualizations and demonstrations (using Java applets, VRML, and Shockwave). Here you can visit Jupiter and its moons, excite an atom, explore the physics of a rainbow, or visit the Little Shop of Physics. The site contains sections for student-oriented study resources and forums.

Microworlds

www.lbl.gov/MicroWorlds/

Exploring materials science: This interactive site, designed for kids in grades 7 through 12, is based on research at the Ernest Orlando Lawrence Berkeley National Laboratory of the University of California. Through visual displays and text, students discover what the lab's Advanced Light Source is and how it works, what polymers are and why they are useful, how even minute quantities of trace elements can change a material for better or worse, and how materials science helps scientists understand environmental problems.

Nobel Prize Internet Archive

www.nobelprizes.com/

Winners throughout history: See who won Nobel Prizes for chemistry, physics, and other categories and get to know more about the winners and their research. Although you may think that this site would be a rather formal, stodgy place to visit, its frames-based design is colorful, easy to use, and fun. You can also search only for women who've won and get an interesting history about the prize. (Find out why no prize is awarded in mathematics.) Read about the "First Step to Nobel Prize in Physics," the international physics research paper competition for high school students. The Nobel Prize Internet Archive is not affiliated with the official Nobel Foundation. The site is best viewed with Netscape Navigator.

Renewable Energy Education Module

solstice.crest.org/renewables/re-kiosk/
   index.shtml

Alternative-energy technologies clearly explained: Through this multimedia exhibit, you can click through virtual education tours covering solar, windpower, geothermal, biomass, and small hydro technologies. The tours let you go forward or back at your own pace and are designed for kids, parents, and schools to use. It uses very basic words and pictures to teach the theoretical and practical basics of renewable energy. I strongly recommend that you use a graphical browser (such as NCSA Mosaic or Netscape Navigator) with automatic image loading turned on.

RoboTuna

web.mit.edu/towtank/www/tuna/
   index.html

Mechanical tuna: Meet RoboTuna! Designed to mimic the shape and movements of its biological counterpart, this Lycra-covered engineered version was developed by David Barrett for his doctoral thesis at the Massachusetts Institute of Technology. See through the use of images and clear explanations how RoboTuna was constructed and what makes it move. As Barrett explains, for about 160 million years, fish have been evolving to move effortlessly in water. By understanding what fish do, someone may one day be able to design minisubmarines with similar qualities.

Waseda University Humanoid Project

www.shirai.info.waseda.ac.jp/human-
   oid/

Robot research and development: This project was established at Waseda University in Japan in 1992. Its goal is to build a human-like robot (nicknamed "Humanoid") that will have sensing, recognition, expression, and motion

110 **Specialized Explorations**

capabilities so it can develop a semblance of a working relationship with real humans — rather like Data, the android on *Star Trek: The Next Generation*. Get to know through narratives and images what is known so far about "Humanoid."

Whelmers

www.mcrel.org/whelmers/

Teach scientific principles in fun ways: Try projects such as Balloon in the Bottle, Floating Bubbles, and Heat Sink, all designed to reach and excite students. Veteran science teacher Steven Jacobs tries to reactivate the natural curiosity that kids have when they're young but seem to lose for various social and personal reasons as teenagers. By using simple, fun demonstrations nicknamed "Whelmers" because they "whelm" without "overwhelming," Jacobs began reaching students very effectively. Here he shares his years of experience and his experiments with other teachers, parents, and kids. Grown-ups need to be involved to oversee safety and learning.

Women in Science and Technology

www.anl.gov/WIST/links.htm

Selected links of interest to females who are or want to be engineers: Part of the overall site of the Women in Science and Technology Program at Argonne National Laboratory in Illinois, the links here include those science and engineering associations and societies for women, as well as newsgroups and education and

funding programs. This is a good resource list for any young woman contemplating a technologically based science career.

Other Stuff to Check Out

Web sites
www.grin.net/~zgolden/
www.superscience.com/
www.ch.ic.ac.uk/GIC/
dizzy.library.arizona.edu/library/teams/set/
   virtual.html
www.tufts.edu/~jlarsen/sds.html
www.imagination-engines.com/
   corporate.htm
solstice.crest.org/online/aeguide/index.html
www.ornl.gov/ORNL/Energy_Eff/
   EE_links.html
www.esd.ornl.gov/bfdp/
www.igc.apc.org/awea/
www.csn.net/solar/
www.nrel.gov/
www.inel.gov/
www.nanothinc.com/NanoWorld/Kids/
   NanoKids/index.html
www.execpc.com/~skaufman/book.html
ericir.syr.edu/Projects/Newton/9/slink.html
sprott.physics.wisc.edu/wop.htm

Newsgroups
k12s.phast.umass.edu/gui/newsgroups/
   scied.htmlother URL

Mailing list
www.igc.apc.org/awea/mlist.html

Online service areas
America Online: LEARNING & CULTURE

Suggested search-engine keywords
Yahoo!: Physical sciences, chemistry,
   engineering, physics, technology,
   YAHOOLIGANS — Science and Oddities
Infoseek: Physical sciences, chemistry,
   engineering, physics, technology

Virtual Libraries

No more trips to the library. No more card files. No more "Shhhhh!" from the librarian. You can giggle out loud, listen to your favorite music, or have a cup of coffee or soft drink. You can even pore through research material in you pajamas. No matter what your attire, sleeping habits, or silly sense of humor, you can visit these libraries 24 hours a day, seven days a week. It is almost too easy to drop in a search word or phrase and have these virtual libraries do the legwork for you. But, hey! That gives you more time to write a brilliant piece of research that will escalate your name and manuscript into the virtual libraries of the Internet. Are you ready to handle the notoriety?

Electric Library

www3.elibrary.com/s/nettest/search.cgi

  $

Search engine devoted to reference and research: This subscription based search engine devotes itself to online and library research sources. Just type a question in plain English into the search box to begin a comprehensive, simultaneous search through more than 150 newspapers, hundreds of magazines, two international newswires, 2,000 classic books, and bunches of maps, photographs, works of art, and literature. It's like having your own electronic librarian, plus the content is reviewed for quality, reliability, and kid-safety. And it's constantly updated via satellite. Sources of information include Reuters, Simon and Schuster, Gannett, World Almanac, and Times Mirror, as well as a number of ethnic, international, and special interest publications. Take advantage of the 30-day free trial period. Schools, libraries, and individuals each have their own subscription rates. You can even purchase gift subscriptions for those special friends.

My Virtual Reference Desk

www.refdesk.com/

Timely updated information compendium: This is a wonderful place to find the latest and most reliable resources for research. This site contains a weekly update and review of newly added sites, an internal search box so you can access any site by title or keyword, a trouble-shooting guide so you can resolve any access or navigation woes, a feedback form so you can suggest new sites or ideas, and an incredibly well-presented library of research, financial, sports, entertainment, scientific, and news resources. You can find links to current times, dates, worldwide weather, calculators, dictionaries, and a continuously updated look at the U.S. National Debt and world population, plus almanacs, atlases, maps, and over 270 direct sources to facts and data. (Some links may require plug-ins.) A homework helper section for kids allows them to contact experts for online and e-mail assistance. You can even link to 260 search engines. There is also a whole section devoted to computers and online use from freebies and shareware, to devices, gadgets, games, applications, plug-ins, and Internet helpers. It's amazing.

Research-It!

**www.iTools.com/research-it/research-
    it.html**

Well-organized research resource links: Find dictionaries, encyclopedias, transla-tors, convertors, atlases, maps, and monetary and financial tools, and that's just for starters. Research tools and information are sorted into categories of language, library, geographical, financial, shipping, and Internet. Each area offers research, terminology, and compilation resources that rival any library's research section. Use search boxes or click links to get where you want to go and find what you need.

World Wide Web Virtual Library

www.w3.org/vl/Overview.html

Links to subject libraries on the Internet: Probably the most massive research collection on the Internet, the WWW Virtual Library consists of specialty research categories maintained by various Internet Web sites. You'll always notice the WWW Virtual Library logo on any site that has been approved for inclusion. At this site, you find a master

index of all the categorized topics contained in the library and the links to get you there. You must scroll to believe the vastness of this resource. If you want a site devoted to links on Aboriginal Studies, AIDS, or Amateur Radio, on down to Women's Studies, Writers' Resources, Yeasts, or Zoos, look no further. This outstanding resource is a bookmark must.

Other Stuff to Check Out

Web sites

    www.oxford.net/~ocbe/subject.htm
    www.schoolwork.org/
    www.st.rim.or.jp/~kanada/lib.html#online-
        dic
    www.loc.gov/

Online service areas

    America Online: REFERENCE DESK,
        LEARNING & CULTURE
    Compuserve: GO ENCYCLOPEDIA, GO
        DICTIONARY

Suggested search-engine keywords

    Yahoo!: Reference
    Infoseek: Reference

Part III
News, Weather, and Current Events

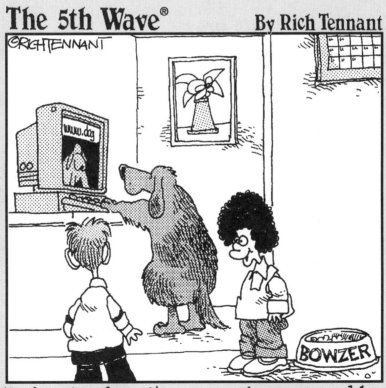

"He found a dog site over an hour ago and has been in a staring contest ever since."

In this part . . .

Keeping up-to-date on what's happening in the world can be a chore, especially when you need to know something at 3:00 and the news doesn't come on TV until 5:30. The World Wide Web has made it possible for you to get the latest regional and national news and weather forecasts whenever you want. You can even find out about world events at some of the sites listed in this part. For that matter, you can even visit some sites to discover the (relatively) current events going on in Solar System!

Current Events

One of the most amazing and educational aspects of the Net is its international resources — and the speed with which you can surf or send e-mail across the world. Beaucoup! (www.beaucoup.com) is a Web site that offers an English-language list of search engines organized by category (education, health, politics, and so on), geographic location, and language. This page, as well as others listed in this section, can help you find information about topics such as holidays, geography, national and international news and views, or historical trivia — while giving you a peek at the huge international scope of the Internet.

Holidays and Other Celebrations

No matter what country, culture, or period in time, people have always celebrated holidays — days when you take time to reflect, celebrate, honor, and share. These sites explain the history behind the holiday and the current way it's celebrated; some sites even offer games and activities related to the featured holiday. So whether you are researching holidays in a foreign country or just delving into the whys and hows of some good old American traditions, you'll find many, many answers here.

An American Thanksgiving

www.night.net/thanksgiving/

The history and traditions of Thanksgiving in the U.S.: Who was Massasoit? You can come to this neat site to find out. The page reminds us that this American holiday for giving thanks, which takes place on the fourth Thursday in November, "is a time for family, food, and football and marks the unofficial beginning to the winter holiday season." The page also recounts the history of the first Thanksgiving in Plymouth when the Pilgrims shared their bounty with the Native Americans who had helped them survive. The document section of this page has a copy of the Mayflower compact (1620), the historic document signed by the men who established the Pilgrim settlement, as well as the first Thanksgiving proclamation (1676) and other related documents.

Bastille Day

www.premier-ministre.gouv.fr/ENG/
HIST/FETNAT.HTM

Background on Bastille Day: July 14 is Bastille Day in France, and the observance includes solemn military parades, fireworks, and streets decked out with flags. The holiday commemorates the beginning of the French Revolution, specifically the day the people stormed the Bastille, or French State Prison, demanding the end of the monarchy. What they got once the dust settled was a republic. Today the holiday is very important in France, and this Web page not only retells the story of the storming of the Bastille but suggests some additional reading if you're really interested.

Celebrate Chinese New Year on the Net

www.dae.com/cny/

Observe the Chinese New Year online: The date of the Chinese New Year falls between January 21 and February 19, and this Web site was created to celebrate the Chinese New Year online. The page describes the Year of the Ox and the Chinese Zodiac. The site includes photos of the Diaspora, Chinese people around the world, and an exhibition featuring descriptions of Deities with art, artifacts, and photographs.

Christmas

www.christmas.com

Christmas around the globe: Christmas is celebrated in Europe and Asia, in North America and South America, in Africa and Australia, but each country's traditions are different. This page describes the Christmas carols, food, and decorations of various countries. In Bethlehem, the Church of the Nativity where Jesus was

thought to be born is decorated with flags and decorations, and pilgrims come from around the world. Greek children travel from house to house on Christmas Eve offering good wishes and singing *kalanda,* the equivalent of carols, while they play on little clay drums. In South America, Christmas is a deeply religious event, so the main focus is the *presepio,* or manger. Unusual links on the site include Santa Sightings and, for those who need to know how long until Christmas, a countdown section tells you how many days, hours, and minutes you have to wait.

Day of the Dead

www.tulane.edu/~latinlib/
   deaddays.html

Observing Day of the Dead: In Mexico, Day of the Dead is November 2. It is a day for honoring one's ancestors; in fact, children in Mexico often picnic near their ancestors' graves so that they can be remembered and "share" in the feast. This holiday has a long history in Latin America: It lets the people laugh at death and express love for their families — while enjoying a delicious feast! Check out this site to find out more about the history of Day of the Dead.

Earth Day

www.earthsite.org/

Observance of the plan to save the planet: When Gerald Ford was president of the United States, he announced that "all individuals and institutions have a mutual responsibility to now act as Trustees of Earth. . . ." The occasion was Earth Day, which is now celebrated every year around the world. This page by John McConnell, the founder of Earth Day, keeps awareness high by reminding us of the ideals behind the campaign for Earth.

You can support McConnell by becoming part of a global plan to support and sustain the earth. Just fill out the online form and become a Certified Earth Trustee.

Hanukkah, the Festival of Lights

www.ort.org/ort/hanukkah/title.htm

The Jewish holiday of Hanukkah: Hanukkah is celebrated for eight days, in the month of Kislev (November/December), to commemorate the victory of the Jews over the Hellenist Syrians in 165 B.C.E. This page explains the importance of the holiday to Jewish families and to those of the Jewish faith; it also discusses the significance of the menorah and describes songs and games that are a part of the traditional celebration of Hanukkah.

The Haunted House

members.aol.com/harley101/private/
   hween/hween1.html

Step into the haunted side of the Web: Even though some of the graphics and stories may need a little parental scrutiny, this site rates right at the top of Halloween Web sites. From the haunting "Welcome" and spooky music on the home page to the various haunts that you can

visit, you'll want to leave no door unopened. The page titles almost speak for themselves. The Haunted House link takes you on a narrative tour of an actual haunted house that the webmaster participates in yearly. Sound Bites and Haunted Midis provide you with lots of downloads of scary screams, howls, and music. Bloody Links can connect you with other Web sites that focus on Halloween stories, games, clip art, and more. You can retrieve gruesome TrueType fonts to use on your computer from the Dastardly Downloads page. Lastly, don't forget to sign in at the Book of Lost Souls. As the head ghoul says, it may be the last time that anyone hears from you!

Holidays on the Net

www.holidays.net/

Activities for special celebration: This site lists holidays ranging from Jewish Pruim and Yom Kippur to Christian Easter and Muslim Ramadan. You're probably familiar with many of the nonreligious holidays — such as Martin Luther King Jr. Day, Thanksgiving, Mother's Day, and Father's Day — listed at this site, but this page also describes less familiar holidays and suggests different activities to do to celebrate. "Best of 96" is a hyperlinked list of the site author's favorite online holiday celebrations.

Kathy Schrock's Guide for Educators — Holidays

www.capecod.net/schrockguide/
   holidays.htm

A cornucopia of celebrations: From the U.S.A.'s Memorial Day and Thanksgiving celebrations to the Chinese New Year to African American Kwanzaa, these sites contain enough information, recipes, and

118 **Current Events**

festivities to keep you celebrating all year. The KIDPROJ Multicultural Calendar is especially nice, and the site offers a link to the Black History Page for additional African holidays.

Kwanzaa

www.tike.com/celeb-kw.htm

Celebrating first fruits of the harvest: Kwanzaa, meaning "first fruits of the harvest," is an African American celebration. It is a time of reaffirming African American people, their ancestors, and culture. Celebrated from December 26 to January 1, the holiday is based on Nguzo Saba, or seven guiding principles: unity, self-determination, collective work and responsibility, cooperative economics, purpose, creativity, and faith. If you are interested in exploring the customs of this holiday, come visit this page. The site includes a description of a Kwanzaa Karumu, or traditional feast.

The World Book of Holiday Traditions

mgfx.com/holidays/

Make your holiday contribution: You can contribute to this special holiday site! Holidays on this site are not limited to the traditional Christmas, New Year's Day, or Fourth of July. Your birthday, wedding,

christening, or graduation also qualify. Fill in the blanks of the easy-to-complete online form and your holiday is posted. Simply select the month, date, and description of your fondest memory, and submit the form with your name and other personal information. Whatever you submit gets posted under that month's heading. To get an idea of the other postings, click the link to look at the up-to-date book.

Yahooligans — World Holidays

www.yahooligans.com/ Around_the_World/Holidays/

Kids' guide to holidays: Yahooligans, the Yahoo! guide for kids, has a good section on world holidays, including Kwanzaa, Hanukkah, Christmas, St. Patrick's Day, Bastille Day, and others. You also find sites that help you send electronic greeting cards to your online pals.

National and International Events

Many Web sites and pages go into detail about current events, or give views that differ from the traditional or mainstream. Though the News and Views section of this part profiles sites that report on current events, the sites in the following section view national and international events from particular (often political) perspectives or with an alternative point of view. ***Note:*** Because of the controversial nature of the topics and the sites themselves, parents are strongly urged to review these sites before letting the younger crowd browse freely.

American Spectator

www.spectator.org

The online version of a popular magazine: The counterpart to the print journal, this site has a distinctly conservative slant — but don't be put off. It claims to be one of the country's fastest growing magazines of investigative reporting and commentary (this fact is of interest in itself) and offers much food for thought. The journal is 30 years old and was founded by R. Emmett Tyrrell, who boasts, "It embraced much that was once right with historic American liberalism as well as what was increasingly right and relevant with the emerging conservatism of the late Twentieth Century." You get the picture. If you like the contents of the current issue, or just can't believe the strident tone, you can find archives of past issues.

Atlantic Unbound — Politics, Society, the Arts, and Culture

www.theatlantic.com

Online version of *Atlantic Monthly:* Atlantic Unbound contains reprints of select *Atlantic Monthly* features, plus links and notes created especially for the online version. Known for its thoughtful discussions of politics and current events, the journal's impressive — and marvelously diverse — online archive includes articles on Black History Month, baseball, the U.S. budget, health care, the decline of film, troubled Ireland, the tobacco industry, NATO, copyright piracy, Picasso, Nazi plunder, extraterrestrial life, and the death penalty. Readers who find the variety and quality of such articles irresistible can subscribe to the print journal via the web site. Other online sections include Post & Riposte, a reader forum for discussions devoted to arts and literature, science and technology, and

religion and spirituality, as well as global views, politics, current events, community, and society. This site even has a small online "shop" where you can purchase back issues, article reprints, books, t-shirts, and more.

Boston Review

www-polisci.mit.edu/BostonReview/

Politics and poetry on the same page: New to the current events/literary magazine list, the *Boston Review* is off to a good start. This online site includes commentary and book reviews and has interesting folks contributing essays and commentary on culture and politics with a broadly progressive outlook. Political issues, economics and literature, fiction and poetry, and book reviews make up their bimonthly fare. The variety and overall quality is especially notable, as are the list of contributors ranging from Noam Chomsky and Joseph Brodsky to Robert Pinsky and Martha Nussbaum.

Consortium Online

www.delve.com/consort.html

Dedicated to truth in reporting: The Consortium specializes in investigative reporting and covers crucial stories that it feels the mainstream media has ignored. Published by award-winning journalist Robert Parry (who broke many of the Iran-contra stories), The Consortium focuses on national politics and international affairs. Exposés and essays have included "Dark Side of Rev. Moon: Drug Allies," which looked into this cult leader's political connections and into alleged links to the Russian Mafia. The full texts of the stories that are listed on the home page are available only to those who subscribe to the service.

DeepSeeker

www.deepseeker.com

Insight and opinion on current events: DeepSeeker takes the news on American society, science, technology, politics, and history, examines it for bias, and serves it up to you with their opinion. Titles include: "Imitations of the Primateez: Battlefield Cyberspace," "On the loss of TWA Flight 800," and "On the loss of Amelia Earhart and Frederick Noonan." This is a thought-provoking site — one you may disagree with, but well worth visiting. Parents may want to supervise young ones or approve this site ahead of time.

FAIR (Fairness & Accuracy In Reporting)

www.igc.org/fair/

Journalism's watchdog: Fairness & Accuracy In Reporting (FAIR) is the national media watch group attempting to correct media bias and imbalance via documented criticism. Recent hot topics include: the *San Jose Mercury News* exposé linking the CIA-backed Nicaraguan Contras to the spread of crack cocaine in urban America; and a probe of Channel One, the news show/advertising vehicle beamed daily to millions of students, which FAIR found to be of dubious educational value. The FAIR radio show, CounterSpin, is available every week via RealAudio in its entirety! If you have picked up a free RealAudio Player, you can listen to Counterspin on the Web. Transcripts will evidently be available soon, for those who prefer the written word.

George

www.georgemag.com

Not just politics as usual: George online is as controversial as the print version, probably because they share resources. (Parents may want to keep an eye out because some of the photographs are "colorful.") But it is more than just fashionable politics. George offers a different view of topics such as the phase-out of affirmative action at the University of Texas law school and the 20 most fascinating women in politics (you get only a sample online, though). The most interesting section here is probably Virtual Politics and the interesting list of political links (federal government links, for example, which are very information-rich, and United Nations links including the World Bank and World Health Organization pages).

Liberty Unbound

www.LibertySoft.com/liberty/

News from the Libertarian point of view: Liberty Unbound is dedicated to reviewing culture and politics from the Libertarian point of view. Simply put, according to its founders, Liberty Unbound "uses the lens of freedom — individual liberty, personal responsibility, limited government — to 'see through the political realm.'" Regular features include Medianotes, an examination of global news and entertainment or "the press, pressed," and reviews that are touted as unconventional by the editor. The site also has features such as Nathan Crow's "Leave them kids alone," educating the educators on what kids really need in the summer, or "Witness at the inquest," in which R.W. Bradford calls in Mikhail Gorbachev for a second opinion on the death of communism. Thoughtful and distinct.

LIFE

www.pathfinder.com/Life/

Modern life in pictures: For decades *LIFE* magazine has recorded our triumphs and tragedies, from the battles of World War II to the death of Princess Diana. Sports, music, politics, and famous personalities are just some of the diverse subjects explored in the *LIFE* photo essays. This handsome site features a picture of the day, This Day in *LIFE,* and photo essays drawn from the comprehensive *LIFE* archives. Allow some time for the images to download and prepare to enjoy images of modern times: The Bolshoi Offbalance, American Astronauts in Russia, Zoo Babies, Light in the Desert (on the monks of Christ in the New Mexico Desert), and much more. Not only does *LIFE* tell the story behind the pictures in words, but it also shares interesting bits about the photographers as well.

Monde Diplomatique

www.monde-diplomatique.fr/md/en/

 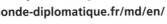

A Francophone perspective: This bilingual publication (click the small phrase "edition en englais" to read the page in English) has particularly good coverage of African politics, the Middle East, and Russia. Subjects include politics, social and economic developments around the world, and technology. Features have included "Hard times for working women" by Margaret Maruani, underlining unemployment, underemployment, and other facts of life that render women many of the working poor, and "A strange inheritance" by Claude Wauthier on the role of Freemasonry in the democratization of Africa. Don't miss this site for thought-provoking reporting.

Mother Jones

www.mojones.com

Review of current events, with an attitude: The writers who contribute to *Mother Jones* magazine, online or print, are a pretty impressive — and opinionated — bunch. Here you can read Jeffrey Klein on race or Jamaica Kincaid on happiness. MoJo updates will give you the latest developments on older stories. There are also features like "Visions," showing the Mother Jones International Fund for Documentary Photography exhibit of winners. Don't miss "Hot Threads" with its list of consumer-conscious businesses, and "Get Involved" for a list of groups you can contribute time and effort to such as the American Friends Service Committee (better known as Quakers) or Mothers & Others For a Livable Planet, a nonprofit organization promoting safe, ecologically sustainable consumer information. While you are here, you may contribute to the latest poll and subscribe to the print version.

122 Current Events

The Nation — Digital Edition

www.thenation.com/

A Liberal tradition: Established in 1865 by a group of abolitionists, *The Nation* is America's oldest weekly magazine and one of the premier journals of opinion and commentary. *The Nation* has an impressive history of publishing a diverse selection of major poets, novelists, and essayists, including Langston Hughes, Sylvia Plath, Henry James, Thomas Mann, Alice Walker, Calvin Trillin, Gore Vidal, Molly Ivins, Toni Morrison, William Styron, and many others. Its reporting presents a range of hard-hitting, idea-rich opinions. The online version contains a selection of each weekly issue (and lists the other contents) — including excerpts from the wonderful section on books and the arts.

Noam Chomsky Archive

www.worldmedia.com/archive/

Is capitalism just?: That is just one of the political and cultural issues discussed at the Noam Chomsky Archive. Chomsky also takes on what he terms the class war ("The Attack on Working People"), prospects for democracy, the Clinton vision, and free market fantasies (capitalism in the real world). The full texts of the articles are not at the archive — although you can order the tapes here — but summaries, segments, and RealAudio files (for both 14.4 and 28.8 modems) are available to introduce Chomsky's perspectives. Other audio and video files of his speeches are here, and you can hear and see them with a RealAudio plug-in: Chomsky on East Timor (from November 1995), and his interviews with Matthew Rothschild of the *Progressive* (audio/video) and Charlayne Hunter-Gault (audio).

Pathfinder

www.pathfinder.com

Prime magazine links: Time Warner, Inc., is the company that publishes a slew of great magazines including *Time, Sports Illustrated, Money, People, ParentTime, Cooking Light, Entertainment Weekly,* and a lot more. Pathfinder itself has late-breaking stories, bulletin boards, and chat rooms, but you'll probably want to link directly to the magazine of your choice. The publisher has made it easy to find articles on specific subjects: The search tool searches all the publications in the Pathfinder Network. This online site does have another advantage over the print venues: daily updates, including quick quotes, people daily, CNN headlines, as well as time and weather.

Progressive Review

www.princeton.edu/~progrev/

A political monthly — with humor: *Progressive Review* is Princeton's journal of alternative news, analysis, and critical critique. Both the print version and the online version (loudly) proclaim a dedication to social justice and, indeed, the contents reflect this. Topics of note have included "Civic Freedom" or Mark Krumholz's critical review of Sandel's treatise on American social problems;

and "Quiet Exodus," Robert McIlvaine exploring the fears — racial, economic and otherwise — that caused four generations of his family to yield to "white flight." Students are encouraged to submit work to the Progressive, and there are some excellent links to "progressive stuff."

Reader's Digest World

www.readersdigest.com

Online version of the world's most widely read magazine: The interactive "World" version of *Reader's Digest* combines favorite elements from the print journal (like inspiring stories, help articles, and favorites such as a Shockwave version of Word Power and Laugh Lines) with services especially tailored for the online audience (shopping online, advice on cooking, gardening, food, health and fitness, and so on). Of course, you can subscribe here, but the online services include home shopping and advice about online privacy. You can also find online contests.

RollCall Online

www.rollcall.com/

Online guide to Congress: *Roll Call,* the newspaper of Capitol Hill since 1955, has created a visually dull but information-rich Web site. Here you find all that you need to know about Congress — and then some. Take a look at the news scoops for the latest in legislative news and controversy, politics at large (Cook & Rothenberg Square Off or who's going to win in Election '98), issues (cyberpolitics; the 2000 election, as first of the digital era), and the hard stuff (Committee Assignments for the 105th Congress). You also can find a Hill Directory for you to chase down that congressman or congresswoman, classifieds, and — believe it or not — a one-minute contest where you, the citizen, can add to a representative's opening lines (for his or her daily one-minute speech).

Z Magazine — A Political Monthly

www.lbbs.org

A political monthly — with humor and great graphics: *Z Magazine* sponsors ZNet which brings you analysis and commentary on politics, economics, culture, foreign policy, and day-to-day life. More than a magazine, ZNet is a community of people interested in dialogue and change. ZNet regularly features robust educational offerings and a list of responsible internet guides, audio and publishing archives, socializing facilities, and activism updates. Don't miss the research tools and interactive forums, or the *Z Magazine* archives and search engines. Contributor-members include Noam Chomsky, Katha Pollitt, and Barbara Ehrenreich.

Online Pen Pals

Because e-mail is so fast — and doesn't need postage — having an online pen pal is very easy. If your parents ever had a pen pal, they probably waited for weeks before receiving a response to their

124 Current Events

letters. The following sites show that online pen pals are becoming pretty popular. Some of the resources ask that your whole class participate, but others let you register alone. In any case, be sure to tell your parents about your pen pals so they can share the excitement.

eMail Classroom Exchange

www.iglou.com/xchange/ece/ index.html

Search the world for a pen pal: eMail Classroom Exchange (ECE) allows you to search for registered classrooms looking for e-mail pen pals; alternatively, you can add your own class information (called a class profile) to the database. A small fee is charged after the first free 30 days of use. The 2,500 classes, searchable by school name, language, grade, or location, are in schools in the U.S., Australia, Europe, and Africa. Hurry up and connect — your pen pals are waiting.

Internet for Learning

www.rmplc.co.uk/

A pen pal service that plays it safe: Internet for Learning (IFL) is a Net education site that develops information systems for educational purposes: Using EduWeb, these folks set up Web pages for schools. Kids can use NetPals to interact with pen pals in a unique environment where all messages are read and checked for appropriateness. You can search for a pen pal specifically for you by selecting an age group, by choosing a boy or girl, and by selecting a preferred nationality. You can also fill in the online registration form to post your profile for others to choose. The page has other interesting features, but it is unique in its development of the online kids community.

KidPub KeyPals

www.kidpub.org/kidpub/keypals/

Pen pals by the thousands: KidPub KeyPals is a place to find keypals. (A *keypal* is a pen pal who sends you e-mail instead of a letter.) To find a pen pal, you just fill out a form, and you automatically join the growing list of KeyPal Kids! This page has more than 5,000 names on the KeyPal list; many of them live in the United States, but some of them hail from Australia, Burunei Darussalam, Latvia, New Zealand, the Ukraine, and more.

Other Stuff to Check Out

Web sites

www.worldvillage.com/ideabox/index.html
peacock.tnjc.edu.tw:80/ADD/TOUR/
   keep1.html
www.unicefusa.org/issues96/sep96/
   trick.html
www.benjerry.com/halloween/index.html
www.arborday.org/
www.peaceonearth.org
powered.cs.yale.edu:8000/~miller/hog/
   map.jpg
www.geocities.com/Heartland/2328/
   stpatty.htm
www.beaucoup.com/
www.gsn.org/
www.un.org/pubs/cyberschoolbus

Newsgroups

soc.culture.jewish.parenting
alt.parenting.solutions
soc.culture.german
soc.culture.jewish
misc.education.home-school.misc

Suggested search-engine keywords

Yahoo!: Holidays, plus keyword (France, Greece, Middle East, Japan, African, and so on); pen pals, education, keypals, writing

Lycos: Holidays, plus keyword (Thanksgiving, Kwanzaa, and so on); pen pals, kids penpals

www.vsa.cape.com/~powens/Kidnews.html

What's the buzz? Tell me what's happenin'! These sites afford you the opportunity to check the news — kidstyle and adult-oriented — as it happens around the globe. Online editions of respected news publications are catalogued and sorted here. Just find your favorites, bookmark them, and build your own international news network.

Electronic News Magazines

Electronic news is the most up-to-date news in the world; in fact, the magazines, newsletters, and journals listed in this section are helping redefine the concept of up-to-the-minute news. In America — and increasingly elsewhere — major daily papers now compete with a slew of online journals, some of which are partners of print magazines, but others that are intriguing models of news and current event publications available only on the Net.

AfricaNews

www.africanews.com/

News from Africa: This magazine presents "The Nile File — International Edition: A Political and Communications Policy Review" and several columns by Charles Onyanbo-Obbo. The columnist focuses on Ugandan politics and foreign policy, and his columns paint a clear picture of the ongoing tumult in that African nation. You can also purchase the CD-ROM "The Daily Monitor," which features Uganda, "the Pearl of Africa."

AJR News Link

www.newslink.org/menu.html

Global news resource: The list of more than 3,500 magazines and newspapers compiled by the *American Journalism Review* includes college papers (such as UC-Berkeley's *Daily Californian*), as well as major metropolitan dailies (*Los Angeles Times, Washington Post,* and *Christian Science Monitor*), small town presses, specialist papers, and more. The magazines include news magazines

(*US News and World Report, Time, Newsweek,* and *LIFE*), as well as less renowned — but interesting — publications on news, culture, and politics. AJR News Link also lists television and radio stations.

Beijing Review

www.cibtc.co.cn/China/bjreview/
BJREVIEW.HTML

China, the new frontier: This weekly news magazine was founded in 1958 under the guidance of the late premier Zhou Enlai. Published in five languages (it's in English and Japanese at this site), the journal covers China's economic and social developments, and reproduces important documents of the Chinese government and speeches made by China's leaders. Sections covered in each issue include a cover story, national affairs, world events, society and people, and in-depth reports on business and trade. Earlier issues from 1997 are archived here, as well.

Bharat Samachar

www.bharatsamachar.com

News from India: This information-rich site — in English — will bring you the latest news of India, including business news, as well as reports on art, culture, and travel (with information on destinations, hotels, and tour operators). The section devoted to business opportunities in India is particularly unusual and discusses public issues, joint ventures, and properties. The site has a monthly feature article; one recent article was titled "Second Freedom Struggle." News and business news sections are updated daily.

Business Wire

www.businesswire.com/

Local, national, and global business news: Business Wire brings you the latest news for a range of businesses — high tech, entertainment, health, and more — by the hour and on the hour. You can click a tiny link to read the latest news of the past 24 hours, or go directly to today's photowire, to corporate news on the Net, to IPOs on the Net, to corporate profiles, or to trade show and conference news. The site has no search tool, but you can set up a personal news box to cull articles on the topics that most interest you. Business Wire is a leading source of news on major U.S. corporations, including Fortune 1000 and NASDAQ companies — and all Business Wire articles are brought to you in full text.

Geneva News and International Report

www.gnir.ch/

News from the heart of Europe: This interesting news site presents a different perspective. Topics range from the European Art Collectors' Fair in Basel and Wired classes (students equipped with laptop computers) at the International School to 77 proposals to relaunch the

Swiss economy and CERN's new great project (relating to the Big Bang theory and scientific debate over the end of the universe). The site features separate sections for business and finance, Zurich, and news reports on the UN. The Swiss news reports (summaries) will be of interest to international business people, but many of the brief cultural articles will be useful for students of all ages.

Interfax News

www.interfax-news.com

$

The latest from Russia: Interfax News agency presents the latest news and information on Russia, CIS, and the Baltic Countries. News includes today's news and editorials, as well as business and industry daily and weekly reports on diverse industries (such as food and agriculture; communications and electronics; petroleum, mining, and minerals; and finance and banking), and more. You also find links to Russian news sites. The site offers a subscription service, and you can request a free sample and price information online.

Jerusalem Post

www.jpost.co.il/

News direct from Israel: This online news resource is, of course, related to the famous newspaper, but it offers immediate updates and opportunities for feedback. You can find interesting opportunities at the site that are not in the print version, such as the Post's offer to fax Israeli businesses via the Internet without charge (sponsored by Yellow Pages Israel). The heart of the site, though, is its Middle Eastern coverage. Sections include news, business, opinion, tourism, sports, features, and real estate; the whole of the site is searchable. There

are select links that link largely to Israeli sites.

Maclean's

www.macleans.ca/

A Canadian perspective: Maclean's presents global news from a Canadian point of view and covers the latest developments in the politics and culture of that country as well. Features include Health Monitor and Keepers (which posts articles from previous issues that show particular breadth and depth). Like *US News and World Report,* Maclean's ranks universities but restricts its list to Canadian universities. And Maclean's also selects Web sites related to each week's issue. Additional features include an unusual archive of writing from 100 years of war around the world with pieces by some of Canada's finest writers, as well as authors from other counties. The archives are particularly rich in stories from World Wars I and II, but contains pieces on Korea, the Gulf War, and Yugoslavia.

Megastories

www.megastories.com

Beyond the headlines: The award-winning Megastories site explores the implications of the stories that hit the front page. From the Northern Ireland talks to the

128 News and Views

death of Diana, Princess of Wales, this online journal explores the news from multiple perspectives. Megastories' editors use RealAudio sound bytes to evoke the mood or tone of each story and to bring the quotes alive. The site includes polls so that readers can help determine what is a "megastory" versus everyday news, and chat rooms are available for feedback.

MultiNational Monitor

**www.essential.org/monitor/
    monitor.html**

Multinational news: This news magazine contains articles on politics, the environment ("The Barons of Bromide: Poisonous Pesticides and Poisoned Politics"), and labor. Recent features include "Tobacco Talks," and editorials on taxes. MultiNational Monitor sponsors the Lawrence Summers Memorial Award interviews: This year, they featured Dr. Judith Mackay, Dr. Witold Zatonski, Eric LeGresley, and Dr. Hatai Chitanondh on "Tobacco Imperialism." Other favorite features are book reviews and Good Works, a national directory of social change organizations (with staff and internship information) and profiles of individuals who are building public interest careers. The site also features links that are related to the topics covered.

One World Online

www.oneworld.org/

Human rights news: One World presents global news from a different perspective. It is published by a collaboration of more than 150 worldwide justice organizations working for human rights, global justice, and sustainable development. Their beat is the world; their subjects range from women's rights in Zambia to the water

supply in Manila. Many of the stories concern the plight of children in the third world; parents should share this publication with their children but be there to explain and discuss. The sections are organized into "Headlines" for the most urgent issues, "This Week" for recent pieces, and by country and theme for logical overviews of the world's news.

Paine News

painenews.com

Net news and uses: This journal aims to provide decision-makers with a valuable resource to more effectively use the Internet, and to acquaint visitors with the services of Paine News. (They create custom intelligence reports and executive briefings.) A recent issue contained intriguing reports on the government and the Internet — an irresistible pairing — such as "U.S. Government Spends $350 Million on Internet without Clear Guidelines to Curb Waste or Abuse." It's hard to not like a journal that begins an article by observing "Search engines are powerful, dumb machines. If you ask a stupid question of these powerful machines, you will likely get a stupid response." And, as the authors point out, there *is* a wealth of information online that needs someone to make sense of it.

PointCast

www.pointcast.com

Desktop newscast: PointCast boasts that it will bring you all the news you can use, personalized and up to the minute. Oh yes, it's free and comes to you via audio and video files that play through the software plug-ins you download from this site. So, if you are interested in a particular industry or in receiving news about your region only, PointCast can take care of you! Not only do headlines dance across your computer screen, colors blazing, but you don't even have to surf. PointCast broadcasts national and international news, stock information, industry updates, weather around the globe, sports, and more from sources such as *Time, People,* and *Money* magazines, and news services such as CNN, Reuters, PR Newswire, and BusinessWire. Wow!

reportage @

www.users.interport.net/~akreye

Documentary news: This bilingual site (German and English) features reportage, a gallery for photojournalism, news, and resource links. Stories can range from the Moscow Mafia to urban control in Los Angeles. A recent photo essay on forced labor and rebellion in Burma was composed of several black-and-white images with brief captions and juxtaposed to a Sebastio Salgado photo essay on Brazil's landless movement. These thought-provoking issues are simply and eloquently presented. Reportage also sells U.S. photojournalism books.

Tower Magazine

ourworld.compuserve.com/homepages/ Harvey_Morris/

A British perspective: *Tower* is a regularly updated review of international affairs written by established journalists and commentators. Topics of interest here include reports from the European Union and elsewhere in the world (such as a story detailing Tony Barber defending Germany's federal system against critics who see it as a cause of the country's current political paralysis, and Jon Mitchell's reports from Panama that massive mining projects in the region are failing to benefit local inhabitants). The site includes regularly updated headlines from Reuters. You can search for foreign affairs reports on either Infoseek or Yahoo from this site. Moreover, if you would like to exchange news and views about any aspect of international affairs or comment on articles, you can post a message on the *Tower Magazine* bulletin board. The archive holds a wealth of articles on the Middle East.

Timecast

www.timecast.com

Media guide of the future: Timecast is a guide to RealAudio and RealVideo reports on the news including more than 500 radio and television stations (including 76 news and talk stations and nine Public Radio stations). Favorite news coverage — such as ABC World News Tonight, and C-SPAN (for political speeches) — are only part of the riches here. When you've had enough news, you can switch to music (literally hundreds of stations ranging from country to rock to classical) or sports (a whopping 63 stations!).

US News Online

www.usnews.com/usnews/main.htm

Politics and current news: At the main US News Online page, you find News & Views, News You Can Use, and the U.S. News Forum (for discussions of the latest issues). Extra, Extra has features such as "Does Class Size Really Matter?" and "Campaign Finance: A List of Senators to Call to Create Change." The site has a link to the print publication's famed — and controversial — yearly ranking of colleges. US News is thorough and detailed: The e-zine's HMO feature ranks the best values in HMOs state by state and offers additional advice for dealing with the folks who run them. Recent issues have lots of job-related features (how to stand out from the pack of job hunters, the booming job market, and so on). If you missed an issue, don't worry. All back issues are archived right here.

World Statesman

www.worldstatesman.kenpubs.co.uk

For politicians of the world: This political and current-affairs magazine is read by leaders around the world. As you may expect, the magazine is serious (visually dull) in format, but it is filled with news features (for example, a recent South African issue featured a Nelson Mandela interview; South Africa's Finance Minister Trevor Manuel on fiscal discipline versus social spending; Alec Erwin, Minister for Trade and Industry, on South African investment, and so on). The site also features sections dedicated to industry and business perspectives and keynote features from around the world. Each issue has a country profile, and all issues are archived by country and/or keyword.

General Sources

Imagine a newsstand with thousands of newspapers and news publications, plus a wall of TV sets for every major news broadcasting network. And you get to sit with a cup of coffee or tea and pick and choose. Well, welcome to your own cybernews café! Find your favorite news sources, bookmark them, and have daily happenings at your fingertips.

The Daily News — Just the Links

www.cs.vu.nl/~gerben/news.html

Straight-to-the-point list of news links: Not fancy, but easy to use. Select from World, North Western Europe, South Western Europe, Eastern Europe, Africa, Asia, Oceania, U.S.A., the rest of North and South America, and Other lists of news sources to get links relevant to those areas. For the U.S.A., links include the ABC Hourly news update (audio), African American News Service, Associated Press Wire search, NPR News programmes (audio), USA Today, Voice of America's News and English Broadcasts wire, Voice of America Audio Files, White House Summaries, The Christian Science Monitor, Muslim World Monitor, and the San Francisco Chronicle and Examiner. Both mainstream and secondary media are represented, and this site has a strong flair for European and other international news.

Editor & Publisher's Directory of Online Newspapers

www.mediainfo.com/ephome/npaper/
  nphtm/online.htm

Newspapers from around the world with online editions: You may be surprised to learn that many newspapers have only recently begun developing editions for the Internet. Worldwide, about 2,000 now have some online presence. The newspaper industry publication *Editor & Publisher* has cataloged most of them here. This site offers one of the most complete lists of print publications with online editions or sections that you can find. Browse the country lists or search for any particular newspaper you're trying to find.

The Newsroom

www.auburn.edu/~vestmon/news.html

Timely news links: Serving the Internet since 1994, this site catalogs up-to-the-minute news sources. Under U.S. & World, for example, you find current reporting from such sources as CBS News Up-to-the-Minute Headlines, Pathfinder's News Now, Reuters News Summary, USA Today Nationline & World News Stories, CNN & CNN Newsroom, TIME Daily News Summary, New York Times TimesFAX, and ABC Radio News (requires RealAudio player). Other subjects are handled the same way. Get daily (or more frequent) financial news (Current Dow Jones Industrials Average, Stock Quotes, Kiplinger's News of the Day, Reuters Business Summary, Hoover's Online, and The Wall Street Journal Interactive Edition). Find additional resources, from something as basic as a copy of the U.S. Constitution to links to major government and legislative offices. This site is great when you need sources fast.

Omnivore

way.net/omnivore/index.html

Strong timely news and links: This daily news and information service offers QuickNews, regional news, subject-based news, weather, and links to magazines. It's fast, comprehensive, and easy to use, as well as global in perspective. Get quick and concise coverage of events around the world as they happen. In-depth follow-ups are generally available through Omnivore's menu system. It's free and not affiliated with any commercial product or service, having started through a university. One unique aspect is this site's emphasis on traditionally underreported or ignored regions. Stories come from numerous sources and many points of view. Get a wide-ranging look at many top issues.

Virtual Daily News

www.erols.com/sopfer/daily.htm

Topical index of news and information sites: The Virtual Daily News focuses on resources that require no fee or registration and are primarily targeted toward a national U.S. audience. From the home page, you can link directly to some news heavyweights, including CNN Interactive, MSNBC, and USA Today. Check out Quick News, U.S. National News, International and Business news, Sports, Weather, Entertainment news, Technology, Education, and Modern Life news and features. Under Home and Family, for example, you find links to resources on pets, retirement, and health, as well as sites for publications such as *Redbook, Country Living,* Home and Garden TV, and many other popular lifestyle magazines and shows. You can search to find online CNN stories.

WORLD News Index

www.stack.nl/~haroldkl/

International, national, and state coverage: Get good graphics, frames or nonframes delivery, and news sources from the U.S.A., Canada, Latin America, Europe, Asia, Africa, and Australia, as well as world publications. Coverage by a news source is featured (such as CNN's remembrance of Diana, Princess of Wales). Under U.S.A., national sources include ABC News (Audio), Access Business News, The Boston Globe, Excite headlines, National Public Radio, and Newsbytes. After the national listings come media sources sorted by state. You must scroll down a long list to get to Wisconsin! Not all major newspapers have free online services, so some major state papers may not be represented, but the selection is still good. Seeing how local papers cover major events in their communities is interesting. You can get all the headlines from the big publications and then scroll down to the states for a more localized look.

Kids' News

These resources offer kids their brand of news: info on choosing lifestyles, making friends, being creative, and making the world a better place. Oh, and you can get the latest news on bugs making headlines.

Bugs in the News!

falcon.cc.ukans.edu/~jbrown/bugs.html

Bugs making headlines: Who says the news has to be about people? This online news service (of sorts) about bugs is geared to kids to help them gain insight into bugs that make the news (for example, recent feature articles were entitled "What the Heck is a Virus?" and "What the Heck is an E. coli?" after a series of meat-related illnesses occurred, many affecting kids). You can find links for the Curious & Interested and for General Interest. For the Curious, Interested & Who Like to More Than Scratch the Surface, you can take Bug Bytes (links) to highly technical sites. All sites help to further demonstrate article themes.

KidNews

**www.vsa.cape.com/~powens/
   Kidnews.html**

Good news, good fun: Creative and kid-oriented news, sports, profiles, and heroes are covered here. Sections also feature kids' reports on their own lives, highlight their creative endeavors, and give them the chance to exchange views and advice online with other kids. Submit your writing or reviews of movies, music, TV shows, foods, video games, and books. This high-quality environment encourages kids to explore the world around them and within themselves. Editor Dr. Peter Owens is an English and Professional Writing Professor at the University of Massachusetts Dartmouth. KidNews is a member of NESPA, the National Elementary Schools Press Association. Check out the figure at the beginning of this "News and Views" section to see what this site looks like.

Kids' Stuff

digmo.org/kids/frontpage.html

News site produced by journalism college: Produced by the Missouri School of Journalism, this fun, graphically rich, musically adorned site features articles and links of interest to kids in today's world. It's a great mix of news and features for kids coupled with an upbeat design. Click The MiniMO Online: A newspaper just for Kids. Although it has many campus and Missouri references, it still contains articles and links of interest to kids everywhere.

TIME for Kids

www.pathfinder.com/TFK/index.html

Kids version of a popular newsstand magazine: This online edition of *TIME* magazine focuses on kids making news and interactively presents big news stories of interest to kids (such as robots and exploration of Mars). Snappy text and graphics, lots of interaction, and a zippy pace make this site the kind of high-quality yet comprehensible resource you'd expect from such a major news provider. Both Shockwave and non-Shockwave versions are provided.

Other Stuff to Check Out

Web sites

now2000.com/bigkidnetwork/
    kidschron.html
www.mindnet.or.jp/kidsclub/kmceng.htm
www.aaa.com.au/Kids_Radio.html
www.newsforkids.com
crayon.net/using/links.html
www.soundbites.com
www1.trib.com/NEWS/APwire.html
www.cnn.com
www.abcnews.com
www.msnbc.com

www.itn.co.uk
www.canoe.com
www.washingtonpost.com
www.nytimes.com
www.latimes.com
www.pathfinder.com

Newsgroup
schl.news.nethappen

Online service areas
America Online: NEWSSTAND, TODAY'S NEWS
CompuServe: GO CNN, GO CNNFORUM, GO TALKBACK, GO APONLINE, GO PAO, GO NEWSGRID

Suggested search-engine keywords
Yahoo!: News, current events
Lycos: Top news

Weather and Other Natural Events

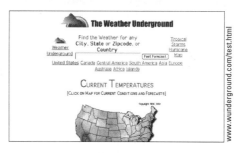

No need to wait for the nightly news or even turn on the TV to get up-to-the-minute weather forecasts and storm information. Find instant information online. And if you want to know how weather is tracked and reported and what makes weather happen, here are in-depth sources of information about atmospherics, climate, and meteorology.

Earthly

Planning to travel? Need to know whether it's going to rain on the soccer team's game? What about that picnic you're supposed to go to on Saturday? Take the guesswork out of weathercasting by utilizing these superb weather sites.

Weather Channel Homepage

www.weather.com/

Official site of the 24-hour Weather Channel: Get current updates for your area or anywhere you plan to travel. Find U.S. forecasts, international forecasts, weather maps, storm warnings and watches, hurricane tracking, and insight into weather forecasting and meteorology. This terrific site has the same high production standards as the TV channel itself. Special forecasts are geared to boaters, people with certain health problems and allergies, pilots, and gardeners!

Weather Underground

www.wunderground.com/test.html

Incredibly fast, well-organized instant weather report site: Immediately, you can comprehend the layout of this site and find the weather report you need. Use the search box to find the weather for any city, state, zip code, or country. Click tropical, storm, or hurricane sections for timely updates. View tracking and forecast maps of the world. Or choose from continental, country, or state listings, all accessible from the main home page. Another search option is to click the world map to get current conditions and forecasts for a region. Among other features: temperature and radar maps, metric and English forecast measurements, and instant access to

weather warnings. The figure at the top of this "Weather and Other Natural Events" section features the Weather Underground Web site.

Intergalactic

How often have you said, "Wow! The weather today is out of this world"? And just what did you have to compare it to? Were you confident that your comment was remotely accurate and not just an exaggeration? Now you can be sure. Visit these sites to get the lowdown on what to pack for those long interplanetary trips or just use them to qualify your statements about the weather. Maybe someday in the future, you'll have to check the weather on other planets just like you check it for your vacations.

Daily Martian Weather Report

nova.stanford.edu/projects/mgs/ dmwr.html

Produced by the Mars Global Surveyor Radio Science Team: Get daily martian weather report information and sample temperature and pressure profiles, find out about seasons on Mars, and meet the MGS Radio Science Team. You can also link to related sites. This site details both the Mars Global Surveyor and Pathfinder landing site missions.

Space Environment Center

www.sel.bldrdoc.gov/

Space weather and conditions: What's cookin' in space? This site provides actual up-to-the-moment monitoring and forecasting of solar and geophysical events, conducts research in solar-terrestrial physics, and develops techniques for forecasting solar and geophysical disturbances. You can track what's hot on the Sun and what events there may affect people or technology on Earth. Incidentally, SEC's Space Weather Operations is jointly operated by the National Oceanic and Atmospheric Administration (NOAA) and the U.S. Air Force. It's the warning center for solar disturbances. Click Today's Space Weather, Solar Images, Data Directories, or Real-Time Solar Wind for updates.

Other Stuff to Check Out

Web sites
www.nws.mbay.net/marine.html
thunder.met.fsu.edu/~nws/buoy/
www.theweathernetwork.com/
www.cnn.com/WEATHER/
www.foxweather.com/
www.weatherpost.com/
www.intellicast.com/
www.cp.duluth.mn.us/~sarah/index.html

Newsgroup
www.weatherman.com/newx.htm

Chat area
pages.map.com/~dactyl/IRC.html

Online service areas
CompuServe: GO WEATHER

Suggested search-engine keywords
Yahoo!: Weather
Infoseek: Weather

Volcanoes, Earthquakes, and Major Storms

The earth is dynamic and fabulous, but the natural processes of evolution and change can wreak havoc on humans. Understanding the natural forces that create the lands and weather is vital to human survival. Atmospheric scientists study conditions above; oceanographers study the ocean and its floor, currents, winds, waves, tides — whatever makes

seas be and influences weather and climate. Geologists study earthly processes, too, both on land and under the sea. Vulcanologists are not people from the planet Vulcan, as in *Star Trek,* but geologists who study volcanoes. These sites introduce you to experts and research in many of these fields.

Earthquake Information from the USGS

quake.usgs.gov/

or

quake.wr.usgs.gov/

All about earthquakes: Get details, maps, and lists of recent earthquakes. The What's New or Interesting section spotlights a selected subject weekly; for example, Earthquake Hazard Reduction and the role of the Global Positioning System. Previous What's New features, such as Late Night Musings of an Earthquake Seismologist, Hawaiian earthquake activity, quick access to all earthquake lists, thickness of the outer layer of the earth, and earthquake FAQs — frequently asked questions about earthquakes — are archived on this site. Get tips on earthquake hazards and preparedness, find out how earthquakes are studied, and link to related resources. The United States Geological Survey, Geologic Division, runs this site.

National Oceanic and Atmospheric Administration

www.nws.noaa.gov/

The National Weather Service: The mission of this official weather and climate agency is "to provide weather and flood warnings, public forecasts and advisories for all of the United States, its territories, adjacent waters and ocean

136 Weather and Other Natural Events

areas, primarily for the protection of life and property." The Weather Service provides data and products to TV weather services and other private meteorologists. They in turn pass the updates along to the public. At this site, you can see what your favorite TV weatherperson may be reporting tonight. Click Current Weather to get the latest official weather warnings, forecast discussions, weather maps, and site observations. You also get current and archived climatic data statistics, government publications in the atmospheric sciences (meteorology, the environment, and geophysical tables), and links to various national weather centers.

National Severe Storms Lab

www.nssl.uoknor.edu/

Official NSSL site: This government laboratory studies and tracks major storms in the United States. Get the inside scoop on current projects and research. The Weather Room is a fantastic resource for kids, providing well-researched and well-written articles on weather careers, science, and natural phenomena. Find out about weather symbols, maps, systems, storm chasing, meteorology school, tornadoes, hurricanes, lightning, and thunderstorms. Link to other weather-related sites. Did you know that the practice of tornado warnings began some 50 years ago? Get to know the history of weather predicting and a whole lot more weather-related facts.

National Snow and Ice Data Center

www-nsidc.colorado.edu/

Research and education about snow, blizzards, and ice: What causes blizzards? This data and information center focuses on studying snow and ice and their importance to Earth systems and subsequent impact on life. Snow and ice data is collected, cataloged, and distributed to scientists. Click ColdLinks, which offers articles and listings of sites dealing with snow and ice. Many of these articles are suitable for student use. Of primary interest to the public are the Education Resources that can be found here, including materials for students. Review booklets (on glaciers, snow removal, and so on) and other resources. Some are on the Web site, while others can be sent to you by contacting the Center at the University of Colorado in Boulder.

Perilous Times Earthquake Links

www.teleport.com/~jstar/earthq.html

Links to in-depth earthquake information: Useful to students and science buffs, this site features earthquake-prediction research, a place where you can report an earthquake if you think you felt one, a daily record of the latest "big one," and a quick overview of recent global occurrences (click a location and get a map of where the recent larger events have happened worldwide, complete with depths and magnitudes). Or you can get updates covering the past two weeks for the continental U.S.A., Canada (and Alaska), South America, or elsewhere. Read up on plate tectonics and the earth's insides and link to some other high-quality earthquake safety, science, and history sites.

Tropical Storms Worldwide

**www.solar.ifa.hawaii.edu/Tropical/
tropical.html**

Track major tropical storms: Click an area of interest to receive a regional map. This tropical cyclone data is presented for personal interest only and not as any official warning system, so don't rely on it in real emergencies. As the site producer puts it, "If you are in the path of a storm, you should be listening to official information sources." Still, the index is easy to read and follow and makes for interesting perusing. Current storms are listed by type (such as HUR for hurricane), name (such as Erika), date, time, latitude and longitude, wind direction, and speed measured in knots. Review potential strike areas and read tropical advisories. You can view storm maps and link to other tropical storm sites. You can also get archived information about past storms.

USGS Near Real Time Earthquake Bulletin

**wwwneic.cr.usgs.gov/neis/bulletin/
bulletin.html**

National Earthquake Information Center: Click Current Earthquakes, Earthquake Information, Earthquake Search, or Earthquake Links to locate event, scientific, or historical information. You can look down a list of earthquake events, which are usually posted right after an event occurs. Earthquakes are listed by date, time, latitude, longitude, depth, magnitude, and location. Get current earthquake maps and explanations of event parameters, including duration, body wave, surface wave, movement, and location. You can also link to more earthquake information from the United States Geological Survey.

VolcanoWorld

volcano.und.edu

or

volcano.und.nodak.edu/

All about volcano research, history, and news: This site has both a frames and a non-frames version. Categories here include volcanoes of the world, currently erupting volcanoes, volcano images, volcanoes of other worlds, volcanic parks and monuments, and volcano video clips. Read through the archives of common questions that people ask volcanologists. If you can't find the answer to your question, you can ask a volcanologist yourself. You can search the Bulletin of Volcanology or the Volcano Indexes (lists of the volcanoes on VolcanoWorld and links to pages about them). Click for a list sorted by world region, country/area, or volcano name. Check out volcano stories, games, quizzes, and activities for kids, including Kids Volcano Art, Volcanic School Project Ideas, Virtual Field Trips, and Schools' Volcano Homepages.

What is an El Niño?

www.pmel.noaa.gov/toga-tao/el-nino/

Information on this major weather disrupter: Produced by the federal government, this site (in English and Spanish) explains the science behind and impacts of El Niño, using maps, text, and graphics based on continuously updated data from an array of moored buoys in the Equatorial Pacific Ocean. El Niño is a disruption of the ocean-atmosphere system in the tropical Pacific that has big consequences for weather around the globe (including too much and too little rainfall). Get lots of information about predicting its impacts and monitoring its presence. And find out how El Niño got its name.

138 **Weather and Other Natural Events**

Other Stuff to Check Out

Web sites
wxp.eas.purdue.edu
www.indirect.com/www/storm5/
    twisterhomepage.html
www.disasters.org/weblink.html
vulcan.wr.usgs.gov/home.html
facs.scripps.edu
www.hawaii.edu
civeng.carleton.ca/cgi-bin2/quakes

Suggested search-engine keywords
Yahoo!: Weather, earthquakes, volcanoes,
    atmospherics, climatology
Infoseek: Weather

Weather Whys and Wonders

When you go outside and look up to decide whether you need a sweater or a raincoat, you're predicting weather. Meteorologists use radar, planes, computers, and many other tools to understand and predict weather tomorrow and years from today. *Meteorology* is the study of atmosphere, weather, and climate. It's important because our lives depend on adapting to weather and climate conditions. But it's also fun because who hasn't found forms in the clouds? So get to know why and how weather happens. These sites will keep your sunny side up!

Dan's Wild Wild Weather Page

www.whnt19.com/kidwx/

Interactive Weather Page for Kids: Meteorologist Dan Satterfield of WHNT-TV, Huntsville, Alabama, hosts this delightful site for kids (and parents). Click the weather icons or terms to get vibrantly written articles from Dan about atmospherics and meteorology (what are clouds, what makes tornado weather, and so on). Categories include clouds, temperature, pressure, humidity, climate, wind, lightning, forecasting, radar, tornadoes, hurricanes, and Ask Dan. Link to the fantastic *USA Today* A to Z Weather Index, which provides lots more articles from its news archive about weather and climate.

Galaxy's Meteorology and Climatology Links

www.einet.net/galaxy/Science/Geo-
    sciences/Meteorology-and-
    Climatology.html

Mega-linking site: Find an absolutely amazing list of links to some of the Internet's best meteorology and climatology sites. Categories include academic university programs and organizations worldwide (Scripps Institution of Oceanography, University of California – San Diego, and Virginia State Climatology Office), articles, cartography, collections, conferences, current weather maps and movies, publications, directories, surveys, archives, gophers, government organizations, and links to sites for ecosystems and the environment.

National Drought Mitigation Center

enso.unl.edu/ndmc/

Helping people and institutions manage drought: By working to develop and implement measures to decrease human vulnerability to drought, the NDMC stresses prevention rather than crisis intervention. See how this philosophy is applied in practice by clicking Drought Watch, the Enigma of Drought, Mitigating the Impacts, or Climatology and Drought. In the Climatology section, for example, you find out what climatology is and how it's used to help prepare for drought. See climographs for various U.S. cities, generated by the NDMC. Discover the history, science, and challenges of planning for and managing drought.

Northern Lights

www.uit.no/npt/nordlyset/
   nordlyset.en.html

Discover the Northern Lights: The Northern Lights Planetarium opened in 1989 as Norway's first public planetarium. As sponsor of this site, the planetarium offers articles describing the Northern Lights and the physics involved. View the impressive picture collection and QuickTime movie (which is 1.1MB in size and lasts about 30 seconds when you view it). Northern Lights, or Aurora Borealis, is nature's ultimate light show. See why here.

Some Like It Hot

www.blm.gov/education/sonoran/
   hot.html

Adapting to drought: See what drought brings ultimately to the earth and discover how even in a harsh environment, life goes on, if rather precariously. The Bureau of Land Management produces this attractive and informative site, with sections on American Indian traditional cultural places, riparian habitats, traces of ancient people, and desert land management for the future. One section of the site looks at the Sonoran Desert, the hottest desert in North America, where "a person stripped of clothing, water, and shade in the morning could be dead by evening." How is survival of any living thing possible under such conditions? This site offers insights in an informative and thought-provoking way.

Weather Science Hotlist

sln.fi.edu/tfi/hotlists/weather.html

Great weather links: An outstanding collection of weather-related links awaits you here. Explore topical, media-produced, research-oriented, and real-time weather sites sorted into categories covering background information about weather, atmosphere, severe weather, El Niño/La Niña, historical weather, career connections, weather forecasting, and weather-oriented learning activities. These well-selected links will keep you in weatherland for hours.

Other Stuff to Check Out

Web sites
   www.meteo.fr/e_index.html
   www.weatherman.com/
   zebu.uoregon.edu/joshua/index_old.html
   www.commerce.digital.com/palo-alto/
      CloudGallery/home.html
   www.unidata.ucar.edu/staff/blynds/
      Skymath.html
   covis.atmos.uiuc.edu/guide/guide.html
   www-kgs.colorado.edu
   asp1.sbs.ohio-state.edu/

Suggested search-engine keywords
   Yahoo!: Weather, meteorology, climatology
   Infoseek: Weather

140 Weather and Other Natural Events _____

Part IV
Family Life

The 5th Wave® By Rich Tennant

"SHE JUST FOUND OUT SHE'D RATHER BE A JET PILOT THAN A FAIRY PRINCESS, BUT SHE DOESN'T WANT TO GIVE UP THE WARDROBE."

In this part . . .

Today's fast-paced world makes taking care of the nuts and bolts of family life a more difficult challenge than ever before. From the time you get out of bed until you hit the pillows, you're constantly moving. Work, school, social activities, and other responsibilities can keep all family members so busy that you never take time to reflect on your school plans or career choices, family finances, health issues, or the family pets. This part has many resources on those topics. I even included a section on genealogy, in case you want to climb your family tree.

Careers, Colleges, and Education

Now is the time for that big step into adulthood. High school is over, and you're ready to move on to college or a job. Dependence metamorphoses into independence, and the next choices that you make should be well-planned and extensively researched. No matter which avenue is chosen, these sites can give you the skinny on where to go next in your search for fame, fortune, education, and happiness. Just don't let the door hit you on your way out!

Please note that, while I've taken exceptional care to ensure the quality and reliability of the sites listed in this section, I have no idea whether the commercial sites have sterling reputations or not. A site's listing here does not imply endorsement, and it's up to parents and students to assess the reliability of commercial services whose sites are included in this section's profiles.

Career Choices and College Prep

Getting ready for college-entrance exams? Trying to decide what your college major should be? Wondering whether college is the way to go? These sites can help.

AdOne Classified Network

www.adone.com

Index of classified sections of many national newspapers and other publications: More than 400 want-ad sections are represented in this easy-to-use search vehicle. Simply choose a category (for example, employment, business opportunities, or real estate), choose one or more regions in which to search, and then click the Begin Search button. Corresponding results show up automatically. The site is easy to use and offers a well-organized way to look for a house, a job, or a business to buy (as well as a lot of other things).

AHS On-Line Learning Center

www.milwaukee.tec.wi.us/ahs/
   career.htm

Produced by the Milwaukee Area Technical College: This site is based on a program used by students in a Career Exploration/Preparation class to gather information, identify choices, and make decisions about their professional futures. You can use it, too, to evaluate talents, interests, strengths, needs, and wants. You can communicate via e-mail with experts in fields such as paralegals, office technology, nursing, graphic arts, welding, bakery production, customer relations, and dental hygiene. Using resources and links here, you can assess careers, see what the job markets are like, begin to create a job-finding plan, and discover skills necessary to get hired. Sections cover career exploration/ preparation, personality assessment, choosing colleges, finding financial aid, and seeking jobs.

144 Careers, Colleges, and Education

American College Testing (ACT)

www.act.org/

Info on college-test preparation: Ah, the dreaded ACTs. This site describes test-prep books, software, and videos and offers free tips on preparing for and taking the ACT exam. You'll find this site well worth a visit to help with the pretest jitters. Make sure to check out the information on the ACT Work Keys program, which helps people make the transition from school or unemployment to work, or from one job to the next.

Career Mosaic

www.careermosaic.com

Career-oriented employment site: This site carries employment notices for a number of companies (for example, Bechtel Corporation, Canon Business Machines, Circuit City/Carmax, Denny's, Federal Home Loan Bank of San Francisco, L3 Communications Corporation, and Lockheed Martin Aerostructures & Naval Launching Systems) and in a number of career specialties (such as accounting and finance, electrical engineering, healthcare, and insurance). The site also includes areas devoted to certain segments of the career marketplace (for example, the Advancing Women Career Center, the National Urban League — Diversity Workforce, and WITI Online Jobs – Women In Technology). Search thousands of jobs in several ways and post or update your resume for free. Find out about online job fairs; visit the Career Resource Center for tips on job hunting, resume writing, wages, and salaries; or view job opportunities and entry-level resources for college grads.

CareerPath

www.careerpath.com

Search more than 200,000 help wanted ads from across America: If you're thinking of another job, this site offers you want ads from publications throughout the nation, as well as profiles of some of America's leading employers. The profiles also link job seekers to the employers' sites and e-mail addresses. This site posts about half a million new jobs a month and is updated daily by participating newspapers. The site is best viewed and searched by using Netscape.

College Board

www.collegeboard.org/

Guidance on preparing for college: Get the latest on college entrance exam resources, such as software and books, and find online applications, career counseling, and information on admissions and financial aid. The internal search box makes your topic hunting easier. Read college-oriented news and frequently asked questions (FAQs). Register for the SAT online and try a free demo of study software prepared by the College Board. Check out college rankings and test-performance rates. This site has a text version for computers that are slow to handle graphics.

College PowerPrep

www.powerprep.com

Free SAT software: Get good, objective advice and tips on getting admitted to college, choosing the right college, and finding financial aid. This site offers strategic tips for test taking, along with freebie software, demos, and online games and activities to help with test preparation. Any information pertinent to the SAT test gets good coverage here.

Educational Testing Service Network

www.ets.org/

Practice, practice, practice: Attempt some sample test questions, link to college Web sites, access an online college magazine, and get knowledgeable about making career choices and locating financial aid. ETS Net provides information about college and graduate-school admissions and placement tests. Select links to the test for which you are preparing and get sample test questions, study tips, and registration information. The site also contains advice on college planning and financial aid, and links to college and university sites.

Kaplan Educational Centers

www.kaplan.com

Get ready for college: Lots of information about careers, colleges, financial aid, and college-prep tests and plenty of useful links. After you sign in by filling out a long questionnaire, you can play test-prep games. Click on college, financial aid, or any of the special college-oriented features. You can also click the names of the tests for which you are trying to prepare to find links, software, and other supportive resources.

Monster Board

monster.com

Big job-hunting site: This massive resource offers connections to career counselors, jobs in the United States and overseas, newsgroups, job-search agents, and employer profiles. The Job Search section features more than 50,000 jobs to peruse. Other site features include a special section for health-care professionals, a resume posting service, career tips and employment trends, and a relocation service guide. Jobs for every level are available here, from those for beginners out of college to opportunities for long-time career professionals. This site is frames-based.

Outlook for Specific Occupations

www.jobweb.org/Catapult/oco1000.htm

Promising careers: Here you can find very straightforward evaluations of jobs — including duties, necessary training, and legitimacy in today's marketplace. Use an alphabetical glossary of jobs or browse categories of jobs (such as service occupations). Get current data on salaries, benefits, working conditions, and prospects for future earnings. This site is a good place to get insights into careers in emerging technologies as well as into traditional jobs.

Princeton Review

www.review.com

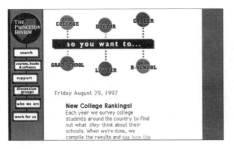

College rankings and readiness information: Find out how colleges rank, get application deadlines, and score the latest information on how to get ready for tests and how to choose the right career. Self-evaluate your career strengths and get the word on the ACT, SAT, and PSAT, and find a really good selection of college and testing links. This site also tells it like it is in terms of training, job opportunities, and the challenges and rewards of certain high-paying professions (such as lawyers and doctors). Its clean, concise layout and wealth of information make it a must-see site for exploring your future.

TestPrep

www.testprep.com

Free online test-prep course: Get comfortable with the college prep test process by trying this sample software that you can download and keep. You also get useful practice-drill materials here to build your confidence. This award-winning site features free test preparation and ways for you to build your own training course.

Other Stuff to Check Out

Web sites
 ericir.sunsite.syr.edu/
 www.learningco.com
 www.hoovers.com
 www.cweb.com

Newsgroups
 soc.college.admissions
 soc.college.financial-aid
 misc.education.adult

Mailing list
 www.neosoft.com/internet/paml/groups.C/
 career-l.html

Chat area
 206.86.214.238/

Online service area
 America Online: LEARNING & CULTURE

Suggested search-engine keywords
 Yahoo!: Career and Vocational Education,
  College Preparation
 Infoseek: Careers

College Advice and Information E-zines

Here are some of the different e-zines dedicated to college students and college life. Some of these sites focus on finding a college you like and getting in; others are survival manuals; still others help with the transition to "real life." All are aimed at students — or perhaps the young at heart. In some instances, a bit of parental supervision before the young adult views the site is recommended.

Black Collegian Online

www.black-collegian.com

Colleges and careers for people of color: The *Black Collegian* was founded more than a quarter-century ago, and the online version not only archives past issues but holds a wealth of useful current information. One link leads to a listing of open positions, information on graduate and professional studies, career-related news, and a place to post resumes. Another link leads to announcements for global studies, and yet another leads to sports pages. The quote of the week (by various African Americans) is inspiring for everyone. Black Collegian Online hot links include a number of college-oriented sites, such as a guide to preparing your doctoral dissertation, the Study Shack, Writing Central, and Silicon Graphics College Connection.

College Bound

www.cbnet.com

Interactive college guide: College Bound is the interactive guide for high-school and college students. It starts with some college profiles but also includes sports (with a newsletter, trivia, and a recruiting coach to answer your e-mail), music (several features to show you what's cool on the college music scene), a digital guide (for those computer problems), food (you guessed it — recipes), and a help line. Student Cafe is the student bulletin board where collegiate types can be creative and/or let off steam. The guide has select schools listed by location [New York, for example, links to SUNY (State University of New York) campuses, St. John's University, and a few other schools]. The listings are just getting going, though: College-rich California has but one listing for the (very fine) Academy of Art College in San Francisco.

College Jam

www.collegejam.com

An interactive site for teens: College Jam reflects today's college life with its range of stories, news, and high-tech stuff. Articles can be sentimental ("Remembering Diana") or cool ("Mac OS 8 . . . the upgrade"). Very nice graphics lead you to college home pages and newspapers as well. Besides, who could resist an articles titled "Beetle Popcorn" or "No More Clones"? College Jam publishes a fairly long list of student home pages, some of which its editors have reviewed and deemed the best of the crop. One week, an aspiring entrepreneur was selected, as was m@net (pronounced *mat net*), which contains a little off-the-wall humor. Parents please note: College Jam defines "the best" as the most interesting and innovative, not the safest for viewing.

148 Careers, Colleges, and Education

College News

www.collegenews.com

Connecting students and campuses: College News has a huge list/map of colleges and universities, an index of college papers, practical advice (on campus crime, financial aid, and getting a job), and fun (very nice area, including chat rooms, free stuff, and NCAA sports). The idea is to provide useful information and also to connect students and campuses. The school selection is pretty detailed (U.S. listings are state-by-state and divided into public and private schools), with links to lists of international colleges as well. College News also invites collegiate types to become campus correspondents for the Web page. This site takes time to consume but has much to offer high-school kids thinking about college, as well as those who have made the leap to higher education. Parents should note that most of the humor is pretty collegiate.

Enter Magazine

www.entermag.com

Life after college: Enter Magazine promises to ease that difficult transition from college life to the real world. Much of its content is job focused. It has several interesting sections: Features, Cars and Cash, Work (including FAQs, or Frequently Asked Questions, about job hunting), Play, and Digital Kitchen. If you have a business presentation to prepare and wonder how this assignment is different from the exposés you did in school, Enter Magazine is the place to go. You can ask questions and let off steam at ENTERactive, the powerful discussion and chat system. Don't miss the helpful columns by Bradley Richardson called Job Smarts, and when work has just about overwhelmed you, click into the magazine's Gridiron Challenge for a little (deserved) escapism.

Straight Talk about School

www.balancenet.org/

Straight answers for teens: Straight Talk has information from the experts. Just as its name implies, this site for high-school kids aims to give direction to their lives and advise them on everything from college choices to careers and money. Look for the monthly advice column (one month, it concerned improving organizational skills, dealing with stress, and getting everything done), personal finance information for teens (the site helps you create a personal budget automatically), and, of course, the latest info on schools, both public and private. Experts include psychologist Mike Riera (author of *Surviving High School* and a frequent speaker on NPR)

and Charlie Berman, a specialist in stress management. Most important, you can ask kids your own age how they survive juggling school and sports, how can you run for student council, or how to start community service projects. The site also offers information for teachers and a kit with instructions and magazines for their students.

Student.Net

www.student.net

College news and entertainment: Student.Net has a good balance of the fun (crossword, Seinfeld-o-matic, TV search and remind) and the practical (meeting new friends, Mom-o-matic, Yenta the Matchmaker).You can also find cool links related to collegiate sports. Now, the only drawback comes in the feature section, where "Brew beer in your dorm room" vies for attention with "Penn State Dries Out" (in the aftermath of the LSU and MIT drinking-related deaths of students). However, the site has some really interesting stuff (how to get free airline tickets grabbed my attention, and I *am* curious as to what students think about college athletes being paid). But parents should check out this site before letting the kids at it. It does offer a dose of reality — collegiate reality, that is.

U.Magazine

www.umagazine.com

The national college magazine: This very hip site (flashing graphics, creative fonts) has university searches (for Web pages and admissions info), university news, network info, entertainment, contests, and surveys (for example, "Death Penalty — Yea or Nay?" and the all-important "Mac or IBM?"). The College Life section ranges from Buddhism to loan information, and the Sports section links you to a range of sports stats, sites, and controversies (such as the drinking-related tragedy at Louisiana State University). Issues of *U.Magazine* are searchable back to 1995: Just enter the name of your favorite school and discover how — and why — it made its way into collegiate history.

WhatNext

www.whatnext.com

Precollege prerequisites: This site contains some pretty useful and funny information about going to college and preparing to get there. You can find articles on collegiate topics of note, such as Chelsea Clinton's first week at Stanford (now, could *this* be a spoof?) and nightmare-roommate survival, as well as practical stuff, such as college searches (the ultimate way to find your right school), underground reviews (*not* the same as the reviews appearing in the Princeton Review), financial aid and admissions, and essential stuff such as how to make a home page, what movies to go see to forget it all, and where to chat. Parents may need to check this site out for younger kids — but teens will love it. It's cool looking, too.

College- (Or Student-) Produced Magazines and Newspapers

As the Web leaped onto college campuses, student publications began to leap onto the Web. The following is a selection from the dozens of student publications already online. Many of these publications use the latest graphics, audio, and/or video technology. Some rely almost solely on words and images. All paint an intriguing picture of contemporary college life.

alt.journal

www.emory.edu/ALTJNL/

The literary magazine enlivened: Produced by the graduate students in the Comparative Literature Department at Emory University, *alt* indicates an attempt at being something different, an alternative to those dull, uncomfortably narrow journals often produced by academics. This group wants to bring life to the literary tradition, and it does so with such editorials and articles as "Calvin Klein's Pornographic Gaze" and "Your Horoscope" as told by Mlle. Aredhel Proudhon, a thousand-year-old vampire from Baltimore. You can also find more serious articles, such as "Writing On," an analysis of graffiti. This site is best appreciated by connoisseurs of the imagination.

College Press Network

www.cpnet.com

Collegiate-news resource: This guide to college presses offers (in addition to the list of college papers and magazines) arts and entertainment, sports, jobs and internships, games, free stuff (a collegiate biggie), and a bookstore. The list of newspapers is international, and the authors have selected their top 25 online collegiate papers, including the Kentucky Kernel (University of Kentucky at Lexington), the Digital Collegian (Penn State), and the University of Minnesota's Daily Online. College Press recognizes university presses for developing online journals and papers that take advantage of the medium and aren't simply weak copies of their print counterparts. Also, don't miss the related story from Editor & Publisher Interactive, titled "What newspaper pros can learn from the college online press," written by Steve Outing.

College Street Journal

www.mtholyoke.edu/offices/comm/csj/

New and notable: Mt. Holyoke College produces this weekly journal, which focuses on political and social issues as well as campus activities. Features include such titles as "Educating Inner-City Students," "Faye Wattleton Calls Women to Action as Leaders," "LITS Takes Survey Results to Heart: Institutes Changes," "Vanessa James Brings High-Powered Background, Low-Key Manner to Theatre Design," "New History Course Explores Role of African American Women in U.S. History," and "Lecturers to Discuss Brazilian Slave Relationships." Brief sections are dedicated to the changes around campus and a calendar of activities.

Darpan

www.prairienet.org/darpan/

Reflections of India: *Darpan* is the Sanskrit word for mirror. *Darpan,* the publication, is an annual journal, with two issues online here for you to view. One intention underlying the site is to disprove the myth that identifies Indian Americans as highly scientific but not literary. This site, published by students at the University of Illinois at Urbana-Champaign, goes a long way toward disproving that myth: It's both visually lovely and of high literary merit. Contents include poetry by Anand Menezes, Subina, and others and prose works by Abhijit Ghosh, Steve Wisz, and Chirantan Desai. The page's subtle design is also the creation of Urbana students.

The Digital Collegian

www.collegian.psu.edu/arts/arts.htm

Published by students at Penn State: You may not like this journal's cartoon home page, but its contents are first-rate. Local news touches on both the Philadelphia region and the campus. Sample features include "Binge drinkers risk serious health problems," "National Coming Out Day tells gays they are not alone," and "Alumni revisit student haunts." The weather section gives you the local forecast and a great bunch of weather links; the sports section gives you a number of in-depth updates on Penn State teams (and links you to a special Penn State Football page); the arts section includes local shows and issues and touches on the Penn State music scene. Like most college journals and papers, the Collegian has an opinion page, but this one includes a complete listing of important governmental and university officials — in case you have a grievance to air.

The Eagle's Web

www.eagle.american.edu

Collegiate multimedia journalism: Sponsored by the American University (Washington, D.C.), this site is extensively hyperlinked and uses RealAudio and QuickTime to jazz up its content. The authors point out up front that their university was listed as number 47 on *Wired* magazine's list of the most wired campuses; the journal reflects this status pretty clearly. The Eagle's Web is pretty sophisticated, and its content isn't limited to campus issues or to technology. Speakers are highlighted, and regular features include metro news and sports. This publication manages to achieve a fine balance between the lighthearted and the serious, as well as between the collegiate and the real-world.

Enormous Sky

newsrm01.main.temple.edu/sky/ index.html

152 Careers, Colleges, and Education

Literature from Temple University: Enormous Sky is a magazine of student poetry, prose, artwork, and photography produced by the students of Temple University — and it is fantastic. The table of contents for the current issue lists more than two dozen poems, stories, and works of visual art. You can also find a short list of literary pages (including Yahoo!'s list of literary magazines and a German master list that has many English-language pages). The heart of this site is the energetic prose written by undergraduates at Temple. Submissions are accepted, but only from Temple students.

Feedback Magazine

www.feedback.org.uk

Follow the Yellow Duckie (the icon, that is): This British magazine is full of information for students around the globe — especially if you like rugby. It's a monthly student-culture magazine, containing band interviews (one issue had an in-depth interview with Silver Sun), competitions (just answer some questions about *Quadrophenia*), chances to be on TV, and other pretty cool stuff. The site has some news, too, specifically community-related news, such as an education and safety project going on in a student-populated area of Leeds, where the journal originates. Visit for a different view of what British students like and are busy doing.

Flux 96

ballmer.uoregon.edu/Flux96/

A bold presence: The University of Oregon at Eugene produces this sophisticated news magazine, which has features on archaeology (an Oregon archaeologist digs for clues to the first Americans), ballroom dancing (one of the latest

student passions), life for some disabled students in the '90s (or an unusual camping trip in the Oregon mountains), "model" prisoners (does fashion have a place in felony?), and a whole lot more. Interviews are a semiregular feature here; Spaulding Gray was one interviewee. Some of these features are quite powerful: "Lioness in Winter," a story of breast-cancer survival, is vivid and moving.

HarvardCrimsonOnline

www.thecrimson.harvard.edu/ index.html

View from the Quad: *The Crimson* has been part of daily life at Harvard since 1873, and this online edition makes clear its serious tone and thoughtful content. Style tells a great deal about a journal (and a university), and this style is subdued. But the contents are diverse, and if you probe, you find that the voices are not only scholarly but distinct. Sections include news, opinion (naturally), sports, arts, college, faculty (a creative addition, given that Harvard's faculty is so intriguingly diverse), university, student life (the fun stuff is here), city (occasional humor, along with Cambridge politics and drama), science and technology, and a section called "Fifteen Minutes," where students can have their — brief — say. The Crimson gives a characteristic sample of Harvard news and Harvard noise.

Johns Hopkins Newsletter

www.jhu.edu:80/~newslett/

Baltimore's brightest: The Johns Hopkins weekly newsletter is restrained and mature-looking. Still, it has pretty detailed sports coverage (collegiate, of course), along with arts, features (space probes, for example), news, and, of course, science. You can also find forums and bulletin boards — in fact, it has a great deal of depth for a "newsletter." No huge surprises here, but a pretty straightforward presentation of what's going on and what the newsletter staff has to say about it.

Kentucky Kernel

www.kykernel.com

News from the Bluegrass State: The Kentucky Kernel brings you news, opinions, sports, and diversions (games and art stuff), and though it looks like a newspaper transported online, its creators take advantage of technology to allow you to search their substantial archives. On Thursdays, the Kernel publishes *The KeG,* or Kernel Entertainment Guide, to help students and others in the Lexington region find the hottest things going on that weekend. Selected by College Press Network as one of the top five online student papers, the Kernel offers a variety of features and viewpoints: "Study: Students admitted preferentially perform equally" from a UC Berkeley report on Affirmative Action students and performance; "Doctors warn of spreading STDs"; "Journey of an agnostic in a Christian world." Besides its high-level content, this site offers easy navigation.

The Miscellany News

misc.vassar.edu/

Not for women only: Although Vassar is no longer a women's college, having opened its doors and classrooms to a select body of men, women have clearly shaped this interesting journal. Sections include news ("VSA Council investigates

possibility of lower phone rates for students"), features ("Octoberfest a huge success"), sports ("Box seats — Baseball: after the division's realignment"), arts ("Celebrity Spotting 101: Famous people can go to college, too"), and so on. Though the scope of the journal is pretty much limited to the campus, this publication offers a strong sense of Vassar's character through the voices of its undergraduates. In addition, the unusual grid format of the Miscellany News makes it refreshingly easy to read.

The Other Voice

www.trincoll.edu/~othervoi

The best of student journalism: The Other Voice is the counterpart to the print magazine published by undergraduates at Trinity College in Hartford, Connecticut. It was begun in 1993 and accepts contributions, specifically essays on politics or culture. (Submission guidelines are available at the site.) The journal is looking for the voices of its generation — but only if they're serious about journalism. An average issue may include essays on the environment, vegan diets, or local politics and typically includes some photography or fine art as well. The site also has chat rooms if you want to comment on the essays, as well as links to other literary magazines and an archive of articles.

Planet News

www.hyped.com/planetnews/

More than college news: This award-winning online news and information site is brought to you by San Francisco State University, but it doesn't report collegiate news only. Recent features have included "Hype on Heroin," an examination of the lives of three addicts; "Copyright and Wrong, or how can you break the law when no one knows what it is?"; "Power and Pain," a multimedia conversation between a painter, a poet, and a musician; and "Enabling Technology," focusing on "electronic muscle, digital eyes and ears." Planet News encourages feedback and has a link to the journalism department for those readers who are so inspired that they want to enroll.

Stylus

infoeagle.bc.edu/bc_org/svp/st_org/
    stylus/

Student literature from Boston: Boston College's art and literature magazine is a fun blend of old (fake manuscript illustrations dress up the home page) and new (strong, modern prose forms the content and is presented in red print on a lemon-yellow background). Only Boston College undergraduates can submit to Stylus — which has long been around in print version — but everyone can read it. The contents are mature, vivid, and very much in touch with today's world. Past issues are archived to give a fuller sense of the journal and the college. Aspiring writers and artists, as well as any students considering attending Boston College, should visit here.

Three-point-seven

scs.student.virginia.edu/~3point7/
    threepointseven.html

Virginia's finest: Produced by the non-profit Thoughtlines, Inc., this journal is affiliated with the University of Virginia but states up front that the views contained herein belong solely to the guest authors. Then the fun begins. Three-point-seven contains interviews, essays, and poetry of a very nice level and invites submissions from those smitten by its lovely green format and literary reputation. Interviewees have included Sharon Olds, Cake trumpeter Vince DiFiore of MTV fame, the bands Jon Spencer Blues Explosion and Sebadoh, and other interesting folks. If you like the current issue, you can peruse earlier ones as well.

University Magazine at Cal State Long Beach

www.csulb.edu/%7Eunivmag/
    frame.htm

Update from Southern California: Cal State Long Beach's magazine is pretty, if a bit wordy. But the hidden contents (hidden because you must wade through introductions and apologies to find them) are a bit unorthodox and, as such, worth reading. Recent subjects have included a controversial sociology professor; a feature profile of Tatsuro Abe, a Michael Jackson impersonator; and an article about the Web at the university's new media center. This magazine, though short, gives a sense of the campus issues and will be interesting to watch to see how the two-decades-old style of the print *University Magazine* evolves in this new media.

Colleges, Training, and Distance Learning

Before the advent of the Internet, visiting every college or university in the world before making an admissions choice was pretty much impossible. But not anymore. These sites link you to the world's institutions of higher learning, or if you're the homebody type, explain how to study for a real degree from home.

1998 College Rankings: U.S. News & World Report

www4.usnews.com/usnews/edu/
    college/corank.htm

www4.usnews.com/usnews/edu/
    college/coranknf.htm

Evaluation of America's best colleges: *U.S. News & World Report* magazine ranks the top national universities, liberal arts colleges, fine arts and performing arts schools, service academies, public schools, and regional schools (Midwestern, Northern, Southern, and Western). It also ranks schools according to subcategories including campus diversity; numbers of international students; those with the highest proportion of business,

education, and engineering majors; and the caliber of those programs. You can search for a particular school's ranking by entering the school's name in the search box. To find out how rankings are determined, read sections explaining the various criteria. The site also has a Guide for Parents and a Loan Center. (Note that the first URL given for this site is a frames version, while the second URL is for a nonframes version of the site.)

Braintrack

www.braintrack.com

Massive education index: Track down institutions of higher learning in Africa, America, Asia, Australia, and Europe. This site offers more than 3,800 links to college, polytech, and university home pages in 136 countries. It originates in Switzerland, so it has strong European links.

College Counsel's Colleges and Universities

www.ccounsel.com/states.htm

Quick, thorough assessments and access to admissions forms: Pick a state, pick a college from the state list, read descriptions, request an admissions packet, e-mail a college counselor, and get travel instructions to campus. These concise, complete, and objective descriptions detail such things as school history, enrollment levels, degrees offered, expenses and fees, most popular majors, number of faculty (and education levels), freshman admission levels (and their high school academic rankings), and what percentage receive financial aid. Click Ohio, for example, and then click Kent State University, and read in part that the school is "Public. Founded 1910. Setting: Rural — small town. Degrees offered: B, M, D. Calendar: Semester, extensive undergraduate summer courses available. Undergraduate student body: 14,660 full time, 3,151 part time; 43% male, 57% female; 1% Asian, 6% Black, 90% Caucasian, 1% Hispanic, 1% Native American, 1% other, 1% foreign nationals; 80% are from in-state."

Community College Web

www.mcli.dist.maricopa.edu/cc/

Searchable index of 730 community college Web sites: Link up with two-year, post-secondary institutions that offer certificate programs and Associate of Arts (A.A.) degrees. This site will link you to more than 700 of the 1,114 community colleges in the United States so you can get more information about programs, fees, and admissions. It also includes links to schools in Canada and other countries. Search alphabetically, geographically (country/state/province), or by keywords (college name, location, URL). This site is frames-based.

Community Colleges

www.utexas.edu/world/univ/
index.html#comcol

List of links to community colleges: Find a very plain-looking, but easy to access and use, list of links to community colleges organized to cover new sites added to the database, an alphabetical linking list of U.S. community colleges, or a linking list organized by states. Click any title to connect with the listed home page of the community college. From there, you can find out about programs, fees, and admission requirements, as well as related information.

GreekPages

www.greekpages.com/

Comprehensive listing of links to fraternities and sororities: Go Greek courtesy of this searchable (by campus) site, which lists thousands of chapters from nearly 400 fraternities, sororities, and coed organizations. Find relevant news and events, famous "Greeks," and chapters for more than 660 colleges and universities in seven countries. Connect with Greek career, research, message, and in-house information. This site has an online store of Greek-related merchandise.

Greek Home Pages

www.mit.edu:8001/afs/athena/activity/
i/ifc/www/greeks.html

Home pages of Greek organizations: Find national fraternities, national sororities (women's fraternities), and local organizations. You can also utilize a list organized by schools. Get order information for the manual on all national fraternities, sororities, and societies (Baird's Manual of American College Fraternities). Almost 100 fraternities, as well as 35 sororities and 22 local chapters (those not having a national affiliation), are listed at this site, as are links to other index sites of Greek home pages.

Historically Black Colleges and Universities

www.webcom.com/~cjcook/SDBP/ hbcu.html

Linking index of Historically Black Colleges and Universities (HBCU's): Link directly to the home pages of a long list of educational institutions, including Alabama A&M University, Benedict College, Bethune-Cookman College, Clark Atlanta University, Delaware State University, Fisk University, Howard University, Jackson State University, Kentucky State University, Meharry Medical College, Morehouse College, Morehouse School of Medicine, Spelman College, Stillman College, Texas Southern University, University of Arkansas at Pine Bluff, University of the Virgin Islands, and Voorhees College. Link to related resources, including organizations and publications (such as Black Collegian, Black Excel, United Negro College Fund, and historically black fraternities and sororities).

Independent Higher Education Network

www.fihe.org/fihe/college/search.htm

Links to private colleges and universities: Get tips on searching for the right private college and finding financial aid. Point and click a U.S. map to connect with a college or search alphabetically by state. This organization, incorporated in 1958, specializes in joining philanthropic and corporate entities with independent colleges and universities sharing similar goals and complementary educational programs. What's really useful about the site is that it provides names, phone numbers, and addresses of the schools instead of just the link. You'll find this site useful to find the details of private schools that don't have Web pages.

Internet University

www.caso.com

Extensive list of college-level online courses: Discover close to a thousand online courses leading toward degrees in all kinds of standard majors. Visit any of five sections: articles by noted authors; online-course descriptions, with tuition and contact information; profiles of more than 30 online-course providers; links to thousands of online courses and resources; and the latest news in online-course technology and offerings.

Learning on the Net

homepage.interaccess.com/~ghoyle/

Legitimate study programs online: Click Training or Colleges to find resources and links to online training or college-study programs that have proven credibility and quality. If you want to attend college or develop your career from home, this site is the place to start looking.

158 Careers, Colleges, and Education

Medical School Admissions Information, Resources, Links

www.accepted.com/links.htm

Links for Med School Applicants

The Web is a cornucopia of valuable information for medical school applicants. Whether looking for help with the MCAT, suggestions on interview techniques, material on different medical schools, or the latest on those much maligned--and watched--rankings, it's somewhere on the Web.

List of resources of medical school applicants: Find assistance to prepare for the MCAT, suggestions on interview techniques, material on different medical schools, and various school rankings available on the Internet. Includes links and reviews so that you'll know what to expect if you visit any of the sites. This very extensive list of medical student-related materials, background, and resources includes dental, physical therapy, and osteopathic links. Other sections of this site cover choosing a school, writing for medical school, completing applications, getting recommendations, and surviving the interview processes.

Minority On-Line Information Service

web.fie.com/web/mol/index_.htm

Database of 164 minority institutions: MOLIS provides in-depth information about research and educational capabilities of Historically Black Colleges and Universities (HBCUs) and Hispanic-Serving Institutions (HSIs). Key federal agencies support MOLIS under a cooperative agreement and use MOLIS to identify potential beneficiaries of available federal resources. This site gives information about faculty, research centers, facilities, equipment, administrators, degrees and enrollment, and scholarships and fellowships. The site has a FAQ (frequently asked question) section, which is a good place to start your research.

Peterson's Education Center

www.petersons.com

Comprehensive listing of colleges and universities: Get detailed information about U.S. institutions of higher learning and other educational resources, including graduate studies, study in other countries, careers, job opportunities, summer programs, special schools, distance learning, financial aid, learning adventures, enrichment programs, vocational and technical schools, and tests and assessment. Check out the original features or shop at the online bookstore.

ScholarStuff

www.scholarstuff.com/colleges/
    colleges.htm

Worldwide directory to colleges and universities: Click anywhere on the world map to get links and information on that region's colleges and universities. Link directly to those institutions' home pages. Other features include links to financial aid, Greek Life, research tools, chats, testing aids, and job leads. An extremely user-friendly site.

Universities.com

www.universities.com

> ### Universities.com
>
> #### Search
> our database of
> over 4,000 college and university home pages
> across the globe.
>
> #### Add
> your university.
>
> **Don't forget to add a bookmark!**
> Check back later to see how we expand our services to further meet your needs.

Connect with universities around the world: This searchable database contains more than 4,000 links to universities worldwide. Use the internal search box to enter any part of the university's name or location. Get Web sites that pertain directly or secondarily to your selection. A quick and handy site.

U.S. Two-Year Colleges

www.sp.utoledo.edu/twoyrcol.html

Index of two-year colleges: This database is sorted geographically and includes colleges with and without Web sites. More than 920 U.S. campuses are listed; just select a state and click it to find colleges and contact information or links there. In addition to community colleges, you'll find technical colleges, junior colleges, branches of four-year colleges that focus on associate degrees, and accredited two-year proprietary schools. Link to other indexes of colleges in the U.S. and elsewhere, as well as related resources.

WWW Virtual Library – Distance Education

www.cisnet.com/~cattales/ Deducation.html

Mega linking site: Best viewed with Netscape 2.0 or higher. Very matter-of-fact listing of sites relevant to distance learning. Please remember that this site is an attempt to gather links and that the links are not screened for legitimacy, price, or other factors. You must rely on your own judgment. Categories include distance education offerings; distance education journals, newsletters, and newsgroups; distance education organizations; distance education articles; and related World Wide Web subject catalog listings.

Other Stuff to Check Out

Web sites

www.artsci.wustl.edu/~jrdorkin/GUWeb/ GUWeb.html
www.college-prep.com/
www.cfpi.com/
www.job-hunt.org
www.csu.edu.au/education/library.html
www.mit.edu:8001/people/cdemello/ univ.html
www-net.com/univ/
www.prepdoctor.com/
www.collegexpress.com/experts/
www.state.gov/www/about_state/schools/ txt.html
www.scientia.org/
www.wesleyan.edu/spn/ranking.htm
www.collegefund.org/
www.collegenet.com/
www.ponyexpress.net/~saleh/

tdg.uoguelph.ca/~zhirani/homepage1.html
www.virtualu.ca.gov/
www-net.com/univ/
www.edonline.com/cq/hbcu/
www.jorsm.com/~triage/
www.studentservices.com/
www.ukans.edu/~upc/sa_list.html
www.geocities.com/CollegePark/Quad/
    6288/Fraternities.html
www.greek.com/
www.occ.com/

Newsgroups
alt.college.fraternities
alt.college.sororities
alt.fraternity.sorority
www.linkmag.com/union/
    college_usenet.html

Online service areas
America Online: LEARNING & CULTURE
CompuServe: GO PETERSON

Suggested search-engine keywords
Yahoo!: Higher Education, Colleges and
    Universities, Distance Learning,
    Intramurals, Student college organiza-
    tions, Fraternities and sororities
Infoseek: Colleges and universities

Financial Aid for Education

Have the smarts, the drive, and the
desire, but no money? These sites link
you to legitimate funding agencies that
can help you pay for your education.

Financial Aid

www.finaid.org/finaid/fastweb.html

Huge searchable database: Find close to
200,000 privately underwritten fellowships, scholarships, loans, and grants.

The main site provides you with scam
alerts, assistance for specialty groups
(such as the disabled), and information
about admissions, government resources,
and personal finance.

Student Guide

**www.ed.gov/prog_info/SFA/
    StudentGuide/**

Sponsored by the U.S. Department of
Education: Here's a massive guide to
financial-aid resources, including how to
find federal programs, how to determine
qualifications, how to apply, and how
financial aid does and doesn't work. This
site is clear, complete, and easy to
navigate despite its size and depth.

Other Stuff to Check Out

Web site
www.salliemae.com

Newsgroup
www.finaid.org/finaid/overview/
    forums.html

Mailing list
www.finaid.org/finaid/overview/
    forums.html

Online service area
America Online: LEARNING & CULTURE, RSP
    Funding Focus

Suggested search-engine keywords
Yahoo!: Financial aid for school
Infoseek: Financial aid & grants, Grants for
    school

The Internet and the World Wide Web are amazing sources of information on families and genealogy. Libraries, heritage societies, and other groups have created Web pages filled with information about how to research your family tree — online and off. Many of these pages focus on specific groups, such as the Quakers Corner Page (www.rootsweb.com/~quakers/index.htm) or Ancestors from Norway (www.geocities.com/Heartland/Plains/5100/). Most of the information is free, but software programs for creating multimedia family albums also can be purchased online.

The following sections deal with various aspects of family history and research. Although some excellent commercial sites are listed in the first section, I suggest exploring the other sections, especially "Family History — General Resources," for free information about genealogical studies. Most of these general resources have excellent introductions for beginners.

Commercial Sites

You may want to create your family history from scratch, but if you'd welcome a little help, these sites describe software that can help you research your ancestors, locate long-lost relatives, and document your unique family history. The sites provide some excellent free resources as well.

Family Tree Maker Online

www.familytreemaker.com

$

Multimedia family albums: This site promotes the popular Brøderbund software, Family Tree Maker, which is designed to help you trace your family history and create unique multimedia scrapbooks by using an extensive genealogical library. But this Web page offers several free services including the Internet FamilyFinder, which searches the Net for your relatives, and the World Family Tree Project, which encourages you to submit information on your heritage to the World Family database. Beginners should read the Genealogy "How-To" Guide.

Everton Genealogical Helper

www.everton.com

$

Researching your family tree: *Everton's Genealogical Magazine* has created a site that combines subscription databases with free advice and information for researchers (for example, Getting Started, U.S. and International Genealogical Resources, Queries, and PhotoFind

Database). For those new to the Net, Everton's has links to key introductory sites (for example, the Electronic Frontier Foundation's *Big Dummy's Guide to the Internet*, Brendan P. Kehoe's *Zen and the Art of the Internet*, and *Using the World-Wide Web*, a list of FAQs, or frequently asked questions, for genealogists).

Ethnic, Religious, and Social Groups

Several pages on the Web are dedicated to diverse ethnic groups, religious organizations, clans, tribes, and clubs such as the Descendants of Mexican War Veterans or the Daughters of the American Revolution. Most of their pages link to related sites with a wealth of historical and cultural information.

CompuServe Hispanic Genealogy

ourworld.compuserve.com/homepages/ alfred_sosa

A network of Hispanic history and culture: This straightforward page contains information on how to start genealogical research, a list of Hispanic genealogical sources, information about Spanish heraldry, a discussion of the terms *Hispanic* and *Latin,* a list of events relating to Hispanic genealogy, and a bulletin board, The Ancestor's Exchange, where you can post simple queries pertaining to surnames.

The Genealogy Connection — Native American Links

www.native-american.com/nagene.htm

Native American cultural heritage: This page holds files on the Cherokee, Choctaw, and Lakota tribes, and the authors of the page aspire to build sites for all the American Indian nations. There are links to Native American bookstores and maps (including tribal maps, Montana maps of Reservation lands, U.S. Geological Survey maps, and so forth), as well as miscellaneous Native American genealogy materials (for example, Kevin Cloud Brechner's Lecture on the white buffalo calf). The list of Cherokee links is particularly diverse and impressive.

The Imperial Family of Japan

www.geocities.com/Tokyo/Temple/3953

Japanese royalty and genealogy: This fascinating page illustrates the history of the Japanese imperial family and its branches, provides copies of historical documents relating to the family, and offers links to other sites on Japanese history, government, culture, royalty, and genealogy. The biographies of the Imperial family include the Emperor and Empress, the Empress Dowager, Children of the Emperor, Imperial Princes and Princesses, and other family members. Don't miss the elegantly written "Imperial Oath Sworn in the Sanctuary in the Imperial Palace."

JewishGen: The Home of Jewish Genealogy

www.jewishgen.org

Jewish genealogy worldwide: This incredible site hosts several servers, or online networks of Web pages and resources, dedicated to Jewish heritage, including the international JewishGen Family Finder (JGFF), and has numerous eastern European and central European genealogical resources. You can also find an international discussion group run by Jewish genealogy researchers, and a volunteer service for free translations of material relevant to Jewish genealogy.

Whakapapa Maori [Maori Genealogy]

ourworld.compuserve.com/homepages/ rhimona/whakapap.htm

Genealogy of native New Zealanders: the Maori are the aboriginal New Zealanders thought to have immigrated from Tahiti during the ninth century A.D. This beautiful page, decorated with Maori artwork, describes the Maori traditions and defines the terms used in Maori genealogy. The authors also describe the connections between human genealogy and the Maori stories of creation. The site concludes with links to worldwide genealogical sites.

Other Stuff to Check Out

Web sites

www.oz.net/~cyndihow/african.htm
www.asiawind.com/pub/hakka
www.rootsweb.com/~quakers/index.htm
www.ozemail.com.au/~jsnelson/ozgen.html
www.tartans.com
midas.ac.uk/genuki/big
www.voyager.co.nz/~ianclap/gennz.htm

Mailing lists

afrigeneas@msstate.edu
quaker-roots@rootsweb.com
menno.rec.roots@mennolink.org

Suggested search-engine keywords

Yahoo: genealogy (plus subgroup, for example: African American)
Lycos: genealogy (plus subgroup, for example: Quakers)

Family History — General Resources

Genealogists use resources ranging from biographies and public records to photographic archives and military histories. They also circulate information in a variety of ways: in journals and newsletters, on personal home pages, and through history centers, to name a few. Many such resources are listed at the following sites.

Cyndi's List of Genealogy Sites on the Internet

www.oz.net/~cyndihow/sites.htm

Genealogy supersite: This megalist of genealogical sites — with more than 21,000 links — includes such categories as Adoption, Biographies, Census, Family Bibles, and Historical Events & People. The listings by country are often divided into regions for easier searching. This site contains a huge amount of fascinating genealogical information, so allow plenty of time to explore.

The Genealogy Home Page

www.genhomepage.com

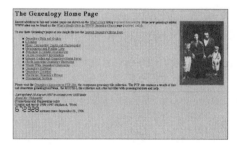

Genealogy resources and events: Libraries, societies, Internet pages, maps, software, and upcoming genealogical events are a few of the aids you can find here. Don't miss the comprehensive list of genealogical newsgroups and mailing lists. To see what makes this page stand out from the rest, visit the What's New link where you'll find goodies such as "Suite 101," a Web guide with a biweekly Genealogy Column, and "Family Dimensions" for information on scanning photographs and documents onto compact discs, as well as special family projects.

Genealogy Toolbox

genealogy.tbox.com

The new genealogists' guide to the World Wide Web: Three sections of this site are guaranteed to get your family history off to a good start: Genealogy White Pages, lists of genealogical links broken down by surname; Genealogy Yellow Pages,

genealogical links by subject, including general references, beginner guides, and commercial resources; and the Genealogy Atlas, international genealogical links by geographical area. You also can find the Journal of Online Genealogy, a history of the site with frequently asked questions, and a What's New section highlighting the newest genealogy sites on the Web.

The Mayflower Society

media3.com/plymouth/ROOTS

Exploring Pilgrim history: Members of the Mayflower Society trace their ancestry back to the pilgrim fathers who sailed from Plymouth, England, in 1620 and established the first permanent colony in New England. In addition to information about the society, this page has sections on the Native American Wampanoag tribes and Pilgrim history. You can also check out links to the Pilgrim Hall Museum, with its many Pilgrim artifacts, and the Plymouth Public Library's Plymouth Collection, a nationally recognized genealogical source, with more than 1,200 items (letters, birth and death records, military records) related to immigrants from the 17th through the 20th centuries.

National Genealogy Organization (US)

www.genealogy.org/~ngs

American resources: This home page includes tips for beginning genealogists and a fantastic bibliography for kids ages 12 to 15 (see the Youth Resources section). You can also take a home-study course, enter a contest in Family History Writing, or simply learn about American genealogy. Numerous links, including

George Archer's NetGuide: Genealogist's Guide to Internet (www.genealogy.org/~ngs/netguide/) and a list of national, regional, and ethnic societies, make it an excellent starting place for people studying American genealogy.

World Genweb Project

www.dsenter.com/worldgenweb

International resources: At Genweb, more than 240 International servers (networks of related Web sites) and individual pages are listed alphabetically by country, from Afghanistan through Zimbabwe. More than one-fourth of these sites have volunteer guides to answer general genealogical queries.

Other Stuff to Check Out

Web sites

pibweb.it.nwu.edu/pib/genealo.htm
www.rootsweb.com
www2.kbyu.byu.edu/ancestors
www.dcs.hull.ac.uk/public/genealogy/gedcom.html
world.std.com/~sheal/sutton/armsbycem.html
www.genealogy.org/~ngs/netguide/
www.geocities.com/Heartland/Plains/5100/

Mailing lists

ROOTS-L-request@rootsweb.com
emigration-ships@northwest.com
gen-newbie-l@rootsweb.com
cemetery-l@rootsweb.com

Newsgroups

alt.scottish.clans
soc.roots
soc.genealogy.misc

Suggested search-engine keywords

Yahoo: genealogy, family history, clans, roots
Lycos: genealogy, family history, clans, roots

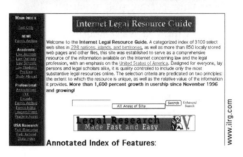

Finances, Law, and Real Estate

Annotated Index of Features:

Running a family's finances is a lot like running a small business. You must know how to budget correctly, plan for the future, and earn and spend wisely. Here are some sites that cover areas of concern to families — from wills and real estate sales to buying the right insurance at the right price and paying taxes.

Consumer Reports' Auto Insurance Price Service

www.consumerinsure.org/

 $

Compare auto insurance prices: Prices for the same car insurance varies by company from hundreds to thousands of dollars. This service finds the least expensive policy for you from among some 70 offerings. You get a personalized report showing as many as 25 of the lowest-priced policies, plus cost-saving tips, a guide to insurance, and Consumer Reports' ratings based on *Consumer Reports* magazine reader surveys. Reports are faxed or mailed the same day. View a sample and then fill out the form online, providing the year, make, and model of each vehicle that you want to insure; the driver's (or drivers') age, sex, and marital status; driving records of all drivers

166 Finances, Law, and Real Estate

(including violations and traffic accidents in the past five years); vehicle use (personal, commuting, business); annual mileage; address and Zip code where the vehicle(s) park; and the amount of insurance you want. You're best off having your current policy handy. The site requires a nominal charge for this service, which varies depending on how many cars you seek insurance for.

Counsel Quest

**home.earthlink.net/~parajuris/
   CounselQuest/**

List of resources for law students and lawyers: Billed as "A Premier Internet Legal Resource Locator," this site can be used to link to law libraries and law schools, or search law review articles. Law schools and related resources are listed with hypertext titles that you click to go to the actual site. For example, under American University (Washington College), you will find links for basic information, the university's home page, the law school, the law review, and three law journals (Gender and the Law, Human Rights Brief, International Law and Policy). This site is a very long but well-organized scroll list.

Essential Links to Taxes

www.EL.com/elinks/taxes/

Tax information: Link to resources covering the preparation of income-tax returns, tax rules, tax codes, finding financial planners and forms (from W-2s to Form 1040), publications, instructions, deductions, and filings. Links to major government tax sites (such as the IRS), consumer assistance sites (for example, The Tax Prophet, Tax Wizard, and Taxing

Times), and basic tax information sites (including Tax Law and Tax World). Get forms and information about various state taxes, international taxes, and the federal tax code. And if that isn't taxing enough, the site also offers tax tips, tax newsletters, tax analysts, tax software, links to commercial tax sites, tax discussion groups, and online directories of even more tax sites.

FindLaw: Legal Subject Index

www.findlaw.com/01topics/index.html

Find legal documents and aids: Link to sites organized into categories that include Administrative Law, Antitrust & Trade Regulation, Banking Law, Bankruptcy Law, Civil Rights, Commercial Law, Communications Law, Constitutional Law, Contracts, Corporation & Enterprise Law, Criminal Law, Cyberspace Law, Dispute Resolution & Arbitration, Education Law, Entertainment & Sports Law, Environmental Law, Ethics & Professional Responsibility, and Family Law. Or search for a particular topic; under *wills,* for example, you find information on Wills, Trusts, Estates, and so forth.

Intelligent Investor Directory

**www.intelligent-investor.com/
   directory.html**

List of links to investing: This portion of a larger site offers links and summaries to a wealth of financial investment organizations, businesses, publications, and experts (some of which are commercial and require fees). Find IPO updates; investment discussions; current rates for mortgages, consumer loans, savings, and credit cards from thousands of banks; a consumer banking library; software; trading advice; stock recommendations; brokers; up-to-the-minute stock and financial news sources; information and data about index options; market statistics; forecasts; company profiles; and corporate annual reports. Link back to the main home page (click the words *Intelligent Investor* at the bottom of the scroll-down directory list) for an even more amazing array of market reports, resources, summaries, publications, and expert advice.

Internet Legal Resource Guide

www.ilrg.com

Categorized index of 3,100 law-related Internet sites: Choose from among thousands of national and international law sites to find selected sites that cover all kinds of legal subjects, including family law, estate planning, and taxes. Strictly quality controlled, site selection is based on uniqueness and quality of content. Find legal references, associations, firms, continuing education, expert witnesses and consultants, law journals and other publications, legal forms, government resources, law schools (and rankings), lawyers, law firms, legal directories and search engines, newsgroups, and articles. You can also search for specific topics. A search of the word *wills,* for example, produced will and estate forms, courses, advice columns, news sources, firms specializing in estate planning, and even the wills of some famous people (for example, Jacqueline Kennedy Onassis, Richard Nixon, John Lennon, Elvis Presley, and Walt Disney). *Note:* The site may be somewhat slow in loading because of its voluminous content.

Kids' Money

pages.prodigy.com/K/I/Y/kidsmoney/
    index.htm

Activities to teach kids monetary responsibility: This site includes a free mailing list for kids, surveys, polls, and opportunities for kids and parents to talk about money, save it, and spend it wisely. Topics covered include allowances (how much, should they be tied to chores, should some money be saved each week), wise money principles to teach kids, developing money management skills, and communicating beliefs and values about money. You can find links to articles by noted authors on these and other subjects related to kids and money.

Laborlink

laborlink.simplenet.com

Gateway to sites about labor: Although it can be slow-loading, this site is packed with links, articles, quotes, and resources related to organized labor, workers' rights, employment law, labor relations, workplace issues, employee organizations, labor news and legislation, and other topics of interest to both organized and independent workers. Link to the section on law, for example, and you find links to such sites as the National Employment Lawyers Association, the Employment & Labor Law News, the Labor and Employment Law Update, the Labor and Employment Bulletin, the Workplace Update, the Unfair Labor Practice Bulletin, the Lawcopedia, and references for employment news, employment and benefits laws, Workers Compensation decisions, and disability laws.

168 Finances, Law, and Real Estate

National Association of Realtors

www.realtor.com

Find a home anywhere: This large real-estate site features more than a million properties that you can view by using a variety of search techniques, including searches by location, size, and price range. In addition to exploring the national housing market, you can get professional assistance related to moving, financing, and finding a realtor through sections such as Find a Home, Movers Toolkit, Real Estate News, Home Ownership Tips, Mortgage Information, and Realtor Associations.

National Fraud Information Center

www.fraud.org

If something seems too good to be true, check it out here first: This frames-based site keeps track of all kinds of fraud, especially in telemarketing, on the Internet, and against the elderly. Read the latest reports and news on investigations, link to supportive agencies and investigative authorities, and find out how to report suspected fraud if you're suspicious of an offer you've heard about on the phone, received in the mail, or seen on the Internet. This site is sponsored by

the National Consumers League, a nonprofit organization that acts as an advocate for consumer protection. Don't spend any money if you have any doubts. Visit here first.

Nonprofit Information Gallery

www.infogallery.com

Online directory for nonprofits: Whether you run a nonprofit, serve on a board, or just want to help your favorite community charity find funds, this site offers lots of information on grants, budgeting, management, and other pertinent topics. Find links to resources dealing with human resources, project management, event planning, legal issues, property management, accounting, auditing, financial reporting, sample forms, taxes, grants, and funding (as in planning for, applying for, researching, and finding sources). You can also search 13 search engines at once for even more leads and link to nonprofit support organizations and companies. This site is a frames-based site.

Online Financial Publications

www.csn.net/natcorp/publish.html

Brought to you by National Corporate Services, Inc.: Part of a larger site, this section is an outstanding list of links to online financial newsletters, magazines, and other publications, as well as data resources. As part of this company's mission to be a world leader in providing convenient, free access to important investment resources on the Internet, this service links you to such diverse sources as the National Investor Relations Institute (NIRI), NETworth (with a large number of newsletters and services), Wall Street Online, and lots of individual magazine sites (for example, Research

Magazine, Business Week, Financial World, The Economist, Entrepreneur, Reuters MoneyNetwork, and PennyStocks).

Quotesmith

www.quotesmith.com

Insurance price-comparison service: Save time and trouble by using this service, which provides access to quotes on life insurance, Medicare supplement policies, and fixed annuity rates currently offered by some 300 companies. Get detailed policy-coverage information and safety ratings from a number of independent rating services before you decide what to buy. After you evaluate your choices, you can apply to the company of your choosing online.

Small Business Administration

www.sba.gov/textonly/

www.sba.gov/

Government agency charged with assisting entrepreneurs: The SBA has offices in every state that offer financing, training, and advocacy for small firms. Find out through this site about services located in your area and about how the SBA works with thousands of lending, educational, and training institutions nationally. If you're contemplating starting your own small business or if you own an independent business that's not dominant within its field and falls within SBA size standards, you could find a program here to assist you. Sections include a bulletin board, Disaster Assistance, Information in Spanish, Special Interests, Starting Your Business, Financing Your Business, and Expanding Your Business. Link to related business and governmental sites.

Tax and Accounting Sites Directory

www.taxsites.com

Links to accounting and tax sites on the Internet: This well-organized directory categorizes sites into three areas. Under Tax Sites, you will find Federal Tax Law, State Taxes, International Tax, Tax Forms, Tax Help & Tips, Tax Updates, Tax Discussions, Tax Articles, IRS, Policy Groups, and Miscellaneous. Accounting Sites, has sections for Financial, Auditing & Fraud, Managerial, Governmental, Accounting News, Certification, AICPA, and more. Combined Tax & Accounting Sites include Academia, Organizations, Publishers & CPE, Software, Firms & Employment, Databases, Government, General Law, Financial Markets, and Other Directories. Click Financial Accounting & Reporting, for example, and you get links to certified accountants, governmental agencies, public companies with financial information, and related press releases.

Tripod

www.tripod.com

Internet neighborhood of friends: In the old days, neighbors would sit out at night on their front porches and talk about work, life, and family. This site is the cyber-version of this almost-lost tradition, with its conferencing system that enables Tripod's staff and contributors to discuss such topics with Tripod members. Other features for talking about smart life strategies include daily updated interactive columns, essays, reviews, interviews, editorials, and interactive services (such as the Resume Builder, the Budget Calculator, and the Leisure Quiz). Tripod, Inc., also publishes a print

170 Finances, Law, and Real Estate

magazine for college students, *Tools for Life,* which offers similar content for that age group. Basic online membership is free.

Other Stuff to Check Out

Web sites
www.altestate.com/index.phtml
www.blackenterprise.com
www.ethosmag.com
www.hispanstar.com
www.mbemag.com
www.ftc.gov/
www.barrons.com
www.businessweek.com
www.economist.com
www.financialworld.com
www.forbes.com
www.pathfinder.com/fortune/
www.pathfinder.com/money/
www.talks.com
www.herring.com
www.dowjones.com/smart/
www.worth.com
www.bloomberg.com

Newsgroups
alt.business
clari.biz.*@
clari.biz.economy
clari.biz.economy.world
clari.nb.*@
clari.tw.*@
home.earthlink.net/~parajuris/
    CounselQuest/usenet.htm
misc.taxes
misc.taxes Archive
misc.taxes.moderated

Chat areas
www.thelawoffice.com/chat/chat.htm
www.AllLaw.com/LawChat.html

Online service area
America Online: PERSONAL FINANCE

Suggested search-engine keywords
Yahoo!: Finance and Investment, Business
    and Economy
Thomas Register (entire search engine is
    devoted to business and products)

Health Care

geocities.com/HotSprings/1505/guide.html

A GUIDE TO
MEDICAL INFORMATION AND SUPPORT
ON THE INTERNET

[MEDICAL CHATS] [NEWSGROUPS] [LISTSERVS]

[ONLINE DOCTORS] [MEDLINE] [MEDICAL LINKS]

INTRODUCTION

This guide is primarily written for people new to the internet and computers. I have tried to provide basic technical directions for using the internet to access medical information and support groups. If you have any suggestions or questions, or need help locating information please feel free to e-mail me .

☐ 🆕This site now has its own Bulletin Board Forum and a Real Time Chatroom called Health Chat. For information on how to use the chatroom

Some of the most affecting issues of family life deal with mind, body, and spirit. This section provides sites that will help keep your family healthy. You can use these sites to identify symptoms, locate clinicians, try herbal remedies, deal with family emergencies, analyze nutrition, and get to know that miraculous machine known as the human body.

Children and Family Life

The sites here offer help with child-care issues, and with advice and support for the family with a child or children. Here you can find information about child care and about all kinds of families, including the blended family (in which children from both sides of the marriage now find themselves living together), the adoptive family, and the foster family.

Adopt

www.adopting.org/

Resources to help before and after an adoption: Here's an incredible array of resources, all well organized, ranging from finding and adopting a child to helping your adopted child adapt. You can find workshops on dealing with separation and bonding, publications on surrogates and agencies, local and global links to adoption services, and adoption support services. Read personal accounts of adoption from kids and adults and connect with other adoptive families online.

Adoption Links Page

home.ptd.net/~jgbur/

Lots of resources on adoption: Opening to the happy strains of "Twinkle, Twinkle Little Star" (for browsers that support this function), this site offers lots of links to international and American adoption agencies. Various sections cover interracial and special needs adoptions, medical issues, counseling, tax and legal matters, and foster care.

Childcare-directory.com

www.childcare-directory.com

Guide to finding quality child care: This commercial directory compiles daycare resources for both providers and consumers. Find products, services, advertisements, and advice related to running or using a daycare facility. Chat and forum sections discuss daycare-related topics, and a guide to daycare facilities is organized by state. Click a state and get names and phone numbers of daycare providers there; note that no assessments are offered related to quality. For childcare providers (in-home care, daycare centers, Nannies, Au Pairs) or would-be providers, the site offers information about professional classes, training, and workshops. Link to child-care- and child-safety-related sites. This site is still developing, so you may find some geographical gaps in provider information.

Foster Family Web

www.designport.com/fosterweb/

Support for foster families: Commune with other foster parents and kids through the mailing list and Foster Web features. Read stories about and from foster kids, answers to foster kids' questions about being in foster care, and a parent's page offering guidance and support. The Foster Family Resources Page has state-by-state listings of foster/adoptive government agencies including telephone numbers.

Foster Parent Community

www.westworld.com/~barbara/

Wide array of online resources: Foster parents appreciate all the articles, newsgroups, message boards, chat groups, publications, contacts, links, and mailing list connections here. This site gives foster parents direct access to other foster parents and the support they need.

Organizations Serving Child Care and Related Professions

ericps.ed.uiuc.edu/nccic/orgs/ orglist.html

Brought to you by the National Child Care Information Center: If you're contemplating daycare for your child but want to know more about evaluating quality, safety, and other issues, this site gives you an extensive list of agencies and organizations, along with descriptions and contact information (including site links if available). Among organizations listed here are the Child Care Institute of America, the Child Care Law Center, the Children's Defense Fund, the Ecumenical Child Care Network, the Families and Work Institute, the National Association of Child Care Professionals, the National Head Start Association, the National Indian Child Care Association, and the Interagency Task Force on Child Abuse and Neglect Clearinghouse.

ParentTime

pathfinder.com/@@vp8bqwqa7mzrovtd/ ParentTime/Welcome/welcome.html

Online magazine for parents: Get advice, talk to other parents, and stay current on all kinds of parenting issues, including blending children from separate families, single parenting, and adoption. This subscriber-based online magazine draws its contents from a number of experts and publications, and it features live chats and polls on all kinds of daily issues affecting families. Note that the site uses frames, so browsers that don't support frames may have trouble viewing it.

Stay-at-Home Parents

homeparents.miningco.com

Frequently updated resource: This attractive, informative site gives parents practical and personal assistance with issues surrounding the choice to stay home with the kids and maybe try to work at home, too. Many issues are intelligently addressed here through links to articles and discussions. Living on one income, juggling kids and work at home, finding balance as a couple, and staying happy as a family are among the topics that this site covers. Link to related sites and gather tips from the Moms, the Parenting, and the For Your Kids sections. You also find a section on the home-based business, which looks at time management, creating and marketing your home business, sorting legitimate business opportunities from scams, and getting ideas for needed services (such as home daycare and tutoring). The site has an online bookstore, too, and you can sign up for a free newsletter.

Other Stuff to Check Out

Web sites
> www.childcare-experts.org/
> child.cornell.edu/

Suggested search-engine keywords
> Yahoo!: Parenting; Child Care
> LookSmart: Parenting

General Information

Use these mega-linking sites and you have thousands of sources for physical, mental, and emotional health. But don't get overwhelmed. All these indexes are well organized and easy to use. As you surf these, bookmark the sites within these sites that seem most relevant to your family's needs. Then you'll have them handy next time someone sneezes, falls down, or gets a tummy ache.

Guide To Medical Information and Support on the Internet

geocities.com/HotSprings/1505/
  guide.html

Medical resources, support, and links to doctors: Connect with chats, newsgroups, mailing lists, doctors, and specialized medical sites. This site is geared to people new to the Net and provides clear technical directions that help you access medical information and support groups. Get caring guidance to help you find and use search engines, chats, and newsgroups effectively. Newsgroups cover such interests as alternative health, arthritis, migraines, cardiology, skin diseases, and chronic fatigue syndrome. Anyone wishing to fully understand how to utilize the Internet's medical resources should visit this site. This site has its own Bulletin Board Forum and a Real Time Chatroom called Health Chat to get you started.

HealthAtoZ

www.HealthAtoZ.com

Search engine for health and medical topics: Want to know just what that prescription is doing for you? Scared that your age spots are really skin cancer? Are the beginning signs of Alzheimer's Syndrome creeping up on someone you know? Then this site just may answer your questions. With the broad listing of general categories that have more specific Web sites listed in their links, you can find information about most any ailment or health-related issue. Use the listing provided to find information specific to your concern, or do your own search using the search box. Find more than 300 newsgroups and thousands of sites on physical and mental medically-oriented topics. This is an extremely usable, thorough, and efficient resource.

Health Explorer

www.healthexplorer.com

Find health information on the Internet: Offering an internal search box so you can type in your specific need, this site also alphabetically categorizes links from Aging to Women's Health. It provides informative site reviews and convenient links to primary research and care institutions such as the American Medical Association, Red Cross, Centers for Disease Control and Prevention, National Institutes of Health, and American Dental Association. Because the site has been designed so well, it is a snap to use.

healthfinder

www.healthfinder.gov/

Sponsored by the U.S. Department of Health and Human Services: This consumer health and human services Web directory offers selected online publications, clearinghouses, databases, Web sites, support and self-help groups, health-oriented government agencies, organizations, frequently asked questions (FAQs), chat groups, and medical libraries. Especially notable are the health "tours" which focus on specific topics and bundle related resources together. Tour subjects include AIDS, allergies, breast cancer and other cancers, diabetes, environmental health, food and drug safety, heart disease and stroke, mental health and disorders, and substance abuse. Find specialty areas geared to age, gender, and racial or ethnic status.

Other Stuff to Check Out

Web sites
> www.yahoo.com/headlines/health/
> www.hirs.com/constemp.html
> www.4healthinfo.com
> www.health-library.com
> www.medguide.net/
> www.xs4all.nl/~kyjoshi/
> www.geocities.com/CapeCanaveral/Lab/
> 1775/

Newsgroup
> views.vcu.edu/views/fap/ng.html

Mailing list
> emailhost.ait.ac.th/Search/pubmail-
> subj.html#health

Chat areas
> pages.wbs.net/
> webchat3.so?cmd=cmd_doorway:Medical_Chat
> www.docsonline.com

Online service areas
> America Online: HEALTH & FITNESS
> CompuServe: GO HLTDB

Suggested search-engine keywords
> Yahoo!: Health
> Infoseek: Health

Health-Related Publications Online

You can find a number of health-related magazines, books, and newsletters that are either completely online or have both online and print versions. The sites tell you how to subscribe to the print magazines or buy the books, and you can enjoy features created just for the Internet at all these sites.

Balance Fitness on the net

balance.net/

Fitness and exercise: Explore sports physiology, therapy and medicine, and sports-oriented nutrition, as well as participate in an interactive forum. Check out a registry of international personal trainers and use an internal search engine that lets you track down topics of special interest related to getting and staying in shape. (Be sure to read the online detailed explanation for best search results.) To receive automatic updates on the latest issues (published on the 14th of every month), register your e-mail address. You can also shop the bookstore for best-selling titles related to sports, health, and fitness.

Couples Adventure

www.couples-place.com

Semimonthly interactive newsletter for committed couples: Explore skill training, support systems, publications, discussion forums, and guides to building stronger, more communicative relationships. Click What's Here to learn about the Subscribers Only program, or visit the free nonsubscriber features at the site. This site is graphic intensive, but you can speed page loading by turning off the graphics (the site explains how). Participate in polls and visit selected sites. Try relationship quizzes, role playing, and personality-assessment questionnaires. Couples Adventure is not a therapy site but a skills-based site where couples can have some fun, get encouragement, and share in a confidential learning community to discuss topics openly and benefit from each other's experiences. This site is for adults.

Delicious!

www.newhope.com/magazines/
   delicious/default.html

Magazine of natural living: Get the latest on organic foods, vegetarian meals, herbs and vitamins, women's health issues, and homeopathy. Enjoy original articles and links to natural-product retailers. The purpose of this searchable site is to inspire families to take charge of their health and well-being. Benefit from the latest medical and scientific research and breakthroughs presented in a clear, easy-to-understand way. Discover ways to make positive changes in your lifestyle, in part through the foods you eat and the products you use. Get advice from natural-health experts and link to related sites.

FitnessLink

www.fitnesslink.com

Health and fitness news magazine: Get resources, tips, and assistance whether you're a veteran fitness enthusiast or you're just starting out to improve your health. This site offers original articles ("Eating for Energy," "Richard Simmons: The Pied Piper of Fitness"); tips; listings of books, magazines, newsgroups, and mailing lists; and interactive bulletin boards to find a fitness friend or get your questions answered. Link to related fitness, nutrition, and lifestyle sites.

Answer monthly opinion polls, talk fitness on the interactive bulletin board, share fitness success stories, and sign up for the free newsletter. This site is searchable, so you can track down topics of special interest.

Health Direct

www.healthdirect.com

Health information for the next century: Find current consumer health news and information on drugs, diseases, and common conditions. Follow a checklist of prevalent diseases and symptoms, use the help hot lines, and get a consumer guide to better health care. The mission of this site is to increase people's awareness on health issues and to assist them in becoming better-informed advocates for themselves in all matters of health care. Read up on new drugs, biotechnology, medical-care proposals, and legislation. Sections include Health News, Health Care, Health Check, and Health Direct.

HealthLine

www.health-line.com

Articles written by professionals: Explore health, nutrition, fitness, and personal relationships and growth with forums, discussions, and articles written by medical doctors and scientists from leading medical schools. Healthline provides high-quality, accurate, up-to-date health information with original material from health care professionals. Since 1980, Healthline has published a newsletter, various magazines, and textbooks; many of these health resources are now available online through this site. Topics include food safety, skin care, allergies and asthma, and immunology. Among the professional associations

represented here are the American Academy of Allergy, Asthma & Immunology; American College of Allergy, Asthma & Immunology; and American Academy of Dermatology.

Healthy & Natural Journal Online

www.healthyandnatural.com/ index.html/

Online version of *Healthy & Natural Journal:* This frames-based, searchable site covers natural health and offers the latest news about supplements, herbal products, natural cosmetics, body care, business opportunities, sights, sounds, books, and education. Get up-to-date developments in natural health, natural/ organic foods, consumer activism, and the environment. Read case histories describing natural healing and alternative medicine use, as well as columns by health and fitness writers. The Buyers Guide covers products and services for natural health and food products and related environmental industries. Examine back issues, find out how to subscribe to the print journal, and participate in polls and forums.

Healthy Weight Publishing Network

www.healthyweightnetwork.com

Books and articles related to dieting and weight issues: Find out about publications, research, news, and opinions related to eating and weight issues. Special attention is paid to detecting fad, fake, or dangerous diets and to helping kids eat right, develop positive self-images, and avoid (or deal with) eating disorders. Click the red-thumbtack icons to get to articles and book reviews.

Typical subjects include examining teens' attitudes about food, defining normal eating habits, dealing with dieting myths, and establishing a realistic and healthy weight and eating habits.

Idea Central: Health Policy Page

epn.org/idea/health.html

The politics behind medical care: Through articles and reports, this site examines the politics, players, and controversies surrounding health insurance, Medicare, Medicaid, managed care, the future of hospitals and medical practice, public health, bioethics, and new technology. From standards for Managed Care and impacts of proposed health legislation (such as the Child Health Block Grant) to physician and customer satisfaction, articles cover a variety of health-news-oriented subjects. Read previous issues, click health-policy-related links, and check out reviews of books and online resources. Sections include Health Policy, Welfare & Families, Civic Participation, and Economics & Politics.

The Informed Parent

www.informedparent.com

Child-care magazine with monthly features and columns: This easy-to-comprehend and easy-to-navigate site does parents a service by reviewing and interpreting leading pediatric journals (such as the *Journal of Pediatrics*) and sharing their findings with parents and the interested public. You can also find articles and columns written by medical professionals and covering such topics as

getting your infant to sleep, dealing with potty training, and understanding many other developmental, health, and behavioral issues related to children. See past issues and provide your input.

LifeMatters

lifematters.com

Conversations and articles about life: Enjoy engaging forums, interviews, and discussions regarding the quest for well-being. Sections include CommunityMatters, HealthMatters, FitnessMatters, NutritionMatters, RelatingMatters, and ParentingMatters. Click a forum, read related articles, and find out about subscribing. Each section has many subjects for you to explore. In RelatingMatters, for example, topics include such things as giving birth to a dream, understanding shame, and facing mid-life. In HealthMatters, you can find out about holistic health approaches, talk to a doctor, read the history and practice of Jin Shin Jyustu, or tackle the problem of headaches. Shop for health products and services through the online catalog or assist a nonprofit organization with its wish list. Much is happening here at this creative site, where you can talk with homeopaths, doctors, fitness trainers, and nutritionists.

Living Well Today

www.living-well-today.com

Bimonthly health journal: Get tips on balancing health, work, and family at this lifestyle-exploring site that features articles about health, money, family relationships, child development and behaviors, exercise, and

178 Health Care

self-improvement. Sections include Kids Korner (discussing health and emotional matters of importance to the young), BodyWorks, Balancing Life, Being Your Best, Travel & Leisure, For Women Only, the Plus Years, and Men's World. Find out about subscribing to the print publication and listening to the radio show if you live near Jacksonville, Florida. This site is not terribly sophisticated in terms of its use of the Internet medium, but the articles are well written and useful.

Magic Stream Journal

fly.hiwaay.net/~garson/

Guide to emotional wellness: This frames or no-frames site is devoted to self-help and mental health. Find lots of references to mental health professionals and support resources, as well as information for consumers, family members, and individuals seeking assistance with personal growth or problems. The site's philosophy is "to do what we can to take care of our self, make ourself stronger, accept our self as we are, and seek help when it is needed." Explore a self-help discussion group, articles ("From Pieces to Peace," "A Natural Mood Booster," "Staying Motivated"), inspiring poetry, mental-health surveys, immediate access to counselors (fee required), and links organized by categories such as Addictions, Aging, Autism, Books, Child Abuse, Children, Cults, Death & Grief, Depression, Disabilities, Disaster, Dissociation, Divorce, Domestic Violence, Eating Disorders, Men's Issues, Spirituality, Stress, Women, Support, and Family. This site is for parents for themselves or to use with children; it's not recommended for kids to visit alone.

A Man's Life

www.manslife.com

Exploring health and wealth: Topics of this magazine include male-oriented news; family views; sports; business and finances; fitness and food; relationships with women, bosses, and coworkers; and tips for looking and feeling good. Lively articles ("Perils of Prostate Prediction!" "'Cures' for bad diagnoses!" "Dr. Bob Arnot!" "The Art of the Cheap Date!") plus regular features on subjects such as fashion styles, cars, and home repairs make this site informative and comfortable for men. Check out interviews with celebrity dads and read about dressing to look your best, eating to stay fit, troubleshooting your budget and career, and keeping things happy on the home front. Participate in interactive forums all about guy stuff with other guys. This site is appropriate for mature teenage boys (with parental approval and oversight, of course).

Med-Brief

www.incinc.net/med.html

 $

Daily summary of major medical research and news: Taken from medical journals, news wires, and press releases, the content of this site is geared toward medical professionals but will interest serious health care consumers and concerned, aware patients. Sample a free newsletter subscription. The subscription service comes to you via e-mail and is compiled in coordination with an advisory panel of physicians. Every edition covers breaking news in medical research.

Medicinal Food News

www.medicinalfoodnews.com/

www.medicinalfoodnews.com/
  noframe.htm

News and information on healthy foods and food components: Find out the relationship between what you eat and how you feel by reading about such things as good basic foods, probiotics (friendly bacteria), nutraceutics, healthy foods from other lands, special properties in certain foods and beverages (such as grapefruit and tea), vitamins and antioxidants, and the way certain foods are produced (yogurt for example). What cooking oils are a good source of vitamin E? What's a Fructooligosaccharide? Why may older women need more zinc? These are some of the topics this site explores. Be sure to visit the glossary of terms, which defines such words as *carotene, fiber, kefir, lecithin, oligosaccharide,* and *pH.* You can also post a question to an expert in the Question and Answer section and check out a calendar of events, links to related sites, and book reviews. (Note that the first URL for this site uses frames and the last URL is for a frame-free version of the site.)

Men's Fitness

www.mensfitness.com

Guide to fitness and health: This online version of the print magazine is definitely for adult men only and deals with everything from workouts and muscle strains to sex and sports. Sections include training, fitness, health, nutrition, sports and sports gear, behavior, and sex. Review current and past issues, take quizzes, talk about manly stuff with other men, and see images of guys who are young and in great shape, which will

prove either inspiring or depressing. Link to related sites. Through the Men's Fitness Interactive Forum, you can offer input related to diet or training. And because this site discusses sex (did I say that already?), parental supervision should be exercised.

Men's Health

www.menshealth.com

About guys: All kinds of topics are tackled here, from training with weights and finding a personal trainer to eating right and staying healthy — physically, mentally, and sexually. This site is for dads, not kids. Find nutritional information, easy recipes, and tips on how to order the right kinds of healthy foods when you eat out in restaurants. Ask health-related questions or sex-related questions of the "Sex Doc." From birth control to back hair, you'll find no-nonsense topics of interest to men.

Perspectives

www.cmhc.com/perspectives/

Online mental health magazine: Read current and archived issues, visit the forum, check out book reviews, and consider editorials at this site, which examines issues related to mental and emotional health (child maltreatment and its later impact, the basis of creativity, and so on). Although many of the topics are written by mental-health professionals, one columnist is a Dear Abby type who is not a professional psychologist or therapist but is billed as a "mentor or friend." Feature articles look at current events (the impact of Princess Diana's death) and personal issues (anxiety and panic attacks). Content is geared toward an adult audience.

180 Health Care

Prevention's Healthy Ideas

www.healthyideas.com

From the publishers of *Prevention Magazine:* This online version features tips on natural living (for example, homeopathy), weight loss, fitness and exercise, healthy cooking, family health matters, and vitamins and good nutrition (such as ten delicious tips to save your life). Share your success stories and read about the success of others, subscribe to the newsletter, and search for health-related articles on specific topics of interest to you.

Self-Help & Psychology Magazine

www.cybertowers.com/selfhelp/

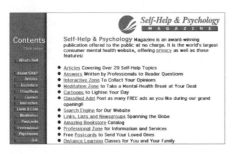

Short articles and practical suggestions for improving and maintaining emotional and mental health: From sports psychology to depression, this site provides guidance and connections to therapy professionals. Articles cover more than 20 self-help topics. You can also find interactive forums, publication reviews, a bookstore, links to related sites, and humor (laughter is healing, too). This free online consumer-oriented publication also features therapist columns and an ask-the-experts section, meditation techniques, and related links, mailing lists, and newsgroups where you can find support and kinship. Shop for therapy-related self-help books and products. Find out about online workshops and subscribe to the free consumer newsletter.

Stanford HealthLink

healthlink.stanford.edu/

Leading medical center's outreach site: Presented by Stanford Health Services and the Stanford University Medical Center News Bureau, this online newsletter reports on current medical research and offers lots of information related to maintaining good health and getting good medical care. Get health tips and health-related links. Search the Stanford Health Library, read patient-information documents, and use the Stanford MedNET Search Facility to query for your area of medical interest.

Today's Caregiver

www.caregiver.com

Dedicated to people caring for ill loved ones: If you or someone you know is caring for a family member with AIDS, Alzheimer's, cancer, or another life-threatening or debilitating condition, this online magazine offers a support network, comfort, and advice. Read interviews with and about other caregivers (a recent interview was with actor Robert Urich, who described how he and his family tackled his cancer). Read the caregiver Bill of Rights for strength and assurance and find out about coping techniques such as meditation and support groups. The resource directory contains toll-free phone numbers to many organizations providing assistance (American Council for the Blind, American Diabetes Association, American Kidney Fund, American Cancer Society, Cystic Fibrosis Foundation, Disability Information & Referral Service, and so on). Participate in surveys and chat with other caregivers. Buy and sell medical items, services, or equipment through the classifieds section.

Trim

www.trimline.com

Health, fitness, and dieting magazine: Get advice from experts about effective training techniques and discipline, find out about fitness-oriented vacations and outdoor adventures, and benefit from tasty recipes that are low in fat and calories. Read celebrity fitness profiles, check out various workout plans, and see how to diet effectively and intelligently.

Vibrant Life Magazine

www.vibrantlife.com/vibrantlife/ index.html

Combining a healthy lifestyle with a practical Christian perspective: Living life in harmony and balance is a central focus of this online magazine, which examines topics such as exercising and controlling weight in both kids and adults; managing addictive habits and behaviors; creating good mental, emotional, and spiritual attitudes; and showing kids how to become positive adults. From allergies to back pain, find out how your body does (and doesn't) work and how to stay

healthy or get healthier. Get better nutrition and more energy and find taste-tempting, heart-healthy recipes. This magazine emphasizes the importance of a connection between good health, happy living, and faith in God. Find out how to subscribe to the print edition, which publishes every other month, and link to health-related sites (National Center for Health Promotion, Loma Linda Medical Center, American Diabetes Association, National Foundation for Depressive Illness, National Council on Alcoholism and Drug Dependence, and so on).

VisionTimes

www.visiontimes.com/pub/public.htm

Understanding proper eye care and the needs of vision-impaired people: This concise, easy-to-use site serves as a primer to proper eye care in the interest of preserving vision and facilitating communication among the vision-impaired, eye-care professionals, and the general public. Find out about vision-related events, facts and myths about the eyes and vision health, the basics of good eye care, and eye terminology (just in case you don't know endophthalmitis from an enophthalmos). Read about famous and aspiring celebrities and athletes with visual impairments. You can also find a section devoted to vision-impairment symptoms in children and adults (such as cataracts, retinopathy, glaucoma, and macular degeneration).

webROUNDS

www.wwilkins.com/rounds/intro.html

Interactive medical journal written by medical students, professionals, interns, and residents: Go behind and inside the world of medicine with this site, which gives you an inside perspective on training for and practicing medicine today. Designed primarily for medical and osteopathic medical students, residents, physician-assistant students, and other health professionals, this site is nonetheless quite enlightening for a lay audience as well. With educational and entertaining content created by medical-school professors, practitioners, medical students, residents, and textbook authors, it shows you what a career in medicine is really all about in today's health-care environment. Needless to say, some of the procedural content may be too graphic or technical for kids.

World of Vitality

www.vitality.com

Diet, fitness, and self-care: Visit chat rooms and forums to discuss losing weight or kicking the smoking habit. Shop online for discounted fitness products and read about how improving health and wellness can be fun. Among the sections are special areas for men and for women, as well as online library selections to help with self-improvement. Typical subjects include lowering cholesterol, reducing stress, sleeping well, walking for fitness, designing workstation comfort, helping an aching back with time-tested daily stretches, beginning an exercise program, managing allergies, lowering healthcare costs, and living with arthritis, headaches, or high blood pressure. The Health

Resources Index provides contact phone numbers for assistance with various health situations. Another section examines AIDS and related issues.

Your Pregnancy

www.yourpregnancy.com

Prenatal newsletter for women: This site focuses on medical issues, prenatal fitness, exercise, personal stories, and related products for pregnant and postpartum women. A monthly publication, both online and in print, Your Pregnancy aims to give emotional and practical support to pregnant women, expectant dads, and other family members. The site also offers complementary tools and interactive resources where families can find advice, encouragement, and answers to questions. Get news and information from medical experts, fitness and nutrition specialists, and other moms. Product reviews look at what's worthwhile and what's not, and you can find useful books, videos, and software to buy.

Other Stuff to Check Out

Web sites
www.addvance.com
www.blackhealthnet.com
www.turq.com/balance/index.html
www.fitcamp.com
plainfield.bypass.com/~pwebb/hth.htm
www.hipmag.org/
www.kencomp.net/internurse/home.htm
www.connix.com/~hygeia/
www.blvd.com/accent/index.html
www.InsideHealthCare.com
vvv.com/healthnews/
www.newmobility.com
www.peakperformance1.com
www.healer-inc.com
gourmetconnection.com/diabetic/
www.midlifemommies.com

Mental and Emotional Health

Staying happy as families and as individuals can be challenging in modern times. These resources lend support and insights on human development and problem solving.

Behavioral and mental development

Get inside your head. These sources explore how human cognition, attitudes, values, and beliefs are developed, how you can help to influence people and, when needed, how you can assist them through counseling.

American Psychological Association

www.apa.org/

Vast collection of psychology resources and contacts: Visit the Help Center for tips dealing with modern life problems related to home, work, and one's mind and body. In the home section, for example, you get guidance to questions about family relationships, single parenting, the teen years, caring for elders, secrets of a good marriage, understanding professional intervention, living in stepfamilies, the warning signs of rage in children, and a whole area devoted to sports psychology. Click PsychNET to access Web documents on psychology including an online version of the APA Monitor and publication information. You can also visit the student-oriented section on careers in psychology.

APA Online

www.psych.org/

Official site of The American Psychiatric Association: This national medical specialty society has 40,500 physician members who specialize in diagnosing and treating mental, emotional, and substance use problems. The Public Information section offers referral assistance and articles on a variety of topics, such as defining mental illness, prescribing medications, and caring for families and children in need.

Personality Test

sunsite.unc.edu/jembin/mb.pl/

Take a personality test: Use this Keirsey Temperament Sorter to take a Jungian Personality Test. Answer 70 questions and receive instant insights into your personality. This is the same type of test used by many clinicians to help evaluate patients. Remember, this online version is just for your personal edification and never a substitute for professional counseling if you feel that you or someone you love needs real evaluation.

Crisis counseling

When the going gets tough, knowing how to find appropriate support can be just as tough. This section offers a solid starting point for guidance and support during personal or family-oriented emergencies.

Animal-Assisted-Therapy

www.aat.org/

Animals helping humans heal: Animal-Assisted-Therapy (AAT) is a therapeutic intervention between an animal and a human in need, with the oversight of a trained human volunteer. You and your canine or other pet may qualify to become certified to visit a variety of settings. Or you can help financially to keep the physical, cognitive, psychosocial, and physiological benefits of this program available. Qualified specialists and animals enhance and assist in the communication process with many kinds of patients, working in hospitals, hospices, special schools, and even homes to bring benefits to people in need. Find out about getting started, attending workshops and events, and contributing to the organization by viewing a wish list of items for help. Get to know some of the service animals and enjoy the touching photo gallery.

National Organization for Victim Assistance (NOVA)

www.access.digex.net/~nova/

Counselors for victims of violence and disaster: Founded in 1975, this organization serves as a national advocate for victim rights and services and provides direct counseling services to victims. The section on crisis reactions is geared to the public and explains what happens physically and emotionally when disaster strikes. Find phone numbers and Web links to organizations and clinical entities that specialize in helping survivors of crime or disaster.

Webster's Death, Dying and Grief Guide

www.katsden.com/death/index.html

Support in times of loss: Need someone to talk to? Connect with newsgroups, mailing lists, and other sources of personal support when you are facing grief or depression or when you need emotional healing. Through links and articles, this site covers a myriad of topics, including aging, care giving, anxiety, suicide, survivors, death in art and literature, coping, and facing practical realities such as funerals, wills, memorials, and hospice and home care. Many areas may not be suitable for children to visit alone.

Youth and Children's Resource Net

www.child.net

Resources for kids in need: Counseling, support, and enrichment sites are organized here, with a special emphasis on services for children and youth. Topics include child psychology, teen empowerment, helping runaways, and dealing with child abuse and family problems. This site is sponsored by the National Children's Coalition and features a long list of links to organizations and agencies known for assisting kids (and families) in crisis.

Disabilities

These days, a lot more emphasis is put on the "ability" in disabilities. These sites connect you with resources for assistance related to learning, mental, or psychological disabilities.

Learning Disabilities Association

www.ldanatl.org/

Support for the learning disabled: This nonprofit organization promotes the education and general welfare of children and adults of normal or potentially normal intelligence who have perceptual, conceptual, or coordinative limitations. Find fact sheets, publications, support groups and organizations, events, and online resources.

Mental Health Net

www.cmhc.com

Guide to mental health online: Featuring more than 6,000 resources, this congenial site provides assistance with such disabling problems as depression, anxiety, panic attacks, personality disorders, chronic fatigue syndrome, learning disabilities, eating disorders, and substance abuse. Link up with professional resources in psychology, psychiatry, and social work, and search journals and self-help magazines. Disorders and treatment strategies are listed alphabetically, and you can link to a search engine to find more. Find books, discussion forums, and appropriate care connections.

Self-Scoring Alcohol Check-up

www.cts.com/crash/habtsmrt/
    chkup.html

Alcohol use evaluation test: Anonymously answer a series of questions pertaining to drinking habits and motivations. Then tally the results to ascertain how your drinking affects your daily life. Please note that this is not a diagnostic assessment tool; it is an informal screening device to promote self-examination, interpersonal discussion, and wise decision-making.

Other Stuff to Check Out

Web sites
    www.nacd.org/
    child.cornell.edu/
    pilot.msu.edu/user/waimh/
    www.onlinepsych.com/treat/mh.htm
    www.geocities.com/HotSprings/1872/
    www.nvc.org/
    www.dyslexia.com
    www.hood.edu/seri/serihome.htm

Chat areas
    www.coil.com/~grohol/chats.htm
    alt.recovery
    www.billh.org/chatnow.html

Suggested search-engine keywords
    Yahoo!: Mental Health, Disabilities, Health
        Chat, Death and Dying

Physical Health

Exercise, proper nutrition, coping with stress, and understanding disease are features of this section. Get strong and stay strong with assistance from these sites. Pump up, don't plump up!

Alternative and complementary medicine

Sometimes in conjunction with traditional medicine, you may want to take matters into your own hands through alternative and complementary medical techniques. My family has a flu tea recipe made from herbs and spices that has gotten us through the sniffles for years. Maybe you can find such a cure in your kitchen, too.

Alternative Medicine

www.pitt.edu/~cbw/altm.html

Major source of information: Explore unconventional, complementary, experimental, and integrative therapies including folk and herbal medicine, diets, homeopathy, faith healing, New Age methods, chiropractic, acupuncture, naturopathy, massage, and arts-based therapy. Find therapies for autoimmune disorders, allergies, joint disease, cancers, and chronic pain. Check out the mailing lists, newsgroups, and related resources involving nutrition, disease, and research.

General Complementary Medicine References

www.forthrt.com/~chronicl/archiv.htm

Straightforward compendium of sites: Categories include treatments, online magazines, journals, newsletters, newsgroups, organizations and groups, diseases, approaches to healing, discussion groups, and mailing lists. You can

find most anything on this site from nutrition to New Age medicine to the Buddhist approach to healing. Homeopathic medicine, acupuncture, Shamanism, and metaphysical and paranormal sciences are here for the asking. Health is not all hospitals and doctors at this site!

Healing Spectrum

www.inforamp.net/~marcotte/
index.htm

Support for healing in traditional and nontraditional ways: Alternative and Allopathic (traditional) medicine disciplines are covered through journals, directories, associations, treatment discussions, symptom and disease presentations, support organizations, and retreats. Organized in their disciplines, hundreds of sites can be searched to find information and support for any number of ailments, diseases, and health issues. This site features links from A (alternative medicine) to Z (Zen) that can keep you healthy and fit.

Diseases and conditions

If you or someone you love has just been diagnosed with an illness and you want to find out more about it, or if you have an existing condition and want to stay current on treatments or breakthroughs, these sites may prove especially helpful.

ChronicIllNet

www.chronicillnet.org/

Updates and support for the chronically ill: Locate abstracts on groundbreaking research and search the bulletin boards, events calendars, guest lectures, news articles, selected links, and a support network. You can find information on a number of chronic illnesses or conditions, including AIDS/HIV, autoimmune disease, cancer, heart disease, Persian Gulf War Syndrome, neurological diseases, and chronic fatigue syndrome.

Diseases, Disorders, and Related topics

www.mic.ki.se/Diseases/index.html

Disease and disorder resources on the Internet: Organized for the public and health care professionals, you can use an internal search box to search for specific ailments, or you can review the alphabetical listings of diseases and disorders. Find Web sites, databases, and medical literature covering several hundred diseases and disorders. You can also explore types of ailments, such as digestive system disorders, eye diseases, and cardiovascular diseases.

Jonathan Tward's Multimedia Medical Reference Library

www.med-library.com

Medical information presented in a variety of formats: Search the extensive links library, or take advantage of online shareware, software, pictures, videos, and sound recordings. You may need plug-ins to use some of these resources. However, you don't need plug-ins to use most of the links. From A (AIDS, allergies, Alzheimer's, and so forth) to V (viral problems), you'll find generous resources and assistance including chat groups, journals, and other medical literature. You can even buy a book in the online bookstore.

First aid

You've just burned your finger on a hot pan. You've been stung by a bee. You twisted your ankle on the front stairs (Sounds like you're having a rough day). What do you do? Keep these sites handy for quick, clear tips on handling medical emergencies.

First Aid Online

www.prairienet.org/~autumn/firstaid/

Get quick assistance: Find straight talk about managing burns and frostbite, accidents, breathing problems, fainting, shock, wounds, poisonings, bites, fractures, sprains, and other common injuries. Know you've done what you can until help arrives. Link to online medical resources.

International Committee of the Red Cross

www.icrc.org/unicc/icrcnews.nsf/
        DocIndex/home_eng?OpenDocument

Organization providing first aid and international crisis assistance: Find out about the mission of the ICRC, which intervenes internationally to aid victims of war and internal violence and encourages implementation of humanitarian rules restricting armed violence. This searchable site, in French and English, looks into topical issues of the day (such as land mines) and outlines the organization's many programs (visiting political prisoners, documenting abuses to civilians, offering relief and health services, providing humanitarian diplomacy and legal work, and fostering public education and outreach). See how you can help, and visit current activities in countries around the world (sorted by region). The Photo Gallery is quite moving.

Rescue 411

library.advanced.org/10624/index.html

Get alert to medical emergencies: Raise awareness about first aid and accident prevention by learning to recognize signs of health emergencies such as heart attacks and pending seizures. Check your savvy by playing the interactive game, "You Bet Your Life." Know when to worry, what to expect from an emergency response, how to deal with sudden illness, facts about CPR and breathing problems, and become familiar with other basic first aid techniques.

Human body

The most amazing computer ever invented can't compare to the awesome construction of the human body. These sites cover the complex inner world that lives inside each of us. We, too, are machines — incredible organic mechanisms of muscle, fiber, and bone. Take some time to appreciate the beauty and wonder of us!

Biomedical Visualization Student Page

www.bvis.uic.edu/student/

Students' medical illustrations of the body and surgeries: View drawings, animations, sculpture, and other medical illustrations created by students. (Some animations bring the act of fertilization to life, which while fascinating, may need parental explanations.) Animations operate with the plug-in Sparkle or with any other MPEG player. View JPEG images of artists' renderings of gallbladder removals, shoulder joint replacements, and other surgical procedures. See computer-generated images in JPEG form of many internal processes. While technical in some respects, the site is well worth visiting.

Cells Alive!

www.cellsalive.com

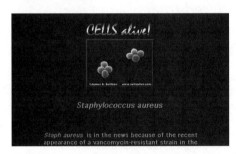

Images of inner space: Discover bacteria that cause ulcers, animated flapping cells, and other things you just don't see every day. Drift through a spectacular inner world of color, moving images, and tutorials from Microscopy and 3D Computer Animation. Check out growing bacteria, cell suicide, swimming E-coli, and other moving scenes from inside the human body. See those little varmints who can make you sick. Your ticket to biological adventures lets you peek in on viruses, red blood cells, and human sperm, view demos of spectroscopic crystallography, and get vivid explanations of how white blood cells fight disease. Be sure to take a look at the related sites for each topic.

The Heart

www.fi.edu/biosci/heart.html

Site with a lot of heart: Hear the pounding heart and begin your adventure of knowledge. Find out how many times a heart pumps in a lifetime, how it works, and why it is such an amazing life sustaining organ. Discover its complexities and follow blood through the blood vessels. (Did you know that a child has more than 60,000 miles of blood vessels?) Appreciate your heart and keep it healthy with insights found here. Review the history of heart science.

Neuroscience for Kids

weber.u.washington.edu/~chudler/
    neurok.html

Get to know the nervous system: Enjoy activities and experiments that expand your understanding of the brain and spinal cord. Make a model of the brain, a neuron, or the retina; play brain games and puzzles (you print these out); test your reflexes and your senses of taste, smell, vision, touch, and hearing. How do we dream? What makes our memories function? How do we learn? Try techniques and activities that demonstrate the whys of our thought processes, as well as the impacts of biological rhythms, brain disorders, and injuries. Link to other neuroscience resources.

Visible Human Project Gallery

www.nlm.nih.gov/research/visible/
    visible_gallery.html

Collection of computerized images of parts of a human body: A project of the National Library of Medicine (NLM), this project is part of an effort to create libraries of digital images that can be distributed over high-speed computer networks and by high capacity physical media. Watch the NLM as it attempts to build a digital male and female including images for cryosectioning, digital images derived from computerized topography, and digital magnetic resonance images of cadavers.

Kids' health

Kids have unique health questions (what is a *mump,* anyway?) and face unique challenges as they grow. These sites contain information about kids' health and safety. Some have been specifically designed for children.

kidsDoctor

www.kidsdoctor.com

This doc makes house calls: Free online service offered by kidsDoctor and Lewis A. Coffin III, M.D., that enables parents or older kids to enter keywords for symptoms or medical problems and get an online fact sheet. Note that this is not intended to substitute for a visit to a real doctor, but you can use it to get an idea of what you may be dealing with next time you cough, sneeze, have a fever, or get itchy bumps. The site covers more than 200 kid-oriented health problems.

KidsHealth.org

kidshealth.org/

190 Health Care

Invaluable resource of kid-related health advice: Click any car on the health train to journey into the land of good health. Presented by the Nemours Foundation and created by pediatric medical experts, this award-winning site is geared to families with a special emphasis on keeping the interest of kids. The site contains sections for kids, parents, and health professionals, and it covers growth, development, food and fitness, childhood infections, immunizations, lab tests, surgeries, medicine, and medical treatments. The whole family can enjoy the health games and How The Body Works animations. Kids can check out the health polls, tips, and articles ranging from feelings, body changes, and proper diet to how the body works and what medicines do. The site contains so much information and is so well designed that it may load kind of slowly on some computers — but it's worth the wait.

National Safe Kids Campaign

www.safekids.org/

Devoted to preventing childhood injury: Unintentional childhood injury is the number-one killer of children under the age of 15. Find out about this organization and receive tips on preventing common household and playground accidents. The site encourages auto, bicycle, and pool safety through fact sheets, frequently asked questions (FAQs), a mailing list, and Health/Safety related links. Take the Family Safety Check List test to see how well your family is doing.

Pediatric Points of Interest

www.med.jhu.edu/peds/neonatology/

Mega-linking site on pediatric medicine: Choose from more than 3,500 links to pediatric organizations, hospitals, practitioners, publications, journals, articles, support groups, parenting resources, sites for kids, patient education, discussion groups, mailing lists, software, information on protecting children on the Internet, and materials on diseases, drugs, and procedures. There are even links to medical humor and art. The site has an internal search box to make your topic hunting easier.

Virtual Pediatrician

www.geocities.com/HotSprings/1364/
    vphome.html

For parents and others involved in childcare: Maintained by a practicing pediatrician and public health researcher, this site features selected links organized for kids, parents, and professionals, plus it offers books of interest on pediatrics and child health. You can order online.

Nutrition for the whole family

You are what you eat, so eat smart. These sites offer nutritional tips for the whole family.

Food Zone

kauai.cudenver.edu:3010/

Interactive nutrition education site: Geared to eighth through twelfth graders, topics include nutrition and understanding the digestive system. Find fodder for discussion and experiments that should be undertaken with adult assistance. Find out how the body turns food into energy and how it utilizes that energy. Meet the cell, that all important building block of the body. Through experiments, see how vitamin C keeps fruit from turning brown

Part IV: Family Life

and take a look at the different forms of fat. Identify monosaccharides, disaccharides, and polysaccharides.

Health Archive

www.2020tech.com/health/

Nutritional articles of interest: Read articles on such topics as little known nutrition facts, getting the most from vitamins in food, and using good nutrition and vitamins to prevent ailments. Get additional resources and link to selected top health sites on the Net.

Rate Your Diet

www.cspinet.org/quiz/quiz_diet1.html rate your diet

Test your nutritional know-how: Here's a quick, easy little quiz the whole family can take to determine how healthily you eat. It's informative, fun, and sponsored by the Center for Science in the Public Interest.

Virtual Nutrition Center

www-sci.lib.uci.edu/HSG/Nutrition.html

Complete guide to nutritional facts and news: If it grows anywhere in the world and humans can eat it, you can probably find it here. From the latest nutrition news to research, articles, journals, relevant links, and other food resources, you can discover how to build a healthy diet. Be sure to see the online nutrition calculators, databases, courses, and updates on genetic engineering. Explore taste and smell, food chemistry, foods of value worldwide, microbiology, food science, and hydrodensitometry (honest, it gets explained). If particular food groups interest you, examine dairy science, meat science, fish science, fowl and poultry science, or more vegetarian sciences. Read about food imports, labeling, food laws, and safety. And get the latest on kitchen cooking equipment, food safety and preservation, menu analysis, recipes, and preparation. Avoid the perils of food poisoning. And if that's not enough, explore the sections on beverages, fitness, and exercise.

Stress relief and exercise

An observant sage, otherwise known as my mom, once sighed and said, "Every day goes faster than I do." If you have that feeling too, use these sites to get into shape, both mentally and physically. (Also check out the Spiritual Health and Growth section later in this part for other ways to reduce stress.)

Best Health and Fitness Web Sites

infotrek.simplenet.com/health.html

Straightforward list of links: Quickly visit some of the Internet's best health and fitness sites by just clicking their titles from a master list. The list may not be completely up to date, but it still offers plenty from which to choose. It also features Java chat rooms. You can even nominate your favorite site for inclusion.

192 Health Care

Fitness Partner Connection Jumpsite

primusweb.com/fitnesspartner/

Original articles, news, book reviews, and links: Get fit and manage stress with the assistance of these articles and features. Topics of interest include getting and staying active, choosing fitness equipment, and understanding weight and nutrition. Check out categories of links that include fitness training, aerobics, bodybuilding, climbing, exercising with disabilities, cycling, endurance events, hiking, backpacking, racquet sports, running, snow and ice sports, surfing, and swimming. The site also covers mind fitness through meditation, yoga, and martial arts, and has sections on keeping kids fit and on eating right.

Other Stuff to Check Out

Web sites
> www.gen.emory.edu/MEDWEB/keyword/
>   alternative_medicine.html
> www.geocities.com/HotSprings/4353/
> www.amherst.edu/~jaloduca/cpr.html
> members.cruzio.com/~hoax1950/
>   KidsFireSafetyTips.html
> www.brain.com/welcome.html
> www.childhealthinfo.com
> www.instanet.com/~sert/
> www.frontpagenow.com/kettenhund/
>   heimlich.htm
> medicus.marshall.edu/medicus.htm
> www.westnet.com/~rickd/AIDS/AIDS1.html
> aids.nyhallsci.org
> www.execpc.com/~stempa/kwhhome
> www.ichp.ufl.edu/
> www.rainbowjoe.com
> www.healthychild.com
> www.axess.com/users/lewis/index.htm
> www.vix.com/pub/men/health/health.html
> feminist.com/health.htm
> sunflower.singnet.com.sg/~cecil/

Newsgroups
> misc.kids.health
> alt.support.diabetes.kids

> sci.med.nutrition
> misc.fitness
> misc.fitness.aerobic
> misc.fitness.misc
> sci.med.diseases.cancer
> news.sci.med.informatics
> sci.med.immunology
> sci.med.aids.
> rec.fitness

Chat area
> chat.healthyideas.com:7080/

Online service areas
> America Online: HEALTH & FITNESS
> CompuServe: GO NATMED, GO NORD, GO
>   AIDSNEWS, GO DISABILITIES, GO
>   DRUGS

Suggested search-engine keywords
> Yahoo!: Alternative Medicine, Children's
>   Health, First Aid, Nutrition
> LookSmart: Health & Fitness

Spiritual Health and Growth

I've always believed that truth comforts the mind, laughter comforts the heart, and prayer comforts the soul. Here are some sites I hope bring you whatever comfort you seek.

Chaplain On Line

**www6.pilot.infi.net/~rllewis/
  chaplain.html**

Help when you need it: It's another late night and it was very bad day. You are troubled and need to unload, seek consolation, or request a prayer for a loved one. Where can you go? The Chaplain On Line site was designed to give help when it's needed. You can post a prayer request or e-mail directly to the Chaplain on call and receive a response back. (Be aware of the wills and won'ts of the site, though.) These on-call chaplains are trained ministers and chaplains and will do everything within their knowledge to help. They won't overstep their training, but instead will refer you to one who knows more. They will even help you on your homework, help you understand the Scriptures, and show you the origin of the Christian faith.

Facets of Religion

sunfly.ub.uni-freiburg.de/religion/

Religions grouped by age: The most prominent world religions have roots dating back thousands of years from many different sources. This home page features a listing of the religions divided by their origination: East and Southeast Asia or the Orient. From this spot, you can explore each of the religions individually. You can read a background and history of the faith before proceeding to Internet links that show you different aspects of the religion today. Some sites list the art of those who follow that religion, and the philosophy and teachings written in literature.

Mysticism in World Religions

www.digiserve.com/mystic/

ysticism in World Religions

This site presents the mystical traditions of Judaism, Christianity, Islam, Buddhism, Hinduism, and Taosim. You can compare and contrast these six religions by going directly to the World Index, or you can look at each religion individually by going to that religion's particular index.

- Jewish Mysticism
- Christian Mysticism
- Islamic Mysticism, also known as **Sufism**
- Buddhist Mysticism

Examine the world's mystical traditions: Explore Judaism, Christianity, Islam, Buddhism, Hinduism, and Taoism by

comparing and contrasting them or examining each individually. Quotations from various disciplines are compared and contrasted by topic. Every attempt is made to remain unbiased and culturally objective. Read about religious leaders and try to apply their teachings. Visitors can submit their own contributions.

Spirit — WWW

www.spiritweb.org/

Focus on spiritual reflection: Guest columnists ponder such questions as what is religion, what is spirituality and what is truth? Link to more than 700 spiritually oriented sites including organizations, institutes, commercial sites, spiritual movements, personal homepages, newgroups, chat groups, and various meditation arts.

World of Religions

religionworld.org/

Understand the beliefs of others: Find religious and sacred texts, documents, teachings, chat groups, histories, worship locations, societies, and links to Christianity, Judaism, Eastern Religions, Islam, and the Baha'i faith. This site is sponsored by Spring of Life Ministry, a non-denominational Christian organization.

World Religions

www.geocities.com/Athens/Forum/ 1699/

Where religion is more than just a belief in a deity: Affecting lives and philosophies and behaviors of millions, religion is a way of life. This site takes an in-depth look at the impact faith has on its believers. Some religions and beliefs are well known; others seem unusual. This site attempts to clarify the beliefs of others and allay misconceptions. Explore ancient European religions, Buddhism, African Religion, the Baha'i faith, Confucianism, Hinduism, Christianity, Wicca, Islam, New Age beliefs, paganism, voodoo, Shamanism, and nondenominational practices. Although much of the site covers historical religions of interest to students, parental involvement is advised.

Other Stuff to Check Out

Web sites
> ccel.wheaton.edu/
> www.biblenet.net/
> www.nauticom.net/users/rafie/judaica-world.html
> www.maven.co.il/subjects/idx111.htm

Newsgroup
> www.torah.org/ (moderated discussion and study groups)

Mailing list
> www.wwcol.com/con/elists.html (listservs)

Chat areas
> chat.christcom.net/
> www.ndirect.co.uk/~clarke/
> www2.jax-inter.net/tc/
> chat.catholicity.com
> pages.wbs.net/
> webchat3.so?cmd=cmd_doorway:Jewish_Chat
> www.4-lane.com/religionchat/pages/judaismchat.html

Online service area
> America Online: LSI - Religion & Beliefs

Suggested search-engine keywords
> Yahoo!: Faiths and Practices
> LookSmart: Religion

Pets and Pet Care

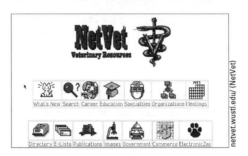

netvet.wustl.edu/ (NetVet)

Lucky you! You just won a goldfish at the community fair, and now you're holding a water-filled plastic bag. All that stands between the helpless little fish inside and certain extinction is — the Internet! Whew! Power up to find current information on all kinds of companion critters. This section can help you find your way to the advice you need about your pet.

But hey, if you can't have a real pet, how about a virtual one? At Dogz (www.dogz.com) you can own and operate a cyberpup. Or you can keep tabs on fish swimming in a real aquarium by visiting the Amazing Fish Cam at www.netscape.com/fishcam. Name them and watch them without ever having to clean the tank, feed the fish, or — dare I say — eulogize them.

Now if someone would only figure out how to give away virtual fish at those community fairs!

Ask a Vet

With Internet access, you can easily find advice on animal health care, nutrition, and other needs. While a cybervet never substitutes for the real thing, you can get a helpful start toward assessing whether or not your pet has a problem that needs veterinary attention. And the information on nutrition, exercise, general care, and maintenance requirements that you find on the Internet goes a long way toward ensuring a healthy pet.

NetVet

netvet.wustl.edu

Compendium of veterinary and animal-health related sites: Veterinary specialists and offices as well as health and general care information for many animals are compiled here. It's the best place to begin any search for veterinary contacts, research, or advice. This site includes sections on e-lists, newsgroups, publications, veterinary career possibilities, and veterinary schools. The best-known sites are listed here, as well as many newer offerings. Parents may want to visit first just to become familiar with all that's here because the myriad links could overwhelm younger surfers.

UC Davis Veterinary Medicine Extension Home Page

www.vetmed.ucdavis.edu/vetext/home.html

Practical help from a leading veterinary college: University of California at Davis provides this site as a conduit between the School of Veterinary Medicine researchers and the interested public, such as veterinarians, farmers, and animal owners. Leading-edge research is covered here, primarily on animals of

interest to agriculture. Some of the site's information is quite technical, but through the FAQs (list of frequently asked questions), fact sheets, outreach, and well-organized animal sections, laypeople can stay current on such topics as disease prevention and animal well-being. Link back to the main Veterinary School home page to find other veterinary links on the Web and to learn more about the school. This site could prove invaluable to the 4-H'er in your household.

Other Stuff to Check Out

Web sites
www.homevet.com
www.avma.org/care4pets

Suggested search-engine keyword
Yahoo!: Ask a vet

Pets

It's reigning dogs and cats on the Net, as these next two sections demonstrate. I'll start with cats; not that I prefer them over dogs or anything. I even have three dogs and one cat. (It's always a three-dog night at our house.)

And speaking of dogs, if you already know that you have the world's greatest dog, make it official. Enter your pooch in the Virtual Dog Show at www.dogshow.com, or become a judge yourself at WorldClassDogs at WorldClassDogs.com.bs/WCD-Contests/Contests.html and vote in unique judging categories (such as World's Cutest Puppy). Be forewarned, however, that a fee is required to participate in certain activities.

Cat's meow cat sites

The sites in this section will help you understand and love cats. Well, maybe not understand them totally, but that's part of their charm.

Cat Fanciers' Association

www.cfainc.org/cfa

World's largest registry of pedigreed cats: You can find the latest on cat shows, breeds, care, and champions. Read about Cat Fancier Association news, history, structure, and goals. Ponder photos of many different kinds of purebred cats and get insights into the temperments and needs of various breeds. Do you want a long-haired cat you can brush or a cat that's practically naked? The wide range of breeds is amazing. Enjoy breed descriptions written by experts and see what the top winning cats in the world look like.

Cats

www.catsmag.com

Online version of the magazine: Features of this online version of *Cats Magazine* include cat care (such as feline feeding and water requirements), population control (articles such as "Trap, Test, Vaccinate, Alter, Release, Maintain groups"), rescue (for example, a look at shelters for homeless cats and the people who volunteer to help), health, training, behavior, and overall feline welfare. *Cats Magazine* is a monthly, international magazine in its 53rd year of publication. Its considerably younger Internet site has

a cat chat, bulletin board, contests, online sales and services section with links to advertisers' sites, lots of cute kitty images (online photos), and even cat cartoons and humor. Find out how to buy or subscribe to the print edition, and see what's in the current issue.

Happy Household Pet Cat Club

www.best.com/~slewis/HHPCC

Hail the common house cat: Fancy purebred cats get all kinds of hype and attention; this site celebrates traditional household cats. The Happy Household Pet Cat Club was organized in 1968 and now has more than 700 members world-wide. The club promotes the exhibition of household pet cats at pet shows. Find out how to enter your good ol' cat in a real cat show, and get tips on going to a cat show and what to expect if you enter. Dates and locations of shows are given. Includes an impressive list of Cool Cat Links that cover all kinds of cat-related subjects.

Panther's Cave: Those Wonderful Cats

www.lava.net/~panther/cats.html

Long list of links about cats. Meet cats with their own Web pages and link to sites with good general information on the acquisition and care of cats. Swap stories through e-mails with other cat owners. What makes this site special is its list of links to people's home pages about — what else — their cats! Meet Socks, the First Cat who lives in the White House, and lesser known but equally loved felines who live in houses like yours. Younger kids will enjoy all the playful cat photos found on many of the sites.

Toilet Train Your Cat

www.rainfrog.com/mishacat/

Feline toilet training technique: This unusual site details the derring do (no pun intended) of one unusual cat named Misha the Wonder Cat. If you think you'd like your cat to give up the litter box for the toilet, the training technique (complete with photos of Misha in action) is detailed here.

Other Stuff to Check Out

Web site
www.acmepet.com/feline/feline.html

Newsgroups
alt.animals.felines
rec.pets.cats

Mailing list
www.neosoft.com/internet/paml/groups.F/
felines-l.html

Chat areas
members.aol.com/sbucciarel/chat.html
www.pergatory.com/chat/data/lisaviolet/
login.html

Suggested search-engine keywords
Yahoo!: Cats, Felines

DOGgone good dog sites

If you need good information about dogs, you're barking up the right tree with these sites.

American Dog Trainers Network

www.inch.com/~dogs

Dog trainers at this site: Trainers here emphasize the humane treatment, and care of dogs and encourage positive training methods. Find the latest dog care and training books, seminars, workshops, publications, events, and advice from training experts. Connect with dog trainers, associations, and organizations (including rescue and adoption agencies). Special sections describe dog-oriented law and the training and use of service dogs for the disabled. You can link up with mail order catalogs. Plus fun pages of dog art, photos, and quotes about dogs are available here. Get firsthand (or paw?) advice through helplines and hotlines. Read tips for dog-related medical emergencies and travel. Visit the dog lost and found. Parents find advice on making sure relations between dogs and kids stay positive. Kids learn more about responsible dog ownership, but in a fun way.

American Kennel Club

www.akc.org

Ultimate pedigree dog site: If you want to find out about dog breeds and dog shows and discover how to choose the right breed based on temperament, mainte-nance, and other needs, visit this site. You also can connect with reputable breeders. This extremely detailed site has lots of pictures to help you discern breeds, make wise choices about owner-ship, and understand the history of dog breeding and showing.

Canines of America

www.canines.com

Dog care, training, and behavior problem solutions: The section on dog behavior lists common problems and offers tips to solve them — from barking, chasing cats, and jumping onto visitors to car anxiety and pulling the leash. For more involved or persistent problems, you can contract online with a dog-training specialist. In addition to behavior problem-solving, training tips, business opportunities, and information on internships in dog training, find Pet News, Pet Chats, On-Line Training and Behavior Seminars, and doggy links to care sites, breeder sites, animal rescue organizations, and pet loss grief counseling.

Dog WORLD Online

www.dogworldmag.com

Largest and oldest all-breed dog maga-zine: This 82-year-old magazine now has an online version that's also written with the serious dog enthusiast in mind. Readers include dog owners, breeders, boarders, trainers, and other profession-als. Issues cover health care, training, nutrition, appearance, grooming, breed-ing, shows, legislation, and breed traits. Find out how to subscribe to the print version, see what's in the current issue,

and interact with fellow dog lovers through the bulletin board and other interactive offerings. The site offers a dog-show calendar, special columns, and an online catalog. Read interviews with experts on dog training and other topics. Enjoy great images (online photographs) and content.

WorldWideWoofs

www.woofs.org/

All the news that's sniffed to print: Find lots of regular articles and features, including the latest news and entertain-ment, current and archived issues, links to dog-adoption centers, a section for and about breeders, a calendar of dog shows and events, information from veterinar-ians, contests, tips on dog training and psychology, and information about dog health and nutrition. The goal of the not-for-profit organization publishing this online newspaper is to objectively present canine-related issues, treatment, training, maintenance, and humane care.

Other Stuff to Check Out

Web sites
> www.canismajor.com/dog
> www.bulldog.org/dogs
> www.dogz.com
> www.dogshow.com
> WorldClassDogs.com.bs/WCD-Contests/
>   Contests.html

Newsgroup
> rec.pets.dogs.info,rec.answers,news.answers

Chat area
> www.acmepet.com/chat/petchat.html?

Suggested search-engine keywords
> Infoseek: Dogs, Dog care

Sites for other critters

Rabbits, rodents, reptiles, birds, fish, and other animals also have homes on the World Wide Web. Start with these great sites and follow their links to even more.

American Equinet

www.ttlnet.com/amequinet/

All-breed equine Internet magazine: Established to promote horses from the U.S., this online magazine comes up with 12 updated online issues a year (on the first of each month). The publication is geared toward breeders, trainers, and owners and covers horses as well as equestrian real estate, feed companies, barn builders, trailer manufacturers, tack stores, and many other products and services. You can find articles, features, equine educational features, and personal stories. Click the category you want to browse, or type a name or subject into the internal search box (for example, typing **paint** gives you access to all Paint breeders, stallions, horses for sale, trainers, and clubs). Submit free classifieds and event notices.

Animal People

www.animalpepl.org/

Monthly news magazine: Dedicated to in-depth coverage of news affecting animals and the people who care about them, this searchable news site features archives of material on all marine animals, land animals, and birds, plus news and commentary on ecological issues of local and global importance. Find information on cats, dogs, tigers, elephants, zebras, monkeys, opossums, raccoons, whales, geese, horses, doves — hundreds of domestic, captive, and wild animals. Issues include animal protection, humane education, legislation, hunting, conservation, research using animals, the fur trade, protection shelters, spaying and neutering, and factory farming. Link to "good" animal sites and "bad" animal sites. Connect with organizations and resource sites for the latest on books, events, movies, and activism. One section explores the relationship between animals and kids. Get details about subscribing to the print edition.

Aquarium Net

www.aquarium.net/

Monthly publication: Read articles on all aspects of setting up and maintaining marine and freshwater aquariums. Get in-depth aquarium information, find help from experienced professionals, and view the Online Atlas, a picture guide of marine fish and corals (using JavaScript). Aquarists at all levels are welcome to join an electronic mailing list for noncommercial discussion of reef aquariums. (Parents will want to participate with kids.)

200 Pets and Pet Care

Visit the archive of previous issues and get lots of aquarium-related tips and helpers (for example, you can convert standard measurements to metric with Java applets: weight, volume, length, and temperature). Check out do-it-yourself projects and interact with experts, article authors, and aquarium suppliers. Find a large list of aquarium-related links (FAQs — Frequently Asked Questions — as well as archives, clubs, public aquariums, personal home pages of aquarists, and so on).

Aviary

theaviary.com

The bird is the word at this massive site: With all kinds of selection, care, and educational tidbits on wild and domestic birds, get oriented by visiting the site map first. The site is divided into well-organized sections for wild birds (focusing on birdwatching and wild-bird conservation) and pet birds (focusing on selection, breeding, and care). Find newsgroups, mailing lists, and massive numbers of links referencing books, publications, resources, supplies and suppliers, activities for kids, even sounds and bird calls. Read bird stories that made the news and shop online for bird books and supplies.

Bird World

www.discoverynetwork.com/ BirdWorld.html

Big bird magazine: Featured in frames or no-frames format, this online magazine is loaded with newsy features, articles, care and training tips, and offbeat stories. Subjects include captive birds, bred birds, wild birds, endangered birds, and

the way humans impact them all for better or worse. Enter contests; find out about bird-related events, supplies, and services; link to other bird-related sites; and participate in bird chats. Find stories related to avian medicine, health, behavior, habitats, and habits. Search the extensive index for past issues and search the directory for avian resources. Submit bird anecdotes or jokes. Link up with bird clubs, organizations, newsgroups, and experts. Get advice related to choosing a bird, keeping your bird safe and healthy, and identifying birds in the wild. Shop the classifieds and link to online stores. For fun, click the mystery Web site just to see where you go.

Cavyland

www.geocities.com/Heartland/7520/ index.html

Devoted to guinea pigs (otherwise known as Cavies): Obtain information on breeding, purebred breeds, health and care, clubs, and events. Get to know some guinea pigs personally, find out how to help neglected guinea pigs, and visit the virtual memorial garden. Kids will delight in the photos of big and baby guineas, as well as many anecdotes and personal cavy pet stories. Links are provided to other cavy pages.

Complete Hamster Site

www.hamsters.co.uk/

British-based hamster fans share their knowledge: E-mail a pet pal halfway around the world. Benefit from friendly, informative articles about hamster species, care, breeding, feeding, handling, bedding, caging, equipment, health maintenance, putting them in shows, hamster genetics, and telling girl hamsters from boys. You can also link directly to hamster clubs and help add to general hamster knowledge by filling out the survey. And if that's not enough excitement, you can order hamster keyrings and refrigerator magnets. Kids will enjoy all the cute hamster photos.

Electronic Zoo

netvet.wustl.edu/e-zoo.htm

If you haven't been able to track down online information about your favorite furry or feathered animal, fear not. If the animal has hooves, fur, scales, wings, or wattles, chances are it's here. Links cover hundreds of animal-oriented sites, including, but not limited to, ponies, emus, tarantulas, horses, chickens, llamas, goats, capybara, sheep, ferrets, and chinchillas. This site is one of the Net's most extensive sources of animal information. It does cover all aspects of animal husbandry, including rescuing, rearing, raising, researching, and retailing animals. For example, I used the internal search box to look for **ostrich** and found sites pertaining to ostrich veterinarians, care, research, zoology, conservation, and farming. (I even found recipes for ostrich meat. Just try to lift the drumstick.) So you may want to help your kids sort the site for the most appropriate pet-oriented links.

House Rabbit Society

www.rabbit.org

All about care, behavior, and responsible ownership. Adopt a rabbit in need, explore a special section just for kids with stories, fun facts (say rabbit in different languages), cute bunny photos, and unpreachy advice on being good bunny owners. Find out about local organizations and clubs. Use the internal search box to find topics quickly. Question and answer pages detail common rabbit care concerns. Link to other rabbit sites. For parents, you'll find a special column on helping kids understand rabbit's needs and sage advice on choosing a rabbit as a pet.

NetPet

www.netpet.com

Searchable online magazine: With articles, links, and pet-product-related ads, NetPet offers online information about services, merchandise, books, videos, and software, as well as classifieds, original articles, a humor section, and a complete alphabetical index. Get breed profiles, connect with animal organizations and rescue groups, and track down nearby veterinary services. Link to animal-health sites and other references and enjoy original reporting on a variety of pet-related topics.

Paw Prints Post

www.netreach.net/~dhoffman/ pawprints/

Animal lovers' newsletter: Find features on pets in general, pet health, working animals, wildlife, and animal behavior, as well as animal-related book and movie reviews, animal welfare news, and much more. Send in your own pet stories, pet or wildlife news, or organization announcements. Among the contents are contests (photo, humorous story, and so on), Creature Features (articles on pets, wildlife, and the animal-human relationship), the Hip Hop Reporter ("insightful rabbit commentaries by the world's most literate bunny"), the BookWorm's Hole (bookstore and reviews of books about wildlife, pets, human-animal relations, and other animal issues), and links to selected animal sites. Explore the forum and a chat section, an extinct animals' memorial section, and columns on health care and training. This site is fun and family oriented, with lots of good content. Find out about subscribing to the print version.

Pet Channel Animal Network

www.petchannel.com

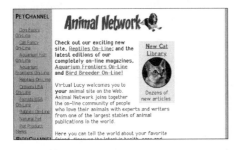

Presenting 25 major pet magazines: This interactive site introduces you to print magazines covering exotic pets, dogs, cats, birds, fish, reptiles, horses, and rodents. Among the publications you can visit that are either totally online or both online and in print you can find Dog Fancy, Cat Fancy, Aquarium Fish, Aquarium Frontiers, Reptiles, Critters USA, Horse Illustrated, and Rabbits. Get

veterinary and pet-product information, tell the world about your favorite pet, discover the latest in health care and nutrition, find a new pet to love, and swap tips and tales with people who care about their special animals, too.

Petlife News

www.petlifenews.com

Online magazine celebrating the human-animal bond: Emphasizing a hard-news focus, this online news publication looks at issues affecting animals in both positive and negative ways. It donates at least five percent of its annual profit from advertising to animal-oriented nonprofit and humane organizations. This online site is fully searchable, so you can track down news stories, as well as resources in the Pet Services Directory. Regular sections include pet-related news, events and legislation, feedback and input from readers, and stories about wildlife and humans. Check out the interesting images (online photographs) and unusual news and feature items (such as a runaway-emu story and an article on pet massage).

Trendy's House of Herpetology

fovea.retina.net/~gecko/herps

Expert advice on reptiles and amphibians: Dozens of dedicated pet owners and researchers who are concerned about the welfare of these animals have joined together here to share information about acquisition and care. They have gone to a lot of trouble to make sure new owners are properly prepared (turtles do NOT eat pizza just because Ninja Turtles do). Find lots of original well-researched articles and links, carefully organized by animal type (for example, snakes, lizards, turtles, and iguanas). Extensive assistance is offered to parents to make sure kids provide proper care for these potentially finicky creatures.

Other Stuff to Check Out

Web sites
www.afrma.org/afrma/index.htm
www.actwin.com/fish
www.xmission.com/~gastown/herpmed
www.rodent.demon.co.uk/gerbils/
homepage.htm
www.cockatiels.org
pathfinder.com/@@Q6BNmgcAR6mGWKzP/
twep/petpath
web.rli.net/herp
www.actwin.com/WWWVL-Fish.html

Online service areas
CompuServe: GO PETS
America Online: LSI - House & Home

Suggested search-engine keywords
For any search engine: Look for species name, for example, gerbil or cockatiel

Passing away: Saying good-bye

There are resources on the Net to help families with the whole cycle of pet ownership, from happily choosing to sadly losing a dear animal friend. Inevitably the time comes when you have to bid beloved pets farewell. Dealing with separation and death is difficult, and the grief that comes from losing a pet is profound and not always sufficiently acknowledged. Sites in this section help family members, especially kids who may be facing their first loss, deal with the experience. If you decide to take another animal into your heart and home, you may consider visiting Mercy Rescue Net at www.aaarf.org to help a homeless pet waiting at a shelter near you.

American Veterinary Medical Association — Pet Loss

www.avma.org/care4pets/avmaloss.htm

Practical yet compassionate help and advice: Here, you get information to help you decide whether it's time to euthanize a pet. You also find out how to make arrangements for a pet upon its death and how to find legitimate grief counselors and strategies for emotional healing.

Pet Loss and Grieving Resource Pages

**www.cowpoke.com/Pages/
Pethome.htm**

Find comfort when death comes: Helps families discuss the loss of a pet, find support, develop memorial ceremonies, and otherwise work through the loss of a companion animal. The site includes sections that you can read aloud to help the family express feelings and memories.

Virtual Pet Cemetery

www.lavamind.com/pet.html

Preserve memories: This site provides a place for your family to post anecdotes, photos, a eulogy, or other remembrances of your departed pet. Take comfort in reading the feelings of others who are going through similar pain.

Other Stuff to Check Out

Web sites
> www.petloss.com
> www.healingforest.com
> www.petmemories.com
> www.aaarf.org

Newsgroups
> alt.support.grief.pet-loss
> rec.pets

Suggested search-engine keyword
> Yahoo!: Pets Death

Part V
Entertainment and Travel

The 5th Wave® By Rich Tennant

©RICHTENNANT

"This afternoon I want everyone to go online and find all you can about Native American culture, history of the old West and discount air fares to Hawaii for the two weeks I'll be on vacation."

In this part . . .

Computers can be relied upon for performing useful tasks, such as doing your taxes, researching term papers, checking on the stock market, or even assuring hypochondriac Uncle Harold about how unlikely it is that his latest symptoms are really life-threatening. ("No, Uncle Harold, I don't think you could get jungle rot just by eating at the Afro-German Tea Room.") But the real joy of owning a computer is when you can use it to have fun! Jump online and surf the sites in these parts to plan a pleasant family trip, to discover neat cooking tips, to find more information about your favorite hobby — or even to enjoy a relaxing shopping experience.

Cooking Up Some Fun

The World Wide Web serves up plenty of food for thought. Need a recipe for spinach dip or for a complete Thanksgiving dinner for 20 of your closest relatives? Some of the world's finest chefs and nutritionists are at your beck and call.

Cook with the kids or whip up something weird! Most sites usually include a vegetarian selection on the menu. See a recipe you like, print it out, and you're cookin'.

Online Cooking Magazines

Here are some online cooking magazines in which you can find great recipes, access to great chefs, and enough mouth-watering photos to build a big appetite.

American Connoisseur

www.americanconnoisseur.com

Recipes, gourmet goods, and articles: Indulge the snob in yourself with this online magazine that celebrates the finest foods, kitchens, restaurants, adult beverages, travel destinations, and notable events (such as the Michaelmas English Harvest Fair at the Biltmore Estate in Asheville, North Carolina; the grape-pressing festival at the Cayuga Ridge Estate Winery in Ovid, New York; the Annual Shrimp Festival in Gulf Shores, Alabama; and the Cranberry Harvest Festival in South Carver, Massachusetts). Find complementary recipes, contests, fine publications, and products (even cigars) and, of course, some good snob humor (things you should never say in a fine restaurant, such as "Do we get refills on iced tea?" or "Hey! My tomato soup is cold!").

Art Culinaire

www.getartc.com/

Great images and recipes from noted chefs: Considered a leading publication for professional chefs, this online magazine enables you to share their secrets and read the latest industry news and trend reports. Enjoy lip-smacking food images and recipes from the greatest culinarians worldwide. Subscribers to the print version hail from 45 countries, so you benefit from interactions among industry professionals on several continents. Get recipes for entreés, side selections, appetizers, and desserts, as well as tips from noted chefs. Read reviews of some of the world's greatest restaurants. Find out how to subscribe to the magazine used by chefs, food and beverage managers, restaurant owners, caterers, and hotel managers. If it's cutting edge in the culinary industry, it's probably going to be reported here.

The Art of Eating

www.artofeating.com/

Food and wine newsletter focusing on U.S., France, and Italy: This print publication covers the best food and wine, with a particular emphasis on traditional methods and food philosophies. This site looks at a time when people spent more time and had a more personal connection to the growth and preparation of foods. In each issue, author Edward Behr explores the impacts of geography, history, sociology, and culture on the creation of great meals, as well as modern improvements that demonstrate a similar respect. Each issue takes you to the source of a great food (for example, the farm cheeses of Province, pizza in Naples where pizza originated, gumbo in Southwest Louisiana, aged North American cheddar, and the world's best dark chocolate). This site tells you about *The Art of Eating,* which has been published four times a year since 1986, and about subscription information. Though the site itself is limited in content, it does provide publication excerpts, notes and queries where you can share or enjoy experiences and insights from others, and a resource list (nonlinking) to organizations that honor food traditions (such as Seed Savers Exchange, which fosters the growing of local plants that are the foundation of traditional eating around the world).

Chile Pepper Magazine

www.chilepeppermag.com/

Spicy food and journeys: The "hottest" authority on spicy and hot foods, Chile Pepper Magazine has been in publication since 1987, and provides anecdotal, practical, and historical information from all over the world, along with recipes ranging from gumbos and salsas to curries, barbecue, stir-fry, and chili. The Hot Flash section gives traditional, new, and off-beat information about the many ways people use chiles, and it updates you on industry breakthroughs. Enjoy a sampling of this bimonthly magazine. See past issues and search the site for hot recipes (in more ways than one) and sauces. You can also find links to other chile-based sites.

Cook's Thesaurus

www.northcoast.com/~alden/
    cookhome.html

Kitchen assistant for home cooks: This online Thesaurus provides potential substitutions for more than 1,500 common cooking ingredients, including low-calorie, low-salt, and low-fat alternatives for specialized diets, inexpensive substitutes for would-be caviar cooks on a fish-egg budget, and creative replacements for ethnic ingredients that may not be sold at the mainstream supermarket. This site also explains drawbacks of substitutes so you can choose whether you want to go with the real ingredient. You can choose to view the Java version or plain old vanilla version.

Epicurious

food.epicurious.com/

International food publication: Frequently updated, this online magazine collection features online versions of print magazines, such as *Bon Appétit* and *Gourmet,* and lots of resources for travel and dining. Epicurious Food's Recipe File features over 6,000 recipes from around the world, and you can find wine tips, restaurant and book notes, and practical kitchen tips. You can plan a trip using the Epicurious Travel six search options for compiling a complete travel agenda (incorporating the resources of *Condé Nast Traveler*). So if you want a good recipe for Hungarian stew, or you want to eat some in Hungary, go to this site to begin your planning. Just for fun, pop into the section called Playing with Your Food where you can find festivals, recipes, and more.

Epicurus Online

www.epicurus.com/

Online magazine of food news and trends for consumers and industry professionals: Review previous issues, find out about membership benefits, search for cooking topics or recipes, and get tips and insights from noted chefs. Enjoy chatting with other people who love to cook or eat. All kinds of recipes are presented, as are courses for formal or less-formal dinners. The site also has a classifieds section and links to mailing lists and message boards. This is a well-organized, attractive, and highly usable site.

Gourmet Connection

gourmetconnection.com/

Food, recipes, healthy living: This site, which covers dining-related entertainment, health, fitness, nutrition, and shopping, is a place to find specialty recipes, cookbooks, and lots of food-related news. From the release of a new cookbook to an investigation by the Food and Drug Administration into an additive, you'll get breaking news of concern to those seeking a healthy diet and lifestyle. Enjoy forums, bulletin boards, and live chats where you can choose from topics such as asthma diets for teens or great wine recipes. You can find a really good daily news section, as well as user-friendly feature sections about cooking and living fit. Regular sections include Eating & Drinking, The Health Spa, Living, and Fine Shopping. The site features Q&As with experts in nutrition and cooking, as well as special sections all about kids' health, nutritional needs, and cooking for them. Search the Recipe Files right off the main page, or go to the Eating and Drinking section where you'll find categories such as the Diabetic Gourmet and the Kids Table. Get evaluations of kitchen and cooking products. Subscribe to the free e-mail newsletter.

Gourmet Fare

www.drspublishing.com/gourmet/

Food and entertainment newsmagazine: Published bimonthly in hard and electronic copy, Gourmet Fare picks a theme to explore with recipes, entertaining tips, and kitchen advice. When holidays approach, get practical help planning and cooking traditional meals or trying new things just to spice up the day. This site provides practical baking hints (for bread, pies, and cookies), looks at related topics (specialty coffees, cooking healthy, and/or for kids), and seeing how the other half of the world eats (foods from Thailand, for example). Get information on good cookbooks and what's happening in the news related to food. Read back issues and find all kinds of well-illustrated recipes.

Internet Chef Online Magazine

www.ichef.com/

Electronic archive celebrating food: Find cooking ideas (for full meals, snacks, and candies), columns by experts, food news and features, message boards addressing a variety of cooking quandaries, links to good cooking sites, and special sections; one recently honored National Honey Month. If you want to contribute tips, hints, or recipes, you'll find a Submit Form. If you need a recipe, try searching the recipe archive or requesting it on The Recipe Box. Go to the main page of the Chef Recipe Archive; the search box is right at the top. Search by category or get more particular by using a detailed search method. Participate in the chat on cooking topics or use the message board to post and request recipes. Meet food lovers from around the world.

Internet Epicurean

internet.epicurean.com/latest/current/

Semimonthly food and dining online magazine: Get interactive articles, food links suggested by readers and editors (sorted into categories such as commercial, recipes, and restaurants), and special features (such as taking high tea in the British tradition, planning a seafood fiesta, using salads as entrees, and making Pfannkuchen). Sit around The Kitchen Table and chat with cooks and epicures (requires a Java-capable browser). The Chef's Forum is a friendly bulletin board for exchanging ideas. Visit the featured menu, exchange or request recipes from others, and read earlier articles.

Roadside Magazine

www.roadsidemagazine.com

Exploration of America's diners: This e-zine offers fun and nostalgia (the site background looks like a vintage Formica countertop) in an effort to celebrate and preserve America's roadside diners. Find out how to help save diners from the wrecking ball and read personal histories of some of America's classic neighborhood dining spots. You'll find book reviews, recipes revealed, and commentaries about respecting history and the simpler pleasures in life. Get news from the roadside, peeks inside diners, evaluations of good — and not so good — diner renovations, the lowdown on buying and running a diner, and information on subscribing to *Roadside Magazine,* the print version. You can also order back issues. The site contains links to related travel and dining sites.

StarChefs

starchefs.com/

Secrets of and for gourmet cooks and food lovers: Crack the secrets of the best cooks. Get guarded ingredients, anecdotes, tips, and recipes from famous chefs and cookbook authors. Visit some of the finest restaurants in the world and get behind-the-scenes tours and insights. Search for recipes, join in on newsgroup discussions, explore a culinary career, check on culinary job opportunities, or help hunger relief efforts worldwide. This really nice-looking site is easy to comprehend and use.

Sugarplums

www.sugarplums.com/ezine.html

Gourmet foods and features: Find food columnists, lots of recipes and restaurant reviews, and a special section for Mom and Dad devoted to food and romance — and bringing the two together. Get ideas for meals when you want to spend time as a couple and create a special evening at home; send the kids to Grandma's!

Supermarket Checker Newsletter

www.pe.net/~checker/

Grocery shopping as seen from inside the store: This amusing site gives you an insider's look at the grocery industry and the 40,000-some products that fill an average supermarket. Written by a real-life supermarket cashier, the content here includes a monthly column about dealing with the public and/or management. You can participate in polls about things that the store management is thinking of doing for (or to) you, the customer. Get the latest on new product introductions that you'll be seeing on store shelves, as well as products that are on the way out (or in the process of being re-"New"-ed and "Improved"). Link to commercial food sites (such as Green Giant) to see what they have to tell you — or ask you — about their product lines. This is an offbeat, entertaining site for anyone who has ever grocery shopped.

Wine and Dine E-Zine

www.winedine.co.uk/

For lovers of wine, food, and travel: This British-based online magazine gives an international perspective to cooking, eating, and traveling in culinary comfort, primarily in the United Kingdom. First published in 1995, this electronic magazine for lovers of wine, dining, and travel provides food- and wine-related news, industry trends and controversies, and features about restaurants and yummy travel destinations.

Wine & Dine Online

winedine-asia.com/index.html

Magazine of Asian cuisine: Explore dining and cooking with an Asian emphasis, from traditional feasts to appetizers. Visit kitchens from Beijing to Bali for recipe ingredients and cooking tips. From street vendors to the finest restaurant chefs, you will benefit from their knowledge of the skillet, wok, or sushi board. This Singapore-based site publishes a print version, which you can also read about, in addition to enjoying special online culinary features.

Other Stuff to Check Out

www.cakemag.com
www.centralmarket.com/links.html
www.cheesewizard.com
www.fix.net/~chiligazette/
www.fruitnet.com/NewsEtc.html
www.pastapassport.com/
table.mpr.org/books/
www.beverage-digest.com/
www.foodanddrink.co.uk/
www.foood.com/
www.nbr.co.nz/Section.cfm?Section=2001
www.keckco.com
www.rbcs.com
www.ids.ac.uk/eldis/food/foo_lele.html

Quick, Nutritious Online Recipes

Egad! You have only a half hour to make dinner before your daughter's soccer practice. How many beanie wienies can one family eat? Once again, the World Wide Web comes to the rescue. Find, print out, or bookmark your favorite sites.

Better Homes and Gardens Online: Kitchen Homepage

www.bhglive.com/survival

Recipes for all occasions: Long geared to families, *Better Homes & Gardens Magazine* now brings you an online guide to all kinds of meals, including quick, healthy, hearty, picnic-style, and special occasion

recipes — you name it. Get recipes kids will eat that are good for them, too. Visit discussion groups and swap cooking tips or recipes. Take advantage of the Interactive Guides, Cook's Helpers, menu planners (to organize meals and food shopping), and other online perks. Seasonal recipes and menus are also offered to help you around the holidays, or when it's just too hot to cook.

Culinary Connection

www.culinary.com

Thousands of links to cooking sites: At this frames-based site (which also uses Java), you can find recipe-swapping and cooking-tip chat groups, newsgroups, mailing lists, and a huge array of recipes. Many of the recipe files can be emailed to you. Hit the links button and an A-Z reference zone of over 800 sites awaits you, with links to Cajun, foreign, vegetarian, soul, southern, and even beer recipes. The list is mind-boggling. Or you can find recipes sorted by type (click the recipes icon) including but definitely not limited to appetizers, desserts, chocolate, cheesecake, main entrees, pasta, meat, salads and dressings, sandwiches, sauces, soups, potatoes, and rice and that's just for starters. Fortunately, this site has its own internal search box. All you do is type in your particular recipe need. Visit this site to get help with family meals, snacks, or that big party. This site really cooks!

Good Cooking

www.goodcooking.com/

Foods and wines: Homestyle and professionally prepared recipes presented by online chefs are among those you'll find here, along with lots of recipe and nutrition links, cooking and consumer tips, and connections to culinary schools, wineries, and cuisine-oriented travel. Check out unusual food facts and food science basics. There are links for vegetarians, vegans, and foreign recipes. Get practical food safety information for shellfish, meats, and seafood. "The Beverage Information Center" features links to beer, home brewing, coffees, and teas. There are several different ways to search the site for specific recipes or general menu planning.

Good Housekeeping — Food

homearts.com/gh/toc/osfood.htm

Recipes galore: This established American family magazine takes you online and into the kitchen with recipes, cooking hints, chats, bulletin boards, and sections related to other aspects of family life. The recipes are presented in article fashion similar to the magazine, so you scroll down the main page to see which topics interest you. Articles range from quick meals, to slimming meals to how to cook with various meats. It's a straightforward listing of features that varies, but always has to do with preparing food, losing weight, or nutrition. To find more specific recipes that may have been featured in the past, link to the unique Recipe Finder, where you can specify requirements (for example, Soup or Vegetarian) and get a list of corresponding recipes and the estimated time it takes to make them.

Kitchen Link

www.kitchenlink.com/

Master index of over 6,993 food-based links: Search the alphabetized category list or use the internal search box to track down recipes, cookbooks, or nutrition- and cooking-related information. Links cover a massive array of information, including famous chefs, consumer tips,

skills for beginners (including kids), culinary careers and schools, diets, recipes for people with food-based allergies, food processors, plants and inspections, helping with hunger relief, food forums, newsgroups, mailing lists and publications, and figuring quantities. Types of recipes (there are hundreds) range from African, American, and appetizers to canning, crockpot, diabetic, fat-free, lowfat, holiday, outdoor, and even solar cooking. If your favorite category isn't here somewhere, it's probably not online yet. What's really nice about this site is that before it links you anywhere, it gives you a description of recipes and dishes you'll find when you link. Additionally, find an online store for cooking products and books, food news, tips on healthy eating, and a cooking club message board and chat room. Get continuous food news updates (recalls, alerts, and business news), fresh recipes hot out of famous test kitchens, and a daily menu planner with links to every course.

Know Cooking?

home.earthlink.net/~daniil/

Links to thousands of recipes: This modest little site erected by a New York restaurant called Vong offers a unique list of links to recipes, books, software, and cookware. Just scroll down the page and click any site that looks interesting. There are links to many foreign food recipe sites (some with cultural explanations about the importance of various foods), many sites with generous links to other cooking sites, and even a link to a site featuring ancient Roman dishes. If you've always wondered how fast-food restaurants cook their secret sauces, there is a "copycat" site that has attempted to duplicate restaurant recipes. Vong's list is an eclectic, high-quality, entertaining selection of sites that will keep cooking fans and recipe hunters busy for hours.

Quick Cook

www.ilands.com/topic/qcook

For good meals in a hurry, rush here: Recipes are organized into the categories of Hors-d'Oeuvres, Soups, Pasta, and Salads. Get cooking tips for "fast foods" from your kitchen, and submit your own favorite quick recipe via e-mail. Each recipe has an estimated completion time and most are quantitated for four diners. This site is very simple to interpret and navigate.

Recipes for Kids to Make

Time for kids to get into the kitchen — with the help of adults, of course! These recipes consist of foods that kids like to eat and ways to prepare them that are fun and uncomplicated.

African Recipes

www.springfield.k12.il.us/schools/
    lincoln/htmlrecipe/Index.recipes

Recipes from African school kids: Working in conjunction with American school kids at Lincoln School in Springfield, Illinois, African children compiled these recipes of dishes that they commonly eat so Lincoln School could post them on its Web site. Try Toad in The Hole, African Feast, or South African Stew (that is, if you can find Water Blommtjies at your local grocery store). It's very informative and fun to see how kids appetites vary and are the same no matter where in the world they live.

Appleby's Treehouse Health Tips

www.mvphealthplan.com/TreeHse/
    TreeTips/TipsHlth.htm

Healthy recipes for kids to make: Find recipes, kitchen safety tips, and advice on eating healthy. Kids can make their own chewy, gooey (healthy but don't tell) snacks using ingredients such as oatmeal, vanilla, applesauce, and walnuts. Or try the rich orange shake or the "incredible" peanut butter sandwich (Elvis would have liked this one). You can find easy to make drinks and after-school or TV-time yummies. Recipes are for one unless otherwise noted.

Cooking With Kids' Recipes!

www.intex.net/~dlester/pam/recipe/
    recipekids2.html

With a little help from mom: This site is brought to you by real, actual mom (and Early Childhood Education and Activity Resources expert) Pam Lester of Plano, Texas. Find her family's suggestions for recipes that kids and grown-ups can make together such as Fruit Soup, Daisy Apple, Strawberry Dip, Vegetable Dip, Cinnamon Raisin Bread, Number Soup, Green Spaghetti, Funny Face Carrot Salad, and Soup Can Bread. Link to other kids' recipe Web pages. All the recipes here are easy to make, and new recipes are added regularly. Kids can submit their own favorite home-tested treats. Other sections of this site feature creative craft activities for children, and parents may enjoy the "coffee talk" chat area. Send the Lesters a family-to-family e-mail.

Kids' Recipes

godzilla.eecs.berkeley.edu/recipes/kids

Sewer soda and monkey tails: Okay, not really, but you don't have to tell your friends that the pox in chicken pox pancakes is really just powdered sugar. Some of the recipe titles may sound yucky unless you're an eight-year-old, but for sleepovers and slumber parties, they get a big reaction. The good news for parents is that all these offerings and more (for example, cat litter casserole) are actually nutritious nibblings kids can help create. (Cat litter casserole is rice-based.) This site is designed to amuse kids, and probably any Calvin and Hobbes fan; remember when Calvin's mom got him to eat cabbage rolls by telling him they were monkey brains? Recipes to use for crafts and creative activities (such as play clay and face paint) are also included — but don't eat those! Parents can help kids tell the difference. Clean up your monkey tails or no dessert!

KidsHealth Kids Recipes

**kidshealth.org:80/kid/games/recipe/
    index.html**

Easy recipes and kitchen safety tips for kids: Here are healthy, tasty meals and snacks that kids can make with adult supervision. Send in your own favorite simple, fun to make, delicious, and good for you recipes to join the list here. If your recipe gets chosen for inclusion, you get a KidsHealth T-shirt! There are dozens of recipes to choose from with kid-cool names like Ants on a Log (celery with peanut butter and raisins) and Mucho Yummy Nachos. Find nutritious, tasty blender drinks, frozen concoctions, baked goodies, breakfast and dinner selections and of course, desserts. The site is graphically pleasing for kids and yet is easy to comprehend and use.

Recipes for Vegetarians

If you've gone vegan or you don't eat meat, these resources can't be beat. Check out these sites for vegan (meat- and dairy product-free) and vegetarian (meatless) dishes.

Vegetarian Pages

www.veg.org/veg

Find recipes and kindred souls: You can find more than recipes here. The site offers links and lists to veggie and/or vegan home pages, world and localized events, restaurants, organizations, electronic mailing lists, USENET newsgroups, FTP/Gopher services, books, and software. You can really veg out here with the latest food news, and all kinds of links pertaining to vegetarian and vegan recipes, nutrition, health, and issues. There is even a long list of famous vegetarians and corresponding online links. Find local vegetarian groups, places to shop and dine, and recipes of American, far Eastern, and Middle Eastern origin.

Veggie Kids!

www.execpc.com/%7Eveggie/tips.html

Meatless recipes for kids: This site has fun-sounding recipes for kids. The recipes focus on legumes, tofu, nuts, soy, grains, vegetables, and fun fruit-based shakes. Look for the section offering practical tips for parents on getting kids to eat healthy foods.

Veggies Unite!

www.vegweb.com

Lots of recipes and food news: Check out an extensive collection of vegetarian and vegan recipes, plus pertinent news and features, a weekly meal planner, a chat group, and a book review section. Get the latest on vegan and vegetarian-oriented events, and find support for your food style decision. The frequently asked questions (FAQ) section provides guidance when it comes to explaining vegan/vegetarianism to others and overseeing your own nutritional health. Join Veggies Unite! to stay informed about the latest news, animal rights action, and of course, recipes. Use the internal search box to find a particular type of recipe, say tofu (over 200 choices) or vegan (almost 100 choices). You can narrow your search even more by typing in specifics such as dairy-free. The search box is fast and easy to understand. The site also lists categories you can explore that cover cooking, as well as activism and animal rights and welfare.

Weird Recipes You Must See to Believe

You can play with your food here and really gross out all your friends. Too cool! Oh, by the way, if you cook as well as I do,

you may want to bookmark MediZine's Heartburn page at www.druginfonet.com/faq/faqhearb.htm!

Fun (Not Exactly Food) Recipes For Kids

www.asfsa.org/students/nonfood.htm

Don't eat these recipes — they're designed for play: Have indoor fun making your own modeling clay or creating treats for wild birds. Make your own bubble solution, finger paint, or playdough. Grown-ups will need to help with providing supplies and overseeing the use of the stove.

Orkin Insect Recipes

www.orkin.com/bugrecipes.html

Now you can eat like a bird, literally: These recipes are guaranteed to set the room abuzz at your next party. And if the family wants a quick snack on the fly, try the Insect Popcorn Crunch or maybe Banana BugCicles. Recipes on this site are for human consumption! Really! (They might come in very handy if you're ever lost in the wilderness, although parents may want to explain that eating freshly plucked bugs out of the yard is not what this site recommends). Read how people in other countries eat bugs on purpose. Then whip up some delicious Bug Bites (you can always share them with the birds). Yummy!

Other Stuff to Check Out

Web sites
www.starchefs.com/
www.dreamdweller.com/webrings/
   chefring.htm
www.wchstv.com/gmarecipes/
www.family.com/Categories/Food
www.druginfonet.com/heart.htm
www.backdoor.com/merritt/
www.kidscook.com/

www.vrg.org
eng.hss.cmu.edu/recipes/

Newsgroups

rec.food.cooking
rec.food.recipes: Index
www.cs.cmu.edu/~mjw/recipes/
rec.food.veg.cooking

Online service areas

America Online: LSI - Everything Edible

Suggested search-engine keywords

Yahoo!: Family recipes, cooking
Infoseek: Ethnic recipes

Hobbies: Busy Hands, Happy Hearts

One of the best ways to have family fun is to collect, make, or do things together as a family. My son and husband are talented potters, and I love displaying their handiwork. Last year we made some of our holiday presents for Gramma, Aunt Ginny, Uncle Jim, and Aunt Alison. All the gifts (especially the refrigerator magnets made from jar lids) received rave reviews. Spend a few hours or set aside regular time to create the most important thing of all — the lasting memories of the good times that you had while sharing a hobby.

In addition to the great jumping off points that you'll find in the sites listed here, try any search engine by using the search box to type in the exact sort of collectible, hobby, or craft you like — for example, art glass, prints, pottery,

limited-edition plates, or antique dolls. Remember that if you type in models or dolls, you may get the human kind, which are not always G-rated. So be as specific as possible. Try ceramic dolls or model trains. The "Cooking Up Some Fun" section in this part has sites offering concoctions for homemade modeling dough and other crafty things.

Collecting

My very practical mom calls them dust collectors, but people with prized collections of beer steins, cereal boxes, Barbie dolls, seashells, teddy bears, Beanie Babies, water globes, ceramic figurines, miniature horses, baseball cards, thimbles, and, in my case, Kermit the Frog memorabilia call them treasures. (For some reason, I'm thinking of starting a feather duster collection, too.)

Part of the fun of collecting is unexpectedly finding your favorite treasure at a garage sale or antique shop. Now the Internet gives you another avenue of adventure and the additional bonus of connecting online with fellow collectors.

Car Collector Online

www.carcollector.com

For serious car connoisseurs: Car collecting is an art and a passion, and those who are interested in (but may not have the funds for) classic cars can also learn about them at this site. The online version has very brief versions of feature articles that appear in the print magazine. Hotwire, the news section, contains items on a variety of topics, such as Roger C. Johnson's "A Gage For Classic Cars" and Dennis Adler's notes on (and photo of) a 1930 Cadillac V16 all-weather Phaeton. Useful pages here include the Calendar of Events, which covers three months of classic-car events as well as highlights of the coming year; and Departments, which has a brief note on such topics as museums, the show circuit, and restoration. For those who own classic cars and who want to find fellow enthusiasts, the site lists several national classic car clubs.

Collecting

www.odysseygroup.com/collect.htm

From autographs to match covers: *Collecting m*agazine has put a sample of its features and monthly columns online. (You can find more information about your favorite collectable by searching the back issues section of the site.) What you find on the Collecting Web site may induce you to subscribe to the print journal. The magazine features a wide range of collectibles: Autographs, Movie, Television, Rock & Roll, Sports, Space Collectibles, Animation Art, and more. Articles available for you to read online include topics such as "Princess Diana: A Giver to the End" and "COLLECTOR SPOTLIGHT: All Fired Up Over Matchcovers." If you are searching for that special item (as collectors so often are), you can post your query on the message board. You'll also find links to several professional collectors and dealer sites.

CollectNet

www.talcott.com/collectiblenews/figurine.htm

Hundreds of links to figurine sites: Search for your favorite figurine collectible by brand name, manufacturer, or category (such as angels, animals, gargoyles, or lighthouses). Sites include suppliers, retailers, collectors, appraisers, figurine

values, and publications of interest. If you're trying to track down just the right miniature horse, owl, frog, music box, or limited-edition ceramic teddy bear, this site is a reliable place to start.

Collector's SuperMall

www.csmonline.com/home.html

One-stop shopping site for every collectible imaginable: This site, shown in the figure at the beginning of the section "Hobbies: Busy Hands, Happy Hearts," is well worth collecting as a permanent bookmark. Here's where you can buy and sell all kinds of collectible items, evaluate the worth of collectibles, and find information about stores, shows, publications, and what's hot in the collecting world these days. Forums offer you the chance to discuss your collecting passion with fellow enthusiasts and discover more about collectibles from experts. If that's not enough, you can enjoy the benefit of all the links to related sites. Wow!

Collectors Universe

www.collectors.com

Collectors' information paradise: You can't go wrong with this site, which is conveniently organized so that you can search specialty areas including (but not limited to) sports, coins, stamps, records (you know, those flat, vinyl, circular things that baby boomers listened to as a needle passed through the grooves in the rotating vinyl), and antiques. The site contains details about upcoming auctions, dealers, publications, and relevant sites. Joining the free Collectors Club entitles you to participate in online auctions and other Internet-related perks.

Doll Page

www.dollpage.com/

Major doll collector's site: If you like new dolls, old dolls, huggable dolls, or fine porcelain dolls, chances are you'll find one here that's just perfect. Describing itself as the Internet's largest doll site, this pretty-in-pink online catalog has areas set up for many of the world's major doll manufacturers and designers. Chat with fellow doll lovers or connect to bulletin boards to exchange doll news. Read what the latest doll trends are, both for play and for collecting. The site's Internet mailing list will keep you informed on shopping specials and discounts. See images of the dolls, get background information on the dolls and doll makers and, if you like what you see, call a toll free number to order.

Philatelic Resources on the Web

www.execpc.com/~joeluft/
resource.html

Mega-index of stamp collecting Web pages: Trying to track down or sell a rare stamp? Want to know more about starting a stamp collection? This site enables you to explore organizations, events, auctions, and stamp values and availability worldwide. Linking categories include: philatelic shows and societies, postal authorities, contacts in many countries, downloadable stamp images, stamp pages, online and offline stamp buying services, and useful collectors software. View images of many of the most sought-after stamps.

WWW Virtual Library — Coin Collecting

www.coin-universe.com/sites/
coinvlib.html

Resource of numismatic links: So many sites are here, there is a fully searchable database to make your hunting easier. Or you can browse categories that cover coin clubs, associations, collector home pages, commercial sites, products, services and software, and related sites that may deal with everything from the history of coins to the world's rarest coins. Lots of images are on the various sites so you can see what the coins look like.

Other Stuff to Check Out

Web sites
www.thebee.com/aweb/aa.htm
kslab-www.pi.titech.ac.jp/~supoj/supoj/
  antiq.html
users.aol.com/barbie747/barbie.htm
members.aol.com/bartfan/index.html
www.mindspring.com/~ejcave/griffey.htm
www.ninga.com/E-comic.html
www.arabian-horses.com/models/
www.barbie.com/
www.stamplink.com/
www.netstamps.com/
www.wwcollectibles.com/art/

Newsgroups
rec.antiques
rec.collecting
rec.models

Mailing lists
model-horse-approval@qiclab.scn.rain.com

Online service areas
America Online: KIDS ONLY - Hobbies & Clubs; LSI - Hobby Central

Suggested search-engine keywords
Yahoo!: Recreation, hobbies, crafts, collecting
LookSmart: Hobbies & interests

Crafts

Don't let a rainy day get you down. Find a craft project on the Internet for the whole family. Or consider making gifts for the holidays. From elaborate to easy, you can find creative, fun ideas courtesy of the Internet. Many of the projects require no special materials and cost very little to complete. I collect empty oatmeal boxes, jar lids, buttons, and many other ordinary household items for projects that I discovered while surfing. You can find favorites, too.

Aunt Annie's Craft Page

www.auntannie.com

Over 80 detailed projects just for starters: Find craft software and idea exchanges with other crafters (including Aunt Annie). You can use a neat search box to type in specific craft projects that you want help with finding or finishing. In addition to plenty of support, this site features great projects geared to adults and kids of all ages.

Classic Stitches

www.dcthomson.co.uk/mags/cstitch

The art of embroidery: No denying it, embroidery is an art. Classic Stitches is a Scots-based embroidery magazine full of great ideas for stitchers of all skill levels. Regrettably, they have put only a very little amount of their content on the Web, preferring to entice you into subscribing via colorful descriptions. You'll find a good illustrated stitch glossary (with entries such as Algerian filling stitch, Jacobean trellis stitch, and so forth). The Charts & Arts section illustrates and allows you to download full-sized stitching charts and full instructions. Despite the paucity of in-depth articles, this magazine is clearly first rate. (Check out the past issues images and notes — Wow!)

Crafts Galore

www.massachusetts.net/nozzle/crafts/

Lots of craft links: Find links to craft suppliers and ideas, from model sailboats, to embroidery, sewing, knitting, toy making, stenciling, woodworking, basketry, jewelry making, and silkscreening to pottery and ceramics. Many of these links are to online shops where you can order various craft projects or supplies. You can also find links to professional and amateur arts and crafts associations and groups, classes, and events.

CraftSearch.com

www.craftsearch.com

Search engine devoted to craft sites: Use this resource, which is divided into areas for crafts, quilting, sewing, and hobbies, and you can happily surf the Net for hours. You can explore over 3,200 links of favored sites in the "Links We Love" section alone. If you don't find a fun site to keep you busy here, you're searching with your eyes closed. A clean, well-organized design makes this site easy to use.

Etcetera

www.eebeads.com/Webzine/

For artists and craftspeople: This bi-monthly electronic newsletter contains interesting notes on topics such as beadwork (several articles have instructions, on different pieces you can make), weaving on a loom, making holiday stamps and cards, and, for the very patient, making clay roses. Articles are very detailed and well-illustrated. You'll also find many interesting projects for children, including "Make a Rainbow Garden," "See Through Card for Kids," and "Marbleized Pencils." Etcetera has some links to other crafts sites and encourages you to submit your craft tips.

Michaels

www.michaels.com

Major arts and crafts project and supply source: If you need to find a Michaels store location near you — or get tons of inspiration, helpful hints, and, of course, craft projects galore — check out this site. A Crafts Calendar features in-store events. Especially terrific is The Kids Club, packed with cool stuff to do provided you have Shockwave. (One fun activity is an online coloring book.) A few other activities, such as the powered kaleidoscope that you can play with online to create beautiful patterns, require a Java-capable browser. But with others you can also click to a generous assortment of uncomplicated kid-oriented craft projects. Make a foam play hat or design projects using felt. The site also has kids projects for beads, buttons, stencils, and many other easily acquired materials. Many can be accomplished in just a few hours, making them perfect for scout troops, rainy day activities, or classrooms. Grown-ups need to help by accumulating supplies, reading directions, and supervising the use of scissors with younger crafters.

World Wide Quilting Page

ttsw.com/Quilt.html

Patterns, instructions, and online support: Find basic quilting techniques and advanced how-tos. There are quilt blocks, diagrams, foundations, directions, and a special Block of the Month (actually two, since one is 6 inches and one is 12 inches). Opportunities to link up with other quilters is vast thanks to features such as the quilters bulletin board for posting questions and requests; the Trading Post, where quilters can exchange fabric and blocks; and Quilting Hints, where quilters can post creative and practical finds. Buy, sell, or trade quilts through the classifieds, or publish original articles, essays, stories, and patterns. Enjoy images of quilters' works and talk to artists, teachers, and other experts. Links to other quilting pages, covering such topics as history and folklore, are included. In the regional information section, quilters or would-be quilters can track down area teachers, classes, and supplies.

Other Stuff to Check Out

Web sites
www.rapidramp.com/Users/toolman/crafts.htm
www.vistek.com/html/kidcraft.html
intranet.ca/~dlemire/craft.html
www.craftweb.com/
www.datt.co.jp/Origami/

Newsgroups
rec.crafts
rec.models

Mailing lists
h-costume-request@andrew.cmu.edu (historic costumes)

Online service areas
America Online: KIDS ONLY - Hobbies & Clubs; LSI - Hobby Central

Suggested search-engine keywords
Yahoo!: Recreation, hobbies, crafts, collecting, kids crafts
LookSmart: Hobbies & interests

Hobbies

Shoot off a rocket, build model vehicles, or find out how to construct your own furniture. Take up pottery or photography. If you know that you need a hobby but don't know what you like, the Internet gives you the chance to explore loads of options. Hobbies are good for your health, as well as lots of fun. So climb on your hobby horse and roam the range of possibilities.

Focus on Photography

www.goldcanyon.com/photo/
   index.html

Hints and links on photography: Like taking pictures? Want to know more about photography? This site offers a little click-through course on the history of photography, on choosing and using the right equipment, and on understanding basic techniques, styles, lighting, and composition. You can find answers to frequently asked questions (FAQs), a reference section, a listing of courses on photography, and additional helpful sites on the Internet. Take a pretest to see how knowledgeable you already are.

The Information Seaway

www.seaways.com

Ship building and nautical research: *Seaways' Ships in Scale* claims to be the leading workshop and research magazine for the ship modeler. This site tempts you to subscribe to the print magazine with its sample articles; the real gem of the site, however, is the Information Seaway,

a useful resource center of links for ship modeling and nautical research, which connects you to museums, galleries, model clubs, naval history sites, and commercial sources for kits and supplies, plans, tools, and books. Even if you don't subscribe to the magazine, you can peruse the Seaways Nautical Research Archives and the links to other Nautical Research and Shipmodeling Sites.

Kofods Railroad Links

www.ifi.unit.no/~anderpe/engelske/
   railroads.html

Sites for model train enthusiasts: If your hobby involves real or model trains, discover a vast, easily accessible list of links from A-Z. Just scroll down the page to find model train suppliers, hobbyist clubs, museums and attractions, historical information, and other sites of interest to anyone who loves the sound of a train whistle. Link to interactive railway sites, sites that sell train videos, sites that produce train publications, and sites for leading model manufacturers. All aboard!

My Virtual Encyclopedia — Recreation and Hobbies

www.refdesk.com/sports1.html

Well-organized library of hobby sites: Conveniently arranged and alphabetized, this site allows you to simply click any letter in the alphabet and get a list of corresponding hobbies and hobbyists. From the American Numismatic Association to World of Wheels, hundreds of hobby groups and activities have resources online, and you can get there from here.

National Association of Fine Artists

www.nafa.com/

Support for artists: Whether you are an accomplished professional artist or an art hobbyist wishing to improve or network with other artists, NAFA focuses on providing access to savings on services and supplies, as well as serving as a clearinghouse for art-related contacts, events, and experts. You must pay a fee to join, but you get the NAFA newsletter "Arttalk" and a chance to display your work in the online gallery. Various classifications of NAFA memberships are available to the fine arts professional, student, and hobbyist. You also can find links to art museums worldwide.

National Association of Rocketry

www.nar.org/

Countdown to rocket fun: Design or buy, build, and launch your own rockets with the assistance, advice, and kinship of the reported oldest and largest sport rocketry organization in the world. Since 1957, over 65,000 serious model makers have participated in the NAR, and you can find out how to join, too. Locate a rocket club near you and follow organized sport and fun launches, conventions, publications, special insurance rates (after all, these are real rockets, just smaller than astronaut size), and tips on safety, construction, and certification. This hobby definitely requires some grown-up oversight, but it's a blast!

RC Soaring

biomednet.com/rc-soar/index.htm

Calling all fans of radio-controlled soaring: Visiting this site is like joining a secret club: Articles as straightforward as "How to build a workbench" quickly give way to features like "Programming the Futaba 7UGFS for F3B/F3F." A recent special feature shows you how to build Marcel Guwang's sensational radio-controlled foamie (polystyrene foam glider); the article has pictures, diagrams, and clear instructions. Departments of the magazine include Events and Places, Safety Matters, and Models and Technique. Check out the expansive Links to Other Sites. Note that most project measurements are metric on this United Kingdom-based site.

The Virtual Birder

www.virtualbirder.com/vbirder

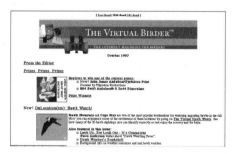

E-zine for bird-watchers: The Virtual Birder has regional info for birdwatching in the United States and Canada, feature articles, and a new virtual birding trip/game each month. The feature articles

224 Hobbies: Busy Hands, Happy Hearts

here are positively inspiring — and the lovely pictures don't hurt either. Check out such interesting tidbits as the "Virtual Hawk Walk," in which you can "visit" Hawk Mountain and Cape May (two of the most popular destinations for watching migrating hawks in the fall) and see how many of the 30 hawk sightings you can identify correctly. Check out the bird-inspired art of Shorebird Gallery and comment on this e-zine in Rants and Raves.

Virtual Hobbies

**www.click-here.com/getalife/
hobbies.htm**

Perfect hobby page for the couch potato: Think a hobby is too much trouble? Are you too busy watching TV? No problem. Pick a virtual hobby you don't actually have to do. Through e-mails, you can hear from others who have equally imaginary but fulfilling hobbies. You can download exciting images of all your virtual activities to impress your real (or courteously provided) friends.

WoodWorker West

home.woodwest.com/wood/

 $

Celebrating woodworking: *WoodWorker West* is a bimonthly publication covering woodworking news, events, exhibitions, competitions, organizational activities, profiles, and so forth. Contents of a single issue list Western Woodworking Organizations, a Woodworking Suppliers Directory, The Woodworking Shows, Wood Notes by Ian Kirby, Turning Topics, and The Market Place - Classified Ads. *WoodWorker West* hopes that you'll subscribe and keep them in business, but the free information on the site is pretty detailed and very useful. Site links include Davis & Wells - Machinery; Micro Fence - Router Edge Guide System, and Tropical Exotic Hardwoods.

Other Stuff to Check Out

Web sites
www.datt.co.jp/Origami/
www.ninga.com/E-comic.html
www.internode.net/HoneyBee/BeeChatter/
   disc2_srch.htm
www.aaca.org/
www.mcs.net:80/~weyand/nmra/
mvp.net/~fred/
www.ram-productions.co.uk/
www.photosecrets.com/Links.html
exo.com/~jht/
www.xtra.co.nz/visitor/lifestyle/hobbies/
   index.html

Newsgroups
alt.autos.antique
rec.hobbies
rec.photo

Mailing list
h-costume-request@andrew.cmu.edu
   (historic costumes)

Online service areas
America Online: KIDS ONLY - Hobbies &
   Clubs; LSI - Hobby Central

Suggested search-engine keywords
Yahoo!: Recreation, hobbies, crafts,
   collecting
LookSmart: Hobbies & interests

Shopping

www.jcrew.com

In the next millennium, e-commerce — buying electronically — may well become the most popular kind of shopping. Already clothing stores, electronics manufacturers, automobile dealers, and specialty shops are providing goods and services, complete with guarantees and home delivery, to Internet surfers.

Online malls gather together numerous stores or vendors and are usually searchable. These malls make an interesting place to start if you want to discover the variety of shops and different types of merchandise available online. However, if you know exactly what you're looking for — Levi jeans or Gap shirts, for example — you can search the Net using just those keywords. Two of the major search engines have good shopping sections: Excite Shopping and the Magellan Internet Guide. A word of caution, however: A parent should always supervise any youngsters making purchases over the Web. Always be sure that you send your personal information to a secure commerce site.

Automobiles and Trucks

You can't test-drive a new car from your computer, but you can do just about everything else! You can research the value of your old car, advertise it in an online classified section, find a dealer near you, negotiate a price, or apply for a car loan. Buying or selling cars and trucks may never be the same again!

AutoWeb Interactive

www.autoweb.com/

Hassle-free car buying: Whether you're searching for a new or a used car or you want to sell your own — fast — AutoWeb may be able to help you. Buyers and sellers of used cars can consult Kelley's Blue Book for a list of car prices and use the free loan calculator to compute payment schedules. One link, AutoTalk, is a discussion forum on various automotive topics.

Dealers Online

www.dealers-online.com

Online auto marketing: Dealers Online is the online community's premier automobile marketing Web service. The site serves car, truck, motorcycle, recreational vehicle, and boat dealerships and publishes weekly updates of all inventory. To use Dealers Online, you simply search for the type of car you're looking for or enter the city where you live. The site also includes a master list of dealerships if you want an overview of everything that's available here. Other links contain information on leasing, used car purchasing, and insurance quotes.

Microsoft Carpoint

carpoint.msn.com

New-car buyer's guide: This site is the complete guide to car buying, whether you want a luxury car, a sports car, a van, a minivan, or a pickup truck. The site has information on automakers, makes and models, dealer locations, and the latest news and consumer reports. By using Microsoft's new-car buying guide, you can even negotiate buying a new car directly online.

OW Distributors

www.owdist.com

Handmade tools at wholesale prices: OW Distributing brings you American hand-made tools at wholesale prices. Computer and DeVilbiss air tools are available as well; they are imported and, according to OW, of the highest quality. Wrench sets, socket sets, and air tools perfect for automotive use are all described and priced. You can order by e-mail or through OW's toll-free number. Don't miss the specials page for sale items or the links to the author's favorite sites, which include Web Magazines, Southern Oregon Tours, and World Wide Classified.

Other Stuff to Check Out

Web sites
>www.volvocars.com/
>www.saturn.com/index.html
>www.honda.com/
>www.landrover.com/
>www.jaguarcars.com/
>www.harley-davidson.com
>www.yahoo.com/Recreation/Automotive/
> Makes_and_Models/

Newsgroups
>alt.autos.antique
>rec.autos.makers.honda
>rec.autos.marketplace
>rec.autos.4x4
>rec.autos.sport

Suggested search-engine keywords
>Yahoo: Shopping, plus specific subtopic (for example: automobiles, rv, Honda, Volvo)
>Lycos: Shopping, plus specific subtopic (for example: used cars, classified, Porsche)

Clothing

Brand-name clothing manufacturers are offering more and more services online — from sales transaction and inquiries to consumer-related queries and other services. The best sites add a touch of entertainment — and maybe even a contest or prize!

Eddie Bauer

www.ebauer.com

Shop for everything from luggage to loafers: Eddie Bauer sells casual clothes, sportswear, travel equipment (check out the handsome soft luggage), and shoes and boots. The folks at this store also care about the environment: They've planted over 855,000 trees with some of their profits. The products are covered by the Eddie Bauer guarantee, and you can order online or from the print catalog. Be sure to peruse the excellent selection of loafers, moccasins, oxfords, and sandals.

The Gap

www.gap.com/

Clothes for GapKids of all ages: Many people of all ages love the clean, simple clothes made by Gap. At this site, you can buy your favorite sweats, jeans, or khakis, and see the latest designs of the season. To keep your visit fun, you can play videos of the latest Gap commercials. If you prefer to shop in person — after you've checked out the merchandise here — you can find a store near you by using the store locator.

J.C. Penney

www.jcpenney.com/

An American favorite: For a shopping site, the J.C. Penney page is fun, with contests and scholarship information, as well as notes on what will soon be on sale. You can order electronics, clothing (including school uniforms), and accessories such as jewelry and hats, online by using your J.C. Penney charge card or major credit cards, or you can request a print catalog. The site also can help you locate a store in your area.

J. Crew

www.jcrew.com/

 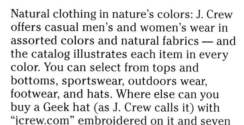

Natural clothing in nature's colors: J. Crew offers casual men's and women's wear in assorted colors and natural fabrics — and the catalog illustrates each item in every color. You can select from tops and bottoms, sportswear, outdoors wear, footwear, and hats. Where else can you buy a Geek hat (as J. Crew calls it) with "jcrew.com" embroidered on it and seven kinds of socks?

Other Stuff to Check Out

Web sites

> www.llbean.com/
> www.apparel.net
> www.coat.com
> www.levi.com
> www.fashionmall.com/
> www.mckinley.com/magellan/Reviews/
> Shopping/index.magellan.html
> www.excite.com/channel/shopping/
> clothing/

Newsgroups

> alt.clothes.designer.armani
> misc.kids
> alt.fashion

Suggested search-engine keywords

> Yahoo!: Shopping, plus keyword (for example: clothing, jeans, shirts, Nike, sportswear, and so on)
> Lycos: Shopping, plus keyword (for example: coats, shoes, Clinique, Avon, and so on)

Electronics

Online electronics sales are booming! From small household tools to computers and major appliances, you can purchase your favorite brands, get information, and arrange for service from your home computer. Consumer reports also are available.

Circuit City

www.circuitcity.com

Buy a home theater from your home: Check out the latest promotions and sales at Circuit City from the comfort of your home. You find new computers, home entertainment systems, and major appliances illustrated and described in detail along with their prices. The AnswerWeb section has technical information on virtually every computer product at Circuit City, including updated drivers and technical specifications. Don't miss the section on Web TV!

Internet Shopping Network

www.internet.net/

Computer superstore: The Internet Shopping Network, owned by the Home Shopping Network, sells computer-related products for Macs and PCs. You can use your credit card to buy computers, monitors, hardware, software, printers, scanners, and accessories.

ONSALE

www.onsale.com/

Bargain shopping auction: Buy great stuff at great prices that you set. This site is divided into two large categories:

Computer Products and Consumer Electronics. The Computer Products section includes everything from computer systems, monitors, scanners, memory, and modems, to hard drives, motherboards, and mice. On the Consumer Electronics side, you can find phones, TVs, camcorders, stereo components, small office equipment, and cameras. Operated like a Yankee-type silent auction, you find the product you want to bid on and sign in. Each item gives you a summary of the product, how many are available, the minimum bid and the current bid. Bidding will be closed at the date and time posted. If you are one of the high bidders when the bidding is closed, you get what you want! Be careful, though; some of the items are refurbished units, so you should look over the product descriptions carefully.

The Sharper Image

www.sharperimage.com

Sophisticated electronics: Whether you need a dual-voltage travel iron, an automobile tool set specifically for your vintage car, or a treadmill with a television, this site offers a unique selection of high-quality products. You can select from electronics and fitness equipment, home entertainment systems, personal care items (such as the latest electric toothbrushes), outdoor equipment, and games. Travel accessories range from a three-person tent to a G2 tracker, which is a hand-held device that uses Global Positioning Satellites to determine your location. The Gift Finder suggests imaginative gifts in four different price ranges, from less than $50 to over $200.

Other Stuff to Check Out

Web sites

www.bestbuy.com
www.thegoodguys.com/
www.800batteries.com/

Newsgroups
rec.audio.marketplace
sci.electronics.design

Suggested search-engine keywords
Yahoo!: Shopping, plus keyword (for example: small electronics, computers, home entertainment, sound systems, and so on)

Lycos: Shopping, plus keyword (for example: televisions, VCRs, and so on)

Family Fun

Shopping can be fun for the whole family. The merchandise sold at these sites encourages family activities and shared adventures.

Amazon Books

www.amazon.com

Book heaven: Amazon lets you select from over 2 million titles, including an excellent selection of children's books. You also can find interviews (recently, author Patricia Cornwell talked about her latest mystery), book reviews, and recommended reading lists for topics ranging from art and architecture to novels and nature. Amazon also has special contests and sales.

Gardener's Advantage

www.gardeners-advantage.com/

A garden site the whole family will love: Gardener's Advantage has loads of pictures of flowers and plants and information. You can order seeds, plants, and books online. The Book of Lists answers questions such as "What grasses grow giant?" and "What plants do well in wet places?" and "What plants attract butterflies?" If you sign the guest book here, the authors will e-mail you when they add new products.

REI — (Recreational Equipment Incorporated)

www.rei.com/

Outdoor gear for family adventures: Whether your family likes casual walks on the seashore or serious hikes through the Grand Canyon, REI can outfit all of you! REI is a cooperative that has been selling outdoor gear since 1938. The site is crammed with everything from knives, boots, and clothing to canoes and electronic compasses. You may even want to join — a year's membership is $15 — for a yearly refund on your full-price purchases.

Ticketmaster

www.ticketmaster.com/

Tickets galore: Ticketmaster's online box office and store is clearly organized and easy to use. You can search for events several ways: by searching by keyword, by using a regional map, or by clicking a category such as art, music, weekly events, or venues. Whether you want to see Aerosmith, Walt Disney World on Ice, the Atlanta Braves, or the Colorado Ballet, you can find information and tickets right here.

Other Stuff to Check Out

Web sites
www.flowernet.com/
clickshop.com/speak
www.hallmark.com/
www.treasure.com/calgold/calhome.htm
www.dickblick.com/

Newsgroups
rec.gardens
alt.treasure.hunting
rec.arts.books.childrens
alt.mothergoose

Mailing lists
LISTSERV@RUTVM1.RUTGERS.EDU
LISTSERV@COLUMBIA.ILC.COM
LISTSERV@UKCC.UKY.EDU

Food and Drink

Just looking at these sites makes you hungry! Fortunately, most of them can ship directly to your door. The sites here are only the tip of the iceberg though; be sure to search the Net for specialty shops selling your favorite foods. From Ben and Jerry's ice cream to Harry and David's fruits, mouth-watering merchandise from many merchants is available online!

The Chocolate Shoppe

www.shoppingplace.com/chocolates/ links1.html

A chocolate-lover's delight: Over a dozen shops here sell different chocolate treats — from gourmet truffles to simple chunks of dark Swiss chocolate. You also can find out about the history of chocolate, "visit" a chocolate factory, and, for a special treat, order a cookie bouquet.

Dean and DeLuca

www.dean-deluca.com/

A New York landmark for gourmands: Dean and DeLuca, for two decades a famed merchant of gourmet items from all over the globe, now sells online. Truffles, cheese, oils, olives, dried mushrooms, fruits, coffee, tea, chocolate, bakeware, and espresso machines, are just some of the items you can order. The site also features a brief history of Dean and DeLuca and a description of their cookbook, which is available for purchase.

Epicurious

www.epicurious.com/

For gourmets only: This site, sponsored by *Epicurious* magazine, has recipes, travel features, and food-related articles. For example, you can find lunch menus to beat the back-to-school blues or you can read a list of favorite menu "bloopers." The 250-plus cocktail recipes are exotic and fun, but the most impressive section here is the searchable database of over 5,000 recipes. Children may enjoy "Playing with Your Food," a virtual reality experiment in table manners. Be aware that the site has a section on alcoholic beverages.

Hannaford's HomeRun

www.homeruns.com

Grocery delivery on demand: HomeRuns offers next-day delivery on high-quality groceries. Deliveries are free if your order is over $60. (Minimum order is $30.) Available products include fresh produce, deli products, chicken, sliced-to-order cold cuts, salads, health foods, and gourmet cheeses. Although the delivery area is limited to Boston, Cambridge, and nearby areas, take a look at this site and see where the future of grocery shopping is headed.

Peet's Coffee

www.peets.com

Joy for coffeeholics: Peet's coffee is online and delivers to your door. If you don't know this San Francisco Bay Area coffee specialist, it may be time you meet. The coffee at Peet's is strong and flavorful, and the selection of loose teas, incomparable. Detailed descriptions introduce new types of coffee, and simple instructions explain how to set up an account. You can also enter your coffee tales in the Peet's guests' journal.

Sam's Wine and Spirits

www.sams-wine.com/

For that spirited something extra: Sam's Wine and Spirits has served Chicagoans for nearly 50 years. This site has an extensive selection of wines, beers, and spirits from which to choose. Sam's also can send fine cigars and accessories or gift baskets to you or your friends. You can retrieve an order form online and then fax it in, or you can place your order by phone.

Other Stuff to Check Out

Web sites
> www.wholefoods.com/
> www.godiva.com/
> www.tea-time.com/
> www.suttongourmet.com/store/catalog/
>   enter.shtml
> www.harryanddavid.com
> www.benjerry.com/

Newsgroups
> rec.food.historic
> rec.food.drink
> rec.food.cooking
> rec.food.chocolate
> rec.food.baking

Suggested search-engine keywords
> Yahoo!: Food, drink, recipes, and specific
>   foods (for example: chocolate, tea,
>   coffee)
> Lycos: Shopping, plus keyword (for
>   example: coffee, candy, fruit)

Shopping Malls

The nicest thing about Internet shopping malls is their variety. You can browse through antique malls, ethnic malls (African, Irish, Asian, and Swedish, to name a few), theme malls, supermalls, flea markets — if you can think of it, an online mall probably sells it!

Asian Mall

www.asianmall.com

From Anime (Japanese animation images) to spices: The Asian Mall has books and media (including Hong Kong movies), personal and professional services, food and beverages, computing and electronics, and a section on traditional Asian medicines that features teas, herbs, and food supplements. The charming illustrations may especially amuse children, but the contents are for everyone. The site also has links in categories for Jobs in Asia, Kids Corner, and News and Events.

Mother Mall

www.inforserv.com/mall.html

Online mall supersite: The Mother Mall connects you to over 400 online shops and malls, where you can order clothing, house and garden supplies, pets, toys, kids' clothing, computers and business needs, automobiles — gosh, did they leave anything out?

Three-D Mall

www.3dmall.com/index.html

FutureShop: Although it is slow to download, this 3-D mall gives you a glimpse of the future of shopping. Featured merchants include: Compverv, Alpine Steel (makers of Swiss Army knives, watches, and sunglasses), Meriwether & Sons, and XL Ultimate Home Fitness. Each merchant has a separate link, but the whole site is searchable.

Other Stuff to Check Out

Web sites

www.irishmall.ie/irishmall/
www.AfricamVillage.com/
www.cache.net/westmall/
www.biggestmall.com/

Suggested search-engine keywords
Yahoo!: Shopping, plus specific subtopic (for example: malls, flea markets, books)
Lycos: Shopping, plus specific subtopic (for example: antiques, African, Swedish)

Whether your vacation plans involve driving to Gramma's house or going to the top of the Eiffel Tower, you can get there from here. This section gives you resources for every aspect of travel. And if you want to see the world without leaving home, you can do that, too — take a virtual vacation!

Travel E-zines

Many of the finest travel magazines, like *Epicurious Travel* by Condé Nast, have online versions; but other wonderful travel e-zines (Orbit, HotWired — the Rough Guide, and Wanderlust) exist only on the Web. You can find journals for luxury travel and budget travel, for families and women flying solo, for those who wish to be pampered, and for those who won't go unless they are roughing it! Diving, hiking, cruising, sailing, you name it — it's online.

21st-Century Adventure

www.10e-design.com/centadv/

Traveling in the new millennium: The most wonderful thing about the 21st-Century Adventure site is its amazing variety. This site has features called PennyWise Alaska (an advice piece), Extreme Photography (several pieces including "Panning for Gold — A Rush for Some" and "A Walk in Cornwall"), The Virtual West (a virtual adventure), an Interactive Travel brochure, and, our favorite, Cowboy Trivia. Thus, this adventure travel site looks both forward and backward — and will probably inspire you to go on a splendid and unexpected adventure yourself. Other sections contain a travel quiz, a bulletin board with travel reports, and queries about China, Mexico City, and Greece, among others. Don't miss the background sound files that play while you are here. RealAudio soundtracks are also featured on this site. Enjoy.

Atlantic Explorer Magazine

www.whatasite.com/explorer/

Come to Canada: This monthly journal combines travel deals — you know, money-savers! — with savvy and interesting information on the Canadian Atlantic provinces. If you are curious about Nova Scotia or have always wondered if you should visit Quebec City in the winter (the answer is yes!), this site will answer your questions. You'll also find travel tales from visitors who've braved these northern regions, and you can submit your own. *Atlantic Explorer* has also compiled an interesting list of official and commercial Canadian travel sites (don't miss Parks Canada), as well as global travel pages including the Networthy Travel page, and Global Passage for still more travel resources on the Net.

Atlas Travel and Geography Magazine

www.turknet.com/atlas/

Turkish delight: *Atlas Travel* focuses on Turkey and other select regions around the world (such as the Caribbean and Cuba). It is updated monthly and each issue contains a variety of articles on unexpected aspects of travel. Examples include: "In the Eye of a Flying Man" on paragliding from the peaks of Dedegöller, Tahtali, and Baba Dag; "Two Worlds — One Country" on modern Cuba; and "Aristocratic City" on Edinburgh, Scotland. The archives go back to December 1995 and are searchable by keyword.

Coastal Traveler Magazine

www.coastaltraveler.com/

Discover the *other* west coast: As Northern Californians know, there is much more to the west coast than Los Angeles's fine beaches. This magazine may well inspire your next trip to the coastal shores of Marin County, to Monterey Bay, to the "rugged" Sonoma coast, to Lake County, or to other northern California wonders. The magazine is sponsored by Point Reyes Light and has a strong naturalist bent, but you will no doubt be inspired by its pictures and stories of these quiet places. Inverness, Stinson Beach, Olema, and other small but memorable areas are discussed (with brief histories and notes on amenities), as are local attractions like the Point Reyes Lighthouse. You'll find a commercial directory as well if you need information on places to stay in these inspiring areas.

Discover India Magazine

www.pugmarks.com/d-india/

Destination India: This monthly e-zine is filled with tales of Indian culture, food, festivals, travel spots — and is wonderfully illustrated. From famed monuments to the Garhwal Himalayas and other lesser-known regions, this journal introduces the magical, history-rich cultures and landscapes of this diverse country. Whether you wish to explore art and architecture (such as the rock carvings at the Unakoti Hills or Amarpur's larger than life-size statues), discover natural wonders (Runachal Himalayas or the beautiful wooded valley full of lakes near Imphal), or pilgrimage to religious sites (Tenzingao's tranquil Buddhist monastery or Manipur, the ancient kingdom renowned in the Mahabharat epic as the home of Princess Rukmani, chief consort of Lord Krishna), you can learn about that facet of India here.

Down Under Travel

www.south-pacific.com/travel-zine/

The Moomba Site: "Moomba" is Aboriginal and means "Have Fun," and the authors of this simple but useful site intend for you to do just that. They have compiled some interesting observations, charming (and funny) pictures, and features related to traveling in Australia, as well as a solid set of Down Under travel links including Anza Travel, specialists in Australian travel tours. The Beat travel column will give you a casual introduction to the land down under and detail different methods for getting around. (They suggest using railways for the sake of efficiency.) The Features section has articles on attractions such as Coober Pedy, an opal-mining town. For those having trouble with Aussie "English," you'll find a dictionary to help with translations. This site also contains links to Discover *New Zealand Magazine,* Tourism & Travel in New Zealand, Travel, and the Port Douglas Visitors Bureau.

Destinations

www.travelersguide.com/destinations/destcovr.htm/

Traveler's tips: *Destinations* magazine offers tips for travelers — gleaned from the State Department and arranged in an orderly fashion (alphabetically by country) — as well as travel specials and information on the latest airfare wars. Hawaii seems to be a specialty: Don't miss the list of discounted diving tours. The list of special events — Happenings — is a kick: It includes events ranging from rodeos, wine festivals, and bluegrass concerts to a Judy Garland festival! Past issues are archived online, but please note that for the most part, *Destinations* covers U.S. travel.

Epicurious Travel

travel.epicurious.com/

The gracious traveler: This elegant travel site from Condé Nast teases you with gorgeous photos and contests. It also holds some information about elegant places to stay around the world, as well as wonderful places to visit while staying there. From Ski New Zealand to Touring Tunisia and Malta, Epicurious has tours and cruises for all kinds of tastes — although few of them are low budget. Still, this site contains weather information and a great interactive atlas, both of which may be useful if you decide to plan your own vacation to one of the 500 locations included in the Epicurious database. You can also find links to Microsoft Expedia for accommodations and flight reservations, to a Forum section with discussions of travel issues such as travel with tots and where to honeymoon, and, of course, a link to the Epicurious Food site. Not sure where you want to go? Ask Wendy and she will answer.

Focus

www.focusmm.com.au/~focus/

Mediterranean delights: Focus is dedicated to providing up-to-date travel information on Italy, Turkey, Israel, Greece, Morocco, and the rest of the Mediterranean region. It is an outstanding and rich site. You'll find historical information here, as well as practical advice for traveling (hotels, music, and cuisine). You can read about Ancient Egypt, the Trojan War, and more before you take your trip. Don't be surprised when you click to the country of your choice and are treated to a brief concert! The site's creators have also put together a Kids Focus section that links to games and other fun things for kids (they publish stories kids submit as well). For adults, this site includes business news, as well as special articles on, for example, Turkish glass. This fantastic site takes a while to download (it is Australian in origin), but it's well worth the wait.

Global Passage

www.globalpassage.com/

Travel megasite: Global Passage has a searchable travel directory and tons of travel links, as well as articles and features. Among the articles, you'll find "Lopsided Map" with stories from Buenos Aires, Mozambique, and other unusual places; "Rodley's travels" with the author's amusing accounts of a day in Malawi or a bushwalk in Tasmania; and "Armchair Travel Guide" with reviews of travel books, guides, and magazines. (Rodley also links to his wonderful page on Africa, if that's where your passions lie.) This site has numerous travel adventures, and readers are invited to submit their own stories for publication. The Global Passage Newsstand will lead you to the latest travel e-zines on the Web: Unusual ones include Get Lost Adventure Magazine and Outside Online. If you want to follow the R2N (Road to Nowhere) link, you need the RealAudio plug-in.

HotWired — Rough Guide

www.hotwired.com/rough

Travel from the irreverent ones: We like *HotWired* in spite of itself — 'cause the authors have put together a fine online guide! So far, the *HotWired* searchable travel site includes Australia, Europe, Canada, Mexico, Hong Kong, India and, of course, the U.S. Interactive maps (just click the country of your choice) give you the basics, such as country-by-country statistics, including embassy information and weather, as well as travel hints for women, gays, and families; and information on money, maps, police, and so on. Look to this site's features to entertain and amaze (don't miss Threads, a chilling account of an American's unexpected stay in a Czech prison). *HotWired* even includes information on customs, studying abroad, and International Ferry routes — in fact, this site doesn't seem to miss much at all!

Journeywoman

www2.journeywoman.com/
   journeywoman/

For women only: Journeywoman is news for women travelers, from cities that welcome the solo female traveler, to women's travel tales, tips, and classifieds, to a section on the adventurous. The types of travel featured in this online magazine range from spas to ecoadventures and everything in between. Female visitors can subscribe to a free online newsletter or enter a contest to win tickets to a lecture by Deepak Chopra. The section titled Love Stories may surprise you: One issue contained an article on "Love and Marriage — Hong Kong Style" and an amazing tale of a woman giving birth — prematurely — in the air over Dulles International Airport.

Lonely Planet

www.lonelyplanet.com

Travel keeping the earth in mind: Lonely Planet is more than a travel guide. It is a Web site dedicated to responsible trips that honor the character of the country being visited. The site has three main sections: Destinations, an alphabetical menu of countries (each has information on environment, climate and character, accommodations, events, and so on — with images); Eyewitness, for pictures that speak a thousand "blurbs;" and On the Road, for tales by travelers. You'll also find a bulletin board to share your experiences. One of the best elements here is "Off the Beaten Track," for unique travel experiences in each country or region. You can order the Lonely Planet print guides here, too.

OneWorld

www.envirolink.org/oneworld/

The environmental tourist: OneWorld focuses on global environmental issues and travel. Its aim is to reveal through images, sounds, and stories both different and shared aspects of the world's cultures and environments. Its section on Antarctica presents in-depth viewpoints on different aspects, including Antarctica's history ("The Explorers"), geography ("The Continent"), political issues ("The Treaty"), and travel ("The Adventure"). What's more, the writers are clearly experts in their respective fields. This site is stunning and has amazing photos and gripping articles, such as Wade Farley's "Ice Paddles: The Excitement of the Unknown."

Orbit

www.pi.se/~orbit/welcome.html

Travel down under: Orbit's special focus is Asia, Australia, New Zealand, and the Pacific Islands — although for some reason they have posted some nifty information on Sweden as well. Orbit won the "Cool Site of the Day" for its good-looking exploration of these regions. Its section on Australia features that country's dense forests, deserts, and coral beaches, as well as her two bustling modern metropolises, Sydney and Melbourne. You'll find separate links to each Australian province and additional information on where to stay and attractions not to miss. One of the unique features of Orbit is the photos and movies used to introduce each country: They will take your breath away — and have you running to the travel agent to make reservations!

Mungo Park

www.mungopark.com/

Unexpected adventure: Each month, Expedia's Mungo Park presents a new adventure. The adventure may be watching whales off Newfoundland or Laborador, diving to view the coral walls of Fiji, or a Panamanian jungle trek

recreating Balboa's journey across the rugged Darin Gap. Other features have included Muriel Hemmingway tracing her great-grandfather's steps through Cuba, and journalist Robert Scheer's return to Vietnam and Cambodia (including 360-degree surround images of Angor Wat). Correspondents for Mungo Park include Stephanie Powers and Martha Stewart, travel topics have included Dinosaurs, and interviews have tapped into the imaginations of Oliver Stone and Ziggy Marley. This site is deep, so allow lots of time to enjoy it.

Shoestring Travel

www.stratpub.com/

Travel on a budget: Shoestring's goal is to help you travel inexpensively whether you are going solo, traveling with a pal, or taking the entire family. You'll find practical information, including a list of cheap accommodations, but also interesting articles, such as John Tessensohn's "Angkor & The Killing Fields." Shoestring posts notes from readers on particularly great buys around the world. The site also boasts the Web's most comprehensive list of travel links and, with 26 categories (Study Abroad, National Parks, Sports, Travelogues, States/Provinces, Food, Advisories, and World Facts, among others), they may be right.

Soft Adventure Almanac

SoftAdventure.com/

Preparing for your own adventure: Whether your tastes run to hiking, sailing, whitewater rafting, or other outdoor adventures, you would do well to prepare for your adventure by reading this online magazine. Soft Adventure — so-called because of a belief in treading softly upon the earth — offers sound advice, including how to prepare provisions for a sailing voyage, how to select a white river raft guide, and so on. You'll also find sections with general tips on hiking and rafting, and, best of all, true life stories of outdoor adventures (triumphing over the Green Wall rapids on the Illinois River in Oregon and a mismanaged sail off the coast of Maine), including some that were less than perfect. This thoughtful magazine also links to you other soft adventure sites.

Travel Weekly Online

www.traveler.net/two/

A practical resource for travelers: This magazine may not be much to look at, but it is crammed full of information for global travel. Departments include news (with consumer-oriented travel updates), railway and air travel information, travel agencies, and tours. Perhaps the most unusual features are the U.S. links and Worldwide Links, which not only connect you to travel sites based on geography, but also contain highly distinctive trip information — a hints and tips section to get help with utilization and other questions, for example. Parents will want to lead the visit here in relation to age-appropriateness and suitability of various games and the chat area.

TravelMag

www.travelmag.co.uk/travelmag/

Not your traditional travel e-zine: This award-winning and easy-to-read travel site hosts unusual feature stories (for example, "Saved in Southern Africa — A safari with a difference in Namibia's backlands," "Great railway journeys," and "China Crisis: Stan Diamond heads out to the wilds for this report of offbeat travel"). You'll also find a section devoted to travel deals in the U.S. and the U.K. and a "regulars" section with news from around the world (based on the premise that truth *is* stranger than fiction and the concept that travelers ought to be prepared), photo tips for travelers, health tips, product reviews, and book reviews of travel books with a different twist.

Wanderlust

www.salonmagazine.com/wlust/ feature/1997/10/00expat.html

For the hip traveler: The brainchild of those folks who create the "Wanderlust" column in the print magazine *Salon*, Wanderlust is smoothly written and makes entertaining reading. A typical issue may contain an article on Veritable Venice, the city of contemporary contradictions; Travels along the Edge, or cruising Antarctica; or Crooning the Expat Blues, on the difficulties of the expatriate life. You'll find tips for travelers by travelers, articles on gourmet food and business travel, but the heart of Wanderlust is the personal recollection, sometimes unexpectedly insightful, often self-indulgent, but usually interesting and more than enough to set your thoughts toward that next trip of our own.

Wide Wired World

www.worldworks.net/widewiredworld/

Four corners of travel: Wide Wired World brings together four different travel publications: The Connected Traveler features travel reports edited by Russell Johnson; Travel Takes features news from the world and business of tourism; Flights of Fancy has recommendations for armchair travelers; Site Trips offers links for thoughtful travelers. One nice aspect of this site is its searchable archive, which will lead you to reading on the topic or country of your choice: A search for "France" yielded 17 titles by luminous and varied writers like Gerald and Lawrence Durrell, Jan Morris, Mark Twain, S.J. Perlman, and Paul Theroux.

Vacation Planning

Choosing, organizing, budgeting, and packing for a vacation can be more work than school or the office! These sites make the preparation process a whole lot easier.

Air Traveler's Handbook

www.cs.cmu.edu/afs/cs.cmu.edu/user/
    mkant/public/travel/airfare.html

Comprehensive, annotated collection of travel links: Not at all fancy, but easy to load and great to use, this compendium of travel links is organized into categories such as airlines, airports, frequent-flyer programs, travel agencies, online reservations, tour operators, charters, cruises, newsgroups, mailing lists, embassies, car rental agencies, hotels, bed and breakfasts, hostels, home exchanges, money

and currency, languages, packing, insurance, maps, student/budget travel, round-the-world travel, rails, bus travel, travel industry associations, and travel careers. Click any top-level topic, and scores of helpful links come up.

Letsgo.com

Letsgo.com

Bible of the budget traveler: Traveling can be expensive, especially with kids. This site (with both graphic and text-only versions) focuses on inexpensive alternatives. An entirely student-run operation since the 1960s, Let's Go, shown in the figure at the top of this "Traveling on the (Cyber)Road Again" section, employs about 200 students to write and revise the 28 books, and to apply their curiosity, good humor, hard-earned travel lessons, and terrific discoveries, into the series every year. The links list is an invaluable source related to air travel, hotels, rental cars, credit cards, train travel in the U.S. and Europe, bed and breakfasts, budgeting, governments, currency converters, hostels for youths and retirees, places to camp, visa info, and cultural insights. Features highlight traveling and destinations.

Mapquest

www.mapquest.com

Get an updated destination map online: At this site, you can get so many kinds of maps in so many ways, you'll be astounded. Or if you prefer, you can use the site to get directions to your specific destination. Customize your driving-trip map by requesting routes with either the fastest speed or the shortest distance. Select route display options, including text only, text with overview maps of the origin and destination points, and text with turn-by-turn mini maps. You can also print out your maps, and find lots of other fun and practical directional services and travel-related products.

Travelocity

www.travelocity.com

Large site of travel resources: From the site's home page, you can see the vast selection of references awaiting you (the daily check on lowest fares is neat). But what makes this site especially valuable for families is its extensive section called Children's Activities; to get there, click Destinations & Interests. In a search box, you can enter any activity or term related to what you'd like to do with the kids (roller coasters, swimming, ecology, and so on). You can regionalize your search, too. From close to a thousand possibilities, the site's search mechanism selects and shows those that meet your interest. Of course, the rest of the Web site is searchable, too!

TravelWeb

www.travelweb.com

One-stop trip planning: One of the many unique services offered here is Hotel Search, which lets you find and reserve a hotel in TravelWeb's database of tens of thousands of hotels worldwide (search by city, amenity, name, hotel type, price range, and so on). After you've found lodging, let Flight Search make online flight reservations through one of some 380 airlines. Got your reservations, but now you can't remember your flight number or the hotel address? Review Hotel/Air Plans to see what you did and make any modifications. Also check out Click-it! deals and Travelscape, the online magazine of TravelWeb, which looks at cities and cultures. If your browser is Java-ready, the Low Fare Ticker Java applet shows you the lowest fares that users of the system are finding.

Travlang

www.travlang.com/

Brush up on foreign languages the fun way: Choose any of about 30 languages and get pronunciations via sound files, expressions and phrases tourists commonly need, and lots of other useful language-based information (names of coins, what street signs mean, and so on). Find translating dictionaries, a chat so you can practice up, and a huge amount of information on language enhancement, translation, comprehension, exchange, and general travel services, as well as links. This page is *trés magnifique!*

Other Stuff to Check Out

Web sites

www.city.net/
www.gorp.com/gorp/trips/main.htm
www.curiouscat.com/travel/index.htm
www.spacecamp.com/
www.randmcnally.com/home/index.htm
www.aaa.com/

Newsgroups

rec.travel.air
www.cs.cmu.edu/afs/cs.cmu.edu/user/
mkant/Public/Travel/html/
newsgroups.html

Mailing lists
> www.cs.cmu.edu/afs/cs.cmu.edu/user/
> mkant/Public/Travel/html/lists.html

Chat area
> chat.travlang.com/

Online service areas
> America Online: TRAVEL
> CompuServe: GO AIT, GO GOLFGUIDE, GO
> TRAVSIG, GO TRAVAD, GO USTRAVEL,
> GO CANADA, GO MEXTRAVEL, GO
> FORLATIN, GO ISRAEL, GO UKTF, GO
> JAPAN, GO PACFORUM, GO ASU, GO
> OAG, GO SABRE, GO WORLDCIM, GO
> CRUISE, GO INNS, GO STATE

Suggested search-engine keywords
> Yahoo!: Commercial and summer camps,
> family travel
> LookSmart: Travel & vacations

Virtual Vacations

Need an instant getaway? These
cyberadventures provide you with
beautiful scenery and the chance to
experience new places without ever
opening your wallet or leaving your seat!

Great Adventure

**www.cmcc.muse.digital.ca/cmc/cmceng/
childeng.html**

Virtual adventures for children: Kids of all
ages can capture the spirit of world travel
and friendship as they choose and take
interactive adventures. From Japanese
tatami rooms to Nigerian gidas, kids can
experience cultures and places available
to them in no other way. Pick up your
passport, plan your itinerary, and begin
your discovery of far-off lands and
interesting new people. Parents will want
to copilot the trip for younger travelers to
help them stay on course.

Viewseum

www.cmg.hitachi.com/

Journey for the mind's eye: This fantastic
collection of images and sounds covers a
variety of subjects. Choose the level of
graphics that your system can handle
(minimal for slower loaders). For best
results, adjust your browser to fill the
whole screen. Some of the high-quality
images may take time to load, but they're
worth it. Click Viewseum Travel Adventure, Listening Booth, Photography
Exhibitions, or Viewseum Fine Art
Exhibitions to get started. Visit the
sections on Digital Image System (DIS)
and tips for better image quality to find
out about the reproduction methods used
and the best ways to utilize the site.

VirtEx: Virtual Expeditions

www.coil.com/~jhegenbe/virtex.htm

List of travelogues and travel dispatch
sites: Join these free, happening-now (in
real time) online expeditions. Explorations involve real people on real adventures that they share online as they
travel. Destinations have included several
parts of Africa, Zion National Park, the
ruins of the ancient Mayans, the Nile
River by kayak, Russia, and space aboard
the Space Shuttle! Jump into present
adventures. Previous adventures, while

not live, are archived so you can enjoy them, too. Archived trips include Laos, Cambodia and Vietnam, Antarctica, the Appalachian Trail, a sailing trip on the Caribbean, an Ironman Death Rally across the Andes, and a climb up Mt. Kilimanjaro. All the treks are presented differently and may require various helper applications and plug-ins. This site describes what you need in order to link to any of the other sites.

Virtual Image Archive

imagiware.com/via.cgi

Create your own destination: Some of the Net's best images, covering every subject imaginable, are a click away. From 15 centuries of Korean art to skydiving, fantasy graphics, and original comics, you can spend hours just letting your mind's eye wander. This collection includes offbeat actioncams, in which a camera is set up someplace in the world and transmits images of what is currently happening in that location to a Web page. Categories to explore in addition to art include comics, computers, digital animation, fantasy, space, and nature. You may need various helper applications or plug-ins, depending on where you wander.

Other Stuff to Check Out

Web sites
www.alaska.net/~steel/kidsfun.html
www.jasonproject.org/
www.goals.com/
www.whitehouse.gov/WH/kids/html/home.html
www.10e-design.com/

Newsgroup
imagiware.com/via/Usenet/

Online service areas
America Online: KIDS ONLY, TRAVEL

Suggested search-engine keywords
Yahoo!: Travel
Infoseek: Travel

People the world over spend many hours each year watching television, movies, and videos. And fans by the score are checking out the Web sites of those shows and of the actors appearing in them. Most popular television shows have dozens of Web sites that explore the series' characters, collect information on the stars who play them, recall favorite episodes, and in general give fans the chance to continually enjoy those programs. Some of the entertainment pages have chat rooms where fans can meet other fans, and some of the children's pages encourage kids to write in expressing their opinions about shows and movies.

You also can find some wild and wonderful music sites in cyberspace. Great folks create and use these Web resources, which offer plenty of information on Bach and Beethoven alongside Little Richard and the Rolling Stones. However, parents need to remember that many music pages reproduce the recording artists' lyrics and CD covers; you may want to explore these rich and colorful sites with your children.

Movies and Videos

Are you a movie buff? Got a favorite actor or actress? Do you know all the movies they have been in? What are the hottest videos that you can rent this weekend? Noticed that most movies released now seem to have their own Web sites? Studios sometimes include the Web address right on the playbill and in their television commercials. There's no doubt that the Internet is a veritable treasure of information on old movies, new movies, and movies that haven't even been released yet. All you have to do is know how and where to find them.

American Cinematographer Online

www.cinematographer.com/magazine/

  $

Moviemaking magazine: American Cinematographer balances film history, contemporary film projects, and practical filmmaking information. You can read Sponsored Articles such as "Once Upon a Time There Was Beauty and the Beast," about Jean Cocteau's 1946 film classic; or "High Noon Hits the Jersey Turnpike"; an analysis of *Copland;* or several other exclusives archived here. A section called Wrap Shot gives a history — with illustrations — of a great director at work on a notorious project (for example, Erich von Stroheim's version of Frank Norris' novel *McTeague,* which was released as the film *Greed*). One part of the film e-zine is for subscribers only; but, if you like, you may subscribe online for immediate access. Shockwave files are used here, so be prepared with the plug-in.

Boxoffice Online

boxoff.com

All the news from Hollywood: *Boxoffice,* the print journal, has been bringing readers the Hollywood scoop for more than 45 years. Boxoffice Online covers new releases (with lengthy reviews), gives the advance word on films in the works, and has a special section dedicated to sci-fi films. The Classic Movie section offers more than 75 reviews from the print archives; films range from the War of the Worlds (1953) to the original release of Star Wars (1977), and from The Big Sleep (1946) to Psycho (1960). This movie magazine also features filmmakers (Francis Ford Coppola) and movie icons (Mann's Chinese Theater). The Industry Links section, which includes all major distributors, is amazing. If you can't live in Hollywood, this magazine will keep you in touch.

Coming Attractions

corona.bc.ca/films/homepage.html

Film guide from Canada: Unsure about which movie to see? Curious to find out what's up on that big budget movie in the works? This is the place to come. Besides the profiles and reviews of recent re-leases, Coming Attractions has an extensive film archive and a column summarizing the thousands of movie "scoops" visitors have sent via e-mail. Choose the best version of this site for you: frames, no frames, or text.

Internet Movie Database

us.imdb.com/

Facts about 95,000 movies: This site contains information about movies from the early days of films to the present. You can find plot summaries, trivia, quotes, character information, famous mistakes, sound tracks, and lots more. The section on Academy Award winners may help you decide what to rent at the video store. Note that though this site doesn't require a plug in, some sites to which it links do require plug-ins such as RealAudio.

Indian in the Cupboard

www.paramount.com/Indian.html

From the hit movie: Nine-year-old Omri has a terrific secret — a magic cupboard that can bring toys to life. The toy Indian that he places in the cupboard comes to life as a small Iroquois Indian from the 1800s named Little Bear. The story of Little Bear's experience in twentieth-century England is amazing but somehow believable, and what the two learn from each other is the heart of this story. The video has some neat special effects, and this page explains how they were done. The most amazing trick, of course, is making Little Bear appear so very small!

Millennium Film Journal

www.sva.edu/MFJ/

Moviemaking magazine: Sponsored by the School for Visual Arts, *Millennium Film Journal* has published articles of film and technology since 1978. Topics vary with each issue. The magazine has covered Surrealist film; Feminism/Dream/Anima-tion; The Script Issue; Dance/Movement/ Performance/Theater; Independents; Video Installation, and others. These scholarly articles are also cross-refer-enced by author, which includes such notables as Paul Arthur, Sally Banes, Jonathan Buchsbaum, Noel Carroll, Ann E. Kaplan, and others.

Muppet Treasure Island Video

www.disney.com/DisneyVideos/ MuppetTreasure/index.html

The Muppets' pirate adventure: Shiver me timbers! This Disney-sponsored site retells the story of *Treasure Island* with "an archipelago of clips, interviews, production shots, fun, and games." The Behind the Seams section tells a bit about how this swashbuckling film was made. Perhaps the most fun feature is reading the ship's log to find out what really happened on board. You also can explore links to other Disney films and videos.

Skywalker Sound

**www.thx.com/thx/skywalker/
skywalker.html**

How movie sound effects are created:
Have you ever wondered how movie
producers come up with those wonderful
Star Wars sounds — such as the *Star Wars*
laser blasts or R2-D2's squeaks and
whistles? This site answers your questions and explains how these various
sounds are mixed together to create a
movie sound track. You can find out
about sound effects in other movies, too,
including *Jurassic Park* (remember the
dino roars?) and *Toy Story*.

T'Bone Fender's Star Wars Universe

www.internexus.net/~tambone/

A mecca for *Star Wars* enthusiasts:
Besides the usual *Star Wars* archival
material, this *Star Wars* page contains
some cool behind-the-scenes stuff and an
archive of cut scenes. It also has the
latest images from the prequel being shot
in the Middle East. T'Bone, the page's
author, has posted autographs of *Star
Wars* actors. The site includes some funny
pages and links to other *Star Wars* sites.
Don't miss this one!

World Media

www.worldmedia.fr/cine/

All about film festivals: The trend for
many major cities these days seems to be
hosting an important film festival. The
World Media Live site (sponsored by
Le Monde) will bring you the news about
each festival as it happens, whether it's in
Mill Valley, California, or Cannes, France.

One fun feature here is the "Cafe des
Fans," where you can ask questions that
reveal the evolving direction of movies
today (for example, "Should there be
more nudity in blockbuster action
movies?" or "If all the past winners of the
Golden Palm were on a sinking life raft,
who should be tossed overboard to save
the others?" or even "Would William
Shakespeare like Kenneth Branagh?").
You can also ask more trivial questions
about your favorite stars ("What is
Liv Tyler's favorite food?"). One section
of the site, in which celebrities are
morphed, requires a QuickTime plug-in.

Other Stuff to Check Out

Web sites

www.filmsite.org/
allmovie.com/amg/movie_Root.html
echo.simplenet.com/
www.mgm.com/bond/
www.turner.com/tcm/index.htm

Suggested search-engine keywords

Yahoo!: Movies or video, plus specific
subtopic (for example: cinema, film,
black and white, Wizard of Oz, Star
Wars)

Lycos: Movies or video, plus specific
subtopic (for example: Marilyn Monroe,
African, Swedish)

Music for the Whole Family

With the development of audio files for
the Net, music sites became far more than
huge information databases or, at the
opposite extreme, sites for fan to celebrate their idols, whether they are the
Rolling Stones or Beethoven. Music
history sites educate you about lost or
little-known forms of music; event sites
tell you where and when you can buy
concert tickets; and the best sites

combine abundant factual information about the music and the artists with the joy of the music itself. These pages give you a glimpse of the rich variety of online music pages, including classical, country, jazz, pop, rock, ethnic, and world music.

Addicted to Noise

www.addict.com/

Music e-zine online: You can find a fair number of music e-zines out there, but Addicted to Noise is considered to be one of the best. Besides Music News of the World, an impressive beat, Addicted contains feature articles such as "Beating the 'Sophomore' slump" (on Green Day's attempt at a comeback) that vie for your attention with columns by Greil Marcus, Cynthia Fuchs, and others. Addicted doesn't limit its content to music: Features and columns touch on radio, the politics of entertainment (affirmative action in film casting and plots, for example), and television as well. Movies are covered by a section called Cinemachine, which leads to dozens of movie reviews scattered throughout the Net. If you have a little time, stop by Sonic Lodge, where you can log on and talk about your latest peeves and passions in the entertainment world. This page has two versions: Hi-Fi comes complete with flashing GIFs, Shockwave files, and QuickTime movies; Lo-Fi is for those with less powerful modems — or a little less time to spare.

AllStar by Rocktropolis

www2.rocktropolis.com/rt/
    main.asp?area_id=2&venue_id=16

Alternative, rock, and more: Don't confuse this site with sports — it is visually crowded but cool and well worth a visit. Flashing signs will direct you through the site: Find your favorite band

in the section called Hunt; use the ichat plug-in to participate in the discussion groups; or get the Microsoft Netshow plug-in to play and watch cybercasts. AllStar has intelligent reviews, up-to-date news ("Metallica plans free Concert"), and interesting notes on culture that are not just limited to music. You can also chat with other music fiends in the Buzz Cafe or buy the hottest CDs on Music Boulevard, and you'll also find links to David Bowie's site and the (Rolling) Stones World.

Beatles Life — Entertainment Web

www.entertainmentweb.com/

Celebrating the Fab Four: This Web site has lyrics and sound files (naturally) and the first online Beatles newsletter. The site's articles combine Beatles news (information on Paul's rumored TV appearances turn out to be false) and trivia (updated weekly), with Beatles Chat (real-time discussions for Beatles fans), Beatles Postcards (you can send one directly to all your friends), the Beatles Life Store (CDs at low prices), the Beatles Bulletin Board, a list of all the Beatles' Grammys, and a huge photo archive with images from the Beatles' childhoods and early tours through the 1995 Paul, George, and Ringo reunion photo. One fun feature is "Paul is Dead," which explains that strange chapter in Beatles history. The more than two dozen Beatles links include Neil's Beatle Page, BEATLEFEST, and the unusual Non-Musical Writings of John Lennon.

Blues Web

www.island.net/~blues/

Talking the blues: If you like blues, you'll probably relish the slow, rich tone of this page as the author walks you through each section, from audio files to biographies to an art gallery. The site offers a lot of information in addition to the music, and much of it is in oral history or interview format. The sound of these musicians talking is almost itself like hearing the blues. Be aware that Blues Web is a slow download. Most of the music samples are in WAV format and can be handled by current browsers.

Country Spotlight

www.countryspotlight.com/

For country music fans: This interactive country music magazine is updated every weekday. You'll find articles (such as the one about Chet Atkins, "Playing from the Heart"), CD reviews, interviews (with the likes of Alison Krauss, Pam Tillis, and Mark Chesnutt), sound clips, interactive games, classifieds, chats, polls and perspectives, opinions on trends in country music, and "Name That Tune." Your browser should be able to handle the AU files, but a RealAudio version is also available. The archives hold previous articles and interviews, and the hot links (don't mind the frying sausage icon) are quite comprehensive. Also available is Ask Cousin Url — whose knowledge of country music seems mighty impressive. Here's a sample question: "I heard that Epic producer and songwriter great Billy Sherrill had a record out in the 1960s on his interpretations of country music

classics. Is it available on CD or tape?" Cousin Url identified the probable album, noted that it was not included in the Country Music Foundation Media Library, and sent the inquiring soul to a dealer knowing just what to ask for. Whew.

The Classical MIDI Archives

www.prs.net/midi.html#index

Only the classic movements from the masters: How about some nice and relaxing music to soothe and calm you? Download and play concertos from Bach, Beethoven, Chopin, Mozart, and more by using your computer. This award-winning site features for your enjoyment thousands of classical music compositions in MIDI format. This site is probably the most complete of its kind on the Internet. If you are looking for the "1812 Overture," the "Ode to Joy," or the "Hallelujah Chorus," it's here. A pretty darn good search engine will help you if you can't remember the composer or composition title.

Classical Net

www.classical.net/

A thousand years of classical music: This beautiful page presents information about classical music performers and composers and explains the basic classic repertoire — that is, classical styles and forms of music from the medieval period through the modern day. This site can also help you identify music that you recognize. You also find a buying guide, recommended CDs, reviews and articles, and classical music links. (One thing you don't find, however, is sound.) The searchable indexes are at the bottom of the home page.

IUMA (Internet Underground Music Archive)

www.iuma.com/

Master music site: IUMA considers itself the one stop for all music surfers. It is a formidable music archive, fully search-able, and very up-to-date. If you want to locate a particular artist, you can search by name, genre, or recording label. Still not sure this is the page for you? Well, IUMA features hundreds of artists and has partnered with 25 recording labels to bring you the best music resources online. Right now you can find informa-tion on classical, country, techno, rave, children's music, rock, hard rock, easy listening, folk, punk, instrumental, hip hop, New Age, jazz, Thrash, Weird, soul, R&B, and World music. Performers range from Ella Fitzgerald and Elton John to Altered Vision and Sublime. This site requires either a RealAudio plug-in or one called Liquid MusicPlayer and offers a place to download either plug-in from the home page. Samples of the music are AU and MPEG files.

John Roache's Ragtime MIDI Library

members.aol.com/ragtimers/index.html

Site devoted to Ragtime: The slogan on this site says, "Some of the Finest Rag-time, Stride, and Swing Piano Music on the Internet" — and that's absolutely

true. Classics from Scott Joplin like "Maple Street Rag" and Hoagy Carmichael's "Georgia on My Mind," are featured. The Web site is run by John Roache, like the title says, but he is also the man performing a lot of the files posted here. Great pianist! Great site!

The Lighthouse electronic Magazine

tlem.netcentral.net/

Celebrating Christian music: Lighthouse is a monthly contemporary Christian music magazine that contains artist interviews with leading vocalists such as Lisa Bevill and Rebecca St. James, album reviews, upcoming release lists, news, and much more. Besides individual singers, groups such as Six Foot Deep are featured here as well. The articles are newsy but have a definite Christian focus. Editorials include topics such as "A Message to the Media," and "What Exactly Is a 'Good' 'Christian' Video?" The section DIG is about "unearthing the under-ground"; in other words, it is the place to go to read about "up-and-coming and otherwise noteworthy unsigned acts." The reviews cover Christian folk through Christian alternative rock, and the reviewers are detailed but not overly long in their writing, and are refreshingly casual. If you have the RealAudio plug-in or your browser can play AU files, you can listen to audio samples while you're visiting.

The Midi Farm

www.midifarm.com

Music for the entire family: All things MIDI are on this site. Not only can you down-load all sorts of free MIDI files, but you can get all the technical information on how the MIDI file is constructed, the instrument names, and even download a MIDI player if you're not satisfied with the one you're using. A lot of this site is really advanced for the common user. If you want to skip all the techno mumbo-jumbo, just jump into the Free Files section and get some tunes to play on your computer. This site contains over 4,000 files and a handful of links to even more MIDI file sites.

Music from Africa and the African Diaspora

matisse.net/~jplanet/afmx/ahome.htm

Information about music from numerous African countries: You can select the countries from an alphabetical list; general facts and figures about some countries supplement the information about music. This comprehensive site is a bit slow to download, but if you want to find out about African percussion, the music of Benin, Kenyan popular music, the Kanda Bongo Man, or Master Musicians of Jajouka, you must see this page. Most of the sound clips are WAV format and will play on most current browsers.

Music Interactive

musicinteractive.com/

Musicians' home page: This comprehensive music page may be of special interest to musicians, music industry professionals, and serious music students. The site

is free, although visitors need to register. Here's where you can find music news, tips on life as a musician, and chat rooms to discuss music developments, as well as links to legal information, professional resources, publishers, and a product showcase section.

The Musicals Home Page

live.mit.edu/musicals/

Playbill online: This site is made for actors, singers, and fans of musicals. You can find everything from *Brigadoon* and *Big* to *Les Miserables* and *Phantom of the Opera*. Each musical listed on this site has a page containing links to a song list, to lyrics, and to a history of the musical in question. You can even find links to other sites specifically featuring that musical. You can cast your vote to rank each musical on a scale from 1 to 9. Some audio files are available in a compressed Zip format; others are WAV format.

Offbeat Online

www.offbeat.com/

Blues, soul, and jazz in Louisiana: *OffBeat* is New Orleans' and Louisiana's monthly music and entertainment magazine that specializes in interviews and features on the music and music-makers in New Orleans. Contents include special coverage of the Louisiana Music on Tour, Jazz Fest information, and dates of Louisiana fairs and festivals. This site has garnered a number of awards, including making the top 1001 sites selected by PC Computing. The site is understated in style (muted colors and few images), but a glance at the Club Descriptions (more than 70 establishments) will remind you how seriously music is taken in Louisiana. The section called News Flash has the latest-breaking New Orleans and Louisiana music and music industry news, including new music deals, music awards, and obituaries. You'll find outstanding jazz, blues, and Louisiana links, a music board where you can post messages, back issues (with select features posted in their entirety) if you need to read more, and subscription information.

Rock and Roll Hall of Fame and Museum

www.rockhall.com

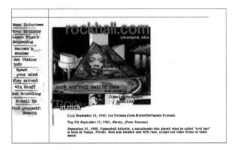

Profiles and audio files of rock legends: The Rock and Roll Hall of Fame and Museum is in Cleveland, Ohio, and the launch of its Web site was one of the highlights of the Net in 1996. This is a comprehensive site; besides the profiles of rock legends like Aretha Franklin, Elton John, Buddy Holly, Elvis Presley, Little Richard, and the Beatles (with accompanying WAV, AU, and/or RealAudio audio files, of course), you can listen to audio files of 500 songs that, according to the experts in Cleveland, shaped rock and roll. One section focuses on the cities that formed rock and roll (Detroit, Los Angeles, and Liverpool, England). Those who need a contest to be happy can try to win a T-shirt by submitting their own classic rock and roll memory — in 75 words or less.

The Ultimate Theme Song MIDI Page

mrdata.simplenet.com/midi.htm

Great TV and motion picture themes: Old and new TV and movie theme songs are here for the picking. Enjoy scores from *Star Wars, Les Miserables, The Summer of '42, West Side Story, Jurassic Park,* and more. Television shows from the past and present include *The Addams Family, Baywatch, Melrose Place,* and even the *Rush Limbaugh Show.* A healthy list of links for MIDI junkies is available if you can't get your fill here. And if that isn't enough, you can even link over to movie and television sites and to general Internet resources.

Unfurled

www.unfurled.com

Music for the MTV crowd: With the technical savvy of Yahoo and the spirit of MTV, this site is totally awesome. You can find almost every musical topic that you can think off, from labels and artists' tours, to charts, genres, live interviews, chats, and gossip. Of course, the site also has information about recording studios, music magazines, lyrics, and tabs (kinda like sheet music for guitars). Although this site doesn't use plug-ins, some of the sites to which you can link from here require RealAudio and Shockwave, so be prepared.

WebNoize

www.webnoize.com

Web music only: Don't miss this handsome Web e-zine, the first magazine dedicated exclusively to music on the

Web: WebNoize covers the music industry and the Web music scene, and offers daily news, features, exclusive reports, and commentary. News headlines include such topics as digital video offerings, site developers, generative music, High-Tech enforcing performance rights, women generating Noize in music, media and the Web, electronic music labels report, and so on. You'll find reviews and special reports, such as the in-depth analysis of how the Internet has revolutionized the concept of a musical event — tours will never be the same. Each week, WebNoize has different departments (Happenings, Business, Sitings, Technology), and you can always visit one of the following: Current Issue, News, Search, Archive, and Newsletter. A section called Buzz, for the editor's reflections on the latest musical inventions online, has truly excellent links to other related sites. This site is timely and intelligently done.

Other Stuff to Check Out

Web sites
www.jsbach.org/
www.wnet.org/mom/
www.ubl.com/
syy.oulu.fi/music/
musiccentral.msn.com

Newsgroups
alt.guitar
alt.music.
rec.music.bluenote
rec.music.classical
rec.music.christian
rec.music.folk

Suggested search-engine keywords
Yahoo!: Music, plus keyword (for example: rock, jazz, classical, country, blues, gospel)

Lycos: Music, plus keyword (for example: record labels, Beatles, Cranberries, Oasis, Wynton Marsalis)

Television Channels and Networks

Some television networks are so good that they become famous in their own right — and sometimes they even have great Web pages. Here are some of the best television network Web sites.

A&E Television Network

www.aetv.com/index2.html

Television that combines education and entertainment: A&E, the Arts and Entertainment channel, is top-notch — like a restaurant with a changing menu but where the food is always the best. For example, A&E's Web links, such as www.biography.com and www.historychannel.com, are good-looking and crammed full of interesting stuff. On the Biography site, you can find profiles of figures from throughout history, including a series of programs on women, including Princess Diana, Amelia Earhart, and Marilyn Monroe. The A&E home page is full of material to intrigue children — such as the Mystery Database, a weekly quiz, and information about the making of *Ivanhoe*.

Discovery Channel

www.discovery.com/

Discover the Discovery Channel: This Web site is almost as cool as the channel itself. Articles and pictures focus on the Discovery Channel's nature, science, technology, and history programs. Most

252 Movies, Music, and Television

of the stories change each week, but they are archived so you can read them again later. The site also includes tours; one takes you to visit Keiko, the real *Free Willy* whale who lives in Oregon. This page also has links to The Learning Channel and Animal Planet.

Disney Channel

www.disney.com/DisneyChannel/

Preview the latest on Disney TV: A can't-miss site, the Disney Channel is great for children of all ages. That's because here you can see *Timon & Pumbaa* or *Aladdin* cartoons. However, this site focuses on what's new on Disney TV and when you can see it. You can watch QuickTime movies and audio clips for each featured show. The site also has some amusing links; each day you can download a new coloring page for your little brother or sister (or yourself if you're a fan). Links to Disney's Star Watch (Web sites of Disney characters) and the Disney Directory (Disney online resources) are other features of this site.

ESPN — SportsZone

espnet.sportszone.com/

Twenty-four hours of sports: ESPN brings you sports news, scores, statistics, rumors, editorials — you name it. You can click directly on coverage of your favorite

sport — baseball, football, tennis, golf, soccer, whatever — or start with the general news updates. The site includes great action shots and live audio files. With over 100,000 pages on this site, something for everyone in the household is bound to be here. Get active with one of the four on-line Zone Games: Fantasy Football, Basketball, Hockey, and Baseball. You can also join the chatter, cast your vote in a poll, or dash off a letter to the editor . . . er, producer.

NBC.com

www.nbc.com/

Television network news and sports: NBC has clearly caught on to the Net. This NBC page links you to online shows (counterparts to their real programs) such as *At the Max, The Pretender,* and *Profiler.* You can also find links to NBC Sports and to a chat room where the NBC stars like Fred Savage of *Wonder Years* fame and Sarah Buxton of *Sunset Beach* connect to you (NBC promises). The best link, of course, is to MSNBC, where the combined efforts of Microsoft and NBC bring you some of the fastest and most detailed news coverage available online.

Nickelodeon

www.nick.com/

Games and more for *Rugrat* fans: Nickelodeon is clever television for kids; not surprisingly, this Web site is also creative. Nick's sections explore the programs (highlighting favorites such as *Rugrats*) and add games, Nick Magazine, and the Big Helper, where visitors young and old are encouraged to make a difference through civic and charitable activities. The site also links to Nick at Nite, where you can read about *The Betty White Show, Bewitched, I Dream of Jeannie,* and other classic television shows.

Other Stuff to Check Out

Web sites
> abc.com
> cbs.com
> www.historychannel.com/
> www.cnn.com/
> www.pbs.org/

Newsgroups
> alt.tv.public-access
> rec.arts.tv

Suggested search-engine keywords
> Yahoo!: Television or TV, plus keyword (for example: channel, network, NBC, Fox, or Warner Brothers)
> Lycos: Television, or TV, plus keyword (for example: sci-fi, horror, Comedy Central, or Weather Channel)

Television Shows

Who would have thought 40 years ago that television would have the impact on our society that it has? Not only has the content of the programs changed, but the number of channels has escalated as well. Now with the personal computer and the Internet, another medium enters the scene and competes for your time. If you find that you can no longer keep up with your favorite TV shows because you're constantly surfing the Web, try these

sites. If your favorite show is not in this list, you can be sure that a site somewhere on the Internet focuses on your all-time favorite show.

The Biggest Simpsons' Links Page

www.geocities.com/TelevisionCity/ 2395/

Links to *The Simpsons:* Famed the world over, the Simpsons — Bart, Homer, Marge, Lisa, and Maggie — have a huge following on the Net. This page lists dozens of Web sites dedicated to this American cartoon family. The author has graded the Web sites: Each has earned a rating of 2 through 5, representing boring to great; a rating of 1 gets a "Really Bad" icon. The site's author has also created icons to tell you which sites have audio clips, video clips, text, pictures, and trivia. The download is slow, but this may be the best site you can find if you enjoy *The Simpsons.* As with anything Simpson-esque, parental supervision is a good idea on some of the sites that are listed here.

Children's Television Workshop

www.ctw.org/

A class act for children: *Sesame Street* has been setting the standard for children's television for two decades. At this good-looking page, children can enter a writing contest, find out about family trips, and play Java games with Elmo. The site is less concerned with references to the television series (although it does present some interesting behind-the-scenes interviews) than with an expansion of the ideas and series characters into the Internet world. Most children will like this site.

Clarissa Explains It All

www.ee.surrey.ac.uk/Contrib/Entertain-
ment/Clarissa/

Your guide to Clarissa and her family: The popular Nickelodeon television series starring Melissa Joan Hart continues to win new fans. Meanwhile, the related site describes the characters, guides you through the episodes, and offers details about the CD that you can buy. "Did Ya Notice?" has trivia about Clarissa and the Darling family — including mistakes made in filming the series! You also can find some questions and answers along with teasers about some of the episodes.

Dr. Quinn, Medicine Woman

www.aspenlinx.com/DrQuinn/

Behind the scenes with the Medicine Woman: This page gives you some behind-the-scenes photos taken during the making of this television series set in the Wild West. The heroine, Dr. Quinn, faces difficulties each week involving her family, her work, and her community, and every week she solves the problem (sometimes with a little help from her friends). On the Web site, you can use the Post Office to send fan e-mail (in care of the site) to the individual characters of the show, or you can drop into the Portrait Gallery for some pictures from different episodes. If you have a hankerin' for some sound or video files from the show, including the theme song and Sully and Mike exchanging their wedding vows, this site has 'em!

Klingon Diplomatic Corps

www.klingon.org/

Klingon database: Inspired, of course, by the fierce Klingon warriors of *Star Trek,* this site holds the Klingon informational archives and brings you the latest Federation news — from a Klingon perspective. Links take you to numerous sites of interest to Klingons and their enemies. The section on Who's Who in Klingon Society features the biographies and filmographies of the actors and actresses who have played Klingons in film and television. Other sections include information about Klingon rituals and traditions and Klingon cultural links on family lines and architectural tradi-tions. You can view an expanding Klingon image gallery, but you won't find many links to other *Star Trek* pages. For those, you have to go to Yahoo!

The Lurkers Guide to Babylon 5

www.midwinter.com/lurk/comic/
index.html

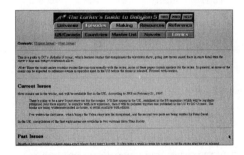

Babylon 5 comic-book site: As the site authors warn, this guide to DC comic's *Babylon 5* series is so closely linked to the television program that the comics can spoil the TV series by giving away secrets! Visit the site to learn about new comics (available in early 1998), Babylon 5's origins (and the Earth-Minbari War), the universe of Babylon 5, episodes from five seasons, the making of the *Babylon 5* television series, the cast, its setting, and a lot more. Of particular interest to teens

are the production links, which identify several principals behind the scenes of the TV show (the producer, writer, director, designer, and so on) and explain what their backgrounds are and what their jobs necessitate. Links connect you to fan clubs, numerous mailing lists, and World Wide Web sites.

Total TV OnLine

www.tottv.com/index.html

Electronic version of a magazine covering American television: *Xena: Warrior Princess, Hercules: The Legendary Journeys,* Cable for Kids, *Mystery Science Theater 3000,* and other subjects and shows are characteristic feature topics. The Web version of *Total TV* magazine also brings you complete TV listings and assorted Web sites dedicated to television. Creative touches include the Browse Bin (with fantastic related Web sites like PBSOnline and ESPN SportZone's Fantasy Basketball) and TV Tactics (with information for parents on TV and your child). You'll also find news related to TV and the Web, such as the recent report about corporate crackdowns on fan Web sites. By popular demand, the site has a stunning link to *Star Trek* Web sites!

TREKNEWS.com

www.treknews.com

Star Trek news across the galaxy: Formerly the Federation Chronicles, this electronic journal combines the latest technology (real-time chats and forums) with good interpretive articles. Besides the major articles appearing in Mission Profile, you'll find the TransWarp Newsletter, created by the editors of TrekScoop and Stardate, and news stories (such as a brief announcement of Patrick "Captain Picard" Stewart's engagement to *Voyager* producer Wendy Neuss). Other links lead to related pages such as FedChron and the TrekNews Book Bin, where you can purchase thousands of science-fiction books online. This site is great for *Star Trek* fans of all ages.

Wishbone

www.pbs.org/wishbone/

Television terrier's Web site: This site spotlights Wishbone, the adorable Jack Russell terrier who stars in a PBS series created to introduce children to literature. Wishbone knows a lot about great books. You find pictures and a discussion of all the stories that Wishbone has "starred" in: "Hercules Unleashed," "Hunchdog of Notre Dame," "Bone of Arc," "Little Big Dog," "Frankenbone," "Cyranose," "The Impawssible Dream," and many other fine tales. You also can obtain scheduling information and watch a QuickTime promotion of the rascally little pup.

The X-Files

www.thex-files.com/

The X-Files official site: As dark and mysterious as the series, this site invites you to inspect the case files — the real substance of the site. The bulk of the site is devoted to an extensive listing of the episodes, listed chronologically. When available, QuickTime movies from the episode can be found at the end of the synopsis. You can also give your feedback on that episode via another link at the end of the episode summary. Also included are information facts on the show and its creator, character biographies, a fan forum where you can compare notes with other *X-Files* fans, and "What's New," a section where you can enter contests and buy stuff such as *X-Files* books for young adults and art inspired by the series.

Other Stuff to Check Out

Web sites

www.foxworld.com/simpindx.htm
www.timelapse.com/tvlink.html
www.epithet.demon.co.uk/
www.prairienet.org/britcom/BD/index.html
www.internetv.com
www.canoe.ca/Jam
www.multichannel.com
www.geocities.com/Hollywood/Lot/2756/
    seinfeld.htm
ourworld.compuserve.com/homepages/
    ntsgr/
www.stgenesis.org/seaQuest
www.primenet.com/~dbrady/
people.delphi.com/slanoue/loisep.htm
www.tvguide.com
www.nytimes.com/etv/
www.holodeck3.com/
www.nbc.com/tvcentral/
us.imdb.com/M/multi-search
www.kids.warnerbros.com/karaoke/
www.primenet.com/~dbrady/

Newsgroups

alt.tv.simpsons
rec.arts.tv
rec.arts.startrek.misc

Suggested search-engine keywords

Yahoo!: Television series, plus keyword (for
    example: Dr. Quinn, Star Trek, E.R.,
    Quantum Leap)
Lycos: TV Shows, plus keyword (for
    example: Mad About You, Wonder
    Woman, Brady Bunch)

Part VI
Mother Earth,
Father Sky

"From now on, let's confine our exploration of ancient Egypt to the computer program."

In this part . . .

Interested in browsing around the universe? Want to know more about dinosaurs or prehistoric people? Or maybe you'd like some information about a nearby national forest? Have you ever considered taking up bird-watching or forming a local environmentally conscious group? Take a look at this part. The sites profiled cover lots of topics related to our earth in the past and present, ecology and environment, recycling, "green" politics, and outer space.

Earth a Long Time Ago

www.bvis.uic.edu/museum/exhibits/dino/images/albert2.gif

We are all curious about the people and creatures who lived before us. On the Net, scientists and specialists can show us what they know about ancient life, answer our questions, and discuss the questions *they* still have about prehistoric animals and ancient civilizations. Whether you are fascinated by woolly mammoths discovered frozen in the Russian Arctic or interested in the Mayans who developed a complex civilization in Central America, individuals and organizations like the Museum of Natural History in Chicago, Illinois (www.fmnh.org./Home.htm), have created dozens of fascinating Web sites with information about life long ago on planet Earth.

Archaeology and Anthropology

Web sites can help you discover the wonders of archaeology and anthropology. *Archaeology* is the study of human history and prehistory through the excavation of sites. *Anthropology* focuses on people, on both their physical development (*physical* anthropology) and their diverse societies and customs (*cultural* anthropology). Of course, these different studies often overlap. Most of the following sites focus on one group of people or geographic area, but all tell fascinating stories of how human beings have adapted to life in diverse environments around the world. (For more information on early peoples, check out the History section in Part II: Cool School Tools.)

General archaeology and anthropology resources

ArchNet

spirit.lib.uconn.edu/ArchNet/ArchNet.html

Archaeology resources for the serious student: ArchNet is the Web's Virtual Library for Archaeology. It lists just about all major Internet archaeological resources and is searchable. The site includes categories such as museums, academic departments, geographic areas, and subjects (for example, ethnohistory, historic archaeology, and software) and can be accessed in six languages. The museum list is especially useful. Don't miss the featured site, which changes on an irregular basis, that makes "a significant contribution to the way in which the World Wide Web is used by archaeologists for research, teaching, and publication." One recent choice focused on the excavation of a 19th century Manhattan slum!

Anita Cohen-Williams's List of Anthropology/Archaeology WWW sites

www.aau.dk/~etnojens/etnogrp/
    anitaslist.html

Archaeology and anthropology from *A* to *Z:* Although the author claims that this list is not totally comprehensive, look what it includes: general Web pages; site-specific resources; Egyptian, North American, and Mediterranean Web pages; physical anthropology sites (including primates); museums, associations, and organizations; underwater anthropology; and technology. Neatly organized and quick (no images), this site may be the most efficient place to start exploring!

Classics and Mediterranean Archaeology Home Page

rome.classics.lsa.umich.edu/
    welcome.html

Explore ancient civilizations: This terrific list of archaeological sites is particularly rich in resources on Greece and the Aegean; it also includes pages on the Near East and world history. Not all of the references are scholarly: Sites such as Exploring Ancient World Cultures or The Greek World of Mary Renault may be of interest to teens. The first site is a splendid collection of poetry, short stories, and history recollections that enable the visitor to embrace some of the ancient civilizations by getting a feel for how life was lived in those times. Mary Renault was a novelist whose most renowned books are based on the ancient Greeks. Mixing history, legend, and myth, Renault brought ancient Greece to life. Don't miss the image resources and online journals.

Peoples from around the world

Arctic Circle

www.lib.uconn.edu/ArcticCircle/
    HistoryCulture/

Life at the top of the world: Several tribes are indigenous to the Arctic Circle, including the European Sámi, the Cree of Northern Quebec, the Nenets and Khanti of Siberia, Russia, and the Inupiat of Arctic Alaska. Here, each is the subject of an ethnographic portrait. You also can read thought-provoking articles about life in the harsh Arctic, the treatment of these tribes by Europeans, and the arts of these indigenous tribes.

Canadian Museum of Civilization — First Peoples Hall

www.cmcc.muse.digital.ca/membrs/
    level01.html

Indigenous life in North America: Early life and indigenous cultures in Canada are displayed and discussed in the Early Peoples Hall and the Archaeology Hall. What clothing did they wear? What type of boats did they use? Who were the Inuvialuit people and how did they live? The past relics and history of the first Canadians are presented here in text and photos. The Canadian Museum of Civilization also has a section on the Mayan civilization (www.cmcc.muse.digital.ca/membrs/civiliz/maya/mminteng.html). This page links back to the museum's pages on North American history.

Chetro Ketl Great Kiva

www.sscf.ucsb.edu/anth/projects/
great.kiva/

Focus on vanished Native Americans: This magnificent 3-D reconstruction of a Great Kiva, or subterranean Anasazi house, is based on archaeological finds in New Mexico. You can choose from minimal interactivity or a visually richer version, depending on the capabilities of your computer. Whichever you select, the detailed text, beautiful graphics, and "Turtle Dance" audio, available as a Quicktime or LiveAudio file, evoke the spirit of this long-vanished Native American people.

Cyber Mummy

www.ncsa.uiuc.edu/Cyberia/
VideoTestbed/Projects/Mummy/
mummyhome.html

An ancient Egyptian mummy comes to life: How can technology help uncover the mysteries of ancient Egypt? Visit this page and discover the secrets of an Egyptian mummy. Through animation and movies, you see a mummy come to life, "pick up" objects, and be taken back in time to its home in Fayum Oasis in ancient Egypt.

Flints and Stones: Real Life in Prehistory

www.ncl.ac.uk/~nantiq/menu.html

Meet Britain's late Stone Age hunter-gatherers: This well-illustrated site takes you back in time nearly 13,000 years to when earth was populated by hunter-gatherers. You meet a *shaman,* or magic man, and discover what the hunter-gatherers ate and how they found their food, as well as how they built their houses, created art, and buried their dead. You can also meet an archaeologist and unearth some misleading myths about prehistoric peoples.

Ice Mummies of the Inca

www.pbs.org/wgbh/pages/nova/peru/
expedition/index.html

Meet a 500-year-old Peruvian child: Nova and WGBH television in Boston have created this wonderful page about 7-year-old Sarita, the 500-year-old Inca mummy discovered near Quilcata, Peru. Photographs show the mummy and other artifacts found near her, as well as contemporary folks at work on the site. The authors explain Inca rituals and other uses of the objects they've found.

MayaQuest 97 — Lost Cities of the Rainforest

www.sci.mus.mn.us/sln/ma/top.html

Ancient peoples of Mexico and Central America: MayaQuest is an exploration of the ancient people who created a rich and complex civilization in Mexico and Central America starting around A.D. 260. The Mayans were great warriors, administrators, inventors, and artists, and their cities dominated this area for nearly 600 years before being mysteriously abandoned. This page explains Mayan history and gives a report on the discoveries of a team of students and archaeologists who are exploring the jungle while studying the sites of this fascinating civilization. The page also discusses the descendants of these great people. If you want, you can submit your artwork and Mayan questions to the team at this Web site. This site offers a lot for the senses, which means you will need several plug-ins in addition to the ones installed by your browser: Quicktime, Shockwave, and RealAudio.

Mysterious Places

www.mysteriousplaces.com/

Sacred sites and ancient cultures: This handsome and succinct Web page introduces several mysterious cultures, including the people of Easter Island, Stonehenge, Chichén Itzá, Egypt, and ancient America. Each has a separate page with text explaining these places and their artifacts. You also find links to Web sites about other mysterious places, including the Lost City of Atlantis and the lost (and recently found) Arabian city of Ubar.

Perseus Project

www.perseus.tufts.edu/

A digital library of Greek antiquity: The classicists at Tufts University have compiled an amazing collection of documents, images, and Web resources for this digital library on ancient Greece. The site contains texts by famous Greeks, such as the philosopher Plato or the historian Herodotus, and Greek dictionaries. You also find a rich database of Greek art and archaeology, with over 13,000 images of ancient coins, Greek vases, buildings, and archaeological sites. For fun, don't miss Nicolas Stringos's beautiful model of the Parthenon sculpted out of 1,300 sugar cubes!

The Traveler

tqd.advanced.org/2840/

Ancient civilizations of the ancient Middle East — and beyond: Travel back through time to immerse yourself in an ancient culture at this beautiful site. You choose your character — either a merchant, a scholar, or a princess — and determine how the character might act on a "journey" through the ancient Middle East! Each character dates from a different period and has a different problem to solve appropriate to that character and that time. After you try one character, you'll want to try them all!

Viking Home Page

control.chalmers.se/vikings/

Bloodthirsty vandals or adventuresome inventors?: This amazing Swedish site can help you distinguish the truth from the myths concerning the Vikings, those famous seafaring raiders. The page lists tons of topics related to Vikings: museums, exhibitions, and festivals; general Viking information (ships, homes, clothing, and social structure); their stories, language, and writing, or *runes;* and Vikings today. The site uses frames, which can be tricky, but it is filled with links, including 14 on Viking longships alone!

Other Stuff to Check Out

Web sites

www.ucmp.berkeley.edu/subway/
    anthro.html
www.memst.edu/egypt/main.html
www.superscape.com/intel/shenge.htm
www.sscf.ucsb.edu:80/anth/index.html
www.umich.edu/~pfoss/ROMARCH.html
www.aboriginalart.com.au/culture/

Newsgroups

sci.archaeology
sci.anthropology
sci.archaeology.mesoamerican
sci.anthropology.paleo
soc.culture.native

Mailing lists

majordomo@rome.classics.lsa.umich.edu
Roman_Sites-L

Suggested search-engine keywords

Yahoo!: Anthropology, archaeology, indigenous peoples, ancient history, cave paintings, peoples (for example: Mayans)
Lycos: Anthropology, archaeology, indigenous peoples

Dinosaurs (Paleontology)

Long before they roared to life in the movie *Jurassic Park,* dinosaurs were a favorite topic for kids of all ages. The following sites describe the different kinds of dinosaurs, explain where their bones were found and how scientists piece them together, and show you other animals that roamed the earth long ago. Most of these pages have fantastic pictures or animation, so be patient while they download.

The Academy of Natural Sciences in Philadelphia

www.acnatsci.org/dinosaurs/index.html

Dino info at a click: Located in the City of Brotherly Love (that's Philadelphia, Pennsylvania) the Academy of Natural Sciences houses a massive exhibit on dinosaurs. You can take a virtual reality tour of the exhibit from this site if you have the Quicktime plug-in for your browser. If you don't have the plug-in, the site has a link so that you can go get it! Shop in the museum gift shop for dino keepsakes or choose the links that take you to the photos and information on the big beasts of the past. Think Tyrannosaurus Rex was the king of dinosaurs? Here you can find which dinosaur was his match!

Dinosauria

www.dinosauria.com

The latest discussions of hot dinosaur topics!: This page is for serious dinosaur students as well as new enthusiasts. The site is divided into four sections: a journal with scientific but easy-to-understand articles on paleontology; an art gallery so that you can see what you are reading about; a dinosaur omnipedia to explain terms and relevant geological information; and a store that sells fossil replicas and dinosaur collectibles.

Dinosaurs in Cyberspace: Dinolinks

www.ucmp.berkeley.edu/diapsids/ dinolinks.html

Dino sites galore: This site may well be the best list of links to dinosaur sites ever compiled: Web sites, museums, projects, art and models, dinosaur movies, and Just for Kids are some of the categories. For example, want to find some funky dinosaur art, or see how they made the dinosaurs so lifelike in *Jurassic Park,* or even order some stuff from Monstrosities, a mail-order company specializing in dinosaur products as well as Godzilla and the like? They are all listed here. Go to it!

Field Museum

fmnh.org./Home.htm

The way it was: Say you can't visit the Field Museum in Chicago, Illinois? You can avoid the crowds, the drive, and the sometimes miserable weather. This site tours the museum through its Exhibits links — and that's where you'll find the dinosaurs! The three exhibits, Life Before Dinosaurs, Dinosaurs, and Teeth, Tusks, and Tarpits!, will take you through the early years of earth when the dinos ruled. In the end, as you will find out at this site, humanity was the overall winner. If you are impatient and want to get straight to the games and videos, you'll find a link to get you there quickly. MPEG movies, interactive games, and an AU file of music conducted on the bones of a mammoth are here for the senses!

National Geographic: Dinosaur Eggs

www.nationalgeographic.com/features/ 96/dinoeggs/

Meet a paleontologist: This virtual tour takes you on an egg hunt where researchers "hatch" dino eggs. You get to meet the hunters (paleontologists or dino specialists) and find where the eggs were discovered. Then you watch as the researchers determine which creatures were probably growing inside these eggs. Don't miss the finished models!

University of California Paleontology Museum

**www.ucmp.berkeley.edu/exhibit/
exhibits.html**

Learn about prehistoric creatures: Paleontology is the study of fossils, dinosaurs, and other prehistoric creatures. At this museum Web site, you find special exhibits on dinosaurs (including Dilophosaurus and Tyrannosaurus Rex), as well as exhibits on such animals as great white sharks, saber-toothed tigers, and woolly mammoths. Just follow the link to Paleontology without Walls. The Subway link leads you to still more online paleontology resources.

Other Stuff to Check Out

Web sites
> www.nrm.se/virtexhi/mammsaga/
> swemamm.html.en
> www.hcc.hawaii.edu/dinos/dinos.1.html
> www.comet.net/dinosaur/
> www.indyrad.iupui.edu/public/jrafert/
> dinoart.html
> www.execpc.com/~maas/extinction/

Newsgroups
> sci.bio.paleontology

Mailing lists
> listproc@usc.edu

Suggested search-engine keywords
> Yahoo!: Dinosaurs, paleontology, fossils,
> trilobytes
> Lycos: Dinosaurs, paleontology, fossils,
> trilobytes

Earth Today

cissus.mobot.org/AABGA/welcome.html

Plant, animal, and watery wonders fill our planet. In this section, you not only find out how and where to best appreciate all these wonders, but you also can get all kinds of information about them as well. The enormous number of species that can be gleaned from the sites listed here represent only a few petals of the flower. The links from these sites can expand your possibilities even more! So stop and smell the roses, trees, fungi, and other living botanical wonders.

Gardens and Arboreta

People around the world study and value plants for their beauty, their potential medicines, and their importance to the welfare of human and animal life (as oxygen producers and food). These sites take you to many of America's premier botanical gardens, as well as to arboreta, herbaria, and public gardens worldwide.

American Association of Botanical Gardens and Arboreta

cissus.mobot.org/AABGA/welcome.html

American links: As the professional association for public gardens in North America, AABGA presents links to member gardens and research programs throughout the nation. Find out more about efforts to study, display, and conserve plants. Its sections include the Publications and Resource Center for gardening and botanical resources. Click Institutional Members to link to home pages of public gardens throughout the United States, many of which display lovely images of plants. Click Related Sites to get links to resources covering such topics as biodiversity; lawns and turf grass; gardening; international gardens; plant research; seeds; trees; rare, native, and cultivated plants; and societies — as well as information on books and discussion groups. If what you see inspires you, click Anyone Can Join!

Internet Directory for Botany: Botanical Museums, Herbaria, Natural History Museums

www.helsinki.fi/kmus/botmus.html

Worldwide botany links: Travel the world to see all kinds of plants and public gardens. This Helsinki-based site provides a huge collection of links that also covers plant research and natural history museums. Select from locations listed such as Africa, Asia, Australia and New Zealand, Europe, Latin America, or North America. Links for Asia, for example, include Gazi University, Faculty of Science and Arts: GAZI Herbarium, Ankara, Turkey; Herbarium, University of Kebangsaan (UKMB), Malaysia; Herbarium, Institute of Botany, Academia Sinica, Taipei (HAST), Taiwan; Botanical Inventory of Taiwan; Herbarium of the

Kochi University (KOCH), Laboratory of Plant Taxonomy, Japan; the North Cyprus Herbarium, Nikosia, Cyprus; and the Herbarium of Tel Aviv University (TELA), Israel. This fascinating site with its worldwide links may really grow on you.

Internet Directory for Botany

www.biol.uregina.ca/liu/bio/idb.shtml

Massive linking network of gardens, botanical organizations, and research worldwide: You can plant yourself here for hours by rooting through subject areas that include Arboreta and Botanical Gardens; Botanical Societies, International Botanical Organizations; Botanical Museums, Herbaria, Natural History Museums; Checklists and Floras, Taxonomical Databases, Vegetation; Vascular Plant Families; Conservation and Threatened Plants; Economic Botany, Ethnobotany; Gardening; Lower Plants and Fungi; Paleobotany, Palynology, Pollen; and University Departments, Other Institutes. You also find newsgroups, mailing lists and other link collections, as well as books and publications, field guides, and lots of good plant images. Search by category, by country, or alphabetically.

Other Stuff to Check Out

Web sites
> www.helsinki.fi/kmus/botcons.html
> www.ualberta.ca/~slis/guides/botany/
>   gardens.htm
> www.ifgb.uni-hannover.de/extern/ppigb/
>   ppigb.htm
> www.trine.com/GardenNet/GardensOnline/
>   state.htm
> www.scisoc.org/

Newsgroups
> sci.bio.botany

Online service area
> America Online: LSI

Suggested search-engine keywords
> Yahoo!: Botany, botanical gardens
> Infoseek: Botany, gardens

Green, Marine, and Animal Attractions

From purple mountains' majesty to the deep-blue sea, these sites emphasize the beauty, complexities, and unique life forms on our planet. Get to know fascinating and often rare plants and animals from other lands. (***Remember:*** To find hundreds — if not thousands — of additional animal and plant links, turn to this book's sections on Life Sciences, Outside Fun, and Pets.)

Natural wonders

The earth is full of beauty, and that statement is evident from the sampling of photos that are available from these sites. Looking at these photos can give you an appreciation for the landscapes that our world offers. From mountains and volcanoes to the beauty of the undersea world, the armchair traveler can see just about every corner of the globe from an Internet browser.

Aquatic Network

www.aquanet.com/

All about the world's seas and inland waters: This site is all wet — and that's terrific! Subject areas include aquaculture, conservation, fisheries, limnology, marine science, oceanography, ocean engineering, seafood, conservation (for example, of whales, dolphins), and maritime history. You can find timely articles, a calendar of water-related events, stories of the sea, and a neat ocean-image gallery. You also find links to hundreds of sites, including aquariums, aquarists (if you have a fish tank, you're going to like this section), conservation groups, notable quotes, school projects, publications, products and services, and issue-oriented topics (for example, whaling, the status of sea turtles, the legacy of Jacques-Yves Cousteau, and so on). Shop for fishy products and books at the online store. Find out about careers, grants, and project funding as well as opportunities to volunteer for research and other programs. You can search the Aquatic Network for specific topics. You can also take virtual tours of the sea if you have the Shockwave Flash animation feature.

Majestic Landscapes

www.kodak.com/digitalImages/
    samples/majesticPix.shtml

Kodak's digital photography site: Kodak's Majestic Landscapes Web page is designed to demonstrate its PhotoCD technology. View high-quality images of Yosemite, Yellowstone, Bora Bora, and other landscapes shot with Kodak's digital cameras. After you select one of the categories, you see small versions of the photos and a list of the photo titles underneath. Following each photo title is a choice of JPEG or Image PAC file. If your browser is capable of viewing inline JPEG files (most current browsers will), or you have software on your computer that can open these files, you can download this version. If, on the other hand, you wish to download the large Image PAC (Kodak PCD format) file, you can choose that link. Not sure if your software will handle the PCD format? Kodak also lists all the applications that they know of that can accomodate PCD format. The images are stunning, and you can link back to Kodak's main page to find out exactly how the pictures were digitized or look at other picture categories.

Natural Resources: Institutions and Organizations

sfbox.vt.edu:10021/Y/yfleung/
    forestry.html

All about the earth's natural resources: Detailed and well-organized, this site contains lots of links to leading nonprofit organizations, research facilities, and government entities that, in one way or another, study, manage, use, or conserve the world's natural resources. Click your country of interest. In Egypt, for example, you can link to the research-based Egyptian Environmental Information Network or the environmental interest group Hurghada Environmental Protection and Conservation Association. Then you're off to Kenya to link with the Mpala Research Centre (which conducts research on tropical ecosystems and sustainable development); the National Museums of Kenya, Centre for Biodiversity; or the East African Wild Life Society. Madagascar links you to the Malagasy Association for the Biodiversity Protection. The United States links are numerous. Search alphabetically for Academic Institutions or click to link lists for Professional/Research organizations or environmental interest groups.

Virtual Image Archive: Nature

imagiware.com/via/Nature/Views/

Images of nature online: Part of a larger site that offers images and other electronic forms of illustration in many categories, this section focuses on sites that offer nature scenes. Click the site to view its images. You find sites for underwater, cloud, landscape, and natural-event images. Most sites use the JPEG format, which can be viewed in most current Web browsers, but some sites may require certain helper applications or plug-ins — such as Adobe Acrobat. You're bound to find something for everyone in this list of links.

Plants and animals of other lands

Prepare for your next safari, vacation, or educational excursion based on the offerings of these sites. From the wildlife of the Dark Continent and the Land Down Under to the beautiful orchids of Canada and China, you can go wild about these sites. Llamas, kangaroos, baboons, and polar bears are just a few of our animal neighbors that you can find out more about.

African Wildlife

www.wolfe.net/~scat/index.html

Articles and links about African animals: As expansive as the African plains, this frames-based site provides a wealth of articles and links. Get new information and updates, a taxonomic index (which you can click to find various animals by order, family, subfamily, species and subspecies), related African links, and a reading list of printed books (literature, nonfiction, and scientific and resource works). The listing of animals includes antelope, sheep, goats, cattle, giraffe, okapi, hippos, swine, dogs, cats, hyena, weasels, otters, genets, civets, mongoose, seals, whales, dolphins, porpoises, the hyrax, zebra, asses, rhinos, bush babies, monkeys, baboons, chimps, apes, elephants, African manatees, and dugongs. In other words, you can have a really wild time browsing here.

Arachnology

dns.ufsia.ac.be/Arachnology/
    Arachnology.html

Spiders of the world unite: Spiders of the world infest this site, including many extinct ones. See the world's biggest, most venomous, most endangered, most beneficial, and most mysterious spiders. This repository and directory of arachnological information and articles helps you weave your way to other great spider sites on the . . . er, Web. A common name guide is available for younger spider fans with listings of, for example, Spiders, Scorpions, Mites, and even some "Special spiders" — black widows, brown recluse spiders, tarantulas, and the hobo spider. Find articles, courses, educational projects, museum and zoo exhibits, phobias, myths, stories, books, poems, songs, art, pictures and movies, conferences and news, research funds, graduate programs, mailing lists, publications, Internet discussion groups and databases, and societies of the world on this site.

Australian A–Z Animal Archive

www.aaa.com.au/A_Z/index.shtml

Community service of the AAA World Announce Archive – Matilda Search Engine in Sydney, Australia: Straight from the Land Down Under comes this alphabetized digest of nearly all Australian animals. (The site is regularly updated, so if you want to suggest to the Webmaster an animal that you don't see here, you're welcome.) Click any letter to find animal drawings and brightly written descriptions of the animals with names that begin with that letter. Under *K,* for example, you find *kangaroo* and *koala* and the *kultarr.* (Huh? You need to read about that one for yourself — no clues.) Find out the animals' habitats, status in the wild, habits, and behaviors.

Canadian Orchid Congress

www.cfn.cs.dal.ca/Recreation/
    OrchidSNS/coc.html

Orchids of Canada and the world: This union of orchid societies is devoted to increasing understanding, propagation, and conservation of their favorite plant, especially in Canada. The Orchid family, with more than 20,000 species, grows from pole to pole, except in the Arctic and Antarctica. But the destruction of native habitats (rain forests, old growth forests), threatens the survival of the species. More than 20 Canadian orchid societies are members of the Canadian Orchid Congress. You can view orchid images, including one of the *Cypripedium calceolus* (in JPEG format), otherwise known as the Yellow Lady's Slipper (*Le Cypripède jaune*). This variety is the symbol of the Canadian Orchid Congress and is native to Canada. Enjoy music, images, and information about wild orchids on this site.

Flora of China

flora.harvard.edu/china/

Research about China's native plants: Make sure that you check out the images on this site, which include plant illustrations and maps. (You can enlarge smaller images by clicking them.) This site reflects an international effort by more than 600 experts to publish the first English-language account of China's native plants and flowers. See which Chinese plants look a lot like our own and which are completely unique. For scientists pondering such topics as the periodic shortage of bamboo for endangered pandas or the search for new human medicines, this undertaking is an important one. For ecologists, the information on this site helps establish the status of many little-known plants. For kids (and parents who like nature), the site offers a neat way to find out about some 30,000 known plant species (twice as many as in the United States and Canada combined) through images and concise text.

Llama Web

www.llamaweb.com/

South America's answer to the camel: Llamas are valued as pack animals and for their wool (not to mention their unique personalities). This site presents the animals for fun and for owners' information. Subjects include llama farms, maintenance and medical care, and ways to interact with llamas (for example, through llama events and services, such as llama trekking). You can find llama games for kids and articles that describe what llamas are, where they come from, their history, their colors and types, how to care for and train them, and how to acquire and raise them. Find out about llama magazines, books, videos, associations, and how to get a llama-loving pen pal!

Plants of the Machiguenga

www.montana.com/manu/

Click through a tour of this Eastern Peruvian rain forest: See how a scientist collects and studies plants in the search for new medicines. Neurologist Dr. Ethan Russo spent two months foraging this spectacular rain forest for plants to treat headaches. (After all, aspirin came from the willow tree.) You find photos of the plants he gathered, along with botanical and medicinal information about them. You also find photos of birds, indigenous peoples, and the rich forests of Peru.

Polar Regions Homepage

www.stud.unit.no/~sveinw/arctic/

Arctic and Antarctic articles and links: Enjoy spectacular images of two spectacular regions and find out about tours and expeditions that take you there in person. Get to know the wildlife, habitats, and explorers of the last great frontiers. Click topics such as The Great Explorers (the history of the polar regions) and Bears, Seals, and Penguins (wildlife near the Poles) for a list and brief descriptions of relevant links.

Tropical Rainforest in Suriname

www.euronet.nl/users/mbleeker/ suriname/suri-eng.html

Clicking tour of a rain forest: Wander through the verdant rain forests, swamps, and Savannah of Suriname to discover its unique people, plants, and animals. You see photos and hear sounds (in WAV format) of the region. Check the map and then read about and view images of various species by clicking their names. Located in South America, to the east of Venezuela, this tropical region faces increasing pressure from timber and mining interests, the results of which you can follow on the bulletin board. You can also link to related sites about Suriname and rain forests.

Other Stuff to Check Out

Web sites
www.aquarius.eds.com/
www.earthwatch.org/ed/home.html
www.tas.gov.au/subject/tourism.htm#flora
www.doe.ca/
clever.net/kerry/creature/creature.htm
www.vni.net/~kwelch/penguins/
www.geom.umn.edu/~jpeng/KOALA/
    koala.html
www.erin.gov.au/erin.html
www.indiana.edu/~primate/primates.html
www.selu.com/~bio/PrimateGallery/
    index.html
rs306.ccs.bbk.ac.uk/flora/welcome.htm
cervid.forsci.ualberta.ca/DeerNet/
    default.html#services
esnet.edu/ican/master.htm

Newsgroups
sci.environment
sci.bio

Mailing lists
dns.ufsia.ac.be/Arachnology/Pages/
    Subscrib.html
www.neosoft.com/internet/paml/groups.C/
    cichlids.html
www.neosoft.com/internet/paml/groups.K/
    killifish.html
cervid.forsci.ualberta.ca/DeerNet/
    DeerMail.html

Online service areas
America Online: Nature
Compuserve: GO EARTH

Suggested search-engine keywords
Yahoo!: Natural wonders, plants, animals,
    aquaria
Infoseek: Nature

National Forests and Other Public Lands

These sites enable you to find national and state-managed lands where you can camp, hike, and nature-watch. Comprehensive linking lists describe locations, rules, access, facilities, fees, amenities, native plants, animals, and terrain. A great way to find county or city public lands is to call your local government's parks and recreation department and ask for the URL of its Internet site! If no Web address is available, you can always ask that someone there just mail you a brochure!

Bureau of Land Management
www.blm.gov/

Official site of the BLM: Both text and graphics versions of this site are available, along with lots of information about this agency, which originally was charged with managing the 270 million surface acres in the country that "nobody wanted." But unlike the nineteenth-century homesteaders who passed this land by, today's society values these areas as desert wilderness, historic tribal land, and grazing, mining, and oil territory. So the BLM's job is to try to make everyone happy. Read what it's doing, express your opinions, and find out how to access BLM lands as a nature-lover or recreationist. You also find a lot of agency-related internal news here, which you may or may not find of interest. But many notable statistics spell out how much of this land is grazed, preserved, mined, trailed, oil-leased, hunted on, and so on and tells you what wildlife is known to exist on BLM lands.

Great Outdoor Recreation Pages - Forests

www.gorp.com/gorp/resource/
US_National_Forest/main.htm

Produced by GORP (the Great Outdoor Recreation Pages): Locate a national forest and get details on how to visit it by using the facilities at this site, which include forest maps, locators, trip planners, books, and related links. Either click the location map or search the state lists. Read up on actual chartered forest trips that you can take (for example, wilderness backpacking, back-country skiing, and snowshoeing in the Rocky Mountains or bicycle tours of Alaska). You can also link to an extensive camping guide and to the U.S. Forest Home Page.

Great Outdoor Recreation Pages - Parks

www.gorp.com/gorp/resource/
US_National_Park/main.htm

U.S. and international parks resources: Plan your trip to the Great Outdoors by using the U.S. Park Map Locator, the U.S. Park Listings, or the list to International parks. Find books, maps, and U.S. Park Jobs or use the search tool to find topics that relate to U.S. parks. Read special reports (for example, *National Parks at Risk: The Grand Canyon – A Case Study from the Natural Resources Defense Council* on issues in the canyon's future). Locate various U.S. national parks and get information about them by clicking a state in the U.S. National Park Locator Map or using the alphabetical listing. (Clicking Alaska, for example, gives you links to the Bering Land Bridge, Denali, Gates of the Arctic, Glacier Bay, and the Kenai Fjords, among other national parks in that state.)

Great Outdoor Recreation Pages - Wilderness Areas

www.gorp.com/gorp/resource/
US_Wilderness_Area/main.htm

Wilderness areas listed for almost every U.S. state: Wilderness areas covered by this site are primarily those located in the U.S. National Forests and National Wildlife Refuges and, to a lesser degree, on Bureau of Land Management lands. Click the state directory to find wilderness areas or use the search function. These wild areas generally offer very limited camping and have specific human-intrusion policies. In fact, you may want to read the Wilderness Ethics section to see just how restrictive the use of these areas really is. Most areas will want you to remove everything that you take in with you (if you pack it in, pack it out). Even biodegradable refuse can take a long time to break down and can be an eyesore to others who use the wilderness area. Find out why these areas are set aside and given such reverent treatment.

Great Outdoor Recreation Pages - Wildlife Areas

www.gorp.com/gorp/resource/us_nwr/
main.htm

Protected areas of U.S. wildlife habitat: Read about specially featured refuges (for example, Refuges of Great Basin – Ruby Lake National Wildlife Refuge in north-eastern Nevada and Fish Springs National Wildlife Refuge in northwestern Utah) and click the state directory to find out more. (Clicking Georgia, for example, provides links to National Wildlife Refuges/Marine Sanctuaries, including Okefenokee National Wildlife Refuge and Savannah Coastal National Wildlife Refuges.) Get all the information you need to visit, enjoy, or come to know these areas online. Read special reports from publications such as *Refuge Reporter,* an independent quarterly journal devoted to increasing recognition and support of the National Wildlife Refuge System. Link to related National Wildlife Refuge System Web pages from the Fish and Wildlife Service.

L.L. Bean's Park Search

www.llbean.com/parksearch/

"The Outdoors at Your Fingertips": Get information to plan your outdoor activities through these factual summaries and good images. Decide where to go to kayak or raft, cross-country or downhill ski, camp, fish, bike, hike, climb, or nature-watch. Get contact and use information for our nation's parks and forests by searching regionally by state, park name, intended activity, or service. Narrow your search by adding geographic locations, seasons, activities, or desired services. The fewer variables you add, the broader are your results. This site covers some 1,500 outdoor areas and provides around 2,000 natural-area and wildlife images. Find state and national parks, national wildlife refuges and forests, and Bureau of Land Management lands at this site.

National Park Service

www.nps.gov

U.S. National Park past and present information: This official site of the National Park Service (NPD) features creative design, good features (for example, the Civil War Collections at Gettysburg) and lots of information and relevant links about the nation's federal parks. (Both text and graphics versions are available, the former for faster downloads.) Visit InfoZone for park information (camping, maps, locations, fees, facilities, and so on, plus legislative updates and background on the NPS), Links to the Past (which relate to preserving America's cultural heritage), NatureNet, (about nature in the parks), and ParkSmart (homework resources and activities for students, such as simple yet really enjoyable image-filled, click-through storybooks on nature, conservation, and cultural history).

State Parks Online

www.mindspring.com/~wxrnot/
  parks.html

All about state parks: Click a finder map or names of states to access relevant links, most of which are maintained by various state departments of tourism or natural resources (and some by individuals). Read the Park of the Week feature to find new destinations (for example, Osbornedale State Park in Derby, Connecticut) or call up past Park of the Week features, which are archived. You can also link to related sites about parks.

USDA Forest Service National Headquarters Service

www.fs.fed.us/

Official site of the USDA Forest Service: After you get past all the bureaucratic stuff (the text of speeches and so on), you find useful information, articles, and internal links about recreation, environmental education, wildlife, wilderness, and tourism. (The site offers both graphic and text versions, the latter for faster downloads.) This agency oversees the nation's public forests for recreational, conservation, and lumbering purposes. You can register your opinions about how it's doing through the Public Forum, where you also can get news of Forest Service activities. The Enjoy the Outdoors section describes recreational opportunities and nature activities. Caring for the Land provides information about ecosystem management, ecological stewardship workshops, forest management, fire management, and forest health. Check out information about ongoing research and link to state, private, and global forestry sites.

Other Stuff to Check Out

Web sites
> www.discoveryweb.com/aep/parks/
> dinosaur/mainmenu.html
> bluegoose.arw.r9.fws.gov/NWRSFiles/
> Contents.html
> www.blm.gov/education/education.html
> www.npsc.nbs.gov/
> www.sws.org/wetlandweblinks.html
> www.wetlands.com/
> chppm-www.apgea.army.mil/gwswp/
> ground.htm

Mailing lists
> www.sws.org/wetlandweblinks.html#lists

Online service areas
> America Online: KIDS ONLY – Hobbies & Clubs

Suggested search-engine keywords
> Yahoo!: Public lands, National forests, camping
> Infoseek: Public lands, National forests, camping

Nature Museums, Zoos, and Aquariums

You know, it's all happening at the zoo — and at the nature museums and aquariums you find through these sites, too. If you can't go out in the wild and see these animals, the zoos and aquariums listed here can give you a close-up experience for the entire family. Either make a cybervisit or check them out before you make a real-life visit.

American Zoo and Aquarium Association

www.aza.org/

Professional organization that brings you wildlife in captivity: The American Zoo and Aquarium Association site provides information about member zoos and aquariums, explains the standards members strive to meet, and details their conservation and exhibit programs. Sections invite you to help with conservation programs and contests, view animal images and hear animal sounds, and link to sites about zoo and aquarium home pages, conservation programs, career opportunities, and zoo-oriented products.

Consortium of Aquariums, Universities, and Zoos

www.selu.com/~bio/cauz/

Dedicated to worldwide conservation: Find out about this organization and link up to member home pages. The Consortium of Aquariums, Universities, and Zoos is made up of an international network of scientists and educators in universities, zoos, aquariums, conservation organizations, and governmental agencies around the world. The design of the site is clear and well-organized and includes membership, activities, and goals information, as well as a membership directory and links to more than 4,000 relevant sites. Categories include animals, plants, aquariums, conservation, research centers, publications, education, endangered species, environment, government, universities, veterinary medicine, wildlife, museums, parks and preserves, libraries, jobs, and even humor. Visit the images section, especially with younger Web surfers, because they're sure to enjoy it. Most members provide a brief description of their current projects (for example, captive breeding or studying endangered species in the wild or captivity) and this information usually proves of interest to kids who are considering careers in the biological or environmental sciences. The information these groups provide really demonstrates what the work entails.

ZooNet

www.mindspring.com/~zoonet/

Giant herd of zoo links: Zoo sites, zoo kids' sites, images galore, and specialty subject sites related to zoos (for example, Deer Week) await you here. Animal images include those of primates and all

kinds of other mammals, plus images of birds, reptiles, and amphibians. Some parts of this site require JavaScript and frames-capable browsers, and certain zoo home pages may have their own plug-in requests, because these sites do tend to be quite interactive. But you can still find lots to do and see from categories that include Zoo Indexes (both American and World), Zoo Links, Animal Links, Animal Pictures, Endangered Species at Zoos, and ZooNet For Kids. The latter organizes links according to children's zoos, education programs and activities, (for example, WhaleTimes: Kid's Page and Animal Fact Sheets from the Oakland Zoo), children's programs offered at zoos, and animal pictures and sounds.

Other Stuff to Check Out

Web sites
aazk.ind.net/
www.worldzoo.org/arazpa/
www.si.edu/organiza/
www.fi.edu/
www.mbayaq.org/
www.lib.uconn.edu/ArcticCircle/Museum
www.bishop.hawaii.org/
nmnhwww.si.edu/vert/fish.html
www.fmnh.org./
www.si.edu/natzoo/
www.nrm.se/

Newsgroups
sci.aquaria
sci.bio

Mailing lists
csf.Colorado.EDU:80/consbio/

Online service areas
America Online: Smithsonian

Suggested search-engine keywords
Yahoo!: Nature museums, natural history museums, aquaria, aquariums, zoos
Infoseek: Public aquariums, aquaria, nature museums, natural history museums, zoos

Ecology Begins at Home

PROJECT FEEDERWATCH

What is
Project FeederWatch?

The Value of
Your Contribution

How to be
a FeederWatcher

Interactive FeederWatch
Demonstration
(Netscape 3.0 needed)

www.tc.cornell.edu/Birds/

With all the bad news about endangered species, climate change, and development pressures on wild lands, you may find yourself tempted to think that you can really do nothing about the situation. Wrong! Through earth-friendly living at home, you can help wildlife, decrease pollution and waste, and raise kids who are sensitive about the environment. Over the years, as an environmental writer, I got to know many scientists and ecologists who fell in love with their professions as kids. One scientist I know described himself as a boy who "turned over rocks just to see what was underneath"; he grew up to become a leading pathologist and parasitologist. Here's your family's chance to go green at home with the help of Internet resources — and the adventure may just lead to a life-changing experience.

Bird Attracting and Watching

Watching and attracting birds is fun, and birds appreciate a safe haven. Our family built a backyard habitat for goldfinches, my favorite bird since childhood. We planted nettles (yes, I know that they're weeds, but the big purple seed heads are goldfinch favorites), filled the birdfeeder exclusively with black-oil sunflower seeds, and kept some fresh water safely away from cats. Everyone was excited as the first goldfinch landed and, by summer's end, we had goldfinch fledglings at the feeder (along with woodpeckers and other neat birds). You can explore what birds live or migrate near your home and invite your favorites by using these resources.

Backyard Birding

**www.bcpl.lib.md.us/~tross/by/
backyard.html**

Tips for attracting birds: Presented by the Baltimore Bird Club, this site not only has information for its region's bird fans, but also lots of great general hints about how and what to feed birds, how to buy or construct birdhouses (including some that kids can make) to attract certain birds, how to pick shrubs and flowers that attract birds, and how to find on the Internet related links of interest to backyard birders. Find out which birds inhabit America and the rest of the world. Get info about publications, bird citings, and organizations for bird lovers.

Birdlinks

**www.mth.uea.ac.uk/~h055/headings/
birdlinks.html**

Straightforward catalog of bird links: Well-organized but not showy, this site offers bird links sorted into geographic categories, including Global, North America, South and Central America, Asia, Africa, Netherlands, Caribbean, Europe, and Australia and New Zealand. Also find links sorted by specific birds or families, as well as bird software, books, and birding-related travel. Most sites come with brief content descriptions so that you know what to expect before clicking to the link. Nearly all categories cover images, organizations, governmental agencies, research facilities, universities, and educationally oriented sites.

Birdlinks

www.phys.rug.nl/mk/people/wpv/
    index.html

Another compendium of links about birds and birding worldwide: This frames-based site has organized bird-related sites on the Internet into the following categories: Global, Conservation, North America (general, by geographic location and institutional), South and Central America, Asia, Africa, Netherlands, Europe, and Australasia. Find bird checklists, links to specific birds or families, and bird-related books and resources.

Project FeederWatch

birdsource.cornell.edu/pfw.htm

Be a part of Cornell University's Lab of Ornithology research team: Now you can feed birds at home and contribute to scientific research. A great opportunity for kids (with adult assistance), this project demonstrates how to keep accurate records and contribute data to Cornell. Review the site's Tips for Beginners and other information and then sign up by using the online form (and pay a modest materials fee). Get assistance with identification partly through an alphabetical index of bird resources. Each year, from November to March, thousands of North American volunteers use a set protocol to count the kinds and numbers of birds visiting their feeders on one or two days every two weeks. Such

data helps show how populations of winter birds are increasing or decreasing and where they're distributed across the continent. If you choose not to participate, you're still invited to follow this site for free as it reports apparent population and distribution trends. (House finches, for example, are spreading in the Eastern U.S., where they were introduced in 1940, but not out West.) Some parts of this site are best viewed with Netscape 3.0.

Virtual Birder

www.virtualbirder.com/vbirder/

Birding online: This monthly online magazine about birds and birding features high-quality enlargeable images and well-written articles about birding, birds, trip destinations, supplies and equipment, and books and publications. Three versions of the site are available so that you can choose the best for your computer system (low-band, mid-band, or high-band). Monthly issues adopt and explore a theme (for example, hawks) in-depth yet very entertainingly. Read lots of descriptive first-person accounts, from those of fledgling birders to scientific experts. Whether you "bird" by actively traveling to locations or by hanging up a bird feeder and looking out the window, you can find something here for you. Lots of fun are the virtual birding trips, which give you visual and other clues and then award you points for correct identification. To hear the bird sounds on this site, you need a plug-in — for example, RealAudio 3.0 , WAVE, AIFF.

Other Stuff to Check Out

Web sites

www.audubon.org/
www.phys.rug.nl/mk/people/wpv/
    oldlinks.html
math.math.sunysb.edu/~tony/birds/
    links.html

www.gorp.com/gorp/activity/birding.htm
www.surfnet.fi/birdlife/
www.birdsforever.com/chart.html
www.wildbirdcenter.com/
www.birds.org.il/e-main.htm
www.mc.hik.se/ottenby/hemsidor/how.html

Newsgroups
rec.birds

Mailing lists
www.audubon.org/net/list/index.html

Chat groups
www-stat.wharton.upenn.edu/~siler/
chat.html
nbhc.com/birdmail.htm

Online service areas
America Online: LSI - House & Home
Compuserve: GO EARTH

Suggested search-engine keywords
Yahoo!: Bird houses and feeders, birding,
birds
LookSmart: Birds

Composting and Recycling

Robert Faughum is a charming modern philosopher who wrote *All I Ever Really Needed to Know I Learned in Kindergarten.* Among the wisdom he imparts through this endearing treatise is to "Put things back where you found them. Clean up your own mess." I like to think that, as my family sorts cans from glass from paper and gets it all to the recycling center, we're observing those suggestions. As for our leftover foodstuffs, well, what doesn't pass muster with our goat seems to satisfy the worms in our compost pile. (And you should see the rich soil I get back in return!) Here are some sites on composting and recycling that I find especially useful.

Compost Resource Page

www.oldgrowth.org/compost/

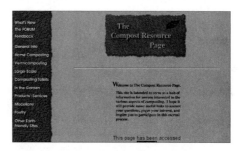

Dig up everything on composting: "Behold this compost! behold it well!" exclaimed Walt Whitman, whose poetry is included in this *annelid-ical* site about worms, dirt, and piling it on — for the good of the garden, of course. Share composting insights and tips and ask questions through the Composter's Forum. Set up the right system for your needs. Utilize the links geared to homeowners at the Home Composting section. And if you really want all the dirt on this subject, information is available on compost-related legislation, history, lore, and oddities (for example, sled-dog manure composting in Alaska).

RotWeb

net.indra.com/~topsoil/
Compost_Menu.html

Basic guide to composting: If you've been worming out of starting a compost pile because you figured it was too much trouble or mess, this family-oriented site can guide you through the process. Get tips on composting, setting up your system, knowing what to compost, and getting composting supplies. Find out about composting demonstrations, books, and other resources. The site also offers teacher resources that families can adapt to make playing in the dirt a project of discovery.

United States Environmental/ Recycling Hotline

www.1800cleanup.org/

"Earth's 911": This public/private partnership with the U.S. Environmental Protection Agency lists centers and resources in all 50 states that specialize in recycling and dealing with household-product waste. You can easily locate community-specific information about recycling programs and centers that handle oil, batteries, and other recyclables — now only a click away. Find out about buying recycled goods, get recycling articles, and link to recycling-related sites. You can choose a high- or low-graphics version of this site, depending on the speed of your computer system.

Other Stuff to Check Out

Web sites
www.pwc.bc.doe.ca/corp/press/eweek/
    grhome/yard.html
www.ozemail.com.au/~natloo/home.html
www.best.com/~dillon/recycle/local/
    index.html
www.gruener-punkt.de/e/tagx/
    frameset.htm
atlenv.bed.ns.doe.ca/udo/paydirt.html
www.nwlink.com/~van/glcomp.html

Online service areas
America Online: LSI - House & Home
Compuserve: GO EARTH

Suggested search-engine keywords
Yahoo!: Composting, recycling
Infoseek: Composting, recyling

Gardening

What are those white sticky things on your favorite camellia bush? Are they good bugs or bad bugs? Can a magnolia do well in your yard? Where can you get advice about growing tomatoes? What can you do for that rather sad-looking African violet clinging to life on the kitchen windowsill? Check the general gardening resources for sites offering useful articles, colorful images, and helpful links. Then go out and play in the dirt with the kids' gardening resources. Gather and share insights on nature, food production, and the joys of gardening. ***Remember:*** If you want to find even more sites about plants and creatures that may be in your yard or neighborhood, visit this book's sections on Life Sciences, Gardens and Arboretums, and Pets.

Biocontrol Network

www.usit.net/hp/bionet/BICONET.html

Integrated Pest Management (IPM) research and solutions: If you release ladybugs rather than spray pesticides on your roses, you're practicing Integrated Pest Management, or IPM, which in effect uses "good" bugs and other natural systems to combat "bad" bugs and diseases. As questions increase about the effects of pesticides and herbicides on health, soil, and air, biocontrols are becoming much more economically viable and environmentally popular. Find resources and methods that you can use at home to supplant or replace pesticides and herbicides with beneficial insects, botanicals, cover crops, insect barriers, and other alternative methods.

The Garden Gate

www.prairienet.org/ag/garden/

Carefully selected links for gardeners: Enjoy the personalized gardening column and a thoughtfully organized compendium of links covering such topics as gardening glossaries; FAQs (frequently asked questions); specialties; collections; plant lists; sources for books, magazines, and catalogs; houseplants (visit the Sun Room); botanical gardens; greenhouses; private gardens; mailing lists; and newsgroups. Newly discovered links are in the Holding Bed, where they're "heeled in until they're transplanted into their permanent spots. Or composted . . .". This site is a noncommercial one that generally lists commercial sites only if they include value-added content about horticulture.

GardenNet

trine.com/GardenNet/

Lots of gardening resources: Visit The Ardent Gardener for tips and advice through this weekly gardening newsletter. Flora's Best online garden shop is one place to buy products or get catalogs and catalog information. Or connect through the Garden Business Home Page Center to find out about guides for quick reference, garden-related travel, magazines, books, gardens, and gardening associations online that are specifically selected for those in the gardening business.

GardenWeb

www.gardenweb.com

Online magazine for gardeners: Original articles and products about gardening await you here. In Sesbania's Gardening Tips, get advice on lots of subjects (for example, starting seeds indoors, preparing a new garden, and correct watering techniques). The Rosarian is all about roses, and the Cyber-Plantsman is a magazine for serious (but fun) gardening. At the GreenLeaves Bookstore, you can shop for books on gardening, wildflowers, or birding. The Garden Spider's Web offers selected links to other gardening-related sites, and The Garden Exchange is where you can post a request for hard-to-find seeds or plants. The Merchant Directory connects you with gardening products. And if you want a foreign flare, visit GardenWeb Europe, with forums in four languages (English, French, German, and Italian). (Other GardenWeb forums are all in English.) Take the Mystery Plant challenge to test your identification skills. Many other offerings are available here as well, related to online shopping and gardening resources.

kinderGARDEN

aggie-horticulture.tamu.edu/kinder/
   index.html

Introducing kids to gardening: Through activities and links picked just for kids, the entire family can begin to explore horticulture together. From therapeutic horticulture to children's programs at school gardens, botanical gardens, 4-H, or community gardens, the site describes and suggests resources to get kids started. The Seeds of Change Garden explores the importance of food crops from both the Old and New Worlds to economics and society. The Fun Page consists mainly of links within the hyperlinked text to garden-related sites that offer content and activities kids enjoy (for example, butterfly gardening, bird watching, gardening books, art and poetry, food gardening, studying insects, and environmental projects).

Missouri Botanical Garden: Just For Kids

www.mobot.org/MBGnet/just_kids.html

Presented by one of the world's finest botanical gardens: Best viewed in Microsoft Internet Explorer, this site introduces kids to the science of plants. Search for subjects or link to sections dealing with such subjects as biomes, field studies all around the world, aquatic plants, reefs, rain forests, and savannas. The section for parents offers ideas for introducing kids to plants and biosystems. Visit exotic faraway places and get information about plants and animals by reading the MBG Field Reports (or purchase the MBGnet CD-ROM). Link to sites related to science and the Internet. You find simple activities for kids and parents to do together that teach plant science principles (for example, rain-making and osmosis).

Pesticide Action Network

www.panna.org/panna/

Nonprofit organization supporting ecologically sound practices in place of pesticide use: This site has weekly updates on approved pesticides and herbicides commonly used by home gardeners. Find out what treatment methods are safest around kids and pets and what alternatives to traditional practices are available. Check out "PANNA's" activities relating to methyl bromide (a common fumigant for houses), sustainable cotton production, children and pesticides, and international clean-up efforts. Link to sites about sustainable agriculture, pesticides, biotechnology, methyl bromide, and environmental organizations.

PlantLink

www.plantamerica.com/palink.htm

Online plant reference locator: Having trouble finding information about a particular plant? This search engine for plant-related sites enables you to type in the correctly spelled plant name to begin your search or to choose a letter of the alphabet that begins your plant's family, scientific, or common name. If you're not sure of the family, you can click to The Royal Botanic Gardens, Kew's Genus Search. If your plant is referenced on the Internet, references and links to those references appear.

Soil And Water Conservation Society

www.swcs.org/

Promoting responsible use and care of soil and water: If people abuse topsoil and water over long periods, once-fertile areas can become desertlike, which is a growing problem worldwide. This society assists gardeners, farmers, and others in understanding and utilizing responsible planting and watering methods. The site also covers research and support organizations and agencies involved in soil and water conservation. Through this searchable site, you can find out about resources and opportunities to become involved in good soil stewardship, and develop good gardening habits. The Other Links section puts you in touch with conservation, governmental, and science-based sources (for example, the Symposium on Soil Erosion and Dryland Farming, the National Association of Conservation Districts, and the Sustainable Agriculture Network).

Tree Doctor

www.1stresource.com/t/treedoc/

All about landscape trees: This well-developed commercial site covers aspects of tree care of special interest to property owners. With emphasis on preventive maintenance and environmentally friendly solutions, site sections cover natural alternatives to fighting tree diseases and pests, the truth about tree topping, ways to stimulate healthy tree growth, and finding professional arborists (and what their training involves), as well offering as publications, products, and relevant links. The Tree Doctor's Favorite Links include research, organizational, and governmental resources, as well as general tree identification and use guides. Jim Cortese (The Tree Doctor) is a certified, university-trained arborist with 20 years of field practice and research. Along with his site associate, certified arborist Marty Shaw, Jim answers your tree questions for a requested $25 fee to help maintain the site. Many of your questions may also be answered through the Fact Sheets links or Tree Care publication links.

Other Stuff to Check Out

Web sites
   www.reeusda.gov/new/statepartners/
      usa.htm
   www.sfrc.ufl.edu/

www.geocities.com/WestHollywood/2445/
   links.html
www.cog.brown.edu/gardening/
www.worldleader.com/garden/index.htm
gypsy.fsl.wvnet.edu:80/gmoth/
ianrwww.unl.edu/ianr/plntpath/nematode/
   wormhome.html
leviathan.tamu.edu/
www.usc.edu/dept/garden
www.palms.org/
www.connix.com/~reingg/links.html
www.bamboo.org/abs/
www.pacificrim.net/~bydesign/acs.html
www.msue.msu.edu/msue/imp/moduf/
   07279513.html
www.odf.state.or.us/UF/0098.html
www.arborday.com/
www.arborists.com/

Newsgroups
   alt.agriculture.misc
   alt.bonsai
   alt.pets.chia
   bionet.agroforestry
   bionet.plants
   rec.arts.bonsai
   rec.gardens
   rec.gardens.orchids
   rec.gardens.roses
   sci.agriculture

Mailing lists
   listserv@ukcc.uky.edu

Online service areas
   America Online: LSI - House & Home
   Compuserve: GO EARTH

Suggested search-engine keywords
   Yahoo!: Gardening, trees
   LookSmart: Gardening

Wildlife in the Back Yard

You don't need to travel to distant jungles to encounter wildlife. Just go into the yard or to your neighborhood park! My mom lives in a gated mobile-home retirement community; at night, foxes raid her fig tree, and raccoons waddle through her carport. During the day, brightly colored orioles, finches, war-blers, moths, and butterflies decorate the sky. Lizards sun themselves on the walkway. Wildlife is all around. Use these sites to discover a peaceable kingdom right outside your own front door. *Remember:* To find even more sites about local wild animals and insects, visit this book's section on Life Sciences.

Bug Club

www.ex.ac.uk/bugclub/welcome.html

Get to know bugs: This endearing, delightfully graphic kids' site is intended to inspire young entomologists to venture out into their own yards and libraries in the name of science and fun. The site comes in both a frames and no-frames version. Appreciate earthworms, beetles, bugs, and insects through the colorful newsletter and features that offer an-swers to questions that may always have bugged you, such as "Where do bugs go in the winter?" This site is British-based, but American kids can have fun here, too.

Butterfly Zone

www.butterflies.com/journal.html

All about butterflies: Large sections of this site are devoted to information about attracting butterflies to urban gardens, whether those gardens are in yards or window boxes. This beautiful, well-written site features an online butterfly-oriented store, lots of practical tips, and inspiring reasons to care about butterflies (for example, that butterfly gardens are environmentally sound, help butterflies and native plants, and make people feel uplifted). Find out how butterflies sense their environments, what flowers are

most effective in attracting them, where to get those flowers, and how to display them. You can also plan your flower spaces with the right plants for caterpil-lars and have permanent repeat business! You also find resources to assist you in identifying butterflies and finding out which ones are native to your area. Enjoy The Urban Gardener's Journal, one butterfly fan's personal history of his small urban garden.

National Wildlife Federation: For Kids

www.nwf.org/kids/

All about American wildlife: This wonder-ful resource for kids, in both English and Spanish, is part of the National Wildlife Federation's home page (which you can access by clicking the Home button on the kids' site). Kids can take fun quizzes, play games, and read brightly written articles all about indigenous wildlife. Try the click-through nature tours about water, wildlife, wetlands, and public lands. See whether you can guess which animals made which tracks as part of the Explore the Outdoors game (designed to excite kids about nature in their own backyards and neighborhoods). This site is really high-quality from a veteran American wildlife organization.

Northern Prairie Other Resources by Geography

**www.npsc.nbs.gov/resource/
geoout.htm**

Plants and animals native to your region: This terrific collection of mostly governmental, nonprofit, and research links compiled by the United States Geological Survey's Northern Prairie Wildlife Research Center features a clickable map, a state list, and a scroll-down title list of links with brief descriptions that help you track down mammals, plants, insects, birds, reptiles, and amphibians native to your area and your own backyard.

Wildlife Rehabilitation Information Directory

**www.ndsu.nodak.edu/instruct/devold/
twrid/html/hp.htm**

People helping wildlife: Sometimes, with people and wildlife living in ever more-crowded conditions, wildlife loses. Songbirds fly into plate glass windows, raccoons get attacked by domestic dogs, and all kinds of animals get hit by cars or displaced by development that eliminates foraging areas. But although we sometimes cause problems for wildlife, we can also try to come to its rescue. This site is a list of wildlife rehabilitation centers and professionals with sites on the Internet. You can also get tips on what to do if you find injured or orphaned wildlife and discover more about laws relating to wildlife. Read personal accounts of people's experiences with wildlife, as well as poetry about the topic and view images of many kinds of wildlife. You can also find news and offer feedback about wildlife-related issues.

Other Stuff to Check Out

Web site
> ourworld.compuserve.com/homepages/
> sbwcn/
> www.npsc.nbs.gov/resource/distr/lepid/
> moths/mothsusa.htm
> monkey.ee.vt.edu/ee/cameron/Mammals/
> mammals.html
> iris.biosci.ohio-state.edu/osuent/home.html
> www.colostate.edu/Depts/Entomology/
> www_sites.html

Newsgroup
> sci.bio.entomology.lepidoptera

Online service areas
> America Online: LSI - House & Home
> Compuserve: GO EARTH

Suggested search-engine keywords
> Yahoo!: Wildlife
> Infoseek: Wildlife

A Native American expression goes "We borrow the land from our children." Whether you're old enough to remember the founding of Earth Day, contemplating a college major in environmental studies, or starting a recycling project at your elementary school, these collective environmental libraries and specialized sites should have something of interest to you. These sites offer activities and resources for people of any age who care about the health of the planet and environmental effects on long-term human survival.

Business and Family Finances

You can change the world one penny at a time with information from these sites, which advocate environmental and social responsibility in the way that companies make and people spend money. If you are considering investing in a company or have questions on the environmental responsibility of local, national, and international companies you do business with, you can find the answers and recommendations on these sites or their worldwide links.

Envirobiz

www.envirobiz.com/

Resource site for environmental professionals: Although this searchable site is geared primarily toward environmental technology, engineering, and waste management, it dispels any myths that the environment is not a booming industry. Find press releases, professional services, the latest equipment and technologies, publications, software, conferences and professional events, business opportunities, environmental news, research, studies, databases, and links covering many subjects, including air quality, Superfund sites, emergency spills, governmental agencies, public interest groups, cleanups, toxic waste, endangered species, and all aspects of business. Other sections cover industry press releases, news, and the business, regulation, and technology of environmental protection.

Ethical Business

www.arq.co.uk/ethicalbusiness/

British-based international resource for ethical and environmental business practices: This site provides a comprehensive, up-to-date directory of ethical business links covering such areas as research, conferences, campaigns, new ventures, news stories, philosophical and economic discussions, archives of papers, books, and articles on ethical business. You can also link to this site's sister site, Investing for Change. Updated every two months, Ethical Business is categorized by world regions (for example, the United Kingdom, Europe, the U.S. and Canada) and topics (such as Books, Investment, Trade, and Research).

OneEarth Gallery

www.1earth.com/

Browsable database of environmentally and socially responsible organizations and companies: This regularly updated site catalogs and features organizations and businesses that care about improving society and the environment through their resources, products, services, and actions. Get updates on environmental technologies and services, natural health news, and links to selected sites reflecting OneEarth's philosophy, which advocates social and environmental responsibility and progressive health practices. In addition to promoting existing sites, OneEarth Gallery also designs and hosts sites. "Ideal" clients who support environmental causes get "substantial discounts."

S-R-Invest

tbzweb.com/srinvest/index.htm

Resource guide to socially responsible investing: Get tips on evaluating good funds with a conscience. Check out the GreenMoney On-Line Guide, Good Money Publications, and Center for Visionary Leadership, plus features such as the True Business Zeal Directory for Entrepreneurs. According to this site, socially responsible investing is "the allocation of financial resources after the consideration of both economic and social criteria with the goals of maximizing the potential financial and social returns to both the investor and the investee." Read the linking list of fund and investment firms (for example, Pax World Fund, New Alternatives Fund, Calvert Group, and Franklin Research & Development Corporation) and find out why they're qualified for inclusion under the criteria. The purpose of this directory is to point out sites maintained by publicly owned companies that are followed by some stock analysts and portfolio managers who specialize in Socially Responsible Investing (SRI).

Students for Responsible Business

www.srb.org/

Aspiring business people with conscience: This group was founded in 1993 for graduate and undergraduate business-school students and alumni who believe that earth stewardship and free enterprise are not incompatible. SRB believes that companies are not only responsible to their shareholders, but also to the larger community of colleagues, employees, towns in which they operate, and the environment. Find out about SRB activities, membership, job and internship opportunities, and who the organization

considers role models. Link to articles and sites covering such topics as responsible business practices and investing. The site offers a discussion forum and a question-and-answer forum so that you can meet leaders in the socially responsible business movement. The site is designed to support frames-enabled browsers such as Netscape 2.0 or higher.

Other Stuff to Check Out

Web sites

www.gaia.org/businesses/index.html
www.envirolink.org/sbn/noframe.html
snyside.sunnyside.com/home/
www.psr.org/
www.cipe.org/efn/bsr.html
epic.er.doe.gov/epic/
www.airproducts.com/care/respcare.html
www.wald.com/office.html

Newsgroup

comp.org.cpsr.talk

Suggested search-engine keywords

Yahoo!: Social responsibility, business ethics
Infoseek: Socially responsible businesses, ethical business

Consumerism

Solar-powered toys and nightlights? Washing clothes without using detergent? Who ever heard of such a thing? You have after you visit these sites, which emphasize environmentally safe services and products manufactured by environmentally and socially responsible companies.

Eco Goods

www.ecogoods.com/

Alternative general store: Get organic, recycled, and nontoxic products (for example, organic cotton) and check out the eco-oriented newsletter, news section, and healthful tips. The online catalog of the store, based in Santa Cruz, California, features hemp, jewelry, cotton clothing, lighting, music, books, magazines, hardware, body products, furniture, garden supplies, paints and building supplies, baby products, pet care products, and cleaners.

EcoMall

www.ecomall.com/

Environmentally safe and sound products and services: Click your way through the virtual town to connect to sections covering Activism Alerts; eco-articles; news and quotes; forums and chats; local, national, and international groups and projects; and eco-products and services (such as renewable energy, veggie restaurants, baby and children's products, books, investments, clothing, cleaning products, lightbulbs, furniture, flowers, food, gifts, hardware, natural-health products, magazines, pet products, office supplies, gardening equipment, and recycled paper products). Shop online or link up with suppliers for more information. Other features on this frames-bases site include energy-saving ideas for the home and office.

Real Goods

www.realgoods.com/

Source of products and knowledge for the eco-home: Products sold through Real Goods stores, catalogs, and online can

increase the home's energy efficiency, start to reduce utility bills, and create a healthier physical and emotional environment without harming the planet with overpackaging, wasteful manufacturing, or harmful ingredients. Find solar-powered toys, solar cookers, and lots of other eco-friendly products, such as lighting, air, and water purifiers, cleaning aids, pest control, clothing, health care, and tools for home and garden. Find out about workshops and other resources that can make you environmentally savvy at home. This site is a frames-based site, so it requires a browser such as the current version Netscape Navigator or Microsoft Internet Explorer.

Other Stuff to Check Out

Web sites
> www.greenshopping.com/invite.htm
> www.natureco.com/
> www.greenmarket.com/

Chat area
> www.ecomall.com/chatx.htm

Suggested search-engine keywords
> Yahoo!: Eco-friendly retail, eco-friendly shopping
> Infoseek: Earth-friendly products

General Environmental and Socially Responsible Resources

Want to save a rain forest or your own neighborhood's last remaining open space? These sites index causes and organizations locally and worldwide that need you. Get involved for a more peaceful, positive, pollution-free planet.

The choice is yours (and hundreds are available here). Find a project just right for your family, church, group, or school class.

Amazing Environmental Organization WebDirectory

www.webdirectory.com/

Internet library of environmental sites: A long-time environmental search tool, this big green eco-machine gets you where you want to be quickly and efficiently. From the home page, you can access alphabetized folders on topics ranging from Agriculture, Animals, and Arts on down to Usenet Newsgroups, Vegetarianism, Water Resources, Weather, and Wildlife. Select the folder topic of interest and you get a secondary collection of folders as well as a scroll-down list of some of the more comprehensive sites. Click Energy, for example, and you get folders for Alternative Energy, U.S. Department of Energy, Indoor Climate Control, Conservation, Energy Efficient Systems, Environmental Homes and Buildings, Fossil Fuels, and Institutes. Sites in the scroll-down list below the folders include private companies; university and research programs; and construction, advocacy, and educational groups. You also find an environmental bulletin board where you can post questions, news of an action, or an announcement.

EcoWeb

ecosys.drdr.virginia.edu/EcoWeb.html

Searchable environmental database maintained by the University of Virginia: An internal search engine indexes all the documents on EcoWeb. Choose a keyword or an idea/concept to search for. Enter your words in the search box and

EcoWeb documents or catalogued sites come back with a summary (click the word *summary* in parentheses) and a percentage of relevance (which may or may not apply all that closely). Type **native plants**, for example, and you get back several titles, none of which actually alludes to native plants. But all do contain references to native plants; for example, in a discussion about a forest plan, you get a summary of the 24 canoe plants of ancient Hawaii, a recycled paper-slide demonstration, and a botany site about plants native to northern California. The more specific your search, the more specific are the sites you're likely to receive as a result. Just click the titles that look relevant to access the sites or articles. Even if the titles aren't exactly what you had in mind, they make for good reading and may give you some good ideas.

EnviroLink

www.envirolink.org/

Mega-index of environmental resources: One of the Internet's oldest, biggest, and most-respected environmental library sites, EnviroLink catalogs eco-sites and presents environmentally based special sections and features. The EnviroLink Library is organized according to earth elements (earth, air, fire, and water) and all living creatures (flora and fauna). Click Water, for example, and you get the subcategories Agriculture, Aquatic Ecosystems, Dams and Dikes, Drinking Water, Ocean Issues, Water as an Energy Source, Water Conservation, Water Cycle, Water Pollution, and Water Sciences. You can click any one of these subcategories to find related sites, or you can scroll down to find additional online resources listed and described under headings that include Education (for example, classroom materials for K-12 or university-level environmental-studies programs), General Info (such as water conservation, water supply, and quality information), Government (for example, national federal and international agencies with jurisdiction over water), Organizations (scientific and activist water-related groups), and Publications. And that's just the library section of this soothingly designed, easily navigated site. Other sections are devoted to environmental news, actions that you can take, forums, eco-arts, and site assessments.

Environmental Protection Agency

www.epa.gov

Official site of the federal agency: Both a beautifully well-designed graphic-intensive version and a text-only version are offered for this extensive government site. Click special features (for example, American Heritage Rivers), select a user category for resources of particular interest (such as Projects, Games, Art and Helpful Tips for kids; Basic Environmental Concepts & Teaching Aids for students; or Tips for Home, Garden, Work and Beyond for families) or choose by topic (for example, Offices, Labs & Regions across the country; EPA Projects and Programs sorted by natural resource; Laws & Regulations; or publications and other resources). This site is also searchable and contains many internal links.

Environmental Science and Engineering Related Web sites

www.envision.net/osites/environ/ envrelat.html

Database for environmental scientists and engineers: Although many of these sites are professional or technical in nature, they may have strong relevance for students researching homework or contemplating a career. Producer

ENVision provides links to research and professionally oriented sites divided into global and local sites. Local is subdivided into sites in the United States and Canada, Europe, Asia, and Australia and New Zealand. Use global links for global information and localized links for more regional information. Use global links for information on climate change, for example, and localized links for data on pollution problems in your area.

Other Stuff to Check Out

Web sites
www.commpages.com/globe/
www.clearinghouse.net/cgi-bin/chadmin/
    viewcat/Environment?kywd++
www.southampton.liunet.edu/library/
    environ.htm
phantom.rec.org/
www.envirosw.com/
www.voxpop.org/jefferson/issues/enviro//

Newsgroups
sci.environment
sci.environment.waste
talk.environment
sci.bio.ecology

Chat area
www.envirolink.org/cgi-bin/WebX

Suggested search-engine keywords
Yahoo!: Environment, nature, environmental science, environmental activism, ecology
Infoseek: Environment

Home Construction and Remodeling

As the world's dependence on lumber and oil becomes more tenuous, creative efforts are under way to find other materials and methods for construction. Although some alternatives are quite new and experimental, others date back centuries and are enjoying a revival. Revive your imagination at these sites.

For more sites on alternative technologies and engineering, make sure that you visit the Physical Science and Technology subsection in Part II.

Earth Architecture Center International, Ltd.

www.unm.edu/~eaci/

Building with earth: An ancient building art gets revived here, where adobe's energy-efficient and cost-efficient properties are explored and praised. The Center is a source of earth-building technical information for architects, builders, homeowners, and planners. Find out about workshops and demonstration events, publications, and other resources and read the Frequently Asked Questions (FAQs) section. Get info on building codes for adobe, rammed earth, and straw-bale structures and connect with related organizations and links. This site is presented by P.G. McHenry of the School of Architecture and Planning, University of New Mexico in Albuquerque.

Ecotopia

www.ecotopia.com/

Building a vision for the millennium: Through well-researched and enjoyable written articles, carefully selected links and publications, plus neat graphics and images, this site presents earth-friendly construction, landscaping, and transportation technologies. The home page divides into two parts: Ecotopia and Ecosystems. The Ecotopia half features the Ecology Hall of Fame (for environmental heroes), Circle Trail (forest, meadow, and beach paths), EcoVisit (ecology and nature-based homestay visits), and the Hydrology and Watershed Project. The EcoSystems half of the home page addresses building a sustainable future through alternatives for fossil fuels, traditional lumber-based construction and tract developments, and wasteful living practices. View solar houses and electric cars as well as new, more energy efficient products and technologies. The site also address environmental and economic ethics.

Mr. Solar

www.netins.net/showcase/solarcatalog/

Friendly first-person advice about going solar: Visiting this site is like talking to your neighbor who just installed a solar heating system. No question is too dumb, and the answers arrive in plain, good-natured, not-too-technical English (or Spanish or French, if you choose). All kinds of information, products, and services about solar, wind, and water power are addressed here. Charlie Collins, "Mr. Solar," lives in southwest Utah with his wife, Fran. Together, they built the Do It Homestead, where they've lived 18 years on free solar electricity. Charlie shares their experiences. You can also find more than 100 articles on alternative energy by energy experts, as well as a solar energy products catalog, instructions on designing and installing your own solar electric system, and links to environmentally friendly sites. Check out examples of residential and office alternative energy projects with accompanying images and text. You can shop while visiting the Mr. Solar site on what the site lists as a secure server.

Rammed Earth

www.hahaha.com.au/rammed.earth/

Alternative housing method detailed: This Australian site provides a clear walk-through with text and images of what building a rammed earth structure entails. The site also offers an archive of Rammed Earth questions. Although rammed earth is a very old process, it's gaining popularity today because of its earth-friendly, relatively economical, and energy-efficient properties. The entire process of creating a structure is outlined here, so you can decide whether this labor-intensive building idea is for you. Along the way, you can get practical tips. (For example, if the soil mixture "falls apart as you squeeze it in your hand, it's too dry; if it doesn't shatter after you drop the ball from shoulder height, it's too wet.") and benefit from the lessons learned by Steve Davis, this adventurous builder. Be forewarned, however, this Aussie's language can be a little colorful, so parents should review the site first.

Rocky Mountain Institute

www.rmi.org/

Nonprofit research and educational foundation: This Institute creates new solutions by using market economics and advanced techniques for resource efficiency and assists private citizens, businesses, and governmental entities in adopting those solutions as well. In addition to research, RMI sponsors and publishes books and other reference materials on a variety of alternative energy and energy-conservation topics. The books are extremely well-researched and not terribly expensive. (Subjects include sustainable building, site and habitat restoration, transportation integration, edible landscapes, energy-efficient design, materials selection,

indoor air quality, weatherization, insulation, heating and cooling systems, windows, hot-water heating, appliances and lighting, solar and other efficient design elements, and resource-efficient home construction.) The pamphlets cost $2 or less and cover topics relating to cost-effective technologies and do-it-yourself measures to cut your home energy bills. You can browse the online catalog for specific titles.

Straw Bale Construction

solstice.crest.org/efficiency/
    straw_insulation/index.html

The Big Bad Wolf can't blow these straw houses down: Straw-bale technology is both ancient and modern. Find out why it's gaining popularity and get lots of links and support from this plain-looking but very useful page (part of the larger Solstice site, which is covered in Part II). Get links to discussion groups and advocates, articles on straw-bale energy efficiency, how-to's, why-to's, outlets for books and other publications, images and text about a two-story straw-bale building built in 1945, a construction slide show, and some practical assistance.

U.S. Department of Energy

www.eren.doe.gov/

Energy Efficiency and Renewable Energy Network (EREN): Find out about ways the government is attempting to improve its own energy efficiency and get answers and publications related to your own energy needs. Ask an Energy Expert enables you to submit questions about energy efficiency and renewable energy technologies to EREN specialists. Link to sites related to "clean" energy and get a listing of news, events, and hot topics through the calendar of energy-related conferences, workshops, and seminars. The site even has an entire section for kids (detailed in this book in the Part II subsection on Physical Science and Technology).

Other Stuff to Check Out

Web sites

solstice.crest.org/online/aeguide/
    metaindex.html
www.asis.com/aee/
www.kauai.net/bambooweb/bamboo.html
www.washingtonforests.com/
www.ifsia.com/ecosense/menu.htm
www.envirosense.org/
greenbuilding.ca/
www.arcosanti.org/
ag.arizona.edu/OALS/ALN/TOC36.html
es.inel.gov/index.html
www.ornl.gov/ORNL/Energy_Eff/
    Energy_Eff.html
www.greenbuilder.com/
www.solardesign.com/~sda/
www.slip.net/~ckent/earthship/

Suggested search-engine keywords

Yahoo!: Alternative energy, alternative
    construction
Infoseek: Alternative energy, earth-friendly
    construction

News and Politics

Do you know how your legislators really vote on environmental issues? What's happening around the world related to commercial fishing, pollution, habitat loss, and waste? What can you do to make sure that everyone has enough to eat without devastating the land and natural resources? These sites look at political and environmental issues, as well as related social issues and historic events.

20/20 Vision

www.2020vision.org/

 $

Get involved easily: You want to save a rain forest, but to borrow a quote from the late John Lennon, "Life is what happens while you're making other plans." This national nonprofit advocacy organization understands how busy, yet caring, people are, and it's developed a 20-minute-a-month activist plan. Every month, 20/20 Vision identifies an urgent environmental and peace-oriented issue. You're advised where your elected representatives stand on the issue. You get an action postcard with the necessary information to write a brief letter, send an e-mail, or make a key phone call. Then, every six months, you receive an update on the results of your actions. The site has a sign-up form and asks a registration fee of $20 a year to cover project costs. You can pick your preferred monthly cause from among the topics of environment, peace, corporate reform, or gun control. Regional causes also are tackled. Students qualify for a free, three-month trial subscription.

Center for Environmental Citizenship

www.cgv.org/cgv/cec.html

Youth-led national nonprofit, nonpartisan group: Founded in 1992, the center trains college students to become citizen activists for better environmental policies. Among its projects are Campus Green Vote, the EarthNet listserv, Blueprint for a Green Campus, and *The Green Voter* newsletter. Find out about recent accomplishments (such as massive registration of student voters, hosting of Earth Day events, and coordination of the Campus Earth Summit) and how you can get involved.

Environmental Information Center

www.eic.org/

Public relations resource for environmental campaigns: Through grassroots organizers, advertisements, press contacts, and events, the Environmental Information Center works with environmental groups to publicize such issues as America's endangered species and ecosystems, safe drinking water, and global climate change. Find out how you can become part of these and other campaigns and see what's been happening in Congress lately with regard to environmental concerns. Link to sites concerned with political action and events, laws and regulations, products and business, environmental research, and societal improvement. Get tips for evaluating whether your congressperson is a committed environmentalist. EIC is a nonprofit, nonpartisan organization supported by donations from foundations, environmental organizations, and individuals.

Environmental News Network

www.enn.com/

Timely environmental news, info, and resources: Get daily reporting of top environmental news from around the world through staff reports by journalists, researchers, and scientists and associated content from Reuters, Knight-Ridder/ Tribune, Associated Press, and other leading news organizations. Each week, *Planet ENN,* the online magazine, takes a deeper look at issues through columns and features by leaders in environmental science and politics. Various subscription services are tailored to user preferences, and the site offers an audio service called ENN Radio. Visit Cyberhiker (a roundup of Web sites), Guide to the Web (selected sites considered the best environmental sites on the Internet), and the Calendar (conferences, workshops, and events).

Environmental Working Group

www.ewg.org/

Content provider for public-interest groups: Read articles about concerned citizens who're campaigning to protect the environment in EWG's online reports, articles, database, and other resources. A writing and computer staff publishes hundreds of newsmaking reports each year, based on EWG analyses of government and other data. EWG, founded in 1993, is based in Washington, D.C., with an office in San Francisco. It provides articles and policy analysis online and off to the general public, environmental organizations, news media, and public-interest groups. Special areas of concern include effects of pesticides and other chemicals on infants and children; the effect of federal farm programs; safe drinking water and wetlands conservation; federal budget and appropriations policies; and the effect of campaign contributions on environmental policy. This site contains many of the organization's publications and other resources.

Institute for Global Communications

www.igc.org/igc/

Web provider for progressive causes: IGC hosts Internet sites that seek to expand and inspire movements for peace, economic and social justice, human rights, and environmental sustainability around the world. This 10-year-old nonprofit organization provides Web hosting, e-mail access, and other Internet services primarily to activists with modest budgets and big agendas. Some of the causes are controversial — even radical — so parents need to supervise site links here to make sure that they're suitable for your particular family. The Institute tries to provide a free-speech vehicle to many kinds of causes, and it welcomes constructive feedback. Sites are organized under five sections: PeaceNet, EcoNet, ConflictNet, LaborNet, and WomensNet. Click one or choose the Members Directory. Linkable site names and descriptions are provided in the individual sections, member directory, and from the home page. Among sites listed, from A-Z, are the Activist Handbook, Africa Faith and Justice Network, Alaska Boreal Forest Council, and so on down the alphabet to Zero Population Growth.

League of Conservation Voters

www.lcv.org/

Nonpartisan political arm of the environmental movement: Polling results show that mainstream Americans of all political stripes place a high priority on environmental protection, at least according to this group, which advocates eco-policies. Sections here include Winning Elections for the Environment (working toward electing a pro-conservation majority in Congress), LCV National Environmental Scorecards (rating environmental votes by the U.S. House and Senate), and LCV Communications (speeches, press statements, news releases, and editorial pieces). You can subscribe to the lcv-update list to receive e-mails of fresh news, including critical environmental votes within 24-48 hours of when they occur. Visit the archives or membership page if you want to consider joining or applying for a job based in Washington, D.C. You can also volunteer as part of the Grassroots network — to contact state and local environmental Political Action Committees (PACs), write your elected officials, and vote!

Other Stuff to Check Out

Web sites
www.deb.uminho.pt/fontes/enviroinfo/news.htm
www.sej.org/env_sej.htm
www.enetdigest.com/
energy.nfesc.navy.mil/pp/rachel/rachel.htm
earthday.wilderness.org/history/history.htm

Newsgroups
relcom.ecology
alt.save.the.earth

Suggested search-engine keywords
Yahoo!: Science: Ecology; Society and Culture: Environment and nature
Infoseek: Environmental news, environmental issues

Kids Who Are Saving the World

Hawaii's Endangered Species, Balancing On A Thin Line

Endangered Species of Hawaii

Researched by Enchanted Lakes Elementary School students
This website is dedicated to educators and students who are interested
in protecting and studying about endangered species in our world.

www.hisurf.com/~enchanted/

Who says that you must be all grown up to make a difference in the world? These sites feature projects by and for kids who demonstrate their leadership potential (with just the right dash of caring support and guidance from adults). Kids are becoming involved by helping with research, monitoring endangered species, and creating school outdoor labs. Air, land, seas, and oceans are all being explored to help the environment and expand the knowledge of not only the students involved in the projects, but also the general public.

Bluegrass Water Watch

www.uky.edu/StudentOrgs/BWW/bww.html

University of Kentucky Chapter of the Kentucky Water Watch (KWW) program: See how students volunteered to become part of a statewide effort to collect environmental data from streams. Take a look at student research, maps, data, graphs, photos, and movies. The Study pages link you to maps that provide an overview of the streams under student investigation. Get to know student volunteers, why they're participating, and

what they're discovering about environmental science and themselves. Actual videos taken in the field are digitized and edited for quick download time. The site also features a mailing list and a links section to science-related sites and resources.

GLOBE Student Data Server

globe.fsl.noaa.gov/welcome.html

Students teaming with atmospheric scientists: See how kids and scientists are teaming up to study the world's atmosphere and monitor climatic change. GLOBE students all around the world take daily environmental measurements at their schools and record their data on the Internet where you can see it. Review what data's been collected in the past and find out about ongoing projects. (Students are currently tracking the weather effects of El Niño. To find out more about El Niño and the National Oceanic and Atmospherics Administration, which oversees this site, visit Part III.) See how your school could get involved. This site is in English, French, and Spanish.

Hawaii's Endangered Species: Balancing on a Thin Line

www.hisurf.com/~enchanted/

Students report on their islands' native species: Fabulously researched by Enchanted Lakes Elementary School students in Kailua, Oahu, Hawaii, this site contains lots of excellent information and art about Hawaii's endangered species. Find out why Hawaiian species are endangered and how the students and other Hawaiians are helping plants, animals, and habitats; get resources for further exploration into Hawaiian species and issues of conservation. Best of all, you can find out how to get involved yourself. Make sure that you visit the photo gallery and Newswatch sections, as well as the Endangered Species Hotlinks. Try the scavenger hunt for fun.

Kids Did This!

sln.fi.edu/tfi/hotlists/kids.html

Hot list of kids' home pages: Link to sites by and for kids that describe their many research and activity projects related to the environment, humanity, the arts, math, and news. This site gives you kid power straight from kids themselves. Under Life Science, for example, you find kids' reports on animal habitats, rain forests, endangered species, butterflies, native plants, bird migration, and genetics! Under Social Studies, you find kid-conducted studies and/or prepared articles on black history, civil rights, and Native Americans. Read student newspapers online and find out what issues are important to the generation that's next to inherit the planet.

Le Moyne College's Virtual Museum

vc.lemoyne.edu/museum.html

Created by students: View online museums created by Le Moyne students using skills and theoretical knowledge that they acquired through their Museums and Social Science course. Student Erika Beckman's museum, for example, looks at a regional lake that's now one of the most polluted in the world. Student Heather Gidney's museum highlights Iroquois women to examine their political, social, and economic roles in this Native American culture. A number of other fine student museum pages also are available

and, because the students change, so do their virtual museums. The selection when you visit may have changed from the ones listed here.

Minnesota New Country School Frog Project

mncs.k12.mn.us/frog/frog.html

Students research deformities in pond frogs: With all the care and quality research of professional scientists, these students took on an ambitious environmental science project that wound up being an award-winning endeavor. (The site details their impressive awards.) From studying local frogs to now launching a national scientific effort (which you can become part of), these students do much more with frogs than dissect them. They're helping scientists determine important environmental data. The effort started in 1995, when a Nature Studies class on a field trip to a local pond noticed that many frogs' legs looked "weird." Since that time, students have studied their local frogs with the assistance of the Minnesota Pollution Control Agency. Read what the students have discovered so far.

Natural Schools Project

www.evergreen.ca/
resnsprojectpage.html

Canadian school campuses go green: See how Canadian school kids and their teachers have turned their school grounds into more natural environments by using native plants and other environmentally sensitive landscaping techniques. Get and share ideas for your own school. Search for schools to visit by province or territory (Yukon, British Columbia, Northwest Territories, Alberta,

Saskatchewan, Manitoba, Ontario, Quebec, New Brunswick, Prince Edward Island, Nova Scotia, Newfoundland), by biogeoclimatic Zone, or by special emphasis (for example, attracting birds, butterfly gardening, forests, ponds, deserts, prairies, rivers, or streams). Maybe your school can become part of the International Natural School Project. Since 1991, the Evergreen Foundation has helped communities and schools connect with nature through outdoor enhancement projects.

The Salmon Page

www.riverdale.k12.or.us/salmon.htm

Comprehensive salmon resource site: Hosted by Riverdale School, this site shows how kids can really utilize the Internet and further environmental science. This terrific site features student forums, well-researched and well-written position papers, lots of great student art and images, and probably the best-organized compendium of salmon-related sites anywhere. Students at this Pacific Northwest elementary school study salmon because of the economic and environmental importance of the fish to their region and to many other places and cultures of the world. The status of salmon is cause for controversy and concern these days, but these young scientists take an honest look from many perspectives, including logging, fishing, manufacturing, and regulation.

Wild Ones

www.columbia.edu/cu/cerc/WildOnes/

Students worldwide working on behalf of endangered species: If you're between the ages of 7 and 14, you're invited to use this site to share information about endangered species, different habitats, and environments. More than 20,000 children, teachers, and conservation professionals in 23 countries around the world participate. Click projects to see the kind of things that kids are doing already (for example, animal behavior study, bird feeder observations, bird-migration study, habitat designs, and nature artwork). Then find out how to propose a new project and enroll.

WylandKids Web

www.wylandkids.com/

Children's art and oceans projects: One child can make a difference. That's the message of this site, sponsored by famous activist and oceans artist Wyland. Visit the children's art gallery of ocean-oriented creations and find out how to get involved yourself in ocean conservation and art activities. You can register your school as a Wyland Pod for even more involvement. Visit the kids' activities here, including the coloring book and "whaling walls."

Other Stuff to Check Out

Web sites

> eelink.umich.edu/
> creativity.net/kidcast2.html
> earthvision.asu.edu/
> www.specialspecies.com
> www.savewhatsleft.org/main.htm
> www.rpi.edu/dept/union/pugwash/
> www.webcom.com/tfk/
> www.eddytheeco-dog.com/

wwwscout.cs.wisc.edu/scout/KIDS/current/
index.html
130.194.180.26/

Mailing lists
www.kidlink.org/english/
general.html#instructions
www.riverdale.k12.or.us/salmon/
listserv.htm

Suggested search-engine keywords
Yahoo!: Kids environmental projects
Infoseek: Kids and environment

Lend a Helping Hand

In our own country, in countries around the world, and globally, environmental action groups are in need of contributions, letter-writing assistance, volunteers, or advice. These sites introduce you to some community groups here and around the world and to large-scale organizations with an international focus. You can assess their causes firsthand through each site's images, articles, and links.

Community and Regional Efforts

In communities around the world, neighbors and other concerned citizens band together to preserve their local environments and open spaces, just as Americans do here. Before the Internet, joining community efforts halfway around the world was next to impossible. But now, you can become a neighbor or community activist in a town five states or five continents away! The Internet gives a whole new meaning to the term "think locally; act globally!" You can now meet the locals in places such as Russia, Belarus, rural England, or France and pitch in with their town or regional-park, playground, clean-air, or water-quality projects! It *is* a small world after all.

Coromandel Watchdog of Hauraki Inc

bitz.co.nz/watchdog/

New Zealand citizens' group: This conservation organization is dedicated to protecting the scenic land and coast of Coromandel (Hauraki) from hard-rock mining. The group's involved in litigation against an American-based mining company doing business on the land. The group is now in need of donations to cover mounting legal costs totaling more than $20,000; under New Zealand law, it could be shut down if funds aren't forthcoming. Find out what's at stake for this group and why it's so determined to continue its fight for the coastal region. Link to other sites of community groups with mining concerns worldwide.

EarthLife Africa

www.earthlife.org.za/

Broad-based group concerned about social and environmental justice: Begun in 1988 by a group of young South Africans, this organization supports reverence for the Earth, grassroots democracy, rejection of discrimination, nonviolence, and the freeing of human potential. To those ends, this site describes current campaigns and the methods employed to achieve the group's goals. The group, located in Johannesburg, requests donations. ("We gladly accept donations of — almost — any sort. No veal or weapons of mass destruction, please.") It posts its expenditures on the site to supply full accountability. A membership form is available online for individuals to print out and mail. (The group accepts no corporate or organizational memberships.) Current issues of local concern include toxic waste, landfills, and medical waste incineration. This site is a frames-enhanced site.

Ecologia

www.ecologia.org/

New citizens' environmental efforts underway in the former Soviet Union: ECOlogists Linked for Organizing Grassroots Initiatives and Action is an independent coalition of Americans and residents of the former Soviet Union. Many major pollution problems exist as the result of policies in force when the Soviet Union was in power. Now, residents of many of the independent states are trying to model their environmental efforts to clean up towns after American nonprofit eco-groups. With headquarters in the United States and offices in Moscow, Russia; Minsk, Belarus; and Vilnius, Lithuania, Ecologia offers technical, organizational, and advocacy expertise to citizens in these regions and in Eastern Europe. Find out about current projects and how you can help if you want to support environmental reform efforts there.

FoE Regional Campaigns

www.foe.co.uk/

Environmental activities in England, Wales, and Northern Ireland: Find out what Friends of the Earth are doing in their local areas to tackle matters of concern, such as global warming, toxic emissions, traffic congestion and auto pollution, and the destruction of wild forests. Test drive the Virtual Java Car. Get information on membership, action items, publications, press releases, and localized eco-campaigns.

Forests Forever

www.forestsforever.org/

Fighting for California forests: As logging pressures edge into some of America's last ancient redwood forests, this group, founded in 1989, is trying to protect and enhance forests and wildlife habitats through educational and legislative activities. A current major campaign involves saving the Headwaters Forest, which is the largest unprotected old-growth redwood grove remaining in the world. Located in coastal northern California, the Headwaters Forest is slated to be chopped down. Forests Forever is trying to halt the logging and arrange some kind of forest-saving deal with MAXXAM CEO Charles Hurwitz to acquire the tract. Find out about this situation and other old-growth and redwood forest issues in the region at this site. Get news updates and action alerts as well.

NGOs in the NIS

solar.rtd.utk.edu/partners/ccsi/
nisorgs.htm

Independent Grassroots organizations based in the former Soviet Union: Browse for organizations by country (for example, Armenia, Belarus, and so on) or by concern (such as Agriculture or

Business). Clicking Environment, for example, brings up country names followed by linkable titles to the causes in their regions. Under Kazakstan, grassroots organizations include the Center in Support of Environmental Education, Ecological Fund of Kazakstan "Initiative," Green Movement Center, and Snow Leopards Lovers Club. Under Turkmenistan, you find the Ashkhabad Ecology Club, the Society for the Preservation of Nature of Turkmenistan, and the Dashkhovuz Ecological Club. Information collected here by the Center for Civil Society International comes from the organizations themselves, U.S. organizations and individuals who have worked with these groups, and CCSI's 1996 publication *The Post-Soviet Handbook,* which includes brief descriptions and contact information for more than 1,000 regional or local grassroots groups.

Surfriders

www.surfrider.org/

Concern about coastal pollution: Few humans come into direct contact with coastal pollution more frequently than do surfers. Logically, therefore, surfers care about the health of the oceans and work to clean up and monitor coastal problems. Find out through this frames-based site where Surfrider chapters are located throughout America and link to affiliate surfer groups in other parts of the world. Dedicated to the protection, preservation, and restoration of the world's oceans, waves, and beaches, local chapters tailor their activities to their region's needs. Because development pressures on coasts increase as resources allocated for coastal protection and maintenance decrease, surfers are trying to bridge the gap. Among issues making waves with various chapters are water quality, urban water runoff, access to beaches, public education, and surf protection and enhancement. Each of these areas is detailed on this site.

Vince Shute Wildlife Sanctuary

www.americanbear.org/

Promoting the welfare of the black bear: This Minnesota-based sanctuary and education site conducts educational and scientific activities on behalf of North America's native bear. Find out how to visit or help the resident bears at the group's Vince Shute Wildlife Sanctuary or discover how to help black bears in general. Vince Shute was a logger in the 1940s who shot marauding bears until he realized that they were just hungry. So instead, he started studying them and became a self-taught expert on their habits, needs, and behaviors. In 1994, Vince's health faded and he became worried about the future of "his" bears. With the help of friends and local experts, a sanctuary was established on his land and on surrounding properties. Today, local volunteers watch over the bears, protect them from poachers, and promote their survival in the wild. You can find out how to "adopt" a bear, become an American Bear member and get the newsletter, volunteer at the sanctuary, or donate items on the needs list. See neat bear images and link to other bear sites, including some for kids.

Welcome To Sherwood

www.sherwoodinitiative.co.uk/

Robin Hood's woods need rescuing: The woods where the Merry Men once roamed are almost gone. This site describes through text and images the legendary history of Sherwood Forest and its rather sad demise today because of intensive agriculture, the industrial expansion of the Nottinghamshire coal fields, and two centuries of population growth and urban development. Some key features and fragmented sections of the original woods remain, including

Birklands and Bilhaugh, listed in land surveys dating back to 1086, and the famous massive Major Oak. The Oak, more than 1,000 years old, is believed to have been Robin Hood's secret meeting place. But all is not lost! The government's Forestry Commission, in conjunction with local citizens, has launched the Sherwood Initiative to acquire and restore substantial amounts of original forest. If you want to help, just sign in, ask any questions you may have on the intake form, and wait for the citizens' committee to contact you.

Global Efforts

Major global concerns are handled by organizations with worldwide contacts and projects. Because pollution, overfishing, and habitat loss know few national borders, these groups and organizations take a big-picture approach (working quite often through local chapters or offices, perhaps even in your area). Most all the sites explain how you can get involved to help protect our environment and its inhabitants for future generations.

Center for Marine Conservation

www.cmc-ocean.org/

Saving the seas internationally: Kids can cavort in the Wading Pool with JavaScript games and then print out activities about whales, dolphins, sea turtles, and fish. Grown-ups can read about CMC programs and projects ranging from shark conservation to establishment of protected marine habitats, such as coral reefs. Find out how to contact public officials, related organizations, and marine sites. Shop at the online gift shop. This Washington, D.C., organization is dedicated to protecting ocean environments and conserving ocean resources through science-based advocacy and public education. Visit the online library and reference areas for more resources and visit What Can I Do? to get involved.

Earth Summit Watch

www.earthsummitwatch.org/

Holding governments accountable: About five years ago, world leaders met at a highly publicized Earth Summit to establish an agenda for environmental, economic, and social improvement. This site has been established by interested citizens to follow up and continue to urge action by each national government to keep its word toward sustainable development. This site also reports on Earth Summit II, held subsequently at the United Nations to assess progress. Read summary reports and calls for renewed attention to the pressing issue of worldwide safe drinking water.

Earth Island Institute

www.earthisland.org/ei/allproj.html

Develops and supports environmental projects: This organization approves and funds efforts by citizen groups and environmental concerns to preserve biological and cultural diversity that sustains the environment. Through education and advocacy, these projects promote conservation, preservation, and restoration. Founded in 1982 by David Brower, the Earth Island Institute outlines through its site many of its past and present projects worldwide, including rain-forest protection; habitat protection for whales, dolphins, and nesting sea turtles; furtherance of the Russian environmental movement; exchanges of citizen environmentalists between the U.S. and Japan; preservation of indigenous sacred lands; promotion of organic agriculture; building of multicultural environmental leadership in urban areas; development of ecological paper-fiber alternatives; and support of United Nations sustainable development goals. You can also link to other relevant sites.

Environmental Defense Fund

www.edf.org/

Using the courts for change: With more than 300,000 members worldwide and a $23.5 million budget (earned primarily by member donations and grants), this nonprofit organization employs more than 60 full-time scientists, economists, and attorneys. The EDF was founded in 1967 by Long Island, New York, community volunteers concerned about the use of the pesticide DDT. Now the group has grown to cover regional, national, and international environmental issues and emphasizes legal and economic incentives to solve problems. Access EDF publications and find out about membership benefits. Read EDF's action guide to more environmentally friendly paper use and printing. Get updates and news on EDF campaigns and read articles about endangered species, habitats, and environmental topics. The Kids section features children's art, poetry, homework helpers, and feedback through kids' e-mails.

Green Globe Yearbook

www.ext.grida.no/ggynet/

Associated with the United Nations Environment Program: What happens after world governments and other institutions get together and make speeches and sign documents that pledge environmental reform and then they all head back home? This yearbook, prepared by The Fridtjof Nansen Institute,

keeps track of the players and their track records. Find International Agreements on Environment and Development and locate any major participants, from governmental concerns to nonprofit groups, participating countries, and related information. Five years after the United Nations Conference on Environment and Development (UNCED), the world still faces big challenges. At this Swiss-based site, you can see who's really doing what to improve things.

Greenpeace International

www.greenpeaceusa.org/

Vocal advocates for oceans: This extensive site covers Greenpeace campaigns on ocean toxics, nuclear testing, atmospheric contamination, loss of biodiversity, overfishing, whaling, and other issues. An independent nonprofit organization, Greenpeace uses events, street theater, demonstrations, and other media-attracting measures to openly expose problems and inspire solutions. Find out through action alerts, updates, and information on contributions how to get involved in protecting species and ecosystems, preventing pollution and waste, and promoting world peace and disarmament. Portions of this site do require Java.

Nature Conservancy

www.tnc.org/

"Nature's real estate agent": This frames-based, searchable site tells about the activities and preserves of the Nature Conservancy, which accesses, purchases, and maintains some of the earth's most precious real estate. This nonprofit group operates the world's largest private system of nature sanctuaries in the world (more than 1,500 in the United States alone). Some are very small, but others cover thousands of acres. See and read about many of these sites and find out how you can help the Nature Conservancy acquire other threatened lands. By protecting habitats, the group saves rare plants and animals. Using member dues and funds raised through special campaigns such as "Adopt an Acre" or "Rescue the Reef," the Conservancy acquires land from willing sellers and donors. The concept began back in 1955 with the purchase of 60 acres in New York. Using the clickable maps and titles, you can see where the Conservancy owns land now.

Sierra Club

www.sierraclub.org/

One of America's oldest environmental groups goes international: Among the premier environmental advocacy organizations in America, the Sierra Club is a nonprofit, member-supported, public-interest group that promotes conservation of the natural environment through legislative, administrative, legal, and electoral means. Still active in the U.S. and Canada (65 chapters are involved in conservation work and outings), the Sierra Club is now taking what it's learned to other nations through international outreach and awards. (The Chico Mendes Award, for example, was recently presented to Nigerian environmental activists.) Find out through this searchable site about local and global activities (for example, international trade and development, global forests, interorganizational alliances, natural resources in developing nations, population, and toxics and pollution).

World Society for the Protection of Animals

way.net/wspa/

Protecting animals in many nations: This site describes the disaster relief, international human-education campaigns, and hands-on projects conducted in countries where the concept of "animal protection" may be unknown. Offices are located in the United Kingdom, the United States, Canada, Costa Rica, Colombia, and Kenya. Find out about current campaigns against many forms of animal cruelty, neglect, or cultural insensitivity. WSPA, a 40-year-old organization, has 300 member societies in more than 70 countries. It consults with the United Nations Economic and Social Council and the Council of Europe. Some of the campaigns are quite controversial, particularly in light of cultural norms in the countries where the animal practices occur (for example, bullfighting or wearing fur). Some reported instances of abuse or neglect, particularly in relation to companion animals that Americans keep as pets (such as dogs), may not be appropriate reading for younger children.

World Wide Fund

www.panda.org/

Major nature organization with worldwide projects: Offered in English, French, and Spanish, this site is very large with its ecology section for kids and resource section for teachers. With activities in 96

countries, the World Wide Fund has millions of members worldwide, 24 national organizations (which carry out conservation activities in their own countries and contribute technical expertise and funding to WWF's international efforts), and 26 Programme Offices (which implement WWF's fieldwork, advise national and local governments, and raise public understanding of conservation issues). The WWF combines field work, policy development, scientific information, and dialogue among concerned parties to encourage environmentally sound actions. It describes itself as global in outreach and local in implementation. Find out in detail about its current campaigns, which cover major land- and sea-related issues. Membership is offered for a fee. Videos are available on the site and require either the VDO or VivoActive plug-ins.

Other Stuff to Check Out

Web sites

> www.webcom.com/~iwcwww/
> whale_adoption/waphome.html
> www.rainforest-alliance.org/
> www.coral.org/
> www.owplaza.com/eco/
> www.iwec.org/
> esnet.edu/ican/
> www.ext.grida.no/

Newsgroups

> alt.org.sierra-club

Chat areas

> www.greenpeace.org/icha.html
> www.tnc.org/chat.html

Online service areas

> America Online: Environment, Network
> Earth, Sierra
> Compuserve: GO OUTNEWS

Suggested search-engine keywords

> Yahoo!: Environmental groups, environmental organizations
> Infoseek: Environmental topics

Outer Space Exploration

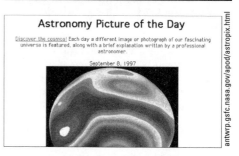

Astronomy Picture of the Day

How far is forever? How high can we soar? What's it like to float out in space? What does Earth look like from up above? How does someone become an astronaut? Are we alone in the universe? If you like staring at the stars and wondering about distant galaxies and our own neighboring planets, these sites will really space you out (and launch you in the right direction with your next far-out homework assignment).

Amazing Space

oposite.stsci.edu/pubinfo/amazing-space.html

Web-based educational activities about outer space: Primarily for classroom use, but easily adaptable by creative parents, activities here are designed to give kids a better understanding of such topics as the solar system, the requirements for becoming a space scientist, the life cycle of stars, and the history and use of telescopes. This site is sponsored by The Space Telescope Science Institute in Baltimore, Maryland, which is responsible for the scientific operation of the Hubble Space Telescope. The lessons, developed in conjunction with educators, involve Hubble space photographs, high-quality graphics, videos, and animation.

Astronomy Cafe

www2.ari.net/home/odenwald/
cafe.html

"The Web site for the astronomically disadvantaged": That's how this cleverly presented site describes itself, and it *is* very user-friendly. Get a feeling for being an astronomer conducting research and hear from actual astronomers. Find out about hyperspace, black holes, time travel, and quantum cosmology; nothing is too far out because space *is* far out, after all. Sections are devoted to space images, space poetry, a career center, and related links.

Astronomy Picture of the Day

antwrp.gsfc.nasa.gov/apod/
astropix.html

Inspiring images of the cosmos: Every day, check this site for a new image or enhanced photograph of stars, planets, galaxies, comets, or constellations, or other fascinating views of the universe. Each image is accompanied by a brief explanation written by a professional astronomer. Visit the archive to see past images, and link to astronomy-related sites. The site includes a glossary of key terms and a subject-sorted archive for broader searches of past images.

Cambridge Astronomy

www.ast.cam.ac.uk/

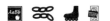

Great space research resource: With its clear, well-indexed design and attention to updating, this site provides plenty of good space resources. You may have to dig through a lot of links and pretty technical information to find the attractions for space buffs and scientists, such as Hubble Space Telescope images and updates and links to observatories and educational activities. A text version is available.

EarthRISE

earthrise.sdsc.edu/earthrise

Photos of Earth from space: This beautifully designed site is about a beautiful subject, our home planet. This large database of photos was taken by astronauts from the windows during space shuttle missions. View photos from the past 15 years, all well organized and accessible by using several different search methods. It's an uplifting resource for kids, parents, and schools. You can enlarge many of the images by clicking them, but they load up small for faster access.

Expanding Universe

www.mtrl.toronto.on.ca/centres/bsd/
astronomy

Impressive search tool for amateur astronomers: This searchable directory of organizations, institutions, associations, companies, and others involved in astronomy and related space sciences is all yours. Thousands of sites and related resources are cataloged here, based on a sort of online Dewey decimal system. Click to the Top Level Classification covering such areas as Astronomy and Allied Sciences, general astronomy sites, periodicals, associations, planetariums, observatories, telescopes and equipment, deep-sky and solar system bodies, and phenomena. After you select a top-level category, subheadings lead you systematically down the sort list to your intended destination. You can also do word searches or search alphabetically.

Images of Galaxies

zebu.uoregon.edu/galaxy.html

Stunning, easy to use image gallery: View amazing images of stars and galaxies. This CCD (Charge-coupled Device) Images of Galaxies site is part of the Electronic Universe Project of the Department of Physics at the University of Oregon. It features astronomy photographs of supernovae, a comet crash, and galaxies taken from observatories. See the planets and examine special phenomena, including dark matter and UFOs. Use this resource if you want breathtaking images of all kinds that are only a click away.

Mir Space Station

www.maximov.com/Mir/mir2.html

History and events related to Mir: This graphically pleasing and well-designed site is packed with information about the Russian space station. For over ten years, the Mir Space Station has hosted cosmonauts and, more recently, guest astronauts, during its approximately 60,000 orbits. Find information about its history, current and past research activities, development and design, and present location and crew. Get current news and dock up with related Mir and space travel links.

NASA Home Page

www.nasa.gov/

Spend time inside America's official space agency: From the home page of this site, you can easily click to all kinds of exciting areas. Today@NASA covers current news and events and can be a very busy section, so you may have to try several times to get in. NASA Organization links to home pages of various NASA operation and research centers. The Questions and Answers section offers replies to such queries as "How can I witness a launch?" and "How can I get NASA space photos?" Space Science describes the science behind the planetary explorations and space trips. You also find a spectacular video, audio, and image gallery of "keepsakes" that you can download. Start by reading the letter from NASA's administrator, who explains the agency's strategic plan and provides complete user tips on various plug-ins, applications, and so on that you need in order to take best advantage of the whole site.

Nine Planets

seds.lpl.arizona.edu/billa/tnp/

Be a virtual space traveler: In bold and creative fashion, this site describes each planet and major moon in our solar system. It uses text, images, some sounds, and movies and provides references to additional related information. The site provides an overview of each planet's known history, mythology, and current scientific knowledge. You can take full advantage of the site if you have the various plug-ins required, or you can take the Express Tour, which is satisfying (and quicker for homework assignments!). The site includes a section devoted to other solar systems, a section about how to view our solar system from your backyard, and a complete glossary of technical terms. It's best viewed with a graphical Web browser that displays the pictures in color and supports hypertext link traversal. But you can also visit the site in text-only ways. A helper page presents good usage tips.

Shuttle Launches From Kennedy Space Center

www.ksc.nasa.gov/shuttle/missions/ missions.html

Detailed descriptions and images of U.S. space launches: Stay current with shuttle flights, crews, and mission highlights. The searchable site also provides related links. From here, you can access information about the Latest Shuttle Manifest, projected upcoming missions, Orbiter Vehicles, and Pre STS-1 missions (STS is an acronym for Space Transportation System). You also can view the Kennedy Space Center's Shuttle Countdown Image Archive, Johnson Space Center's Shuttle Image Library, the Ames Graphical Image Index, or the Dryden's Shuttle Landing Archive. The site has options to help you search, including simply clicking on the date that a mission occurred.

StarWorld: Astronomy and Related Organizations

cdsweb.u-strasbg.fr/~heck/sfworlds.htm

Large, searchable directory of space science sites: Thousands of linking resources are accessible here. All you do is type a "character string" (name or part of the name of an organization, city,

location, title of periodical, part of an e-mail address, or a URL) into the query box and press the Return key or click the Search button. Other search options are carefully explained under usage tips. You can also visit hot news, features, StarHeads for home pages of individuals, or StarBits for acronyms.

Views of the Solar System

bang.lanl.gov/solarsys/

Tour of the solar system: Enjoy images and information about the sun, planets, moons, asteroids, comets, and meteoroids. This site displays over 950 high-resolution images and animations and over 880MB of data. Hypertext your way along by clicking on a desired planet, which brings up information and images. When you're on a planet page, hyperlinks take you to related pages about any moons or other cosmic cousins.

Other Stuff to Check Out

Web sites

www.nss.org/askastro/
school.discovery.com/spring97/themes/
   earthtomars/nasa/
quest.arc.nasa.gov/mars/events/
   shoebox.html
www.spacenews.com/orbit
w3.cea.berkeley.edu/Education/
www.marswest.org/
comet.lbl.gov/~bruceg/
   irsearch_homepage.html
www.gbnet.net/orgs/seds/links/links.html
www-hpcc.astro.washington.edu/scied/
   astro/astroindex.html
www.fedworld.gov/astron.htm
zebu.uoregon.edu/cosmo.html
http://iu.berkeley.edu/iu/
www.astro.Virginia.EDU/~eww6n/

Newsgroups
sci.astro

Mailing lists
www.meteoritecentral.com/
mailing_list.html
www.neosoft.com/internet/paml/groups.E/
earth_and_sky.html

Chat areas
www.meteoritecentral.com/cgi-bin/chat/
met-chat.cgi

Online service areas
America Online: LEARNING & CULTURE
CompuServe: GO SPACE

Suggested search-engine keywords
Yahoo!: Space, astronomy
Infoseek: Space, astronomy

From the comfort of your keyboard, browse the mineral wonders

www.goodearth.com/virtcave.html

If you want to experience some of the
world's most extraordinary natural
expeditions, but your budget, job, family
obligations, physical condition, or other
factors preclude a trek to the Amazon or
Arctic Circle right now, why not experience them virtually through images, text,
and (sometimes) movies and audio at
these Internet sites? Take the entire
family along. You don't even need to pack
first!

Amazon Interactive

www.eduweb.com/amazon.html

Geography of the Ecuadorian Amazon:
Through online games and activities,
discover the rain forest and the Quichua
people who call it home. See how the
Quichua live off the land. Then try to
establish and operate your own commu-
nity-based ecotourism project along the
Río Napo. Along the way, you find out
such things as where the Amazon is
located, how rainy it gets, what lives
there, and how to make a living in
harmony with the land. This site is based
on actual field research into indigenous
ecotourism in the region. Use internal
links to find other adventures at this site.

Ancient Bristlecone Pine

www.sonic.net/bristlecone/intro.html

Visit the world's oldest trees: The earth's
oldest living inhabitant, "Methuselah," at
4,763 years, is one of the ancient, beautiful trees you can see at this graphically
and image-rich site. Find out where these
trees are located, who discovered them,
how they were dated, and how they've
adapted to survive for so many years.
This site is based on the White-Inyo
mountain range of California. Link to
other tree sites. Download spectacular
JPEG images. This site is best viewed by
using Netscape 2.0 (or newer version) on
monitors with 16-bit color. To view this
site correctly, set your browser screen
font to 12-point Times and the fixed font
to 10-point Courier. You can also access a
non-Netscape version from this site.

Earthwatch

www.earthwatch.org/

Virtual expeditions for students and teachers: Founded in 1972, this nonprofit organization teams citizens and scientists in on-site research projects. For kids who can't make actual journeys, the Virtual Expedition section of the site offers them the chance to find out about raptors, wild Mexico, Andrew Jackson's Hermitage, Amazonian katydids, and much more, complete with sounds, images, lesson plans, and scientist interviews. This site is a frames-based site that uses a second browser window for field trips. In the past 25 years, this Massachusetts-based organization has mobilized 2,083 projects in 118 countries. This year, more than 600 teachers and students are heading out to the field. Find out how and where here.

Electronic Field Trips

http://www.aea11.k12.ia.us/public.html

List of science- and environmental-oriented virtual expeditions and project sites: This straightforward, scroll-down list of sites and brief descriptions covers biology (topics such as Live From Antarctica, Texas Threatened, Endangered Species, Missouri Botanical Garden, and JASON Project Voyage V: Planet Earth), Climate and Space (including Atmospheric Ozone and the Space Telescope Electronic Information Service), Earth studies (such as Planet Earth Home Page and The Daily Planet), physics (such as Canadian Meteorological Center), and ocean and seas (such as MSSS Antarctic Research). ***Remember:*** each site on the list may have its own plug-in (RealAudio, QuickTime, or VDO) and browser requirements.

Geologists Lifetime Field List

www.uc.edu/www/geology/
   geologylist/index.html

Tour of essential or desirable locations for geologists or travelers to visit: You don't need to be a geologist to enjoy this visual collection of some of the world's greatest natural attractions, based on an article written by Lisa A. Rossbacher for *Geotimes*. Page producer Terry Acomb has added links to places referenced in the article, such as Devil's Tower, Ayers Rock, and various erupting volcanoes. The site's an uncomplicated but very effective way to showcase a lot of geological Meccas, and the images are of outstanding quality (most enlargeable with a mouse click).

Good Green Fun!

www.efn.org/~dharmika/

Good Green Fun!
Music and
Rainforest Ecology
For Children
of All Ages

Explore *tropical and temperate rainforests* of the world through the internet and the music of *Good Green Fun!*,

winner of a *1995 Parents' Choice Gold Award.*

Virtual expedition for the younger crowd: Via music, audio, images, and graphics, kids can experience tropical and temperate rain forests of the world. This award-winning site combines lyrics, song, activities, research, and related links to present topics such as the strangler fig, sunshowers, rain-forest ants, mushrooms, and frogs. For each song, you can hear a sound sample in either WAV or AU format, and read the lyrics. Look for answers to lots of questions about the plants, animals, ecosystems, and indigenous people of the rain forests. A CD version is available.

Netspedition

sunsite.doc.ic.ac.uk/netspedition/

Interactive scientific expedition to the Amazon rain forest: Discover how a scientific team pioneered research in highly remote regions. Accompany them through the Internet to see how they survived in the jungle and encountered amazing Indian cultures. Experience (from the safety of your computer desk) the injuries, illnesses, and narrow escape from a hostile Yanomami tribe. This site is based on a 1996 expedition involving the Imperial College of London and the University of Zulia of Venezuela. Exploring the Amazon region of southern Venezuela by canoe, the expedition involved a 1,200-kilometer journey through the jungle along the Orinoco, Casiquiare, Guainia, and Atobapo rivers.

To See a World

www.marin.cc.ca.us/~jim/ring/ring1.html

College of Marin's Virtual Hike Up Ring Mountain: This site takes you on a walk up one of the San Francisco Bay region's most scenic and environmentally valuable mountains. Spend time viewing great images and contemplating nature and remarkable views. Check the weather and start your hike by exploring the shores of the San Francisco Bay at the mountain's base. Through images and text, you work your way up a wonderful trail to the crest (gaining many insights about plants, animals, and formations along the way) and experience panoramic views of San Francisco Bay.

Virtual Cave

www.goodearth.com/virtcave.html

Go spelunking from your seat: Discover natural wonders within this virtual cave; its mineral wonders should soon have you saying "Ooh" and "Aah" just as if you'd discovered them inside a real cave. Click image titles such as Aragonite, Baldacchino, Canopies, Bathtubs, Bell Canopies, Bottlebrushes, Columns, Conulites, Death Coral, Draperies, Folia, Gypsum, Flowers, Halite, Flowers, Helictites, Pearls, Popcorn, Stalactites, Stalagmites, or Stegamites to see what the heck these things are. After you emerge awestruck from your cave, visit other sections of the site to find out lots more about the wonders of caves.

Virtual Field Trip through Big Bend National Park

geoweb.tamu.edu/faculty/herbert/bigbend/

Brought to you by Texas A&M's Department of Geology: Travel with geologists who explain the geological beauty, features, and history of Big Bend National Park. Created for an independent study project for the Texas A&M University Department of Geology & Geophysics under the supervision of Dr. Bruce Herbert, this visual and text-based field trip originally took place during spring break in 1996. The journey clearly and interestingly emphasizes the geology of the park and pertinent geologic features. The park is located in West Texas adjacent to the Rio Grande, approximately 69 miles south of Marathon, Texas. The park contains a few small ghost towns and visitor amenities. Click through the tour by choosing various topics (for example, Igneous Processes, Sedimentary Processes, Metamorphic Processes, Structural Processes, Big Bend Through Time, or Related Links).

Whale Songs

whales.ot.com/

Virtual expedition to study whales: Go with the International Fund for Animal Welfare's research vessel, *Song of the Whale,* to study the sea's largest mammals. Click a map of various Azores islands to discover what researchers and one American science teacher saw there in their encounters with various whales. Travel the seas without getting seasick and get to know giant cetaceans. Travel aboard the *Song of the Whale,* which is an Oyster-46 ketch (small double-masted yacht), built in the United Kingdom in 1979. Lots of images and well-written text keeps you sailing along.

Other Stuff to Check Out

Web sites

www.earthlife.org.za
www.safari.co.za/ radio safari.
www.fws.gov/~bennishk/endang/sml/
    sld01.html
www.bigstory.com/swamptalk/swampmain/
    index.html
www.nwrc.nbs.gov/fringe/ff_index.html
www.africanet.com/
ecotravel.com/

Suggested search-engine keywords

Yahoo!: Virtual expeditions
Infoseek: Virtual expeditions

312 Virtual Adventures

Part VII

The Part of Tens

The 5th Wave® By Rich Tennant

"It's a letter from the company that installed our in-ground sprinkler system. They're offering Internet access now."

In this part . . .

In the course of getting to know the Internet from a parent's perspective, I came across special sites that have broad-based content, use the Internet medium creatively, are easy to understand and navigate, and focus on exceptional content and/or links. Some of these sites were very good, but didn't have content so specific that they fit into the particular categories defined in other parts of this book. So without further ado, I'd like to present what I consider (sound the bugle) to be Ten Great Sites for Kids and Ten Great Sites for Parents. And the winners are. . . .

(Oh, by the way, don't underestimate the runner-up sites in the Other Stuff to Check Out section. These selections were not easy choices to make.)

Ten Great Sites for Kids

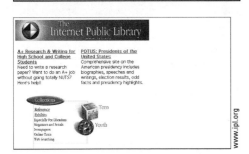

Visit the world, get homework resources, play online, find out about growing up, and make friends. These sites give you action and discovery all in one place. (Heads up, grown-ups! Even though the kids' sites are for kids, links do lead to links that lead to links, and so on, so you'll want to consider an occasional peek over the shoulder at what's on your child's computer screen. All first- and second-level links and any areas within these sites are guaranteed safe.)

4Kids Treehouse

www.4kids.com

From 4Kids Treehouse

Easy to use and lots of good links: Just click anything you see in the tree house to go to links (for example, if you click the goldfish bowl, you go to the Science room with links for animals, the environment, museums, and so on). Under Projects, see kids' home pages and projects they're doing online through schools or organizations. In the Playroom, find online games, shareware, and activities. A show biz/TV section has links to sites about cartoons, movies, television, music, video games, and computer software, and another section helps you with homework.

Berit's Best Sites for Kids

http://db.cochran.com/ li_toc:theoPage.db

Quality links and activities: This neat-looking, easy-to-understand site sorts, ranks (on a scale of 1 to 5), and reviews the best sites for kids on the Internet. You have two main lists to pick from. Clicking a topic from the first list takes you to fun sites about activity centers, crafts and coloring, games and toys, stories, magazines, funnies, sports and recreation, music, TV, and movies. If you click from the second list, you get kids' sites about art, astronomy and other sciences, the environment, government, health and safety, history, math, and world travel. You can find a pen pal, chat with friends, see what kids have created, and visit other kids' and families' home pages. Or link to the best sites about animals, "creepy crawlies," dinosaurs, and hundreds of other topics. Parents, please note: As with any interaction with someone else on the Internet, whether it be through chat rooms or e-mail, keep an eye open for your children's sake.

Cyberkids

www.mtlake.com/cyberkids/

Go shopping and world hopping: Get free multimedia e-mail software for families, chat at the Cyberkids Connection (with

316 Ten Great Sites for Kids

parental supervision, of course), enter contests, and shop at the online store (with parents' permission, of course) for picture or reference books. Read a serial novel, express your views, and show off your creativity. Listen to kids' musical compositions, see artwork, and make keypals (kids who converse through postings in a forum or newsgroup-type area) from around the world. Tackle puzzles and brainteasers that are just for kids. Topics you find covered here include art, entertainment, kids' creations and opinions, fun and games, homework helpers, sports, and nature. (You need Shockwave for part of the site.)

Global Show-n-Tell

www.telenaut.com/gst/

Kids' online art gallery: Even better than the front of the refrigerator, this site lets you post your finest artwork for the whole world to see. Get ideas from what other kids have created and discover from them how they did it. See (or submit) show 'n' tells of favorite art with little stories about them if you want. Link to kids' and schools' home pages. Kids all over the world have home pages, and you can get to know them online. Parents should review the links with their children to be sure that the links are appropriate for the kids. Activities are sorted by age, so you can hang around with kids your own age. This site displays lots of art, so be patient if certain pages take a little while to load. Be sure to have a parent read the page that's meant for grown-ups, for safety.

Internet Public Library

www.ipl.org/

A library you can play in: No one tells you to keep your voice down here — in fact, some of the interactive activities will probably make you "ooh" and "ahh" out loud! Major sections of this library are just for youth and teens, and the exhibit hall has special shows about all kinds of frequently changing subjects, from dinosaurs and lighthouses to history and trains. In the Teen Division, real teenagers and a real librarian select the sites for other teens to enjoy. The Teen Advisory Board makes sure that content is useful and cool. Check out arts, entertainment, books, writing, colleges, clubs and organizations, computers, dating, homework helpers, health and body changes, conflicts and relationships, sports, and style. The Youth Division features a dorky but lovable-looking librarian named J. J. who will point your way to virtual tours (the car factory and museum, for example), fun learning activities, and even let you ask a question of the staff. During story hour, you can read a story or have one read to you online! (You will need to be sure that your browser has a helper application for AIFF audio files.) See the figure at the top of this section to see what this site looks like.

Kid City

www.sftoday.com/enn2/kidcity.htm

Slick city: From the colorful skyline, click the enter sign and find all sorts of parts of town to explore. Kid City Spaceport has astronomy and space links; Kid City Zoo has animal sites; the Mall has corporate sites that make or sell things kids like (cereal, videos, clothes, ice cream). See whether you can guess what kinds of sites these parts of town feature: High School Central, the Toy Store, Science Museum, Kid City Sports Stadium, Children and Youth Library, Computer Lab, Kid City Post Office, Newsstand, Game Castle, Cartoon Cave, Kid City Town Hall, and Kids' Kitchen. This cybercity has even more places than that to explore. It's a clever way to organize a bunch of fun, quality sites.

Kids Korner

www.kids-korner.com

Site for kids of all ages: Teens can check into the Teen Talk page for links most relevant to their interests. Sites for all kids have been examined for safety and quality, and parents are welcome to provide feedback, too, as their kids travel down each linking highway (check out the section on usage and parent resources). Links cover education, reading, world attractions, online activities and crafts, entertainment, toys, games, kids' home pages, online friends, and other topics kids like. Find pen pals and chats just for kids.

KidsCom

www.kidscom.com/

Electronic international playground for kids ages 4 to 15: Offered in four languages (you pick), this chat and activity-filled site lets you offer your opinions to presidents and prime ministers, see how kids live in other countries (and talk to lots of them), visit Neat Links picked out just for you, and take virtual tours of other lands. Tell the world about where you live, and talk to friends with common interests who may live on the other side of the world. Parents will like the fact that anyone who chats at this site is monitored for safety 24 hours a day — but younger children should still be supervised. So chat live with kids from all over the globe. One chat is for kids 11 and younger, and another is for the 12-to-15 crowd. You also find easy games, not-so-easy (but fun) games, and games using Shockwave or Java plug-ins. (Parents can go to the parents' section because it has tips for users and activities that they can do with kids.)

KidsWeb

www.npac.syr.edu/textbook/kidsweb/

A huge collection of sites just for kids: The good news about this site is that it's awesome! The bad news is that the site gets busy because it's so great and so many kids like it. But don't give up trying to connect because the site is worth the time. (And the neat people who set up the site are trying to make it more accessible.) Check out the arts, drama, literature, music, all kinds of sciences, history, games (note the use of plug-ins here), fun oddball stuff (riddles, puzzles, interactive things), homework helpers, and sports. Find whole libraries and links to collections of Web sites for kids, too, plus a list of schools on the Internet. You could go on forever! A version of this site without icons is also available (it loads faster). KidsWeb is brought to you by the Syracuse University Living Schoolbook Project. Because some of the links could lead to areas that parents would rather not have their children visit, parental supervision is suggested.

thekids.com

www.thekids.com

Delightful picture stories: If you like stories of long ago and faraway, along with pretty or funny pictures to go with them, you'll like this site. It works best with Netscape, but you don't need any fancy plug-ins. Just pick a story from the index and then read it or have a grown-up read it to you (you adults will like the really charming pictures). Stories come from all over the world. You find stories with morals, great adventures, funny stories, and mysterious legends. Many of them have weird names, such as "Osoon

Turkey and the Wizard's Heart," a Seneca Indian tale. Explore illustrated stories from around the world that also include rhymes, fables, and folk and fairy tales. Plus, you can talk about stories online with other kids, write stories, play games, and vote in opinion polls. The Best of the Net link takes you to other creative kids' sites.

Other Stuff to Check Out

Web sites

> www.pathfinder.com/kids/
> www.girltech.com
> www.agirlsworld.com
> www.aracnet.com/~charmayn/
>   teenstuf.html
> www.kids-space.org/
> www.erols.com/erols/search/coolkids.htm
> www.lws.com/kidsweb/links.htm
> www.primenet.com:80/~sburr/index.html
> www.vividus.com/ucis.html
> longwood.cs.ucf.edu/~MidLink/
> www.reedbooks.com.au/rigby/kids/
>   kidplace.html
> www.zen.org/~brendan/kids.html

Newsgroup

> alt.kids-talk

Mailing lists

> www.kidlink.org/home-txt.html
> listserv–suvml.bitnet
> kidsphere-request@vms.cis.pitt.edu
> listserv@asuacad.bitnet
> listserv@unccvm.bitnet
> listserv@asuvm.inre.asu.edu

Chat area

> freezone.com:80/join.html

Online service area

> America Online: KIDS ONLY

Suggested search-engine keywords

> Yahoo!: Yahooligans
> Infoseek: Kids & Fun

Ten Great Sites for Parents

Explore your own world and that of your children with these award-winning sites. Some of these sites have sections for kids, but they're mostly for parents. So put your feet up, have a cup of coffee, chat with other parents, get the lowdown on family finances, dream of that perfect vacation, and find a pleasant support network in cyberspace.

Essential Information for Parents

www.mcs.net/~kathyw/parent.html

Provocative look at serious family issues: Part of a larger site that deals also with domestic violence, abuse, trauma, AIDS, and dissociation, this particular section of the site features articles provided by parenting experts and links to their sites. From Habit Smart, for example, come articles on kids and alcohol. You can also link to the main site, which covers addictive behavior. The site is suitable for parents and older children (with parental supervision). Among topics covered are enforcing child safety on the Internet, ensuring girls' self-esteem and positive development, getting general and medical parenting information, raising kids with special needs, parenting effectively, preventing child abuse, understanding preteens and teens, and promoting positive communication.

Family.com

www.family.com

Family matters: The people who brought you Mickey Mouse (yes, Disney) now bring you this expansive, family-based resource. You can customize information to cover the region in which you live, or look at national support, consumer, and news coverage. Among areas featured with original articles and relevant links are recreation, hobbies, computing, food, education, parenting, and travel. Seasonal topics involve back-to-school preparations, winter weather crafts, holiday preparations, and tips on how to play (playing is good for grown-ups, too!). You get plenty of opportunities to interact with other parents through chats and discussion groups. Although the home page may seem a bit daunting at first, spend a few minutes clicking buttons and looking around, and its deft organization gets to you. It's got some really neat navigation touches you won't find elsewhere. Link to programs, plug-ins (Shockwave), and helper applications from the help section to take full advantage of this site, which is frequently updated.

National Parent Information Network

ericps.ed.uiuc.edu/npin/npinhome.html

Intelligent guidance for caring parents: Quality writing, full-text articles by experts, and carefully selected links make this site an outstanding searchable resource. NPIN is sponsored by the ERIC Clearinghouse on Urban Education at Teachers College, Columbia University, New York City; and by the ERIC Clearing-house on Elementary and Early Child-hood Education at the University of Illinois at Urbana-Champaign. Try the Parents AskERIC question-answering service or the PARENTING Discussion List. Topics covered at the site include urban and minority families, assessment and testing, child care, media influences, children's health and nutrition, childhood development and learning, family-peer relationships, gifted children, preteens, adolescents (ages 9 to 14), and teens. Under Teens, for example, find articles and other resources related to pregnancy, teen parenthood, AIDS, drug and alcohol use, and health and development. Other articles cover child safety on the Internet, divorce, single parenting, and many other social, emotional, and learning topics. The figure at the top of this section shows the NPIN site.

Not Just for Kids

www.night.net/kids/

Opening to the strains of Rockin' Robin, this site welcomes you with its cheeriness and whimsy. (Can't hear the music? Get info on the MIDI plug-in at the bottom of the home page.) As you tap your toe, tap your mouse to check out Rosie's Rhubarb Reviews of sites about animals, reading, writing, chats, keypals, science, fun and games, sports, travel, parenting, kid stuff, and entertainment. This site definitely has a childlike feel to it, but its links and activities are meant for kids and parents to experience together. Grandpa Tucker's Rhymes and Tales features silly poems, stories, and activities for the whole family. So if you've had a tough day at work or home and everyone is feeling a little blue or out of sorts, call up this site. If you're not smiling and busy within five minutes, it *has* been a *really* bad day.

Parent News

www.parent.net/

Up-to-date parenting info: The immediacy and current relevance of the information on this site make it uniquely appealing. Plus, the site is not overwhelming, and it's very easy to use. Any new issue or event affecting parents is covered here. The site's layout is neat and to-the-point. Click subject areas that include news, movies, health, books, and homework (great list of links so you can convince your kids that you know everything). Read articles and find general resources or check out the featured item in each category. This site is sponsored by an optical firm, so eyecare topics have a way of showing up, too. The site is updated weekly, and you can read archived coverage in the various topic areas.

Parent Soup

www.parentsoup.com

Emphasis on parent-to-parent communication: Uncomplicated design, good content, and a real desire to get parents talking (chats, discussion groups, feedback forms) are strengths here. Enjoy articles and links in a wide variety of areas, including family activities, babies and toddlers, health and safety, finances, pregnancy, relationships, and education. One especially fun area to visit even if you don't need it is the baby name finder (more than 5,000 entries — find out what your name or the names of your kids mean). You do need to become a member (it's free) and download free software to participate in parent-to-parent activities, such as the chats. In the Parents' Picks section, members describe their reactions to books, baby products, travel, toys, computer stuff, Web sites, and movies (such as thumbs up or thumbs down for kids). A panel of experts takes questions on a range of subjects from concerned parents.

Parent Zone

www.parentzone.com/index.htm

Links to selected site specialties: Click link titles or logos to connect to sites covering sports, finance, family health, parenting issues, child development, pets, and the daily news. One zone on this site is for kids, and another is for parent chats. This site is very techie, graphics oriented, and state-of-the-art, which you'll find either exciting or frustrating. Netscape Communicator Version 4.01 or higher and the Netcaster component are recommended and can be downloaded through the link on the bottom of the Parent Zone home page. Netscape offers a 90-day trial period, after which they ask business and government users for payment. This site covers many topics that you may not see routinely elsewhere (death, emergency medicine, interest-free money and freebies, offbeat travel destinations), so the subject matter as well as the design tend to be cutting-edge.

Parents At Home Page

advicom.net/~jsm/moms/

For parents who stay at home: Feeling a little isolated, perhaps even misunderstood? You've got friends and support at this site (and you can shop for baby stuff through the online catalog). With all the choices women (and men) have to make these days, some choose to stay home with their kids. This site is especially for (but certainly not limited to) those parents who are forgoing full-time paid employment outside the home to focus on their children. It's also aimed at parents who work at home (contract or self-employed) or stagger their work hours to be more available to their kids.

The free online newsletter covers at-home issues and resources. At the discussion forum, you can share thoughts and ideas. Links go to related parenting and kids sites. You can find money-issue information, classified ads, e-mail pen pals, and support organizations waiting for you here.

ParentsPlace.Com

www.parentsplace.com

Timely topics of interest: Check out weekly special features (such as dealing with clutter in the home or with PMS) and see what's happening at the various topic areas, including Sweets (a recipe for banana nugget cookies, perhaps), School-Age, Family (for example, getting along), and Dentist (how often should you replace that toothbrush, anyway?). Check out bulletin boards for parents, pregnant women, expectant dads, hobbyists, cooks, or unmarried partners. You need to join up (it's free) to participate in chats or board activities. You can search the site for topics of interest, and the internal search engine produces relevant articles from its server. Special live chats are announced onsite and cover all kinds of parenting topics (expecting, dieting, working overseas, dealing with kids' and teens' development issues, home-schooling, living as a military family, staying home instead of working, exercising). Additionally, you can get updates on product recalls.

Pathfinder

www.pathfinder.com/welcome/

Incredible all-around family resource: From the home page of this site, produced by Time Warner, you can click to the sites of major print and online publications *(People, Money, Time, CNNSI);* connect to sections devoted to show biz, finances, business, sports, culture, politics, current events, and lifestyles; or click to featured articles in any one of these categories (Back-to-School bargains, Foods to Fight Fatigue). And that's just what you can do from the main page! If you click to the Living section, for example, you find even more links and clearly defined articles (gardening, traveling with kids). And you can link to Living subsections with original, highly creative content of their own (ParentTime, Kidstuff, Sex and Relationships, This Old House). You can find what you need quickly or take time to browse and explore. Either way, this site is dynamic, graphically pleasing, easy to comprehend, and frequently updated, so it's an outstanding resource.

Other Stuff to Check Out

Web sites
www.dailyparent.com
www.familyinternet.com
www.familysurf.com
www1.zdnet.com/familypc/
www.women.com
megamach.portage.net/~rborelli/dads.html
www.einet.net/
www.crc.ricoh.com/people/steve/
parents.html
www.dot-net.net/susanw/lasmadres/
links.htm

Newsgroups
www.liszt.com
www.reference.com
www.dejanews.com

Mailing lists
lawlib.slu.edu/training/mailser.htm
www.liszt.com
www.neosoft.com/internet/paml/
www.reference.com
www.netspace.org/cgi-bin/lwgate/
emailhost.ait.ac.th/Search/pubmail-subj.html
www.cuc.edu/cgi-bin/listservform.pl

Chat areas
www.lifetimetv.com/chat/
unmoderated_chats.html
www.parentsplace.com/genobject.cgi/
talking.html

Online service area
America Online: FAMILIES

Suggested search-engine keywords
Yahoo!: Parenting, Families
Search.com: Parenting, Families

Appendix A

A Surfer's Guide to the Internet

In this section, I dazzle and amaze you with my incredible technological knowledge of the Internet and the World Wide Web. Well, maybe not dazzle. Actually, I'm just going to do my best to explain terms and technology relevant to this book that I've learned as a science journalist, as an educator, as an editor and content specialist for two search engines, and as a mom who had to figure this stuff out just to keep up with my eight-year-old son's computer lab at school!

The Internet and the World Wide Web

I used to think the Internet and the World Wide Web were the same thing, but they're not. The World Wide Web is part of the Internet, but they are different in these ways.

The Internet

The Internet is a linking *network* of computers around the world, a network that is managed by both dedicated volunteers and paid experts and that basically serves as the vital organs of the whole international communications online system.

Like a telephone system, the Internet connects users around the world together using data transmission lines, giant computers called *servers,* and telephone and fiber-optic cable lines.

Originally developed for universities and the military as a quick, dependable form of interfacing, it has now become accessible to the public at large because of expanding, more accessible technology and the introduction of the World Wide Web browsing system. With an address and a password, which you acquire through a commercial, state, or university network or a private company, you can become part of the Internet community.

The World Wide Web

The World Wide Web is a system that allows you to access information and to make sense of it from the Internet. It is designed to be easy for you to understand and interpret (instead of a lot of electronic beeps, numbers, or codes, which is what the Internet would send you directly). The Web uses things such as hyperlinks (different colored, underlined, or otherwise highlighted text), icons (specific graphics), and other visual tools humans understand. Because of the World Wide Web, the Internet isn't just for computer scientists and engineers anymore! Anyone can be a computer geek!

Hardware

To use the Internet and World Wide Web, you need equipment, otherwise known as *hardware*.

First on the list is a *computer,* of course. It's not the purpose of this book to advise you on which brand of computer to buy, and if you've purchased this book, you probably have a computer already. But if you are thinking of making a purchase, talk to people who have computers, consider what type of work you'll do on your own computer, and ask at your kids' schools what kinds of computers they use. When you go to buy a computer, make sure to get one with enough *ooomph* to keep you cruising, not crawling, when you log on to the Internet. Emphasize to the salesperson that you plan to use the Internet — a lot. If you already own a computer, you may want to consider upgrading it with more RAM.

You also need a *modem,* which can be a circuit board installed inside your computer or a funny looking box with polka-dotty lights (I'm not getting too technical here, am I?) that helps your computer talk to another computer. My modem makes all kinds of fascinating noises when I log on to the Internet because that's how computers "talk" to one another.

This next part is very important: Forget 14.4 modems. They are yesterday. They are slow. They are frustrating. All those jokes about waiting a half hour for a site to load are based on 14.4 modems. A 28.8 modem is tons faster (although about three times more expensive). Still, if you are going to really get into the Internet, the 28.8 is worth the cost. Sites come up much more quickly. And if you want to go completely Net nuts, you can get a modem with even bigger numbers like 33.6 or 56 Kbps (which translates to even higher performance — and cost) — but remember to check with your Internet service provider to see whether they can support speeds over 28.8 Kbps.

To read more about modems, visit: www.modemshop.com/.

Web TV is one of the new services attempting to bring the Internet and World Wide Web to you via your TV set. It remains to be seen how ultimately successful this approach will be. (The big TV screen is nice, but I don't think that using a remote control and lap keyboard is as handy as using a mouse.) It's fun to follow these and other developments in the production and delivery of Internet online products and services. Who knows, maybe someday users will be able to call up Internet sites on their picnic coolers or attaché cases!

To read more about Web TV, visit: webtv.net/ (requires Javascript and Macromedia Flash).

To read more about selecting the right computer, I recommend *PCs For Kids & Parents* by the Dummies Press Family and published by IDG Books World-wide, Inc. It's another book in the Dummies Guide to Family Computing series, and it covers such things as buying a personal computer, picking good software and hardware components, and using the Web safely and enjoyably.

Oh, one more thing: you will also need a *browser* (special software to get on the Web) and an *Internet service provider* (a company to connect you to the Web), both of which I describe in more detail later on in this section.

Newsgroups, Mailing Lists, and Chat Groups

Throughout this book, you see references to interacting with other Internet online users. Newsgroups, mailing lists, and chat groups are three primary ways to meet other people on the Internet. Although these activities are fun and many times informative, it's important to remember that parents need to keep a watchful eye on kids, particularly with chats. Appendix C details ways to keep kids safe.

A *newsgroup* is a place where you can post notices, messages, or questions for others to see and reply to with a posting of their own. You type a message and send it along. Then you see it appear. Then you can track responses. The 18,000 or so existing newsgroups are part of a large network called Usenet, which hosts the newsgroups and is part of the Internet. (If you want to know more about Usenet, check out www.columbia.edu/~rh120/ch106.x02.)

Newsgroups are sorted by categories, which is how they get the first part of their addresses. For example, alt stands for alternative, comp stands for computer, K-12 stands for kindergarten through 12th grade, (k12.chat.senior is for high school seniors) and news stands for news. See if you can guess what these would pertain to: rec, sci, soc, talk, misc. If you guessed *recreation, science, social issues, talk on hot topics,* and *miscellaneous,* you're getting good at this.

From these beginning codes, the topics get more specific and the names (also called addresses) get longer. See if you can guess what these newsgroups discuss: misc.kids, rec.arts.movies, k12.chat.junior. If you guessed kids of all ages discussing everything, movies, and topics of interest to juniors in high school, you are now an expert!

Also called conferences or discussion groups, newsgroups are usually monitored to make sure the postings are current and that people are being reasonably courteous to one another. Heads up, parents — the exception here is alt groups where anything goes, so while some alt groups are fine (for example, alt.comics.peanuts), others deal with adult or very controversial subjects and aren't monitored for online language.

You need to know specific codes and rules of etiquette and procedure to follow if you want to join a newsgroup, and these are generally spelled out at the location (usually in a section called *FAQ* or frequently asked questions). To explore the world of newsgroups, check out the following URLs:

- **Liszt of Newsgroups:** www.liszt.com/news
- **Reference.com:** www.reference.com
- **Deja News, Browse Groups:** www.dejanews.com/home_bg.shtml

To use newsgroups, you need software called a *newsreader.* America Online users can just click the Internet button and choose Newsgroups. CompuServe has its own entry system that you utilize by typing **GO USENET** and choosing the newsreader. Netscape Navigator also has its own newsreader. Click the Window menu and click on Netscape News. Microsoft Internet Explorer uses a free add-on called Mail and News, which runs as a separate application.

Another form of online communication is *chat.* When you chat online, you type a message that is immediately read by one person, or a hundred people, who can immediately reply by typing back to you. Everyone sees the sentences at the same time, usually within seconds of the words being typed. I'm not sure why it's called chatting because no talking is involved, but it's just as rapid as talking if you're a fast typist! You just talk with your fingers instead of your mouth.

You can agree to meet someone at a certain time through a certain chat service, or you can just log on to a chat and join in with others. I strongly suggest that parents thoroughly screen chat sites first and give kids guidance about using chats correctly and safely. Chat sites with monitored areas or *rooms* specifically for kids are obviously your safest bets. Read all the instructions about etiquette, appropriate language, and usage. You do need to register to use chats. And you do need to stay safe; see Appendix C for more about that topic.

To get started in a good chat space for kids, visit these sites:

- **Freezone:** freezone.com
- **Jam!Z:** www.jamz.com
- **WebChat Broadcasting:** wbs.net

Another more complicated, multilayered chat system you can use will connect you to people all over the world. It's called Internet Relay Chat (IRC), and it was invented way back in ancient computer times (1988). It became very popular here in the United States during the Persian Gulf War in 1991 because live field updates could be sent immediately to computers anywhere. Now it is not uncommon for people at the scene of any great story or emergency to send out their own dispatches that you can read live. But it's also much more varied a medium, and can involve chats about all kinds of subjects, so parents definitely need to review the rooms in advance of their kids.

If you want to get involved in IRC chatting, you have to connect to a server that carries the network directly, a site that provides IRC chat software, or a site that does it for you. Try these sites:

- **V-Chat:** vchat1.microsoft.com
- **Palace:** www.thepalace.com
- **WorldsAway:** www.worldsaway.com
- **DALnet:** www.dal.net
- **EFnet:** irc.ucdavis.edu/efnet/
- **Undernet:** www.undernet.org
- **WWFIN:** www.wwfin.net/
- **mIRC (for PCs):** www.geocities.com/SiliconValley/Park/6000/
- **IRCle (for the Macintosh):** www.xs4all.nl/~ircle/

To find out more specifics on using family-oriented newsgroups and chats, I recommend *The World Wide Web For Kids & Parents* by Viraf D. Mohta. It's another book in the Dummies Guide to Family Computing series and Mr. Mohta devotes an entire chapter to understanding and using chats and another whole chapter to understanding and using newsgroups. And as most computing gurus do, Mr. Mohta has a Web site; check him out at www.geocities.com/Colosseum/2106/.

The third and final form of online communication I'm going to cover is the *mailing list,* or listserv, or listserver. The mailing list is a special setup using your e-mail system that allows you to automatically receive messages from a group you have subscribed to online. When anyone in the group puts a message into the listserv, it gets sent to you and everyone else in the group. Likewise, if you post a message, it gets sent out as an e-mail message to everyone in the group.

I subscribed to a mailing list started by a graduate of my high school. I get automatic e-mails from former classmates, as well as graduates of more recent years. It's a fun way to keep in touch with those I once went to school with and it's cheaper than traveling to the reunions (plus I can lie about my weight!).

To subscribe to a mailing list, you send a message to the computer that houses the listserv. You must include the name of the listserv and the address of the listserv. Usually, you leave the subject line blank and only put the word *subscribe* on your message. Unless you like tons of e-mail, you'll want to be selective about joining mailing lists. If you get overwhelmed, you can always send another message with the word *unsubscribe* in the message area.

To find out more about mailing lists and how to subscribe, try these sites:

- **Liszts:** www.liszt.com
- **Reference.com:** www.reference.com
- **Publicly Accessible Mailing Lists:** emailhost.ait.ac.th/Search/pubmail-subj.html

Online Services

An *Internet service provider* or *access provider* is a company that gets you online. A *value-added service provider* does that and much more. Probably the best-known value-added online service provider is America Online, which recently acquired the other really well-known value-added service provider, CompuServe. These and other such companies get you online and guide your experience there by providing you with organized categories (for example, Sports or Reference Desk) and access to a lot of additional services (e-mail or newsgroups, for example).

Most "newbies" to the Internet start out with one of these kinds of companies because it's much less intimidating than just signing up with an independent Internet service provider (ISP) that gets you online and then leaves you to sort out the Internet all by yourself. Also, finding a reliable ISP can be tricky if you don't know how to shop for one. It's like buying a car when you've never driven one before and you don't understand how the engine works.

Well-established value-added online services are designed to make you feel welcome and not confused. They try to pay attention to maintaining good customer relations and service. They also try to do a good job of keeping inappropriate sites away from kids. You can expect to pay a flat or sliding rate to use either an ISP or a value-added service. Typically, it will cost you about $20 a month. In some places, you can find a *freenet,* which is a community-based provider that offers very low-cost (or even free) connectivity.

After you have gotten comfortable using the Internet, you may elect to switch to an ISP and take on the Internet independently. Sometimes you can see a cost advantage to this. Other times, you just want more freedom to really explore on your own and not rely on a value-added service to select and organize sites for you. In this case, surfers tend to use a browser and go it alone. When value-added services get too busy for all users to get online when they want to, users are inspired to break from the pack, too.

To find out a lot more about online service providers and value-added online service providers, visit these sites:

- **How to Select an Internet Service Provider:** web.cnam.fr/Network/ Internet-access/how_to_select.html
- **The List: The Definitive ISP Buyer's Guide:** thelist.internet.com
- **ISP Finder:** ispfinder.com
- **Free-Nets & Community Networks:** www.lafn.org/webconnect/ freenets.htm
- **America Online (AOL):** www.aol.com
- **CompuServe:** world.compuserve.com
- **Prodigy:** www.prodigy.com

I also recommend *America Online For Dummies*, 3rd Edition, by John Kaufield; and *CompuServe For Dummies*, 3rd Edition, by Wallace Wang. These two books take an in-depth look at understanding and using these two premier value-added service providers.

Resources for More Information

In addition to the books and Web sites I've mentioned so far in this appendix, a number of other good resources focus on all aspects of Internet content, developments, and use.

I'm partial to books published by IDG Books, not just because I'm writing one, but because it was one of that company's books that first opened my eyes to computers. The book was *Macs For Teachers* by Michelle Robinette, and when I purchased it back in 1995, it changed my professional life. I couldn't believe there was a book written so informatively, but in such a friendly way that even I, a total computer newbie at the time, could understand and instantly use it. I've been a loyal fan of IDG Books and magazines ever since.

Getting to write a *...For Dummies* book for IDG Books is a big thrill for me because I feel that I'm in very talented company. Check out these Internet titles that may enhance your particular Internet experience: *Internet Directory For Dummies* by Brad Hill; *Internet Directory For Teachers* by Grace and Julia Jasmine; *The Internet For Dummies Quick Reference,* 3rd Edition, by John Levine, Margaret Levine Young, and Arnold Reinhold; *The Internet For Dummies,* 4th Edition, by John Levine, Carol Baroudi, and Margaret Levine Young; and *The Internet For Macs For Dummies,* 2nd Edition, by Charles Seiter.

Additionally, IDG publishes a couple hundred magazines throughout the world to give people the latest news on technology and computer-based fun. I've enjoyed the ones listed here; check out the links to their Web sites where you can find even more good stuff:

- **Computerworld:** www.computerworld.com
- **InfoWorld:** www.infoworld.com
- **Macworld:** www.macworld.com
- **Network World:** www.networkworld.com
- **PC World:** www.pcworld.com

Search Engines

Search engines used to be services that helped you find sites. Now, in an effort to distinguish themselves, you may find that some refer to themselves as guides. Such search engines have *value-added content;* they may contain written "tours" that guide you through a subject, say Mars Exploration, and then link you to related sites. Or they may bundle information for you in what the industry calls channels. So if you look up Mars Exploration, you get science-based sites about Mars Exploration, but you also get links to any news stories about Mars.

Different companies take different approaches to finding sites and presenting them to you, so it's best to just take a tour of your own and decide which resource seems to give you the best sites in a format you find comfortable.

I always found it entertaining when I worked for search engines to see how they raced to outdo one another with quantity over quality. Some industry insiders seem to think that when you search for a topic, you want at least 10,000 sites about it. I personally favor search engines that give me quality rankings based on some kind of human evolution, but then I'm just old-fashioned!

Such preferences are very individual, so it's best to just shop around and bookmark a few search engines that you like. If you have a favorite, you can make it your opening site when you load up your browser. With Netscape, for example, click the Options button at the top of the browser and go into General Preferences. You can type any address there and that will become your opening page. Or if you want a whole selection of search engines, click the Net Search button.

Be sure to read any search engine's search tips before using it. Your searching is more efficient when you take time to read these tips. Each search engine uses variations of computer programs that require you to enter words a certain way for best results. Their computers need to be able to make sense of what you type to give you the best results.

Companies that call themselves search engines include the following:

- **AltaVista:** altavista.digital.com
- **AOL NetFind:** www.aol.com/netfind
- **Electric Library:** www.elibrary.com
- **HOTBOT:** www.hotbot.com
- **WebCrawler:** webcrawler.com

Companies that call themselves guides include the following:

- **Infoseek (features good section for kids):** www.infoseek.com
- **LookSmart (emphasizes family orientation):** www.looksmart.com
- **Lycos:** www.lycos.com
- **Excite:** www.excite.com
- **Magellan (with "green light" safe site searching):** www.mckinley.com/
- **SEARCH.COM:** www.search.com
- **DISCOVER WiseWire.com:** www.wisewire.com
- **Yahoo! (features good section for kids):** www.yahoo.com

Companies offering directory assistance include the following:

- **Bigfoot:** www.bigfoot.com
- **Four11:** www.four11.com
- **GTE SuperPages:** superpages.gte.net
- **ON'VILLAGE Yellow Pages:** www.onvillage.com
- **Original Yellow Pages:** 206.141.250.39
- **WhoWhere?:** www.whowhere.com

Companies offering specialized searches of particular subjects include the following:

- **100hot Web Sites:** www.100hot.com
- **Auction Classifieds by eBay:** cayman.ebay2.com
- **AutoWeb Interactive: Buy/Sell Cars:** www.autoweb.com
- **RENT.NET: Apartment Search:** www.rent.net
- **Surplus Direct:** www.surplusdirect.com
- **Thomas Register of American Mfrs.:** www.thomasregister.com

The following sites assist you in evaluating the best search engines:

- **Understanding and Comparing Search Engines:** www.hamline.edu/library/bush/handouts/comparisons.html
- **Evaluation of Selected Internet Search Tools:** www.library.nwu.edu/resources/internet/search/evaluate.html
- **Washington Post's Tour of Search Engines:** www.washingtonpost.com/wp-srv/interact/longterm/safari/compass/compass.htm

Software

To use the Internet you also need a *browser*. Browsers are software that let you see content by assembling images, text, and audio onto Web sites that come up on your computer screen. Microsoft makes Internet Explorer and Netscape makes Netscape Navigator and Communicator, probably the three best-known browsers. You obtain browsers by buying them at the store, downloading them from the companies' Web sites, or asking for one from your independent Internet service (or access) provider.

Additionally, Microsoft, which makes Windows (the operating system that runs most personal computers) has started incorporating its own online browsing tool, Internet Explorer, into editions of Windows. Netscape doesn't have an operating system, but it's working on wiring its Navigator browser to telephones and TVs.

You can also get software to use *e-mail* (for electronic-mail), which is one of my favorite uses of modem-based technology. Just like that, you type a message, click send, and the message is off to someone anywhere in the world with an e-mail address of his or her own. My hubby is a psychologist who travels and teaches worldwide. Within minutes, he can correspond with colleagues in Japan, England, France, and Australia, and they can respond right back! If you have mail waiting for you, you can be alerted by a sound or visual signal. It's amazing.

Besides a modem, you need an e-mail address and e-mail software. Sometimes e-mail software comes with your browser. Or you can use Eudora Light, which is included on the CD-ROM in this book. (For more about Eudora Light and the CD, see Appendix B.)

Throughout the book, I've referenced *plug-ins* that you may need to run certain aspects of various Internet sites. A plug-in is a tool you plug in to your browser to let it do fancier stuff, such as make graphics move or play movies or listen to sounds. If you try to use parts of a site without the right plug-in, you will generally be alerted that you don't have it. Sometimes, you get the option then and there to download it; other times, you are referred to the Internet site that hosts and created the plug-in.

You get all these plug-in options because the major browsers encourage designers to develop new and unique multimedia tools. You may be tempted to download every free plug-in that comes along, but remember, each of these online special effects tools can slow down your computer system because they can run several megabytes in size. So ask yourself first what you mainly use your system to accomplish. If you want to play games, you probably need plug-ins. If you like to search and use e-mail, you probably need a minimum number, and then the most popular ones are best because they are used in more sites. And it's best for security reasons to download only those plug-ins you truly need.

I have encountered the following plug-ins, browser-dependent functions, and helpful programs most often in researching sites for this book:

- **Java:** This programming language is used to create "applets" that automatically download at a site and add to your entertainment by livening up graphic images and making things move. Many of the most current versions of browsers support Java Web applets.

- **GIF animation:** Browsers that support GIF animation can run simple animations and high-quality stills from Web sites.

- **RealAudio:** This program starts playing sounds within seconds of downloading a site or site section that features RealAudio-based music or talking. You can download RealAudio at www.real.com.

- **Shockwave:** This application helps Web-page designers really liven up sites with special moving effects and animated graphics. You can download the Shockwave plug-in that lets your browser run Shockwave animations by going to www.macromedia.com.

- **Helper-apps:** This group of applications gives your browser assistance so it can display GIF animation, JPEGs (another kind of Internet image), many sounds, and movies. When the browser you are using can't open an image or gets stuck trying to interpret part of a site, the browser consults a list of helper-apps to find one of assistance. Plug-ins work within your browser, and helper-apps are externally stored applications.

Surfer Talk

I could personally define all 20,000 or so computer and Internet specific terms known to exist (yeah, *sure* I could), but hey, this is an Internet Directory, right? So instead, I'll give you a list of great sites that cover everything from jargon and technical terminology to acronyms and abbreviations. Before you know it, you'll be a full-fledged nerd. (Don't worry, there won't be a test!)

- **Comparative CyberLexicon:** www.telefonica.es/fat/elex.html (English computer terminology with Spanish equivalents)

- **Computer Currents Online Dictionary:** www.currents.net/resources/dictionary/dictionary.phtml
- **Computer Dictionary:** wagner.princeton.edu/foldoc/about.html
- **Internet Literacy Consultants Glossary of Internet Terms:** www.matisse.net/files/glossary.html
- **Web Words:** www.webwords.net
- **whatis.com:** whatis.com

Appendix B

About the CD

• •

*T*he software on this CD is a collection of useful programs for maintaining your computer, browsing the Internet, working with graphics, and more. Highlights of the CD include:

- ✔ AT&T WorldNet Service, a popular Internet service provider
- ✔ Paint Shop Pro, a great shareware graphics program for Windows
- ✔ Net Nanny and SurfWatch, two parental-control programs
- ✔ Claris Home Page, a trial version of a good Web page builder

System Requirements

Many of these programs require specific features or abilities from your PC or Mac OS computer, so these are the minimum standards that your computer needs for a chance of running the software as it's intended. You probably won't need everything listed here for any one program.

For detailed system requirements for each program, be sure to read the program's "Read Me" documents. You find these documents in the program's folder on the CD or included with the installed program on your computer's hard drive.

At the very least, your computer should have:

- ✔ A PC with a 486 or faster processor, or a Mac OS computer with a 68030 or faster processor.
- ✔ Microsoft Windows 95 or NT 4.0, or Mac OS 7.5 or later. (Some programs on this CD can be used with Windows 3.1 or 3.11, but few new PC programs support those versions of Windows.)
- ✔ At least 8MB of total RAM installed on your computer. For best performance, we recommend that Windows-equipped PCs and Mac OS computers with PowerPC processors have 16MB of RAM or more installed.

> ✔ A CD-ROM drive — double-speed (2x) or faster.
>
> ✔ A sound card for PCs. (Mac OS computers have built-in sound support.)
>
> ✔ A monitor capable of displaying at least 256 colors or grayscale.
>
> ✔ A modem with a speed of at least 14,400 bps or faster. (Some programs may need a faster modem for such things as playing audio and video directly from the Internet.)

If you need more information on the basics for your computer, check out *PCs For Dummies,* 4th Edition, by Dan Gookin; *Macs For Dummies,* 4th Edition, by David Pogue, *Windows 95 For Dummies* by Andy Rathbone; or *Mac OS 8 For Dummies*, by Bob LeVitus (all published by IDG Books Worldwide, Inc.).

Using the CD in Microsoft Windows

To install the items from the CD to your hard drive, follow these steps.

1. **Insert the CD into your computer's CD-ROM drive.**

2. **Windows 3.*x* (that is, 3.1 or 3.11) users: From Program Manager, choose File⇨Run; Windows 95 users: Click the Start button and click Run.**

3. **In the dialog box that appears, type** D:\SETUP.EXE.

   Most of you probably have your CD-ROM drive listed as drive D under My Computer in Windows 95 or the File Manager in Windows 3.1. Type in the proper drive letter if your CD-ROM drive uses a different letter.

4. **Click OK.**

   A license agreement window appears.

5. **Read through the license agreement and, if you accept the terms of the agreement, click the Accept button.**

   After you click Accept, you'll never be bothered by the License Agreement window again.

   From here, the CD interface appears. The CD interface lets you install the programs on the CD without typing in cryptic commands or using yet another finger-twisting hot key in Windows. The first window in the interface is the Welcome screen.

6. **Click anywhere on the Welcome screen.**

   Now you're getting into the action. The next screen lists categories for the software on the CD.

7. **To view the items within a category, click the category's name.**

   A list of programs in the category appears.

8. **For more information about a program, click on the program's name.**

   Be sure to read the information that's displayed. Sometimes a program may require you to do a few tricks on your computer first, and this screen tells you where to go for that information, if necessary.

9. **To install the program, click the appropriate Install button.**

   If you don't want to install the program, click the Go Back button to return to the previous category screen.

   After you click an install button, the CD interface moves to the background while the CD begins installation of the program you chose.

   When installation is done, the interface usually reappears in front of other opened windows. Sometimes the installation confuses Windows and leaves the interface in the background. To bring the interface forward, just click once anywhere in the interface's window.

10. **To install other items, repeat Steps 7, 8, and 9.**

11. **When you're done installing programs, click the Quit button to close the interface.**

    You can eject the CD now. Carefully place it back in the plastic jacket of the book for safekeeping.

To run some of the programs, you may need to keep the CD inside your CD-ROM drive. This requirement is a Good Thing; otherwise, the installed program would have required you to install a very large chunk of the program to your hard drive space, which would have kept you from installing other software.

Using the CD with a Mac OS Computer

To install the items from the CD to your hard drive, follow these steps.

1. **Insert the CD into your computer's CD-ROM drive.**

   In a moment, an icon representing the CD you just inserted appears on your Mac desktop. Chances are good that the icon looks like a CD-ROM.

2. **Double-click the CD icon.**

   You see icons representing the CD's contents.

3. Double-click the Read Me First icon.

This text file contains information about the CD's programs and any last-minute instructions that we don't cover in this appendix, but that you need to know about installing the programs on the CD.

4. Double-click the CD icon to show the CD's contents.

Some programs have an install icon that you need to click to get installation going. Other programs can be installed by simply dragging and dropping a copy of the program from the CD to your hard drive. Icons with the words Setup, Installer, or .sea probably need to be double-clicked from the CD rather than copied.

After you install the programs that you want, you can eject the CD. Carefully place it back in the plastic jacket of the book for safekeeping.

Using the Directory Links

For your convenience, we put all the URLs that are listed in this book on a couple of Directory Links pages that you can open in your Web browser. Any site in this book is just a mouse-click away. To use the Links pages, follow these steps:

1. Launch your Web browser.

2. If you have Microsoft Internet Explorer, choose File⇨Open; if you use Netscape Navigator, choose File⇨Open File.

If you use a browser other than the one listed above, consult your browser's documentation on how to open a file and continue with the next step.

For these two browsers, the Open dialog box appears.

3. Type D:\HOME.HTM in the text box of the dialog box.

If your CD-ROM drive is not D:\, please be sure to use the correct letter for your drive.

The home page for Directory Links now opens. Read the instructions for using the links pages and then click the button to get started.

That's it! To move around the links pages, you can select a Part corresponding to a part in the book by using the buttons at the side of the page. The link Part then appears in the main window; you can move through the selected Part by using internal "jump" links that take you from section to section. (Okay, so this sounds much harder than it actually is; just play with the CD and you see what I mean.)

Clicking a link opens a second browser window. The second window enables you to browse the Web site of your choice without ever losing track of the Links pages on the CD. You can always bring the Directory Links pages to the forefront of your desktop and select another Link. Selecting another link changes the Web site in the second browser window; that way you never have more than two browser windows open at one time.

What You Find

The following sections list the software on this CD. Each entry gives you the following information, in this order: product name, product type and operating system (Mac or Windows); World Wide Web address for the software company or distributor; and the company or owner's name.

If you use Windows, the CD interface provides descriptions and installation instructions for each program, and helps you install the software easily. (If you have no idea what I'm talking about when I say "CD interface," flip back a page or two to find the section, "Using the CD in Microsoft Windows.")

If you use a Mac OS computer, you can find product descriptions and installation information in the Read Me First file, and you can enjoy the simplicity of the Mac interface to quickly install the programs.

Internet tools

- **AT&T WorldNet Service:** Internet service provider (Mac & Win); www.att.com; AT&T

- **Eudora Light:** E-mail program (Mac & Win); www.eudora.com; Qualcomm Inc.

- **Anarchie:** FTP (Mac); redback.cs.uwa.edu.au/PeterLewis/WWW/anarchie/index.html; Stairways Shareware

- **WS_FTP LE:** FTP (Win); www.ipswitch.comZ; Ipswitch

- **Free Agent:** Newsreader (Win); www.forteinc.com; Forte Inc.

- **Starfish Internet Utilities:** Internet utilities (Win); www.starfish.com; Starfish Software

- **Claris Home Page 2.0 Trial:** Web page builder (Mac & Win); www.claris.com; Claris

- **WebWhacker:** Web page downloader (Mac & Win); www.ffg.com; ForeFront Group

- **Web Weaver Lite:** HTML editor (Mac); www.miracleinc.com; Miracle Software Inc.

- **Allaire HomeSite:** HTML editor (Win); www.allaire.com; Allaire Corp.

- **Internet Coach:** Internet tutorial (Win); www.apte.com; APTE

- **SurfWatch:** Parental control application (Win/Mac); www.surfwatch.com; Spyglass, Inc.

- **Net Nanny 3.1:** Parental control application (Win); www.netnanny.com/center.html; Net Nanny Software International

Multimedia tools

- **Adobe Acrobat Reader 3.0:** Portable Document Format (PDF) viewer (Mac & Win); www.adobe.com; Adobe

- **GraphicConverter:** graphics manipulation program (Mac); www.goldinc.com/Lemke/; Lemke Software

- **VDOLive Player:** audio player; www.vdonet.com; VDOnet Corp.

- **VivoActive Player:** audio player (Mac & Win); 206.65.86.113/dload.htm; Vivo Software, Inc.

- **Paint Shop Pro 3.11:** graphics manipulation program (Win); www.jasc.com; JASC Inc.

- **Paint Shop Pro 4.12:** graphics manipulation program (Win); www.jasc.com; JASC Inc.

Utilities

- **ThunderBYTE:** virus scanner (Win); www.thunderbyte.com; ThunderBYTE Inc.

- **WinZip:** compression utility (Win); www.winzip.com; Nico Mak

- **StuffIt Expander:** compression utility (Mac); www.aladdinsys.com; Aladdin Systems

- **DropStuff with Expander Enhancer:** compression utility (Mac); www.aladdinsys.com; Aladdin Systems

- **Complete Program Deleter:** program uninstaller (Win); members.aol.com/leithauser/index.html; David Leithauser

✔ **CleanSweep 3.0:** program uninstaller (Win); www.quarterdeck.com; Quarterdeck

✔ **ClipMate:** Windows Clipboard assistant (Win); www.thornsoft.com; THORNSOFT Development

Fun stuff

✔ **Starfish Sidekick 97:** personal organizer (Win); www.starfish.com; StarFish Software

✔ **HotShot:** game (Win); www.7thlevel.com; 7th Level, Inc.

✔ **MVP Backgammon:** game (Win); www.mvpsoft.com; MVP Software, Inc.

✔ **Snood:** game (Mac); www-personal.umich.edu/~dob/snood.html; David Dobson

✔ **Escape Velocity:** game (Mac); www.ambrosiasw.com; Ambrosia Software

✔ **Eclipse:** screensaver (Mac); www.ambrosiasw.com; Ambrosia Software

If You Have Problems (Of the CD Kind)

I tried my best to compile programs that work on most computers with the minimum system requirements. Alas, your computer may differ, and some programs may not work properly for some reason.

The two most likely problems are that your computer doesn't have enough memory (RAM) for the programs you want to use, or that other programs are running which are affecting the installation or running of a program. If you get error messages like Not enough memory or Setup cannot continue, try one or more of these methods and then try using the software again:

✔ Turn off any antivirus software that you have on your computer. Installers sometimes mimic virus activity and may make your computer incorrectly believe that it is being infected by a virus.

✔ Close all running programs, including the CD interface. The more programs you're running, the less memory is available to other programs. Installers also typically update files and programs; so, if you keep other programs running, installation may not work properly. You can install any program on the CD through the CD directory.

✔ Have your local computer store add more RAM to your computer. This step is, admittedly, a drastic and somewhat expensive one. However, if you have a Windows 95 PC or a Mac OS computer with a PowerPC chip, adding more memory can really help the speed of your computer and allow more programs to run at the same time.

If you still have trouble with installing the items from the CD, please call the IDG Books Worldwide Customer Service phone number: 800-762-2974 (outside the U.S.: 317-596-5430).

Appendix C

A Family-Friendly Guide to Surfing Safely

● ●

*T*he Internet opens new worlds for kids and gives them the chance to interact with people that they would otherwise never get to meet. For the most part, this is a good thing. But, as parents know, some people are not worth meeting, either online or off. Unlike the print media and television, which aren't interactive, the Internet is very much about interaction among people — through e-mail, chats, newsgroups, discussion forums, and so forth.

It's a dichotomy, but both the wonderful and worrisome thing about the Internet is that it's probably the most democratic form of communication on the planet. Anyone can put up a Web site and say or show anything. And in most cases, any of these sites are easily accessible with a few keywords and a search engine.

For example, type the word *pets* into a search box, and you're just as likely to link to a pornographic magazine's nude Pets of the Month as you are to link to a site about hamsters. That's why one of the first rules when using any search engine is to be as specific as possible. Search engines offer tips on how to conduct searches effectively, and these tips are well worth reading. If you search for *pet hamster* rather than just *pets,* you are better assured of getting only the type of sites you want.

Microsoft Internet Explorer, America Online, and CompuServe are making efforts to provide some filtering protections, and search engines such as Yahoo! and Infoseek provide special areas for kids. LookSmart is a search engine that emphasizes family-appropriate sites and original content.

The Seven Be's of Safety

Here are some proven safety tips for families to keep in mind when wandering around the Internet. I call them the Seven Be's:

- **Be** selective about offering any personal information online. You really have no idea where the information may go or who may access it. A person who swears he is a nice 13-year-old boy looking for a pen pal may in fact be a child abuser. The most reputable sites for kids monitor their chats and other interactive amusements to ensure kids' safety and appropriate language. But parents would be wise to monitor conversations as well.

- **Be** nosy. If you are a parent, grandparent, or guardian, ask the kids you love what they're doing on the Internet. Check with them frequently just to share and enjoy what they're discovering and to make sure they haven't accidentally linked from a safe site to one that's not what you consider appropriate. Many, many sites offer links (direct connections) to other sites. Although things may start out fine, 8 or 10 links down the Information Superhighway, the tenor and subject matter may have changed considerably.

- **Be** alert to the potential for viruses, which are software codes purposely implanted just to mess up your life, not to mention your computer. Who knows what motivates the losers who create viruses, but they are out there, putting out their destructive programs onto the Internet. If you decide to download software or plug-ins from the Internet, go directly to the creator or manufacturer's site. Get and use virus-detection software, and always back up valuable data regularly.

- **Be** aware of "cookies." Named for mystical tokens in role-playing games, these crumbs of data get inside your computer's hard drive and help Web designers and marketing folks figure out where you've been on the Net and what you apparently like to visit. The marketing motive behind this is simple: If advertisers, site designers, search engines, and others can figure you out, they can have appropriate advertising waiting for you the next time you log in. Trouble is, they may not tell you they are implanting those cookies and you may think it's an invasion of privacy. Or you may not care because you like seeing stuff automatically come up on your screen that interests you. Either way, you can assess your feelings and find out how to disable cookies by visiting this site: uts.cc.utexas.edu/~ccfr362/index.htm.

- **Be** proactive. If anyone in your family gets abusive online correspondence, print it out and call the police. Gather as much information as you can in terms of what time the offensive message was received, through what channel (e-mail or site chat, for example). *Do not* respond — even anger constitutes attention, which is not what you want to provide. Complain to the webmaster of the site if you want to express an opinion. If the message came via e-mail, ask your Internet service provider to help you or the police trace its origin. Kids, if you ever read something from someone that makes you feel scared or uncomfortable, leave the computer immediately and go get an adult you trust. Show the adult what's on the screen. *Never respond.* Ignoring a scary or abusive remark is okay.

✔ **Be** cautious. You don't have to be scared of the Internet; but just like in real life, you need to be cautious around strangers. Never arrange a meeting with someone you've met online in a secluded place or without telling people you know and trust when and where you're going. Don't let the person pick you up at your house. Meet the person in a safe public setting — a restaurant, for example. Consider taking someone you know and trust with you. You never can be sure the person is who they say they are, no matter how friendly he or she seems online. My personal feeling is that it's wisest to leave online relationships online, especially when it comes to kids.

✔ **Be** protective. Do whatever it takes to ensure children's safety on the Internet. If you really want to go the extra mile, consider installing an Internet filter. In the next section, I tell you how filters do (and don't) work and give you some leads on finding software.

All about Internet Filters

The fact that you've chosen to purchase this book demonstrates that you care very much about children having safe, fun, productive experiences on the Internet. For some parents, Internet filters are an additional way to shield kids from viewing or reading material that is too graphic, upsetting, or explicit for young eyes. Filters are a tool, but they aren't effective without parental oversight. They can't replace the good judgment of a caring grownup.

Filters are technology-based, not values-based. They censor based on keywords, not beliefs. For example, a filter may omit sites that reference the word *breast,* which could omit porn sites, but that would also omit good chicken breast recipes and breast cancer resources for women. In other cases, words that seem completely harmless, such as *pets,* may allow a pornographic magazine's Pets of the Month to load up, at least momentarily. So it pays to try out the software at computer centers or free online trial sites (more on that shortly). Enter words that you want to filter and check the results. Read the product boxes and instruction sheets for even more clarification of what each product offers. In the interest of giving you varying points of view, if you'd like to read what critics of filtering software have to say, check out this site: cgi.pathfinder.com/@@qwcleAUAqxqp1jmN/netly/ spoofcentral/censored.

Besides the fact that I come from a journalism background and have serious concerns about any form of official forced censorship, I have doubts that any single government can (or should) regulate the Internet. For one thing, the Internet represents an international audience and knows no national boundaries. That's part of the greatness of the Internet. Maybe I'm naive, but I think the Internet rightly belongs to the whole world and should be protected as a bastion of free thought and international communication.

But I also have grandkids and a young son who deserve equal protection. So, for all its inherent flaws, safety filter technology is a good choice and, as time passes, I'm sure it will become much more intuitive or simpler for parents to customize. As a mom and grandma, I'd rather err on the side of caution in my own home when it comes to the little ones I love.

Filtering software is not terribly expensive; the general range is from $20 to $40. Most take only minutes to install. You select sites or keywords you want blocked (such as profanity, sex, violence). What gets screened from there can vary widely. Depending on the program you choose, you can prohibit chats, have password protection so no one else can change what you've vetoed, and even limit the time your kids spend on the Net.

Here are some well-known filtering programs and how to find them on the Internet so you can get to know what each product has to offer, where to get it, how much it costs, and how to set it up.

Net Nanny

A 30-day free trial version of Net Nanny is on the CD-ROM that accompanies this book; you can also find information at www.netnanny.com. According to Net Nanny's developers, the software enables you to monitor, screen, and block access to anything residing on, or running in, out, or through your PC, online or off. Net Nanny offers two-way screening in real-time and you decide what to screen with the help of a site list. You can also control access to World Wide Web addresses, newsgroups, IRC channels, FTP sites, e-mail, non-Internet bulletin board services (BBSs), words, phrases, and personal information (address, credit card numbers, and so on).

Net Nanny is a complete Internet and PC management tool that works with all the major online providers (CompuServe, for example) and local applications running on the PC. Net Nanny has no monthly site update subscription fee. Net Nanny screens out sites, words, phrases, and content that you have determined are not appropriate. The Net Nanny Internet site lets you offer feedback about the filtering service and any potentially objectionable sites you've found, as well as get technical support and find out about other related products.

SurfWatch

One of the most popular, best-known brands, SurfWatch has a Web site at www.surfwatch.com. You get a free 15-day trial version of SurfWatch on the CD-ROM that accompanies this book. And you can visit the Internet site to see what happens when you enter a site that you'd consider objectionable into the query system. See if it comes up with a message that says "Blocked by SurfWatch." This company offers its software for both Windows and Macintosh, which can easily be installed and used with any browser. It blocks tens of thousands of explicit sites and is continuously updated using a system of pattern-matching technologies and the tracking of known adult-oriented sites. There are automatic monthly updates of recently blocked sites.

Sites are blocked if they offer a disclaimer indicating restricted access, if they feature a screen or warning that identifies the site as adult-oriented, or if they contain information unsuitable for those underage. They are also blocked if site publishers request it or if the main site has a number of unsuitable links. The SurfWatch site defines what the company considers sexually explicit or what constitutes violent or hateful speech, as well as what it does not consider sexually explicit or constituting violent or hateful speech (for example, it does not generally block sites on the basis of gender preference, sexually transmitted disease information, or sites illustrating and explaining cancers of the breast). Likewise, although it does block sites pertaining to illicit drug use and gambling, it does not block sites discussing medicinal drug use, industrial hemp use, or public debate on the issue of legalizing certain drugs.

Sites are evaluated by SurfWatch staff members and may also be reviewed by an Advisory Committee of parents, teachers, and community members. If you know of a site that should not be blocked but inadvertently was, or if you find a site that should be blocked and inadvertently wasn't, you can submit sites for review through the SurfWatch Internet site. You can also get technical support for any problems or software questions. Related products, such as SurfWatch Manager, allow you to customize filtering even more, according to your individual standards.

CYBERsitter

CYBERsitter is probably the strictest program available. Considered exceptionally cautious by its fans, and ridiculously ultra-conservative by its critics, CYBERsitter uses a content recognition system to identify and block objectionable material anywhere on the Internet. More than 44,000 sites are automatically omitted, including those that deal with homosexuality, as well as certain feminist, political, and social issues.

By visiting the company site (www.solidoak.com), you can preview CYBERsitter and related products, and download a free demonstration copy.

Another interesting product is CYBERtimer. The software for Windows 95 lets you monitor time spent online and disconnect automatically when limits are exceeded. You can specify the number of hours allowed online by day, week, or month, and define what times of day online access is permitted. CYBERtimer is designed for use with Windows 95 Dial-up networking and America Online software.

Get technical support through the site, offer your opinions and suggestions, submit sites for review, and order products (which are best used with Microsoft Internet Explorer).

Cyber Patrol

Cyber Patrol (www.cyberpatrol.com) is blocking software for Windows, Macintosh, and LAN systems. Widely used by Internet industry professionals including service providers, G-rated search services, and browsers, (as well as many businesses related to employee Internet use), Cyber Patrol offers CyberNOTs (Internet sites containing material parents may find questionable), CyberYESes (allowed sites containing completely appropriate material for children), and HotNOTs (sites included on the daily updated blocked sites list).

With the multiuser capability of CyberPatrol, up to nine family members in a household can individually program his or her own blocking selections and passwords. A related product, ChatGard, prevents children from divulging any personal information online (such as name, phone number, e-mail address) and works with all browsers. ChatGard has a "Getting Started" tutorial for first time users. You can also use the software to restrict Internet access to certain times of day and set total time limits.

Cyber Patrol also can be used to limit access to major online services and to local applications such as games and personal financial managers. With a few mouse clicks, grownups can tailor Internet use to fit any kid's maturity level and age. One nice aspect of this software is that it can limit only certain pages of an overall site, rather than the whole site. This comes in handy when a site has a kids' section, but contains other pages of more graphic or mature material. This software also allows parents (or employers) to track use time, which may come in handy if the telephone bill or online provider bills seem out of line.

Cyber Patrol is compatible with Internet applications and Web browsers, including Netscape, Internet Explorer, and Mosaic 2.0. Cyber Patrol loads during start-up and runs in the background. It is accessed via password, offers two levels of parental password control, and prevents children from disabling Cyber Patrol or simply renaming blocked applications — not that any kids I know would ever *think* of doing such a thing.

Cyber Patrol staffers, as well as parents and teachers, help determine whether sites should be blocked. By visiting Cyber Patrol's online site, you can find details about the judging criteria used, as well as additional blocking options for parents and how the service is continually updated.

For more information about pricing, check the Cyber Patrol Web site that appears at the beginning of this subsection. Educational discounts are available and are explained at the site's Cyber Patrol Educators Page. The Cyber Patrol Online Demo Tour lets you get to know Cyber Patrol before you download for a free tryout.

Net Shepherd

Net Shepherd, at www.shepherd.net, is an Internet content selection software tool that enables you to filter Web sites for maturity and quality. You can then rate what you find on the Net and contribute your ratings to Net Shepherd's World Opinion Rating Service. (Please note, however, that Net Shepherd 2.0 may not work with Microsoft Internet Explorer 4.0 or with Netscape 4.0 Communicator, both of which were still being beta tested at the time of this writing.) The World Opinion Rating Service gathers ratings from Net Shepherd users everywhere. It tabulates rating opinions and publishes the rating value chosen by the majority. It doesn't track or connect rating opinions with any information that can identify the person who submitted the rating.

Net Shepherd 2.0 also features IRC chat and newsgroup filtering, and a new, improved administration wizard that you can try out at the site. At the company's Web site, you can perform a sample search and rate a site yourself.

Other Internet Safety Resources

You can find a number of additional resources available on or through the Internet to assist you with online safety concerns. Check out these sites.

SafeSurf

SafeSurf, at www.safesurf.com, is an Internet rating system. This service has developed and implemented an Internet Rating Standard to assist parents, providers, publishers, and site developers in evaluating and denoting site content. By marking sites with the SafeSurf Wave, site producers let parents know that all the content is safe for kids. The section called Kid's Wave lists what SafeSurf considers the Internet's top spots for educating and entertaining children. The site has articles, question and answers (FAQs), and other resources for parents to read and use, as well as some to share with kids about Internet safety. Site producers can rate their sites and submit them, and parents can provide ideas and feedback. You need the new version of Microsoft Internet Explorer to utilize SafeSurf Ratings.

Safe Kids

Dedicated to keeping kids safe on the Net, Safe Kids (www.safekids.com) features an impressive list of links to many of the most credible, informative sites on the Internet that specifically address how to keep kids from getting hurt in cyberspace. From this address, you can access sites that offer safety brochures, activities you can review with your kids, sites for parents and teachers on the subject, and areas for concern you may not have even thought of (such as how marketers approach your kids). You can also find links to sites concerned with general child safety.

Staying Street Smart on the Web

A list of tips for kids: Written for kids and with kids in mind, this site, produced by the search engine Yahoo!, tells kids in how to stay safe when they surf. The site, which is at www.yahooligans.com/docs/safety, contains list of things to remember, which kids can print out and keep by the computer as a reference when they go online. If they ever come across a situation about which they are unsure, this list gives them tips on how to handle situations.

For example, one hint is: "I will never agree to get together with someone I 'meet' online without first checking with my parents. If my parents agree to the meeting, I will be sure that it is in a public place and bring my mother or father along."

Following the kids' section on this scroll-down page is an area that's designed for parents and that contains links to advice, articles, and additional resource sites. Among those listed are Child Safety on the Internet (a site with thoughtful comments and links to other resources) and Internet Advocate (a site featuring a resource guide for librarians and educators interested in providing youth access to the Internet).

Just Remember: It Really Is Supposed to Be Fun!

When kids first learn how to do anything new, they always have cautions and concerns to consider — whether it's shin guards for soccer, drivers' education lessons for using the car, or safety tips for walking to school. Using the Internet is no different than other life experiences for which we prepare. With the right preparation and care, using the Internet is one of the most enjoyable and educational experiences modern kids can have. So get ready as a family and have a great time.

Index

(continued)

(continued)

● **O** ●

● **P** ●

(continued)

AT&T WorldNet℠ Service

A World of Possibilities...

Thank you for selecting AT&T WorldNet Service — it's the Internet as only AT&T can bring it to you. With AT&T WorldNet Service, a world of infinite possibilities is now within your reach. Research virtually any subject. Stay abreast of current events. Participate in online newsgroups. Purchase merchandise from leading retailers. Create your presence on the Internet with a Personal Web Page. Stay in touch with friends, relatives, and colleagues via e-mail, chat and discussion groups.

AT&T WorldNet Service is rapidly becoming the preferred way of accessing the Internet. It was recently awarded one of the most highly coveted awards in the computer industry, *PC Computing*'s 1997 World Class Award for Best Internet Service Provider. Now, more than ever, it's the best way to stay in touch with the people, ideas, and information that are important to you.

Provided you are in the Continental United States, Hawaii, Puerto Rico, or the U.S. Virgin Islands, all you need is a computer with a mouse, a modem, a phone line, and the enclosed software. We've taken care of the rest.

If You Can Point and Click, You're There

With AT&T WorldNet Service, finding the information you want on the Internet is easier than you ever imagined it could be. You can surf the Net within minutes. And find almost anything you want to know — from the weather in Paris, Texas to the cost of a ticket to Paris, France. You're just a point and click away. It's that easy.

AT&T WorldNet Service features specially customized industry-leading browsers integrated with advanced Internet directories and search engines. The result is an Internet service that sets a new standard for ease of use — virtually everywhere you want to go is a point and click away, making it a snap to navigate the Internet.

When you go online with AT&T WorldNet Service, you'll benefit from being connected to the Internet by the world leader in networking. We offer you fast access of up to 28.8 Kbps in more than 215 cities throughout the U.S. that will make going online as easy as picking up your phone.

Online Help and Advice
24 Hours a Day, 7 Days a Week

Before you begin exploring the Internet, you may want to take a moment to check two useful sources of information.

If you're new to the Internet, from the AT&T WorldNet Service home page at www.worldnet.att.net, click on the Net Tutorial hyperlink for a quick explanation of unfamiliar terms and useful advice about exploring the Internet.

Another useful source of information is the HELP icon. The area contains pertinent, timesaving, information-intensive reference tips, and topics such as Accounts & Billing, Trouble Reporting, Downloads & Upgrades, Security Tips, Network Hot Spots, Newsgroups, Special Announcements, etc.

Whether online or off-line, 24 hours a day, seven days a week, we will provide World Class technical expertise and fast, reliable responses to your questions. To reach AT&T WorldNet Customer Care, call **1-800-400-1447**.

Nothing is more important to us than making sure that your Internet experience is a truly enriching and satisfying one.

Safeguard Your Online Purchases

AT&T WorldNet Service is committed to making the Internet a safe and convenient way to transact business. By registering and continuing to charge your AT&T WorldNet Service to your AT&T Universal Card, you'll enjoy peace of mind whenever you shop the Internet. Should your account number be compromised on the Net, you won't be liable for any online transactions charged to your AT&T Universal Card by a person who is not an authorized user.*
*Today, cardmembers may be liable for the first $50 of charges made by a person who is not an authorized user, which will not be imposed under this program as long as the cardmember notifies AT&T Universal Card of the loss within 24 hours and otherwise complies with the Cardmember Agreement. Refer to Cardmember Agreement for definition of authorized user.

Minimum System Requirements

IBM-Compatible Personal Computer Users:

- IBM-compatible personal computer with 486SX or higher processor
- 8MB of RAM (or more for better performance)
- 15–36MB of available hard disk space to install software, depending on platform
  (14–21MB to use service after installation, depending on platform)
- Graphics system capable of displaying 256 colors
- 14.4 Kbps modem connected to an outside phone line and not a LAN or ISDN line
- Microsoft Windows 3.1x or Windows 95

Macintosh Users:

- Macintosh 68030 or higher (including 68LC0X0 models and all Power Macintosh models)
- System 7.5.3 Revision 2 or higher for PCI Power Macintosh models: System 7.1 or higher for all 680X0 and non-PCI Power Macintosh models
- 8MB of RAM (minimum) AND Virtual Memory turned on (or use a RAM emulator software product); 16MB recommended for Power Macintosh users
- Hard Disk Space Requirements for Internet Explorer:
    - For 68K-based Macintosh, installed from CD-ROM: 18MB of available hard disk space (includes OP/PPP 1.0 and Open Transport 1.1.1). If installed from floppy disk, 13MB of available hard disk space (includes MacTCP)
    - Power Macintosh: 20MB of hard disk space (includes OP/PPP 1.0 and Open Transport 1.1.1)
- Hard Disk Space Requirements for Netscape Navigator:
  12MB of available hard disk space (15MB recommended)

- 14.4 Kbps (or higher) modem connected to an outside phone line and not a LAN or ISDN line
- Color or 256 gray-scale monitor
- Apple Guide 1.2 or higher (if you want to view online help)
  If you are uncertain of the configuration of your Macintosh computer, consult your Macintosh User's guide or call Apple at 1-800-767-2775.

Installation Tips and Instructions

- If you have other Web browsers or online software, please consider uninstalling them according to the vendor's instructions.
- If you are installing AT&T WorldNet Service on a computer with Local Area Networking, please contact your LAN administrator for setup instructions.
- At the end of installation, you may be asked to restart your computer.

IBM-compatible PC users:

- Insert the CD-ROM into the CD-ROM drive on your computer.
- Select *File/Run* (for Windows 3.1*x*) or *Start/Run* (for Windows 95 if setup did not start automatically).
- Type *D:\setup.exe* (or change the "D" if your CD-ROM is another drive).
- Click *OK*.
- Follow the onscreen instructions to install and register.

Macintosh users:

- Disable all extensions except Apple CD-ROM and Foreign Files Access extensions.
- Restart your computer.
- Insert the CD-ROM into the CD-ROM drive on your computer.
- Double-click the *Install AT&T WorldNet Service* icon.
- Follow the onscreen instructions to install. (Upon restarting your Macintosh, AT&T WorldNet Service Account Setup automatically starts.)
- Follow the onscreen instructions to register.

Registering with AT&T WorldNet Service

After you have connected with AT&T WorldNet online registration service, you will be presented with a series of screens that confirm billing information and prompt you for additional account set-up data.

The following is a list of registration tips and comments that will help you during the registration process.

I. Use one of the following registration codes, which can also be found in Appendix B of *Internet Directory For Kids & Parents*. Use L5SQIM631 if you are an AT&T long-distance residential customer or L5SQIM632 if you use another long-distance phone company.

II. During registration, you will need to supply your name, address, and valid credit card number, and choose an account information security word, e-mail name, and e-mail password. You will also be requested to select your preferred price plan at this time. (We advise that you use all lowercase letters when assigning an e-mail ID and security code, since they are easier to remember.)

III. If you make a mistake and exit or get disconnected during the registration process prematurely, simply click on "Create New Account." Do not click on "Edit Existing Account."

IV. When choosing your local access telephone number, you will be given several options. Please choose the one nearest to you. Please note that calling a number within your area does not guarantee that the call is free.

Connecting to AT&T WorldNet Service

When you have finished installing and registering with AT&T WorldNet Service, you are ready to access the Internet. Make sure your modem and phone line are available before attempting to connect to the service.

For Windows 95 users:

- Double-click on the *Connect to AT&T WorldNet Service* icon on your desktop.
  OR
- Select *Start, Programs, AT&T WorldNet Software, Connect to AT&T WorldNet Service.*

For Windows 3.*x* users:

- Double-click on the *Connect to AT&T WorldNet Service* icon located in the AT&T WorldNet Service group in Program Manager.

For Macintosh users with Microsoft Internet Explorer browser:

- Double-click on the Internet Explorer icon in the Microsoft Internet Applications folder.

For Macintosh users with Netscape Navigator:

- Double-click on the *AT&T WorldNet Service* icon in the AT&T WorldNet Service folder.

Choose the Plan That's Right for You

The Internet is for everyone, whether at home or at work. In addition to making the time you spend online productive and fun, we're also committed to making it affordable. Choose one of two price plans: unlimited usage access or hourly usage access. The latest pricing information can be obtained during online registration. No matter which plan you use, we're confident that after you take advantage of everything AT&T WorldNet Service has to offer, you'll wonder how you got along without it.

AT&T

Explore our AT&T WorldNet Service Web Site at www.att.net.

IDG Books Worldwide, Inc., End-User License Agreement

READ THIS. You should carefully read these terms and conditions before opening the software packet(s) included with this book ("Book"). This is a license agreement ("Agreement") between you and IDG Books Worldwide, Inc. ("IDGB"). By opening the accompanying software packet(s), you acknowledge that you have read and accept the following terms and conditions. If you do not agree and do not want to be bound by such terms and conditions, promptly return the Book and the unopened software packet(s) to the place you obtained them for a full refund.

1. **License Grant.** IDGB grants to you (either an individual or entity) a nonexclusive license to use one copy of the enclosed software program(s) (collectively, the "Software") solely for your own personal or business purposes on a single computer (whether a standard computer or a workstation component of a multiuser network). The Software is in use on a computer when it is loaded into temporary memory (RAM) or installed into permanent memory (hard disk, CD-ROM, or other storage device). IDGB reserves all rights not expressly granted herein.

2. **Ownership.** IDGB is the owner of all right, title, and interest, including copyright, in and to the compilation of the Software recorded on the disk(s) or CD-ROM ("Software Media"). Copyright to the individual programs recorded on the Software Media is owned by the author or other authorized copyright owner of each program. Ownership of the Software and all proprietary rights relating thereto remain with IDGB and its licensers.

3. **Restrictions on Use and Transfer.**

   (a) You may only (i) make one copy of the Software for backup or archival purposes, or (ii) transfer the Software to a single hard disk, provided that you keep the original for backup or archival purposes. You may not (i) rent or lease the Software, (ii) copy or reproduce the Software through a LAN or other network system or through any computer subscriber system or bulletin-board system, or (iii) modify, adapt, or create derivative works based on the Software.

   (b) You may not reverse engineer, decompile, or disassemble the Software. You may transfer the Software and user documentation on a permanent basis, provided that the transferee agrees to accept the terms and conditions of this Agreement and you retain no copies. If the Software is an update or has been updated, any transfer must include the most recent update and all prior versions.

4. **Restrictions on Use of Individual Programs.** You must follow the individual requirements and restrictions detailed for each individual program in the "About the Disk or CD" appendix (Appendix B) of this Book. These limitations are also contained in the individual license agreements recorded on the Software Media. These limitations may include a requirement that after using the program for a specified period of time, the user must pay a registration fee or discontinue use. By opening the Software packet(s), you will be agreeing to abide by the licenses and restrictions for these individual programs that are detailed in the "About the Disk or CD" appendix (Appendix B) and on the Software Media. None of the material on this Software Media or listed in this Book may ever be redistributed, in original or modified form, for commercial purposes.

5. **Limited Warranty.**

   (a) IDGB warrants that the Software and Software Media are free from defects in materials and workmanship under normal use for a period of sixty (60) days from the date of purchase of this Book. If IDGB receives notification within the warranty period of defects in materials or workmanship, IDGB will replace the defective Software Media.

   (b) **IDGB AND THE AUTHOR OF THE BOOK DISCLAIM ALL OTHER WARRANTIES, EXPRESS OR IMPLIED, INCLUDING WITHOUT LIMITATION IMPLIED WARRANTIES OF MER-CHANTABILITY AND FITNESS FOR A PARTICULAR PURPOSE, WITH RESPECT TO THE SOFTWARE, THE PROGRAMS, THE SOURCE CODE CONTAINED THEREIN, AND/OR THE TECHNIQUES DESCRIBED IN THIS BOOK. IDGB DOES NOT WARRANT THAT THE FUNCTIONS CONTAINED IN THE SOFTWARE WILL MEET YOUR REQUIREMENTS OR THAT THE OPERATION OF THE SOFTWARE WILL BE ERROR FREE.**

   (c) This limited warranty gives you specific legal rights, and you may have other rights that vary from jurisdiction to jurisdiction.

6. **Remedies.**

   (a) IDGB's entire liability and your exclusive remedy for defects in materials and workmanship shall be limited to replacement of the Software Media, which may be returned to IDGB with a copy of your receipt at the following address: Software Media Fulfillment Department, Attn.: *Internet Directory For Kids & Parents*, IDG Books Worldwide, Inc., 7260 Shadeland Station, Ste. 100, Indianapolis, IN 46256, or call 800-762-2974. Please allow three to four weeks for delivery. This Limited Warranty is void if failure of the Software Media has resulted from accident, abuse, or misapplication. Any replacement Software Media will be warranted for the remainder of the original warranty period or thirty (30) days, whichever is longer.

   (b) In no event shall IDGB or the author be liable for any damages whatsoever (including without limitation damages for loss of business profits, business interruption, loss of business information, or any other pecuniary loss) arising from the use of or inability to use the Book or the Software, even if IDGB has been advised of the possibility of such damages.

   (c) Because some jurisdictions do not allow the exclusion or limitation of liability for conse-quential or incidental damages, the above limitation or exclusion may not apply to you.

7. **U.S. Government Restricted Rights.** Use, duplication, or disclosure of the Software by the U.S. Government is subject to restrictions stated in paragraph (c)(1)(ii) of the Rights in Technical Data and Computer Software clause of DFARS 252.227-7013, and in subparagraphs (a) through (d) of the Commercial Computer–Restricted Rights clause at FAR 52.227-19, and in similar clauses in the NASA FAR supplement, when applicable.

8. **General.** This Agreement constitutes the entire understanding of the parties and revokes and supersedes all prior agreements, oral or written, between them and may not be modified or amended except in a writing signed by both parties hereto that specifically refers to this Agreement. This Agreement shall take precedence over any other documents that may be in conflict herewith. If any one or more provisions contained in this Agreement are held by any court or tribunal to be invalid, illegal, or otherwise unenforceable, each and every other provision shall remain in full force and effect.

Installation Instructions

• •

*T*he CD stuck to the back of this book contains all sorts of helpful shareware software and other goodies. Follow these instructions to get more information about the programs on the CD or to install them on your computer. To find out more about the CD contents, refer to Appendix B.

These instructions assume that your computer meets the minimum technical specifications outlined in Appendix B of this book.

To access the programs on the CD, follow these steps:

1. **Insert the CD (label side up) into your CD-ROM drive.**

2. **In Windows 95, click the Start button to display the Start Menu, and then choose Run; Macintosh users double-click the CD-ROM drive icon.**

   Windows users will see the Run dialog box. Macintosh users see a window listing the CD's contents; skip to Step 4.

3. **Windows users, type** D:\Setup.exe **in the dialog box's Open text box and then press Enter.**

   If your CD-ROM drive uses a different letter than D, please replace D with the correct letter.

4. **Windows 95 users: Follow the directions that appear on your screen; Macintosh users: Click the program's installation icon or the program icon itself, depending on which application you wish to work with.**

   You must agree with the licensing agreement in the initial window in order to continue the installation program.

To use the Directory Links pages, put the CD-ROM in your CD drive and follow these steps:

1. **Launch your Web browser.**

2. **Microsoft Internet Explorer users, choose File⇨Open; Netscape Navigator users, choose File⇨Open File.**

   If you use a browser other than the one listed above, consult your browser's documentation on how to open a file.

   For these two browsers, the Open dialog box appears.

3. **Type** D:\HOME.HTM **in the text box of the dialog box.**

   If your CD-ROM drive is not D:\, please be sure to use the correct letter for your drive. The home page for Directory Links now opens. Follow the instructions for using the links pages.

If, after following these instructions, you still have problems installing the programs from the CD, please call the IDG Books Worldwide Customer Service phone number: 800-762-2974 (outside the U.S.: 317-596-5261).

IDG BOOKS WORLDWIDE BOOK REGISTRATION

Register This Book and Win!

We want to hear from you!

Visit **http://my2cents.dummies.com** to register this book and tell us how you liked it!

✔ Get entered in our monthly prize giveaway.

✔ Give us feedback about this book — tell us what you like best, what you like least, or maybe what you'd like to ask the author and us to change!

✔ Let us know any other ...*For Dummies* topics that interest you.

Your feedback helps us determine what books to publish, tells us what coverage to add as we revise our books, and lets us know whether we're meeting your needs as a ...*For Dummies* reader. You're our most valuable resource, and what you have to say is important to us!

Not on the Web yet? It's easy to get started with *Dummies 101*®: *The Internet For Windows*® *95* or *The Internet For Dummies*,® 4th Edition, at local retailers everywhere.

Or let us know what you think by sending us a letter at the following address:

...*For Dummies* Book Registration
Dummies Press
7260 Shadeland Station, Suite 100
Indianapolis, IN 46256
Fax 317-596-5498

BUSINESS AND GENERAL REFERENCE BOOK SERIES FROM IDG

COMPUTER BOOK SERIES FROM IDG